Excel 2003 For Dummies®

BESTSELLING
BOOK SERIES

D0456467

Shortcut Keys for Manipulating Worksheets

Press	To
Ctrl+Page Down	Activate next sheet in the workbook
Ctrl+Page Up	Activate previous sheet in the workbook
Shift+Ctrl+Page Down	Select current and next sheet in workbook
Shift+Ctrl+Page Up	Select current and previous sheet in workbook
Shift+F11 or Alt+Shift+F1	Insert new sheet in workbook
Alt+OHR	Rename current sheet (Format⇔Sheet⇔Rename)
Alt+OHH	Hide current sheet (Format⇔Sheet⇔Hide)
Alt+OHU	Unhide current sheet (Format⇔Sheet⇔Unhide)
Alt+OHT	Select new color for sheet tab (Format⇔Sheet⇔Tab Color)
Alt+EM	Move or copy current sheet in workbook or to new workbook (Edit⇔Move or Copy Sheet)
Alt+ED	Delete current sheet (Edit⇔Delete)

Shortcut Keys for Editing Cell Entries

Press	To
Ctrl+F1	Open and close the Task pane at the right side of the workbook document window
F2	Edit current cell entry and position insertion point at the end of cell contents
Shift+F2	Edit comment attached to current cell and position insertion point in comment box
Backspace	Delete character to left of insertion point when editing cell entry
Delete	Delete character to right of insertion point when editing cell entry; otherwise, clear cell entries in current range
Esc	Cancel editing in current cell entry
Enter	Complete editing in current cell entry
Ctrl+CC	Open Clipboard Task pane
Ctrl+C	Copy cell selection to Clipboard
Ctrl+X	Cut cell selection to Clipboard
Ctrl+V	Paste last copied or cut cells from Clipboard
Ctrl+hyphen (-)	Open Delete dialog box to delete cell selection and shift remaining cells left or up
Ctrl+Shift+plus (+)	Open Insert dialog box to insert new cells and shift existing cells right or down
Ctrl+Z	Undo last action
Ctrl+Y	Redo last action

For Dummies: Bestselling Book Series for Beginners

Excel 2003 For Dummies®

Shortcut Keys for Formatting Cell Entries

Press	To
Ctrl+1	Display Format Cells dialog box
Alt+' (apostrophe)	Display Style dialog box
Ctrl+Shift+~ (tilde)	Apply General number format
Ctrl+Shift+$	Apply Currency number format with two decimal places and negative numbers in parentheses
Ctrl+Shift+%	Apply Percent number format with no decimal places
Ctrl+Shift+#	Apply Date number format with day, month, and year as in 15-Feb-05
Ctrl+Shift+@	Apply Time number format with hour and minute and AM/PM as in 12:05 PM
Ctrl+Shift+!	Apply Comma number format with two decimal places
Ctrl+B	Add or remove bold
Ctrl+I	Add or remove italics
Ctrl+U	Add or remove underlining
Ctrl+5	Add or remove strikethrough
Ctrl+Shift+&	Apply outline border to current range
Ctrl+Shift+_ (underline)	Remove outline border from current range

The following table gives you a quick guide to what words you need to say to get the Speech Recognition feature to enter common symbols and punctuation.

Words Used When Dictating Common Punctuation and Symbols

Word(s) You Say	What Speech Recognition Enters
Ampersand	&
Asterisk	*
At sign	@
Backslash	\
Close paren	)
Close quote	'
Colon	:
Comma	,
Dash	-
Dollar sign	$
Dot	.
Ellipsis	. . .
End quote	"
Equals	=
Exclamation point	!
Greater than	>
Hyphen	-
Less than	<
Open paren	(
Open quote	"
Percent sign	%
Period	.
Plus sign	+
Question mark	?
Quote	"
Semi-colon	;
Single quote	'
Slash	/

For Dummies: Bestselling Book Series for Beginners

Excel 2003 FOR DUMMIES

by Greg Harvey

WILEY

Wiley Publishing, Inc.

Excel 2003 For Dummies®

Published by
Wiley Publishing, Inc.
111 River Street
Hoboken, NJ 07030
www.wiley.com

For general information on our other products and services or to obtain technical support, please contact our Customer Care Department within the U.S. at 800-762-2974, outside the U.S. at 317-572-3993, or fax 317-572-4002.

Wiley also publishes its books in a variety of electronic formats. Some content that appears in print may not be available in electronic books.

Library of Congress Control Number: 2003101884

ISBN: 0-7645-3756-3

Manufactured in the United States of America

10 9 8 7 6

1B/RX/QU/QW

WILEY   is a trademark of Wiley Publishing, Inc.

About the Author

Greg Harvey is a product of the great American Midwest, born in the Chicagoland area in 1949 (thus his saying "I'm only as old as China" — Red China, that is) in the dark ages of the Cold War, before the age of McDonald's, MTV, and, certainly, personal computers. On the shores of Lake Michigan, he learned his letters and numbers and showed great promise in the world of academia (quickly achieving Red Bird reading status after being put back as a Yellow Bird due to an unforeseen bout of chicken pox at the start of the school year). After earning many gold stars along with a few red, he graduated from Roosevelt School (named for Teddy, not that socialist Delano) in 1963.

During his stint at Thornridge High School in the perfectly boring Chicago suburb of Dolton, Illinois (named for Tom Dolton, the gunslinger), he found great solace in Motown music (thanks, Phil) and the drama department (to this day, he can recite every line from the play *Auntie Mame*, verbatim). Bored with what passed for academic studies, he went through high school in three years. Looking back on these formative years, Greg was sure thankful for the great tunes and Auntie's philosophy "Life's a banquet, kid, and some poor suckers are starving."

In 1966 (ah, the Sixties), he entered the University of Illinois at Urbana, Illinois, where he was greatly influenced by such deep philosophers as Abbie Hoffman and Mahatma Gandhi. In the summer of 1968, he purchased his first pair of handmade sandals (from Glen, a hippie sandal maker who'd just returned from the Summer of Love in San Francisco).

During his college years, he became quite political. He holds the distinction of being one of a handful of men and women to attend the "camp-out" protest against women's dorm curfews (back then, not only were dorms not sexually integrated, but also, women were locked up at 11 p.m. on weeknights, 1 a.m. on weekends) and the last one to leave after all the others went back to their dorms. During his subsequent college years he became a regular at the Red Herring coffeehouse, the veritable den of SDS activity on campus

In addition to antiwar protests, Greg attended various and sundry classes in the Liberal Arts (such as they were in the last half of the 20th century). In the end, he took a major in Classical Studies (ancient Greek and Latin) and a split minor in American History and French (Greg showed a facility for foreign language, probably stemming from the fact that he's always had a big mouth). In the course of his classical studies, he was introduced to his first computer-based training, learning basic Latin with a CAI program called what else but PLATO!

At the beginning of 1971 (January 12, in fact), Greg migrated west from Chicago to San Francisco (with flowers in his hair). Deciding it was high time to get a skill so that he could find a real job, he enrolled in the Drafting and Design program at Laney College in Oakland. After that, he spent nine years working over a hot drafting table, drawing (by hand, mind you) orthographic and perspective plans for various and sundry engineering projects. During his last engineering gig, he worked with a proprietary CAD software package developed by Bechtel Engineering that not only generated the drawings, but also kept track of the materials actually needed to create the stuff.

In 1981, following his engineering career, Greg went back to school at San Francisco State University, this time to earn his secondary teaching credential. Upon completion of his teacher training, he bought one of the very first IBM personal computers (with 16K and a single 160K floppy disk!) to help with lesson preparation and student bookkeeping. He still vividly remembers poring over the premiere issue of *PC World* magazine for every piece of information that could teach him how to make peace with his blankety, blankety personal computer.

Instead of landing a teaching job at the high school or community college (because there weren't any at the time), Greg got a job with a small software outfit, ITM, that was creating an online database of software information (well ahead of its time). As part of his duties, Greg reviewed new software programs (like Microsoft Word 1.0 and Lotus 1-2-3 Release 1) and wrote articles for business users.

After being laid off from this job right after the Christmas party in 1983 (the first of several layoffs from high-tech startups), Greg wrote his first computer book on word processing software for Hayden Books (as a result of a proposal he helped to write while still employed full-time at ITM). After that, Greg worked in various software evaluation and training jobs. After a few more high-tech software testing and evaluation jobs in Silicon Valley, Greg turned to software training to get, as he put it, "the perspective of the poor schmo at the end of the terminal." During the next three years, Greg trained a whole plethora of software programs to business users of all skill levels for several major independent software-training companies in the San Francisco Bay Area.

In the fall of 1986, he hooked up with Sybex, a local computer book publisher, for which he wrote his second computer training book, *Mastering SuperCalc*. And the rest, as they say, is history. To date, Greg is the author of more than 30 books on using computer software, with the titles created under the *For Dummies* aegis for Hungry Minds, Inc., being among his all-time favorites.

In mid-1993, Greg started a new multimedia publishing venture called Mind over Media. As a multimedia developer, he hopes to enliven his future computer books by making them into true interactive learning experiences that will vastly enrich and improve the training of users of all skill levels. You can send him e-mail at gharvey@mindovermedia.com and visit his Web site at www.mindovermedia.com.

In 1999, Greg began graduate school at the California Institute of Integral Studies (CIIS) in San Francisco. In the summer of 2000, he received his Master's degree in Philosophy and Religion in the area of Asian and Comparative Studies. In the fall of that year, he entered the Ph.D. program at CIIS, where he is now concentrating on the study of the classical Chinese and Tibetan languages and the study of Chinese philosophy and religion.

Dedication

An Erucolindo melindonya

Author's Acknowledgments

Let me take this opportunity to thank all the people, both at Wiley Publishing, Inc., and at Mind over Media, Inc., whose dedication and talent combined to get this book out and into your hands in such great shape.

At Wiley Publishing, Inc., I want to thank Tiffany Franklin for her help in getting this project under way; Christine Berman as project editor; and Diana Conover as copy editor for making sure that the project stayed on course and made it into production so that all the talented folks on the production team could create this great final product.

At Mind over Media, I want to thank Christopher Aiken for his review of the updated manuscript and invaluable input and suggestions on how to present and handle new features.

Publisher's Acknowledgments

We're proud of this book; please send us your comments through our online registration form located at www.dummies.com/register/.

Some of the people who helped bring this book to market include the following:

Acquisitions, Editorial, and Media Development

Project Editor: Christine Berman

Acquisitions Editor: Tiffany Franklin

Copy Editor: Diana R. Conover

Technical Editor: Tom Farrington

Editorial Manager: Leah Cameron

Media Development Manager: Laura VanWinkle

Media Development Supervisor: Richard Graves

Editorial Assistant: Amanda Foxworth

Cartoons: Rich Tennant (www.the5thwave.com)

Production

Project Coordinator: Kristie Rees

Layout and Graphics: Joyce Haughey, LeAndra Hosier, Stephanie D. Jumper, Michael Kruzil, Lynsey Osborn, Jacque Schneider, Melanee Wolven

Proofreaders: Carl W. Pierce, Robert Springer, TECHBOOKS Production Services

Indexer: Maro Riofrancos

Publishing and Editorial for Technology Dummies

    Richard Swadley, Vice President and Executive Group Publisher

    Andy Cummings, Vice President and Publisher

    Mary C. Corder, Editorial Director

Publishing for Consumer Dummies

    Diane Graves Steele, Vice President and Publisher

    Joyce Pepple, Acquisitions Director

Composition Services

    Gerry Fahey, Vice President of Production Services

    Debbie Stailey, Director of Composition Services

Contents at a Glance

Table of Contents

Introduction

Welcome to *Excel 2003 For Dummies,* the definitive work on Excel 2003 for those of you who have no intention of ever becoming a spreadsheet guru. In this book, you'll find all the information that you need to keep your head above water as you accomplish the everyday tasks that people do with Excel. The intention of this book is to keep things simple and not bore you with a lot of technical details that you neither need nor care anything about. As much as possible, in this book I attempt to cut to the chase by telling you in plain terms just what it is that you need to do to accomplish a task using Excel.

Excel 2003 For Dummies covers all the fundamental techniques that you need to know in order to create, edit, format, and print your own worksheets. In addition to showing you around the worksheet, this book also exposes you to the basics of charting, creating databases, and converting spreadsheets into Web pages. Keep in mind, though, that this book just touches on the easiest ways to get a few things done with these features — I make no attempt to cover charting, databases, or worksheet Web pages in a definitive way. This book concentrates mainly on spreadsheets because spreadsheets are what most people need to create with Excel.

About This Book

This book isn't meant to be read cover to cover. Although its chapters are loosely organized in a logical order (progressing as you might when studying Excel in a classroom situation), each topic covered in a chapter is really meant to stand on its own.

Each discussion of a topic briefly addresses the question of what a particular feature is good for before launching into how to use it. In Excel, as with most other sophisticated programs, you usually have more than one way to do a task. For the sake of your sanity, I have purposely limited the choices by usually giving you only the most efficient ways to do a particular task. Later on, if you're so tempted, you can experiment with alternative ways of doing a task. For now, just concentrate on performing the task as I describe.

As much as possible, I've tried to make it unnecessary for you to remember anything covered in another section of the book. From time to time, however, you will come across a cross-reference to another section or chapter in the book. For the most part, such cross-references are meant to help you get more complete information on a subject, should you have the time and interest. If you have neither, no problem; just ignore the cross-references as if they never existed.

How to Use This Book

This book is like a reference in which you start out by looking up the topic you need information about (either in the Table of Contents or the Index), and then you refer directly to the section of interest. I explain most topics conversationally (as though you were sitting in the back of a classroom where you can safely nap). Sometimes, however, my regiment-commander mentality takes over, and I list the steps you need to take to accomplish a particular task in a particular section.

What You Can Safely Ignore

When you come across a section that contains the steps you take to get something done, you can safely ignore all text accompanying the steps (the text that isn't in bold) if you have neither the time nor the inclination to wade through more material.

Whenever possible, I have also tried to separate background or footnote-type information from the essential facts by exiling this kind of junk to a sidebar (look for blocks of text on a gray background). These sections are often flagged with icons that let you know what type of information you will encounter there. You can easily disregard text marked this way. (I'll scoop you on the icons I use in this book a little later.)

Foolish Assumptions

I'm going to make only one assumption about you (let's see how close I get): You have access to a PC (at least some of the time) that has Windows XP or Windows 2000 and Excel 2003 installed on it. However, having said that, I make no assumption that you've ever launched Excel, let alone done anything with it.

This book is written expressly for users of Excel 2003. If you have a previous version of Excel for Windows (like Excel 2002) running under a previous version of Windows (like 98 or ME [Millennium Edition]), please put this book down and instead pick up a copy of *Excel 2002 For Dummies,* published by Wiley Publishing, Inc.

If you happen to be using Excel 2002 for Windows (either because you just haven't seen the need for upgrading yet, you're just too cheap to purchase the upgrade, or after installing Windows XP, you simply don't have enough disk space left for Excel 2003), you can use this book for the most part to figure out Excel 2002 for Windows. Just keep in mind that are some features such as the new Home and Research Task panes and Side by Side Compare With that simply don't exist in Excel 2002 and others such as the Help and File Search features that work somewhat differently in Excel 2002 from the way they're described in this edition.

How This Book Is Organized

This book is organized in five parts (which gives you a chance to see at least five of those great Rich Tennant cartoons!). Each part contains two or more chapters (to keep the editors happy) that more or less go together (to keep you happy). Each chapter is further divided into loosely related sections that cover the basics of the topic at hand. You should not, however, get too hung up about following along with the structure of the book; ultimately, it doesn't matter at all if you find out how to edit the worksheet before you learn how to format it, or if you figure out printing before you learn editing. The important thing is that you find the information — and understand it when you find it — when you need to perform a particular task.

In case you're interested, a synopsis of what you find in each part follows.

Part I: Getting In on the Ground Floor

As the name implies, in this part I cover such fundamentals as how to start the program, identify the parts of the screen, enter information in the worksheet, save a document, and so on. If you're starting with absolutely no background in using spreadsheets, you definitely want to glance at the information in Chapter 1 to discover what this program is good for before you move on to how to create new worksheets in Chapter 2.

Part II: Editing Without Tears

In this part, I show how to edit spreadsheets to make them look good, as well as how to make major editing changes to them without courting disaster. Peruse Chapter 3 when you need information on formatting the data to improve the way it appears in the worksheet. See Chapter 4 for rearranging, deleting, or inserting new information in the worksheet. And read Chapter 5 for the skinny on printing out your finished product.

Part III: Getting Organized and Staying That Way

Here I give you all kinds of information on how to stay on top of the data that you've entered into your spreadsheets. Chapter 6 is full of good ideas on how to keep track of and organize the data in a single worksheet. Chapter 7 gives you the ins and outs of working with data in different worksheets in the same workbook and gives you information on transferring data between the sheets of different workbooks.

Part IV: Life Beyond the Spreadsheet

In Part IV, I explore some of the other aspects of Excel besides the spreadsheet. In Chapter 8, you find out just how ridiculously easy it is to create a chart using the data in a worksheet. In Chapter 9, you discover just how useful Excel's database capabilities can be when you have to track and organize a large amount of information. In Chapter 10, you find out about adding hyperlinks to jump to new places in a worksheet, to new documents, and even to Web pages, as well as how to convert worksheets into both static and *dynamic* (interactive) Web pages for your company's Web site(s).

Part V: The Part of Tens

As is the tradition in these *For Dummies* books, the last part contains lists of the top ten most useful and useless facts, tips, and suggestions.

Conventions Used in This Book

The following information gives you the lowdown on how things look in this book — publishers call these items the book's *conventions* (no campaigning, flag-waving, name-calling, or finger-pointing is involved, however).

Keyboard and mouse

Excel 2003 is a sophisticated program with lots of fancy boxes, plenty of bars, and more menus than you can count. In Chapter 1, I explain all about these features and how to use them.

Although you use the mouse and keyboard shortcut keys to move your way in, out, and around the Excel worksheet, you do have to take some time to enter the data so that you can eventually mouse around with it. Therefore, this book occasionally encourages you to type something specific into a specific cell in the worksheet. Of course, you can always choose not to follow the instructions. When I tell you to enter a specific function, the part you should type generally appears in **bold** type. For example, =SUM(A2:B2) means that you should type exactly what you see: an equal sign, the word **SUM**, a left parenthesis, the text **A2:B2** (complete with a colon between the letter-number combos), and a right parenthesis. You then, of course, have to press Enter to make the entry stick.

When Excel isn't talking to you by popping up message boxes, it displays highly informative messages in the status bar at the bottom of the screen. This book renders messages that you see on-screen like this:

```
=SUM(A2:B2)
```

Occasionally I may ask you to press a *key combination* in order to perform a certain task. Key combinations are written like this: Ctrl+S. That plus sign in between means that you should hold down both the Ctrl key and the S key at the same time before releasing them. This (sometimes cruel) type of finger aerobics may take some practice.

When you need to wade through one or more menus to get to the selection you want, I sometimes (though not often, mind you) use *command arrows* to lead you from the initial menu, to the submenu and so on, to the command you ultimately want. For example, if you need to first open the File menu to get to the Open command, I may write that instruction like this: Choose File⇨ Open.

Finally, if you're really observant, you may notice a discrepancy between the capitalization of the names of dialog box options (such as headings, radio buttons, and check boxes) as they appear in the book and how they actually appear in Excel on your computer screen. Microsoft has this habit of capitalizing only the first letter of the names of long dialog box options. For example, on the Sheet tab of the Page Setup dialog box, you'll see a check box option called

```
Row and column headings
```

In Chapter 5 where I discuss the use of this option, this heading appears in the text as

```
Row and Column Headings
```

I intentionally use this convention of capitalizing the initial letters of all the main words of a dialog box option to help you differentiate the name of the option from the rest of the text describing its use.

Special icons

The following icons are strategically placed in the margins to point out stuff you may or may not want to read.

This icon alerts you to nerdy discussions that you may well want to skip (or read when no one else is around).

This icon alerts you to shortcuts or other valuable hints related to the topic at hand.

This icon alerts you to information to keep in mind if you want to meet with a modicum of success.

This icon alerts you to information to keep in mind if you want to avert complete disaster.

Where to Go from Here

If you've never worked with a computer spreadsheet, I suggest that, right after getting your chuckles with the cartoons, you go first to Chapter 1 and find out what you're dealing with. If you're already familiar with the ins and outs of electronic spreadsheets but don't know anything about creating worksheets with Excel, jump into Chapter 2, where you find out how to get started entering data and formulas. Then, as specific needs arise (such as, "How do I copy a formula?" or "How do I print just a particular section of my worksheet?"), you can go to the Table of Contents or the Index to find the appropriate section and go right to that section for answers.

Part I
Getting In on the Ground Floor

The 5th Wave   By Rich Tennant

"I think the cursor's not moving, Mr. Dunt, because you've got your hand on the chalk board eraser and not the mouse."

In this part . . .

One look at the Excel 2003 screen (with all its boxes, buttons, and tabs), and you realize how much stuff is going on here. This is no doubt because of the addition of the Windows taskbar to the (already rather over-designed) Excel 2003 screen and then throwing in the Microsoft Office Shortcut Bar to boot! Well, not to worry: In Chapter 1, I break down the parts of the Excel 2003 screen and make some sense out of the rash of icons, buttons, and boxes that you're going to be facing day after day after day.

Of course, it's not enough to just sit back and have someone like me explain what's what on the screen. To get any good out of Excel, you've got to start learning how to use all these bells and whistles (or buttons and boxes, in this case). That's where Chapter 2 comes in, giving you the lowdown on how to use some of the screen's more prominent buttons and boxes to get your spreadsheet data entered. From this humble beginning, it's a quick trip to total screen mastery.

Chapter 1

What Is All This Stuff?

*J*ust because electronic spreadsheets like Excel 2003 have become almost as commonplace on today's personal computers as word processors and games doesn't mean that they're either well understood or well used. In fact, I encounter scads of users, even those who are reasonably well versed in the art of writing and editing in Microsoft Word, who have little or no idea of what they could or should do with Excel.

This lack of awareness is really a shame — especially in this day and age when Office 11 seems to be the only software found on the majority of machines (probably because, together, Windows XP or 2000 and Office 11 hog so much hard drive space that no room is left to install anybody else's software). If you're one of the folks who has Office 11 on your computer but doesn't know a spreadsheet from a bedsheet, this means that Excel 2003 is just sitting there, taking up a lot of space. Well, it's high time to change all that.

What in the World Would I Do with Excel?

Excel is a great organizer for all types of data, be they numeric, textual, or otherwise. Because the program has loads of built-in calculating capabilities, most people turn to Excel when they need to set up financial spreadsheets. These spreadsheets tend to be filled to the gills with formulas for computing stuff, such as total sales, net profits and losses, growth percentages, and those sorts of things.

Also popular are Excel's charting capabilities that enable you to create all types of charts and graphs from the numbers that you crunch in your financial worksheets. Excel makes it really easy to turn columns and rows of boring, black-and-white numbers into colorful and snappy charts and graphs. You can then use these charts to add some pizzazz to written reports (like those created with Word 2003) or to punch up overheads used in formal business presentations (like those created with Microsoft PowerPoint).

Now, even if your job doesn't involve creating worksheets with a lot of fancy-Dan financial calculations or lah-di-dah charts, you probably have plenty of things for which you could and should be using Excel. For instance, you may have to keep lists of information or maybe even put together tables of information for your job. Excel is a great list keeper (even though we tend to refer to such lists as *data lists* or *databases* in Excel) and one heck of a table maker. Therefore, you can use Excel anytime that you need to keep track of products that you sell, clients who you service, employees who you oversee, or you name it.

Little boxes, little boxes . . .

There's a really good reason why Excel is such a whiz at doing financial calculations by formula and keeping lists and tables of information organized. Look at any blank Excel worksheet (the one in Figure 1-1 will do fine) and just what do you see? Boxes, lots of little boxes, that's what! These little boxes (you can find millions of them in each worksheet that you encounter) are called *cells* in spreadsheet jargon. And each piece of information (such as a name, address, monthly sales figure, or even your Aunt Sally's birth date) goes into its own box (cell) in the worksheet that you're building.

If you're used to word processing, this idea of entering different types of information in little, bitty cells can be somewhat strange to get used to. If you're thinking in word-processing terms, you need to think of the process of building an Excel worksheet as being more like setting up a table of information in a Word document rather than writing a letter or report.

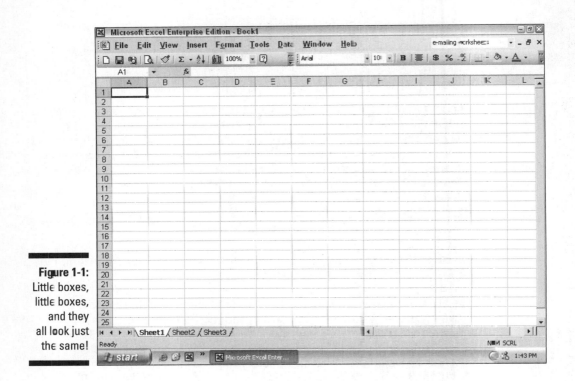

Figure 1-1:
Little boxes,
little boxes,
and they
all look just
the same!

Send it to my cell address

As you can see in Figure 1-1, the Excel worksheet contains a frame used to label the columns and rows. Columns are given letters of the alphabet, and the rows are numbered. The columns and rows must be labeled because the Excel worksheet is humongous. (Figure 1-1 shows only a tiny part of the total worksheet.) The column and row labels act like street signs in a city — they can help you identify your current location, even if they don't prevent you from becoming lost.

TECHNICAL STUFF

Why spreadsheet programs produce nothing but worksheets

Spreadsheet programs like Excel 2003 refer to their electronic sheets as worksheets rather than spreadsheets. And, although it is perfectly acceptable (even preferable) to call one of its electronic sheets a worksheet, you never, never refer to Excel as a worksheet program — it's always called a spreadsheet program. So you can think of Excel as a spreadsheet program that produces worksheets, but not as a worksheet program that produces spreadsheets. (On the other hand I often refer to worksheets as spreadsheets in this book — and so can you.)

Cells: The building blocks of all worksheets

The cells in an Excel worksheet are formed by the intersection of the column and row grid. Technically, such an arrangement is known as an *array*. An array keeps track of different pieces of information stored in it by referring to its row position and its column position (something you see more clearly when I discuss the R1C1 cell referencing system in the sidebar, "Cell A1, also known as Cell R1C1," elsewhere in this chapter). To display your worksheet data in its grid and tabular format, Excel just reads from the row and column position associated with the data that you enter there.

As shown in Figure 1-2, Excel constantly shows you your current position in the worksheet in three different ways:

- ✔ Look at the current cell reference box of Figure 1-2, where it reads G9 (upper-left corner). This box, called the Name box, resides on the Formula bar, which sits atop the worksheet display. Here, Excel lists the current cell location by its column (G) and row (9) reference. (Read more about the so-called A1 cell reference system in the sidebar elsewhere in this chapter, "Cell A1, also known as Cell R1C1.")

- ✔ In the worksheet itself, the cell pointer (refer to Figure 1-2), shown by a heavy border, appears in the cell that's currently selected.

- ✔ In the frame of the worksheet, the letter of the column and the number of the row containing the cell pointer are shaded in a distinct golden color.

You wonder why Excel makes such a big deal about telling you which cell is current in the worksheet? That's a good question, and the answer is important:

In the worksheet, you can enter or edit information in only the cell that's current.

The repercussions of this seemingly innocuous little statement are enormous. It means that if you're paying more attention to what you need to enter in your spreadsheet than to which cell is current, you can end up replacing something you've already entered. It also means that you'll never be able to edit a particular cell entry if you haven't first selected the cell to make it current.

Column letter and row number

Current cell reference

Cell pointer

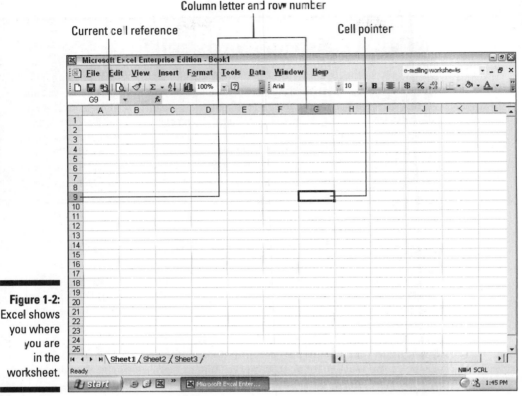

Figure 1-2:
Excel shows
you where
you are
in the
worksheet.

So just how many cells are we talking about here?

I'm not exaggerating when I say that each worksheet contains millions of cells, any of which can be filled with information. Each worksheet has 256 columns, of which only the first 9 or 12 (letters A through I or L) are normally visible in a new worksheet, and 65,536 rows, of which only the first 15 to 25 are normally visible in a new worksheet. If you multiply 256 by 65,536, you come up with a total of 16,777,216 empty cells in each worksheet you use! (That's over 16 million of those suckers!)

And as if that weren't enough, each new workbook that you start comes equipped with three of these worksheets, each with its own 16,777,216 blank cells. This gives you a grand total of 50,331,648 cells at your disposal in any one Excel file that you happen to have open. And should that number prove to be too few (yeah, right!), you can add more worksheets (each with its 16,777,216 cells) to the workbook.

Cell A1, also known as cell R1C1

The A1 cell reference system is a holdover from the VisiCalc days. (VisiCalc was the granddaddy of spreadsheet programs for personal computers.) In addition to the A1 system, Excel supports a much older, technically more correct system of cell references: the R1C1 cell reference system. In this system, both the columns and rows in the worksheet are numbered, and the row number precedes the column number. For example, in this system, cell A1 is called R1C1 (row 1, column 1); cell A2 is R2C1 (row 2, column 1); and cell B1 is R1C2 (row 1, column 2). To switch to the R1C1 system, choose Tools⇨ Options on the Excel menu bar and then click the General tab followed by the R1C1 Reference Style check box before clicking OK.

Assigning 26 letters to 256 columns

When it comes to labeling the 256 columns in a worksheet, our alphabet — with its measly 26 letters — is not up to the task. To make up the difference, Excel doubles up the cell letters in the column reference so that column AA immediately follows column Z. This is followed by column AB, AC, and so on to AZ. After column AZ, you find column BA, and then BB, BC, and so on. According to this system for doubling the column letters, the 256th (and last) column of the worksheet is column IV. This, in turn, gives the very last cell of any worksheet the cell reference IV65536.

What you should know about Excel at this point

Remember the following things about Excel:

- Each Excel file is referred to as a *workbook*.
- Each new workbook that you open contains three blank worksheets.
  - Each of these three blank worksheets contains a whole bunch of cells into which you enter your data.
  - Each cell in each of these three worksheets has its own cell address made up of the letter(s) of its column and the number of its row.

TECHNICAL STUFF

More worksheet size trivia

If you were to produce the entire worksheet grid on paper, you would need a sheet that was approximately 21 feet wide by 1,365 feet long! On a 14-inch computer screen at a screen resolution of 800 by 600 pixels, you can normally see no more than between 10 and 12 complete columns and between 20 and 25 complete rows of the entire worksheet. With columns being about 1 inch wide and rows about ¼ inch high, 10 columns represent a scant 3.9 percent of the total width of the worksheet, while 20 rows fill only about 0.03 percent of its total length. This should give you some idea of how little of the total worksheet is visible on the screen as well as just how much area is available.

- All spreadsheet information is stored in the individual cells of the worksheet. You can, however, enter information into only the cell that is current (that is, selected with the cell pointer).

- Excel indicates which of the over 16 million cells in the worksheet is the current (active) one by displaying its cell reference on the formula bar and displaying the cell pointer in the worksheet itself. (Refer to Figure 1-2.)

- The system for referencing cells in a worksheet — the A1 cell reference system — combines the column letter(s) with the row number.

What you still need to know about Excel

You could easily get the mistaken idea that a spreadsheet program like Excel is little more than a quirky word processor with a gridlock that forces you to enter your information in tiny, individual cells instead of offering you the spaciousness of full pages.

Well, I'm here to say that Bill Gates didn't become a billionaire several times over by selling a quirky word processor. (All you Microsoft Word users out there, please hold your tongues!) The big difference between the cell of a worksheet and the pages of a word processor is that each cell offers computing power along with text-editing and formatting capabilities. This computing power takes the form of formulas that you create in various cells of the worksheet.

Quite unlike a paper spreadsheet, which contains only values computed somewhere else, an electronic worksheet can store both the formulas and the computed values returned by these formulas. Even better, your formulas can use values stored in other cells of the worksheet, and, as I explain in Chapter 2, Excel automatically updates the computed answer returned by such a formula anytime that you change these values in the worksheet.

Excel's computational capabilities, combined with its editing and formatting capabilities, make the program perfect for generating any kind of document that uses textual and numeric entries and requires you to perform calculations on those values. Because you can make your formulas dynamic — so that their calculations are automatically updated when you change referenced values stored in other cells of the worksheet — you will find it much easier to keep the calculated values in a worksheet document both current and correct.

Getting the Darn Thing Started

If you're at all familiar with using Windows XP or 2000, you won't be shocked to find out that you have about a zillion ways to get Excel up and running after the program's been installed on your hard drive. (Okay, only about half a dozen, and I'm going to talk about almost all of them.) Suffice it to say at this point that all the various and sundry methods for starting Excel require that you have Windows XP or Windows 2000 installed on your personal computer. (Excel 2003 won't run under any older Windows versions, such as Windows 95 and 98.) After that, you have only to turn on the computer before you can use any of the following methods to get Excel 2003 started.

Starting Excel 2003 from the Windows Start menu

The most common way to launch Excel is by selecting the program from the Windows Start menu just as you can do to start any program installed on your computer. To start Excel 2003 from the Start menu, follow these simple steps:

1. **Click the Start button on the Windows taskbar to open the Windows Start menu.**

2. **Highlight All Programs at the top of the Start menu.**

3. **Click the Microsoft Excel 2003 option on the Programs menu.**

As soon as you complete these steps, Windows opens Excel 2003. As the program loads, you see the opening screen for Microsoft Excel 2003. When Excel finishes loading, you are presented with a screen like the one shown in Figure 1-4, containing a new workbook in which you can begin working.

After launching Excel from the All Programs submenu, Windows goes ahead and adds Microsoft Excel to the left panel of the Windows Start menu. This means that the next time you need to launch Excel, all you have to do is click the Start button on the Windows taskbar and then click Microsoft Excel on the left side of the Start menu.

Starting Excel 2003 with a desktop shortcut

If you use Excel all the time like I do, you won't want to have to deal with the Start menu each time you need to launch the program. Instead, you can create an Excel desktop shortcut that enables you to start the program simply by double-clicking its icon. If you find that's too much trouble, you can add the desktop shortcut to the Quick Launch toolbar on the Windows taskbar. By doing that, you make it possible to launch the program simply by clicking the Excel button on the Quick Launch toolbar.

To create the Excel desktop shortcut, follow these steps:

1. **Click the Start button on the Windows taskbar.**

   The Start menu opens where you can click the Search item.

2. **Click Search in the lower-right corner of the Start menu.**

   The Search Results dialog box appears.

3. **Click the All Files and Folders link in the panel on the left side of the Search Results dialog box.**

   The Search Companion pane appears on the left side of the Search Results dialog box.

4. **Type excel.exe in the All or Part of the File Name text box.**

   Excel.exe is the name of the executable program file that runs Excel. After finding this file on your hard disk, you can create a desktop shortcut from it that launches the program.

5. **Click the Search button.**

   Windows now searches your hard disk for the Excel program file. After locating this file, its name appears on the right side of the Search Results dialog box. When this filename appears, you can click the Stop button in the left panel to halt the search

6. **Right-click the file icon for the excel.exe file and then highlight Send To on the pop-up menu and click Desktop (Create Shortcut) on its continuation menu.**

   A shortcut named Shortcut to excel.exe appears to your desktop.

7. **Click the Close button in the upper-right corner of the Search Results dialog box.**

   After closing the Search Results dialog box, you should see the icon named Shortcut to excel.exe on the desktop. You should probably rename the shortcut to something a little more friendly, such as Excel 2003.

8. **Right-click the Shortcut to excel.exe icon and then click Rename on the pop-up menu.**

9. **Replace the current name by typing a new shortcut name, such as** Excel 2003 **and then click anywhere on the desktop.**

After creating an Excel desktop shortcut on the desktop, from then on, you can launch Excel by double-clicking the shortcut icon.

If you want to be able to launch Excel by clicking a single button, drag the icon for your Excel desktop shortcut to the Quick Launch toolbar to the immediate right of the Start button at the beginning of the Windows taskbar. When you position the icon on this toolbar, Windows indicates where the new Excel button will appear by drawing a black, vertical I-beam in front of or between the existing buttons on this bar. As soon as you release the mouse button, Windows adds an Excel 2003 button to the Quick Launch toolbar that enables you to launch the program by a single-click of its icon.

Figure 1-3 shows my Windows desktop after creating an Excel 2003 desktop shortcut and adding this shortcut as a button to the Quick Launch toolbar. Note that Windows does not remove the desktop shortcut at the time you add it to the Quick Launch toolbar. That way, you have a choice between using the desktop shortcut (with a double-click) or using the Excel 2003 button on the Quick Launch toolbar (with a single-click).

Mousing Around

Although most of Excel's capabilities are accessible from the keyboard, in most cases the mouse is the most efficient way to select a command or perform a particular procedure. For that reason alone, if you need to use Excel regularly in getting your work done, it is well worth your time to master the program's various mouse techniques.

Minding your mouse manners

Windows programs, such as Excel, use four basic mouse techniques to select and manipulate various objects in the program and workbook windows:

✔ **Clicking an object to select it:** Positioning the pointer on something and then pressing and immediately releasing the primary mouse button (the left button unless, as a leftie, you've switched the buttons around).

✔ **Right-clicking an object to display its shortcut menu:** Positioning the pointer on something and then pressing and immediately releasing the secondary mouse button (the right button unless, as a leftie, you've switched the buttons around).

- ✔ **Double-clicking an object to open it:** Positioning the pointer on something and then pressing and immediately releasing the primary mouse button rapidly twice in a row.

- ✔ **Dragging an object to move or copy it:** Positioning the pointer on something and then pressing and holding down the primary mouse button as you move the mouse in the direction you wish to drag the object. When you have positioned the object in the desired location on the screen, you then release the primary mouse button to place it.

When clicking an object to select it, you must make sure that the tip of the mouse pointer is touching the object that you want to select before you click. To avoid moving the pointer slightly before you click, grasp the sides of the mouse between your thumb (on one side) and your ring and little finger (on the other side), and then click the primary button with your index finger. If you run out of room on your desktop for moving the mouse, just pick up the mouse and reposition it on the desk (which does not move the pointer).

Excel 2003 desktop shortcut

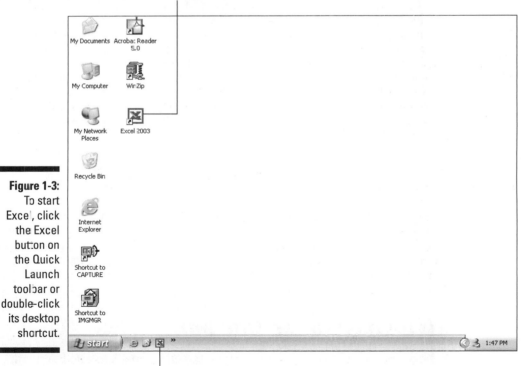

Figure 1-3:
To start Excel, click the Excel button on the Quick Launch toolbar or double-click its desktop shortcut.

Excel 2003 Quick Launch button

When a single click is just as good as a double

Keep in mind that when using Windows XP or 2000, you have the ability to modify the way that you open icons on the Windows desktop on the General tab of the Folder Options dialog box (opened by choosing Tools⇨Folder Options on menu bar of a window, such as My Documents and My Computer). If you use a single-click to Open an Item (Point to Select), you can open programs, such as Excel 2003, along with any of its folders and files on the desktop and in the My Computer and Explorer windows by single-clicking their icons. If this is how your computer is set up, your double-clicking days are pretty much over and done!

Getting your mouse pointer in shape

The shape of the mouse pointer is anything but static in the Excel program. As you move the mouse pointer to different parts of the Excel screen, the pointer changes shape to indicate a change in function.

Don't confuse the mouse pointer with the cell pointer. The *mouse pointer* changes shape as you move it around the screen. The *cell pointer* always maintains its shape as an outline around the current cell or cell selection (whereupon it expands to include all the selected cells). The mouse pointer responds to any movement of your mouse on the desk and always moves independently of the cell pointer. You can use the mouse pointer to reposition the cell pointer, however. You do this by positioning the thick, white cross pointer in the cell that you want to hold the cell pointer and then clicking the primary mouse button.

So What Do All These Buttons Do?

In Figure 1-4, I identify the different parts of the Excel program window that appear when you first start the program (assuming that you haven't selected an existing workbook to open at the same time the program starts). As you can see, the Excel window, upon opening, is chock-full of all kinds of useful, though potentially confusing, stuff!

Turning on to the title bar

The first bar in the Excel window is called the *title bar* because it shows you the name of the program that is running in the window (Microsoft Excel).

When the workbook window is full size (as it is in Figure 1-4), the name of the workbook file follows Microsoft Excel, as in

```
Microscft Excel Enterprise Edition - Book1
```

To the left of the program and filename on the title bar, you see the Excel icon (it appears as a green italic *L* crossed to form an X inside a box). When you click this icon, the program Control menu opens with all the commands that enable you to size and move the Excel program window. If you choose the Close command (the large X in the upper-right corner) on this menu (or press the shortcut keys, Alt+F4), you exit from Excel and are returned to the desktop.

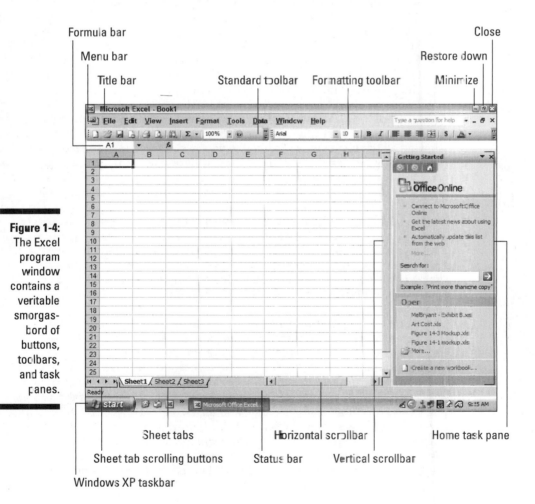

Figure 1-4:
The Excel program window contains a veritable smorgasbord of buttons, toolbars, and task panes.

Formula bar

Menu bar

Title bar

Standard toolbar

Formatting toolbar

Close

Restore down

Minimize

Sheet tabs

Horizontal scrollbar

Home task pane

Sheet tab scrolling buttons

Status bar

Vertical scrollbar

Windows XP taskbar

The buttons on the right side of the title bar are sizing buttons. Click the Minimize button (the one with the underscore), and the Excel window shrinks down to a button on the Windows taskbar. Click the Restore Down button (the one with the image of two smaller, tiled windows), and the Excel window assumes a somewhat smaller size on the desktop, and the Restore Down button changes to the Maximize button (the one with a single, full-size window), which you can use to restore the window to its original full size. If you click the Close button (the one with an X), you exit Excel (just as if you choose Close on the Control menu or press Alt+F4).

Messing around with the menu bar

The second bar in the Excel window is the *menu bar.* This bar contains the Excel pull-down menus, File through Help. You use these menus to select the Excel commands that you need to select when creating or editing your worksheets. (Jump ahead to the section "Ordering Directly from the Menus" for more information on how to select commands.)

To the left of the pull-down menus, you see an Excel file icon. When you click this icon, the file Control menu (much like the program Control menu) opens, showing all the commands that enable you to size and move the Excel workbook window (which fits within the Excel program window). Choose the Close command on this menu (or press the shortcut keys, Ctrl+W or Ctrl+F4), and you close the current Excel workbook without exiting the Excel program.

To the right of the pull-down menus, you see the Ask a Question drop-down text box. You can use this box to ask the Excel Answer Wizard any question you have about using Excel 2003. When you enter a new question in the Ask a Question box, Excel displays a list of possibly relevant help topics beneath the text box. Clicking one of these topics automatically opens the Excel Help window (see "Ogling the Online Help," later in this chapter, for details).

The sizing buttons on the right side of the menu bar do the same thing to the current workbook window as the sizing buttons on the title bar do to the Excel program window. Click the Minimize Window button, and the Excel workbook window shrinks down to a tiny workbook title bar at the bottom of the workbook area. Click the Restore Window button, and the current workbook window assumes a somewhat smaller size on the workbook area. The Excel workbook icon, filename, and file-sizing buttons move to the title bar of this somewhat smaller workbook window; and the Restore Window button changes to the Maximize button, which you can use to restore the window to its original full size. If you click the Close button (the one with the X), you close the current workbook file (just as if you choose Close on the file Control menu or press Ctrl+W or Ctrl+F4).

Excel 2003 automatically adds a button to the Windows taskbar for each workbook file that you open in Excel 2003. This nifty new feature makes it super-easy to switch between workbooks. When you minimize the Excel program with the program's Minimize Window button, a button displaying the name of the current workbook is added to the taskbar.

Scrutinizing the Standard and Formatting toolbars

The third bar in Excel 2003 stacks the two most popular Excel toolbars, Standard and Formatting, side by side. These two toolbars contain buttons (also known as *tools*) for doing the most common tasks that you perform in Excel. Tools on the Standard toolbar include those for doing really basic file-type stuff such as creating, saving, opening, and printing workbooks. Tools on the Formatting toolbar include those for manipulating appearance-type stuff, such as selecting a new font and font size and adding effects such as **boldface**, underlining, and *italics* to worksheet text.

To identify the function of any of the tools on these two (or any other) toolbars, simply position the arrowhead mouse pointer over the button until a tiny text box (called a *ScreenTip*) appears below the mouse pointer. To have Excel execute the command associated with a particular tool, simply click the button under the mouse pointer.

Because the Standard and Formatting toolbars each contain a whole bunch of tools, not all the buttons in either toolbar can be displayed together on the third bar of the Excel screen. This is why the last tool on each of these two toolbars, the Toolbar Options button (indicated by a downward-pointing black triangle), has the continuation symbol (>>) over it. The presence of this symbol immediately tells you that the toolbar is truncated in some way and that not all of its buttons are displayed.

Stack 'em up

If you prefer to have immediate access to *all* the buttons on the Standard and Formatting toolbars at *all* times, you can do so easily by stacking the two toolbars one on top of the other, rather than side by side. (This is the way that these two toolbars appeared in all three previous versions of Excel for Windows). To make this change, right-click somewhere on the menu bar or third bar with the two toolbars, and then select the Customize command at the very bottom of the shortcut menu that pops up. Doing this opens the Customize dialog box from which you click the Options tab. Click the first check box option on the Options tab labeled Show Standard and Formatting Toolbars On Two Rows to add a check mark. I promise: You'll never have need for the Toolbar Options button again.

When you click the Toolbar Options button, Excel displays a palette with the additional tools that don't fit on the toolbar when it's stacked side-by-side with another toolbar. At the bottom of the palette of additional tools, you find two commands:

- **Show Buttons on Two Rows:** Click this to display the Standard and Formatting toolbars on separate rows.

- **Add or Remove Buttons:** This command comes with a pop-up button that enables you to customize which buttons appear on either the Standard or Formatting toolbars.

When you select the Add or Remove Buttons item on the Toolbar Options pop-up menu, Excel displays another pop-up menu from which you can select the Standard or Formatting toolbar. After selecting Standard or Formatting from this submenu, yet another pop-up menu appears, this one showing all the buttons associated with the particular toolbar (Standard or Formatting) that you selected. All the buttons currently displayed on the particular toolbar have check marks in front of them. To add buttons to the toolbar from this menu, click the tool in question to precede it with a check mark. To temporarily remove one of the buttons on the toolbar, click the button to remove its check mark. (For detailed information on customizing the buttons on these and other Excel toolbars, see Chapter 12.)

In Table 1-1, you can see the name and function of each tool normally found on the Standard toolbar when you first install Excel 2003. In Table 1-2, I list the name and function of each tool usually found on the Formatting toolbar. Rest assured: You will come to know each one intimately as your experience with Excel grows.

Table 1-1		The Cool Tools on the Standard Toolbar
Tool	*Tool Name*	*What the Tool Does When You Click It*
	New	Opens a new workbook with three blank worksheets.
	Open	Opens an existing Excel workbook.
	Save	Saves changes in the active workbook.
	Permission	Lists the current permission settings on the current workbook and enables you to set or change these permissions.
	E-mail	Opens an e-mail message header for sending the worksheet to someone via the Internet.

Tool	Tool Name	What the Tool Does When You Click It
	Print	Prints the workbook.
	Print Preview	Previews how the worksheet will appear when printed.
	Spelling	Checks the spelling of spreadsheet text.
	Research	Opens the Research task pane where you can search for online information.
	Cut	Cuts the current selection from the work-sheet and places it into the Clipboard as a prelude to pasting it elsewhere.
	Copy	Copies the current selection to the Clipboard.
	Paste	Pastes the current contents of the Clipboard into your worksheet.
	Format Painter	Applies all the formatting used in the current cell to any cell selection that you choose.
	Undo	Undoes your last action.
	Redo	Repeats your last action.
	Insert Hyperlink	Enables you to insert a hypertext link to another file, Internet address (URL), or spe-cific location in another document. (See Chapter 10 for information on using hyperlinks.)
	AutoSum	Adds, averages, counts, or finds the highest or lowest value in the current selection of cells or enables you to select some other Excel function.
	Sort Ascending	Sorts data in a cell selection in alphabetical and/or numerical order, depending upon the type of data in the cells.
	Sort Descending	Sorts data in a cell selection in reverse alphabetical and/or numerical order, depending upon the type of data in the cells.

(continued)

Table 1-1 *(continued)*

Tool	Tool Name	What the Tool Does When You Click It
	ChartWizard	Walks you through the creation of a new chart in the active worksheet. (See Chapter 8 for details.)
	Drawing	Displays and hides the Drawing toolbar, which enables you to draw various shapes and arrows. (See Chapter 8 for details.)
100%	Zoom	Changes the screen magnification to zoom in or out on your worksheet data.
	Microsoft Excel Help	Displays the Microsoft Excel task pane on the right side of the screen from which you can use the Answer Wizard to search for help or look up particular topics to get help on using various Excel features. (See "Ogling the Online Help," later in this chapter, for details.)

Table 1-2   The Cool Tools on the Formatting Toolbar

Tool	Tool Name	What the Tool Does When You Click It
Arial	Font	Applies a new font to the entries in the cell selection.
10	Font Size	Applies a new font size to the entries in the cell selection.
B	Bold	Applies bold to or removes bold from the cell selection.
I	Italic	Applies italics to or removes italics from the cell selection.
U	Underline	Underlines the entries in the cell selection (not the cells); if the entries are already underlined, clicking this tool removes the underlining.
	Align Left	Left-aligns the entries in the cell selection.
	Center	Centers the entries in the cell selection.

Tool	Tool Name	What the Tool Does When You Click It
☰	Align Right	Right-aligns the entries in the cell selection.
⊞	Merge and Center	Centers the entry in the active cell across selected columns by merging their cells into one.
$	Currency Style	Applies a Currency number format to the cell selection to display all values with a dollar sign, with commas between thousands, and two decimal places.
%	Percent Style	Applies a Percentage number format to the cell selection; the values are multiplied by 100 and displayed with a percent sign and no decimal places.
,	Comma Style	Applies a Comma number format to the cell selection to display commas separating thousands and adds two decimal places.
+.0 .00	Increase Decimal	Adds one decimal place to the number format in the cell selection each time that you click the tool; reverses direction and reduces the number of decimal places when you hold down the Shift key while you click this tool.
.00 +.0	Decrease Decimal	Reduces one decimal place from the number format in the cell selection each time that you click the tool; reverses direction and adds one decimal place when you hold down the Shift key as you click this tool.
⇤	Decrease Indent	Outdents the entry in the current cell to the left by one character width of the standard font.
⇥	Increase Indent	Indents the entry in the current cell to the right by one character width of the standard font.
⊞ ▾	Borders	Selects a border for the cell selection from the pop-up palette of border styles.

(continued)

Table 1-2 *(continued)*

Tool	Tool Name	What the Tool Does When You Click It
	Fill Color	Selects a new color for the background of the cells in the cell selection from the pop-up color palette.
	Font Color	Selects a new color for the text in the cells in the cell selection from the pop-up color palette.
	Toolbar Options	Displays a pop-up menu with a menu item that enables you to show the Standard and Formatting toolbars on two rows (if they currently share one) or one row (if they currently inhabit a single row each) and an item for adding and removing buttons. If the toolbar is truncated (indicated by the addition of >> to this button), this pop-up menu contains a palette with all the tools that can't currently be displayed on the toolbar.

Fumbling around the Formula bar

The Formula bar displays the cell address and the contents of the current cell. This bar is divided into three sections:

- **Name box:** The left-most section that displays the address of the current cell address

- **Formula bar buttons:** The second, middle section that is shaded and contains the Name box drop-down button on the left and the Insert Function button (labeled *fx*) on the right

- **Cell contents:** The third, right-most white area that takes up the rest of the bar

If the current cell is empty, the third cell contents section of the formula bar is blank. As soon as you begin typing an entry or building a worksheet formula, the second and third sections of the formula bar come alive. As soon as you type a character, the Cancel and Enter buttons appear in the shaded Formula bar buttons section (see Figure 1-5). These buttons appear in between the Name box drop-down button (which automatically changes into a Functions drop-down button whenever you edit a cell containing a formula) and the Insert Function button. (See Chapter 2 for information on using these buttons.)

Name box or Functions drop-down button

Cancel button

Enter button

Name box   Insert Function button

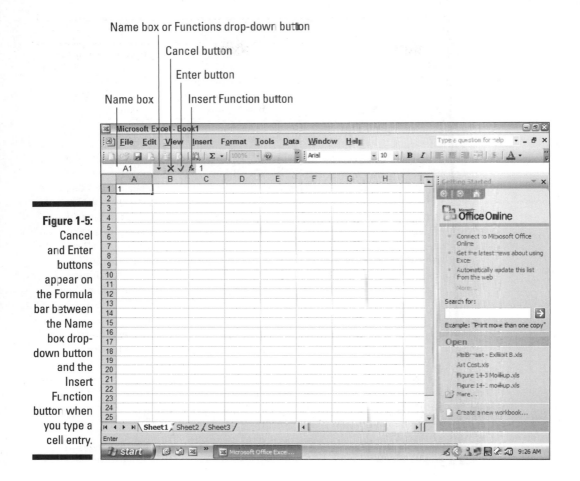

Figure 1-5:
Cancel
and Enter
buttons
appear on
the Formula
bar between
the Name
box drop-
down button
and the
Insert
Function
button when
you type a
cell entry.

After the Insert Function button, you see the characters that you typed in the cell contents section of the Formula bar, mirroring the characters that appear in the worksheet cell itself. After you complete the entry in the cell — by clicking the Enter button — Excel displays the entire entry or formula in the Formula bar, and the Enter and Cancel buttons disappear from the Formula bar buttons section. The contents that you enter into any cell thereafter always appear in the Formula bar whenever you position the cell pointer in that cell of the worksheet.

Winding your way through the workbook window

A blank Excel workbook appears in a workbook window right below the Formula bar when you first start the program (assuming that you don't start it by double-clicking an Excel workbook icon) accompanied by the New

Workbook task pane to its right. As you can see in Figure 1-6, when you click the Restore Window button to make the workbook window less than full size, the workbook appears in its own space to the left of the Home task pane. This workbook window also has its own Control menu (accessed by clicking the Excel file icon), title bar, and sizing buttons. Its title bar also displays the workbook filename. (This appears as a temporary filename, such as Book1, and then Book2 when you open your next new workbook, and so on, until you save the file the first time.)

On the bottom of the workbook window, you see sheet tab scrolling buttons, then the sheet tabs for activating the various worksheets in your workbook (remember that each new Excel workbook has three new sheets to start), followed by the horizontal scroll bar that you can use to bring new columns of the current worksheet into view. On the right side of the workbook window, you see a vertical scroll bar that you can use to bring new rows of the current worksheet into view (keeping in mind that you're only viewing a small percentage of the total columns and rows in each worksheet). At the intersection of the horizontal and vertical scroll bars, in the lower-right corner, you find a size box, which you can use to manually modify the size and shape of the less-than-maximized workbook window.

When you start Excel, you can immediately begin creating a new spreadsheet in Sheet1 of the Book1 workbook that appears in the maximized workbook window. To separate the workbook's title bar as well as the Control menu, and sizing buttons from the Excel menu bar, you click the Restore Window button on the menu bar. Doing this reduces the workbook window just enough to get all this stuff on its own workbook title bar as shown in Figure 1-6.

Manually manipulating the workbook window

When you're working with a less-than-maximized workbook window (like the one shown in Figure 1-6), you can manually size and move the window with the sizing box that appears in the lower-right corner at the intersection of the horizontal and vertical scroll bars.

To manipulate the size of a workbook window, position the mouse pointer on this sizing box, and then, when the mouse pointer changes shape to a double-headed arrow, drag the mouse as needed to adjust the size of the side or sides of the window. Note that the mouse pointer does not change to a double-headed arrow unless you position it on the edge of the window (that is, somewhere on the corner). While the pointer is positioned within the box, it retains its arrowhead shape.

- ✔ If you position the pointer on the bottom side of the window and then drag the pointer straight up, the workbook window becomes shorter. If you drag the pointer straight down, the window becomes longer.

- ✔ If you position the pointer on the right side of the window and then drag the pointer straight to the left, the workbook window becomes narrower; if you drag straight to the right, the window becomes wider.

✔ If you position the pointer on the lower-right corner of the window and then drag the pointer diagonally toward the upper-left corner, the workbook window becomes both shorter and narrower; if you drag diagonally away from the upper-left corner, it becomes longer and wider.

When the outline of the workbook window reaches the desired size, you then release the primary mouse button, and Excel redraws the workbook window to your new size.

REMEMBER

After using the size button to change the size and shape of a workbook window, you must use the size button again and manually restore the window to its original shape and dimensions. Unfortunately, Excel has no magic Restore button available that you can click to automatically restore the workbook window that you changed.

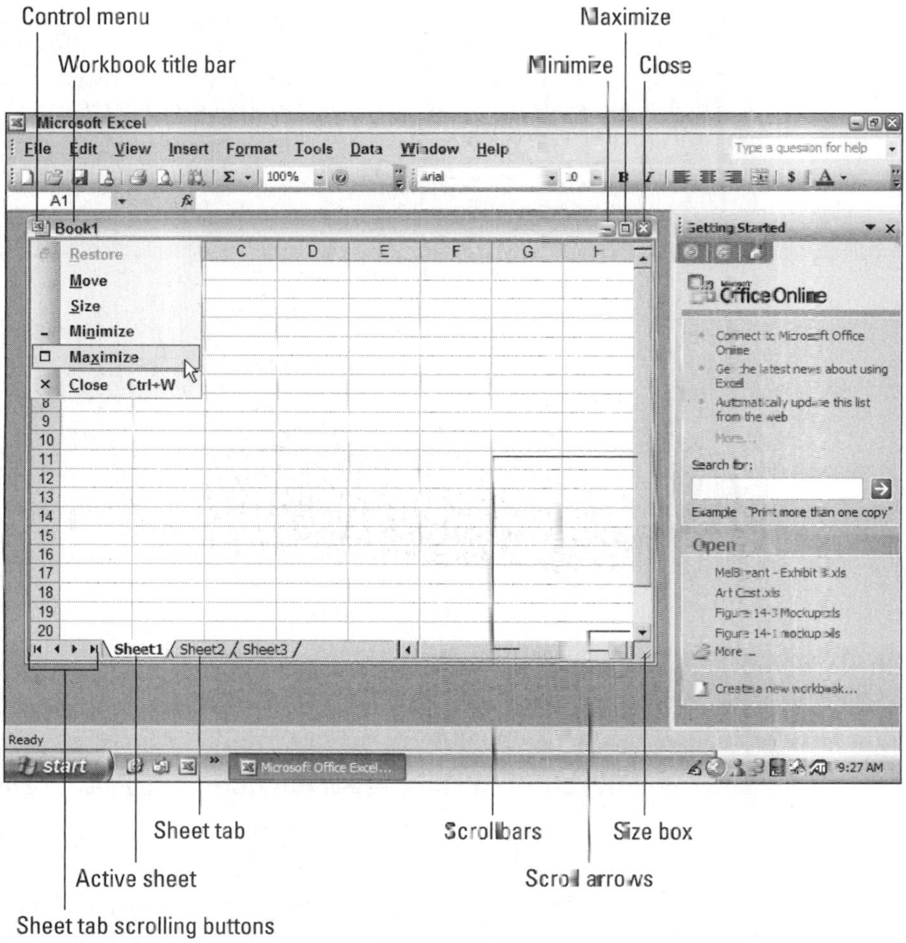

Control menu

Workbook title bar

Maximize

Minimize   Close

Figure 1-6:
Each Excel
workbook
contains its
own Control
menu and
scrolling
and sizing
buttons.

Sheet tab

Active sheet

Sheet tab scrolling buttons

Scrollbars

Scroll arrows

Size box

WARNING!

Musical toolbars!

Don't get too used to the button arrangement that you experience when first using the Standard or Formatting toolbars. Excel 2003 uses the intelli-(non)-sense feature whereby the program automatically keeps promoting the button that you last used to a higher position on the toolbar. For instance, if you use a button on the Toolbar Options palette, the button is immediately added to the regularly displayed portion of the toolbar. Excel 2003 banishes one of the unused buttons that appears near the end of the toolbar onto the Toolbar Options palette. The end result is musical toolbars wherein you can never be sure where a needed button will appear (or not appear if it happens to be exiled temporarily to the Toolbar Options palette)!

Unfortunately, Excel 2003 doesn't give you an option for fixing the position of the buttons on the toolbars so that you can always tell where a needed button appears. You can, however, restore the original arrangement of the buttons on the toolbars (as well as the commands on the menus) by right-clicking somewhere on the menu bar or the bar with the Standard and Formatting toolbars and then selecting the Customize command on the shortcut menu that appears. Doing this opens the Customize dialog box from which you select the Options tab. Click the Reset Menu and Toolbar Usage Data button on the Options tab. Excel then displays an alert box indicating that the record of the commands you've selected in Excel is about to be deleted. Click the Yes button, and the program restores the buttons on your toolbars (and the commands on your menus) to their previous order.

Besides resizing workbook windows, you can also move them around within the area between the Formula bar and status bar in the Excel program window.

To move a workbook window:

1. **Simply pick it up by the scruff of its neck — which, in this case, corresponds to the workbook window's title bar.**

2. **After you have it by the title bar, drag it to the desired position and release the primary mouse button.**

If you are experiencing difficulty in dragging objects with the mouse, you can also move a workbook window by following these steps:

1. **Click the Excel file icon on the workbook window's title bar to open its Control menu and then select the Move command or press Ctrl+F7.**

   The mouse pointer changes shape from the normal thick, white-cross pointer to a pointer with crossed, double-headed arrows.

2. **Drag the window with the arrowheads cross-hair pointer or press the arrow keys on the cursor keypad (←, ↑, →, or ↓) to move the workbook window into the desired position.**

3. **Press Enter to set the workbook window into position.**

   The mouse pointer returns to its normal thick, white-cross shape.

Slipping through the sheets

At the very bottom of the Excel workbook window that contains the horizontal scroll bar, you see the sheet tab scrolling buttons followed by the sheet tabs for the three worksheets in the workbook. Excel shows which worksheet is active by displaying its sheet tab on top in white as part of the displayed worksheet (rather than belonging to unseen worksheets below) with its sheet name in boldface type. To activate a new worksheet (thus bringing it to the top and displaying its information in the workbook window), you click its sheet tab.

If you add more sheet tabs to your workbook (see Chapter 7 for details on how to add more worksheets to your workbook) and the sheet tab for the worksheet that you want is not displayed, use the sheet tab scrolling buttons to bring the worksheet into view. Click the buttons with the black triangles pointing left and right to scroll one worksheet at a time in either direction (left to scroll left, and right to scroll right). Click the buttons with the black triangles pointing left and right to the vertical lines to scroll the sheets so that the tabs for the very first or very last worksheets display at the bottom.

Scoping out the status bar

The bar at the very bottom of the Excel program window is called the *status bar* because it displays information that keeps you informed of the current state of Excel. The left part of the status bar displays messages indicating the state of the current activity you're undertaking in the program. When you first start Excel, the message Ready (far lower-left corner) displays in this area (as shown in Figure 1-7), telling you that the program is ready to accept your next entry or command.

The right side of the status bar contains various boxes that display different indicators telling you when you've placed Excel in a particular state that somehow affects how you work with the program. For example, normally, when you first start Excel, the Num Lock indicator shows NUM in this part of the status bar. If you press the Caps Lock key to enter text in all uppercase letters, CAPS appears to the left of NUM. Press the Scroll Lock key (so as to be able to scroll through the worksheet with the arrow keys), and SCRL appears to its right.

You AutoCalculate my totals

The widest box (the second one from the left) in the status bar contains the AutoCalculate indicator. You can use the AutoCalculate indicator to get a running total of any group of values in your worksheet (See the beginning of Chapter 3 if you need information on how to select groups of cells in a worksheet.) For example, in Figure 1-7 you see a typical spreadsheet after selecting part of a column of cells, many of which contain values. The total of all the values in the cells that are currently selected in this worksheet automatically appears in the AutoCalculate indicator on the status bar.

Not only does the AutoCalculate indicator on the status bar give you the sum of the values in the cells you currently have selected, but the indicator can also give you other statistics, such as the count or the average of these values. All you have to do is right-click the AutoCalculate indicator to display its shortcut menu and then choose from among the following options:

- ✔ To get the average of the values in the current cell selection, you select Average from this indicator's shortcut menu.

- ✔ To get the count of all the cells that contain values (cells containing text entries are not counted), select Count Nums from this indicator's shortcut menu.

- ✔ To get the count of all the cells that are selected regardless of what type of data they contain, select Count from the indicator's shortcut menu.

- ✔ To have the highest value in the cell selection displayed in the AutoCalculate indicator, choose Max from the indicator's shortcut menu. To have the lowest value displayed, choose Min.

- ✔ To have no calculations appear in this area of the status bar, choose None at the top of this shortcut menu.

- ✔ To return the AutoCalculate indicator to its normal totaling function, choose Sum on the indicator's shortcut menu.

The Num Lock indicator and the numeric keypad

The NUM in the Num Lock indicator tells you that you can use the numbers on the numeric keypad to enter values in the worksheet. When you press the Num Lock key, NUM disappears from the Num Lock indicator. This is your signal that the cursor-movement functions that also are assigned to this keypad are now in effect. This means, for instance, that pressing 6 moves the cell pointer one cell to the right instead of entering this value in the formula bar!

Taming the Excel 2003 task panes

When you first launch Excel with a blank workbook, Excel 2003 automatically opens the Getting Started task pane to the immediate right of the workbook (as shown earlier in Figure 1-4). You can use this task pane to edit recently opened workbooks or to create other new workbooks (see Chapter 2 for details). Along with the Getting Started task pane, Excel 2003 supports a fair number of other task panes including a Help, Search Results, Clip Art, Research, Clipboard, and New Workbook along with more specialized task panes such as the Template Help, Shared Workspace, Document Actions, Document Updates, and XML Structure task panes.

Figure 1-7: The sum of the values in the cells currently selected automatically appears in Auto-Calculate indicator on the status bar.

Microsoft Excel Enterprise Edition - CG Media 2003 Sales -1.xls

File Edit View Insert Format Tools Data Window Help

B4   fx 1245

	A	B	C	D	E	F	G	H	I	J
1	CG Media - 2003 Sales by Media and Category									
2		Jan	Feb	Mar	Qtr 1	Apr	May	Jun	Qtr 2	Jul
3	Compact Disc Sales									
4	Rock	1,245.00	1,373.24	1,229.05	3,847.23	1,069.27	1,122.73	1,178.87	3,370.87	1,237
5	Jazz	1,061.47	1,170.80	1,047.67	3,230.14	911.64	957.23	1,005.09	2,873.96	1,055
6	Classical	855.60	943.73	844.64	2,643.96	734.83	771.57	810.15	2,316.56	850
7	Other	642.00	708.13	633.77	1,983.90	551.38	578.35	607.90	1,738.23	638
8	Total CD Sales	$3,804.07	$4,195.89	$3,755.32	$11,755.28	$3,267.13	$3,430.49	$3,602.01	$10,299.62	$3,782
9	Cassette Tape Sales									
10	Rock	945.65	1,418.48	1,241.17	3,605.29	1,154.67	872.93	1,309.40	3,337.00	1,571
11	Jazz	1,035.00	1,552.50	1,358.44	3,945.94	1,624.35	1,228.01	1,842.01	4,694.37	2,210
12	Classical	1,456.00	2,184.00	1,911.00	5,551.00	1,101.12	832.45	1,248.67	3,182.24	1,490
13	Other	987.00	1,480.50	1,295.44	3,762.94	4,935.13	3,730.96	5,598.44	14,263.54	6,715
14	Total Casette Sales	$4,423.65	$6,635.48	$5,806.04	$16,865.17	$8,815.28	$6,664.35	$9,998.53	$25,478.15	$11,995
15	Total Sales	$8,227.72	$10,831.36	$9,561.36	$28,620.45	$12,082.41	$10,094.84	$13,598.54	$35,775.78	$15,777

\2003/

Ready   Sum=3,804.07   CAPS NUM SCRL

start   Microsoft Excel Enter...   1:57 PM

Program status indicator   AutoCalculate indicator

Caps, Numbers, and Scroll Lock indicators

You can turn off the display of any Excel task pane by pressing Ctrl+F1 or by clicking its Close box located in the upper right-hand corner of its window. If you close the Task pane when working in Excel (so as to maximize the number of cells displayed on your computer screen), it remains closed until you press Ctrl+F1 again or choose the View⇨Task Pane or View⇨Toolbars⇨Task Pane command on the Excel menu bar.

When a task pane is displayed, you can select the type of task pane that you want open by clicking the drop-down button on to the immediate left of the task pane Close box and then selecting the type of pane to use. After selecting a new type of task pane, you can scroll between the different task pane choices by clicking the Previous and Next buttons (marked by a left and right arrow icon, respectively). To immediately return to the Getting Started task pane, click the Home button (the one with house icon).

If you decide that you don't want the Getting Started task pane to automatically be displayed each time that you start up Excel, you can turn off this feature by removing (deselecting) the check mark in the Startup Task Pane check box on the View tab of the Options dialog box that you open by choosing Tools⇨Options from the Excel menu bar.

You Gotta Get Me out of This Cell!

Excel provides several methods for getting around each of the huge worksheets in your workbook. One of the easiest ways is to click the tab for the sheet that you want to work with, and then use the scroll bars in the workbook window to bring new parts of this worksheet into view. In addition, the program provides a wide range of keystrokes that you can use not only to move a new part of the worksheet into view but also to make a new cell active by placing the cell pointer in it.

The secrets of scrolling

To understand how scrolling works in Excel, imagine the worksheet as a humongous papyrus scroll attached to rollers on the left and right. To bring into view a new section of a papyrus worksheet that is hidden on the right, you crank the left roller until the section with the cells that you want to see appears. Likewise, to scroll into view a new section of the worksheet that is hidden on the left, you would crank the right roller until that section of cells appears.

Calling up new columns with the horizontal scroll bar

You can use the *horizontal scroll bar* to scroll back and forth through the columns of a worksheet. To scroll new columns into view from the right, you click the right-arrow scroll button on the horizontal scroll bar. To scroll new columns into view from the left (anytime except when column A is the first column displayed), you click the left-arrow scroll button.

To scroll very quickly through columns in one direction or the other, you click the appropriate arrow scroll button in the scroll bar and continue to hold down the mouse button until the columns that you want to see display on the screen. As you scroll to the right in this manner, the *horizontal scroll box* (that big shaded box between the left- and right-arrow scroll buttons in the scroll bar) becomes increasingly smaller — it gets really teeny if you scroll really far right to columns in the hinterland, such as column BA. If you then click and hold down the left-arrow scroll button to scroll quickly back through columns to the left, notice that the horizontal scroll box becomes increasingly larger, until it takes up most of the scroll bar when you finally display column A again.

You can use the scroll box in the horizontal scroll bar to make big jumps to the left and right in the columns of the worksheet. Simply drag the scroll box in the appropriate direction along the bar.

Raising up new rows with the vertical scroll bar

Use the *vertical scroll bar* to scroll up and down through the rows of a worksheet. To scroll to new rows below those currently in view, you click the downarrow scroll button on the vertical scroll bar. To scroll back up to rows above that are no longer in view (anytime except when row 1 is the first one displayed), you click the up-arrow scroll button.

To scroll very quickly through rows in one direction or the other, you click and hold down the appropriate arrow scroll button in the vertical scroll bar just as you do in the horizontal scroll bar. As you scroll down the rows with the down-arrow scroll button, the *vertical scroll box* (that big shaded box between the up- and down-arrow scroll buttons in the scroll bar) becomes increasingly smaller and smaller — it gets really teeny if you scroll way down to rows 100 and higher. If you then click and hold down the up-arrow scroll button to scroll quickly back up through the rows, notice that the vertical scroll box becomes increasingly larger, until it takes up most of the scroll bar when you finally display row 1 again.

You can use the vertical scroll box to make big jumps up and down the rows of the worksheet by dragging the vertical scroll box in the appropriate direction along the bar.

Scrolling from screen to screen

You can use the horizontal and vertical scroll bars to scroll through the columns and rows of your worksheet one screen at a time. To do this, you click the light gray area of the scroll bar *not* occupied by the scroll box or the arrow scroll buttons. For example, to scroll to the right by one screen of columns when the scroll box is snug against the left-arrow scroll button, you simply click the light gray area of the scroll bar behind the scroll box, between it and the right-arrow scroll button. Then, to scroll back to the left by one screen of columns, you click the light gray area in front of the scroll box, between it and the left-arrow scroll button.

Likewise, to scroll up and down the rows of the worksheet one screen at a time, you click the light gray area either above or below the vertical scroll box, between it and the appropriate arrow scroll button.

The keys to moving the cell pointer

The only disadvantage to using the scroll bars to move around is that the scroll bars bring only new parts of the worksheet into view — they don't actually change the position of the cell pointer. If you want to start making entries in the cells in a new area of the worksheet, you still have to remember to select the cell (by clicking it) or the group of cells (by dragging through them) where you want the data to appear before you begin entering the data.

Excel offers a wide variety of keystrokes for moving the cell pointer to a
new cell. When you use one of these keystrokes, the program automatically
scrolls a new part of the worksheet into view, if this is required to move the
cell pointer. In Table 1-3, I summarize these keystrokes and how far each one
moves the cell pointer from its starting position.

Note: In the case of those keystrokes listed in Table 1-3 that use arrow keys,
you must either use the arrows on the cursor keypad or else have the Num
Lock disengaged on the numeric keypad of your keyboard. If you try to use
these arrow keys to move around the worksheet when Num Lock is on (indicated by the appearance of NUM on the status bar), you either get numbers
in the current cell or nothing happens at all (and then you'll blame me)!

Table 1-3	Keystrokes for Moving the Cell Pointer
Keystroke in Question	*Where the Cell Pointer Moves*
→ or Tab	Cell to the immediate right.
← or Shift+Tab	Cell to the immediate left.
↑	Cell up one row.
↓	Cell down one row.
Home	Cell in Column A of the current row.
Ctrl+Home	First cell (A1) of the worksheet.
Ctrl+End or End, Home	Cell in the worksheet at the intersection of the last column that has any data in it and the last row that has any data in it (that is, the last cell of the so-called active area of the worksheet).
PgUp	Cell one screenful up in the same column.
PgDn	Cell one screenful down in the same column.
Ctrl+→ or End, →	First occupied cell to the right in the same row that is either preceded or followed by a blank cell. If no cell is occupied, the pointer goes to the cell at the very end of the row.
Ctrl+← or End, ←	First occupied cell to the left in the same row that is either preceded or followed by a blank cell. If no cell is occupied, the pointer goes to the cell at the very beginning of the row.
Ctrl+↑ or End, ↑	First occupied cell above in the same column that is either preceded or followed by a blank cell. If no cell is occupied, the pointer goes to the cell at the very top of the column.

Keystroke in Question	Where the Cell Pointer Moves
Ctrl+↓ or End, ↓	First occupied cell below in the same column that is either preceded or followed by a blank cell. If no cell is occupied, the pointer goes to the cell at the very bottom of the column.
Ctrl+PgDn	Last occupied cell in the next worksheet of that workbook.
Ctrl+PgUp	Last occupied cell in the previous worksheet of that workbook.

Block moves

The keystrokes that combine the Ctrl or End key with an arrow key listed in Table 1-3 are among the most helpful for moving quickly from one edge to the other in large tables of cell entries or in moving from table to table in a section of the worksheet that contains many blocks of cells.

- If the cell pointer is positioned on a blank cell somewhere to the left of a table of cell entries that you want to view, pressing Ctrl+→ moves the cell pointer to the first cell entry at the leftmost edge of the table (in the same row, of course).

- When you then press Ctrl+→ a second time, the cell pointer moves to the last cell entry at the rightmost edge (assuming that no blank cells are in that row of the table).

- If you switch direction and press Ctrl+↑, Excel moves right to the last cell entry at the bottom edge of the table (again assuming that there are no blank cells below in that column of the table).

- If, when the cell pointer is at the bottom of the table, you press Ctrl+↑ again, Excel moves the pointer to the first entry at the top of the next table located below (assuming that no other cell entries are above this table in the same column).

- If you press Ctrl or End and arrow key combinations and there are no more occupied cells in the direction of the arrow key you select, Excel advances the cell pointer right to the cell at the very edge of the worksheet in that direction.

- If the cell pointer is located in cell C15 and no more occupied cells are in row 15, when you press Ctrl+→, Excel moves the cell pointer to cell IV15 at the rightmost edge of the worksheet.

- If you are in cell C15, there are no more entries below in Column C, and you press Ctrl+↑, Excel moves the pointer to cell C65536 at the very bottom edge of the worksheet.

When you use Ctrl and an arrow key to move from edge to edge in a table or between tables in a worksheet, you hold down Ctrl while you press one of the four arrow keys (indicated by the + symbol in keystrokes, such as Ctrl+→).

When you use End and an arrow-key alternative, you must press and then release the End key *before* you press the arrow key (indicated by the comma in keystrokes, such as End, →). Pressing and releasing the End key causes the END indicator to appear on the status bar. This is your sign that Excel is ready for you to press one of the four arrow keys.

Because you can keep the Ctrl key depressed as you press the different arrow keys that you need to use, the Ctrl-plus-arrow-key method provides a more fluid method for navigating blocks of cells than the End-then-arrow-key method.

When you gotta go to that cell right now!

Excel's Go To feature provides an easy method for moving directly to a distant cell in the worksheet. To use this feature, you display the Go To dialog box by choosing Edit⇨Go To from the Excel menu bar or by pressing Ctrl+G or the function key, F5. Then, in the Go To dialog box, you type the address of the cell that you want to go to in the Reference text box and click OK or press Enter. When typing in the cell address in the Reference text box, you can type the column letter or letters in uppercase or lowercase letters.

When you use the Go To feature to move the cell pointer, Excel remembers the references of the last four cells that you visited. These cell references then appear in the Go To list box. Notice that the address of the cell you last visited is also listed in the Reference box. This makes it possible to move quickly from your present location to your previous location in a worksheet by pressing F5 and Enter (provided that you used the Go To feature to move to your present position).

Lotsa luck with Scroll Lock

You can use the Scroll Lock key to "freeze" the position of the cell pointer in the worksheet so that you can scroll new areas of the worksheet in view with keystrokes such as PgUp (Page Up) and PgDn (Page Down) without changing the cell pointer's original position (in essence, making these keystrokes work in the same manner as the scroll bars).

After engaging Scroll Lock, when you scroll the worksheet with the keyboard, Excel does not select a new cell while it brings a new section of the worksheet into view. To "unfreeze" the cell pointer when scrolling the worksheet via the keyboard, you just press the Scroll Lock key again.

Ordering Directly from the Menus

For those occasions when the Excel Standard and Formatting toolbars don't provide you with a ready-made tool for getting a particular task done, you have to turn to the program's system of menu commands. Excel exhibits a little bit of menu overkill because, in addition to the regular pull-down menus found on the menu bar of nearly all Windows applications, the program also offers a secondary system of *shortcut* (also sometimes known as *context*) menus.

Shortcut menus offer fast access to just those menu commands normally used to manipulate the particular screen object that the menu is attached to (such as a toolbar, workbook window, or worksheet cell). As a result, shortcut menus often bring together commands that are otherwise found on several individual pull-down menus on the menu bar.

Penetrating the pull-down menus

Like when moving the cell pointer in the worksheet, Excel offers you a choice of using the mouse or the keyboard to select commands from the menu bar. To open a pull-down menu with the mouse, you simply click the menu name on the command bar. To open a pull-down menu with the keyboard, you hold down the Alt key while you type the letter that is underlined in the menu name (also known as the *command letter*). For instance, if you press Alt and, as you hold it down, then press E (abbreviated Alt+E), Excel opens the *E*dit menu because the *E* is underlined.

Alternatively, you can press and release the Alt key or function key F10 to access the menu bar, and then press the → key until you highlight the menu that you want to open. Then, to open the menu, you press the ↓ key.

After you open your pull-down menu, you can select any of its commands by clicking the command with the mouse; pressing the underlined letter in the command name; or by pressing the ↓ key until you highlight the command, and then pressing the Enter key.

As you learn the Excel commands, you can combine opening a menu and selecting one of its menu commands Click the menu and drag the pointer down the open menu until you highlight the desired command; then you release the mouse button. You can accomplish the same thing with the keyboard by holding down the Alt key while you type the command letters for both the pull-down menu and its command. To close the active workbook window by choosing the Close command on the File menu, you simply press Alt, and then type **FC**.

Some commands on the Excel pull-down menus have shortcut keystrokes assigned to them (shown after the command on the pull-down menu). You can use the shortcut keystrokes to select the desired command instead of having to access the pull-down menus. For example, to save changes to your workbook, you press the shortcut keys Ctrl+S instead of having to select the Save command from the File pull-down menu.

Many commands on the pull-down menus lead to the display of a dialog box, which contains further commands and options (see "Digging Those Dialog Boxes," later in this chapter). You can tell which commands on a pull-down menu lead to dialog boxes because the command name is followed by three periods (known as an *ellipsis*). For example, you know that selecting the File⇨ Save As command from the pull-down menu opens a dialog box because the command is listed as *Save As...* on the File menu.

Also, note that pull-down menu commands are not always available. You can tell when a command is not currently available because the command name is in light gray (or *dimmed*) on the pull-down menu. A command on a pull-down menu remains dimmed until the conditions under which it operates exist in your document. For example, the Paste command on the Edit menu remains dimmed as long as the Clipboard is empty. But as soon as you move or copy some information into the Clipboard with the Cut or Copy commands on the Edit menu, the Paste option is no longer dimmed and appears in normal bold type when you open the Edit menu — indicating, of course, that this command is now available for your use.

Now you see 'em, now you don't

The pull-down menus in Excel 2003 don't always appear the same way each time you access them. Thanks to another Microsoft intelli-(non)-sense feature, normally when you first open a menu, it appears in a truncated form with some of its commands missing. This "short" form of the menu is supposed to contain just those commands that you recently used, leaving out those that you haven't used in a while. Note that you can always tell when a menu has been shortened by the appearance of a continuation button (marked by two Vs, one on top of the other, creating a kind of downward-pointing arrow) at the very bottom.

If you have the time and patience to do nothing for a few seconds other than continue to display a shortened menu, Excel automatically replaces the shortened menu with the complete (unexpurgated) version. If you have neither the time nor the patience to wait, you can force Excel to display the entire menu's offerings by clicking the Expand button that appears with two downward pointing arrows one on top of the other at the bottom of the menu list.

When the full menu appears, the left border (where icons for some of the commands appear) for the previously missing menu items appear on the complete menu in a darker shade of gray than is applied to the previously displayed items. This lets you tell at a glance which menu items were newly added to the full-blown menu. It does not, however, help you in locating the new positions of the menu items that show up on both the "short" and "long" versions of the menu because many items are displaced by the addition of the newly displayed items!

If you, like me, have no desire to play hide-and-seek with the Excel pull-down menus, you can turn off this "nifty" new feature by taking the following steps:

1. **Right-click somewhere on the menu bar or the bar with the Standard and Formatting toolbars to open the shortcut menu.**

2. **Select the Customize command on the shortcut menu to open the Customize dialog box.**

   The Customize dialog box opens.

3. **Select the Options tab of the Customize dialog box.**

   On the Options tab, the check box reading Always Show Full Menus is not checked (the Show Full Menus after a Short Delay box is checked by default).

4. **Select the** Always Show Full Menus **check box.**

   As soon as you select the Always Show Full Menus check box, Excel automatically removes the check mark from the Show Full Menus After a Short Delay check box below and dims it to make it currently unavailable.

5. **Click the Close button in the Customize dialog box to close it.**

When you're really new to Excel, I highly suggest turning on the Always Show Full Menus option so that you don't keep losing the menu items you do use because the ones you don't use are not displayed until after a short wait.

Note: If you like playing hide-and-seek with the pull-down menus but care nothing for having the full menus automatically appear after a few seconds pause, you can disable this feature by removing the check mark from the check box labeled Show Full Menus After a Short Delay. This check box is located immediately below the Always Show Full Menus check box and is operational only when the Always Show Full Menus box is unchecked.

When changing these types of Personalized Menus and Toolbars settings on the Options tab of the Customize dialog box in Excel 2003, keep in mind that your changes equally affect the toolbars and pull-down menus in every Office 11 program installed on your computer, such as Word 2003 and PowerPoint 2003.

Comprehending shortcut menus

Unlike the pull-down menus, which you can access either with the mouse or the keyboard, you must use the mouse to open shortcut menus and select their commands. Because shortcut menus are attached to particular objects on the screen — such as a workbook window, toolbar, or worksheet cell — Excel uses the *secondary* mouse button (that is, the right button for right-handers and the left button for lefties) to open shortcut menus. (And because you right-handers far outnumber us lefties, this mouse technique has come to be known as *right-clicking an object.*)

In Figure 1-8, you can see the shortcut menu attached to the Excel tool-bars. To open this menu, position the mouse pointer somewhere on the toolbar and click the secondary mouse button. Be sure that you don't click the primary button, or you'll end up activating the tool that the pointer is on!

After you open the Toolbar shortcut menu, you can use its commands to display or hide any of the built-in toolbars or to customize the toolbars. (See Chapter 12 for details.)

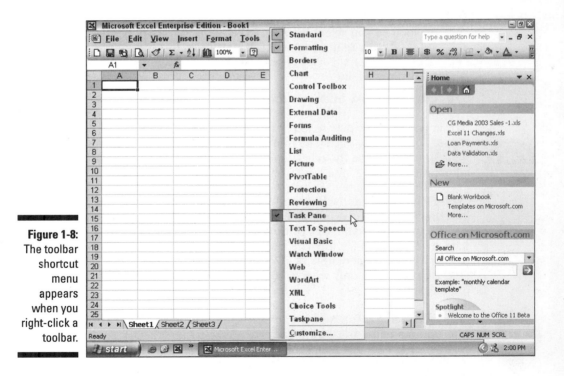

Figure 1-8:
The toolbar shortcut menu appears when you right-click a toolbar.

In Figure 1-9, check out the shortcut menu attached to any of the cells in a worksheet. To open this menu, position the pointer on any one of the cells and click the secondary mouse button. *Note:* You can also open this shortcut menu and apply its commands to the group of cells that you have selected. (You find out how to make cell selections in Chapter 3.)

Because the commands on shortcut menus contain command letters, you can select one of their commands either by dragging down to the command and then clicking it either with the primary or secondary mouse button or by typing the underlined letter to select it. Otherwise, you can press the ↓ or ↑ key until you highlight the command; then press Enter to select it.

The one shortcut menu that you can open with the keyboard is the shortcut menu attached to cells in a worksheet. To open this shortcut menu in the very upper-right corner of the current cell, you press Shift+F10. Note that this keystroke works for any type of Excel sheet except a chart, which doesn't have this type of shortcut menu attached to it.

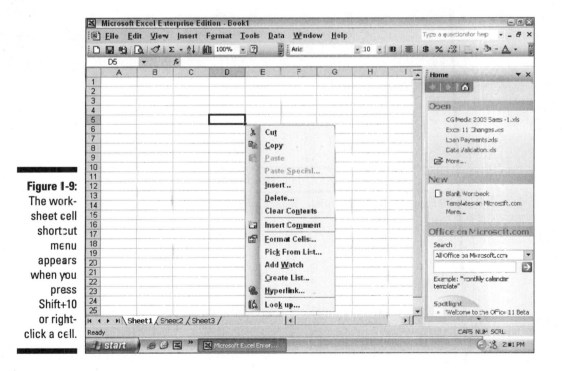

Figure 1-9: The work-sheet cell shortcut menu appears when you press Shift+10 or right-click a cell.

Digging Those Dialog Boxes

Many an Excel command is attached to a dialog box that presents you with a variety of options that you can apply to the command. Take a look at the General and View tabs of the Options dialog box shown in Figures 1-10 and 1-11. In these two figures, you can find almost all the different types of buttons, tabs, and boxes used by Excel in Table 1-4.

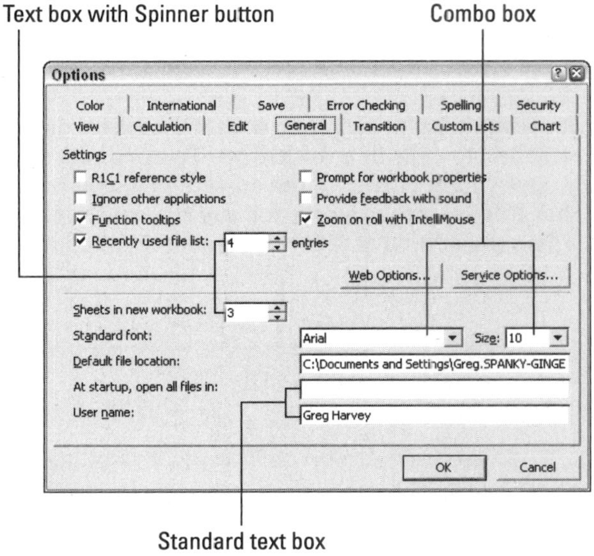

Text box with Spinner button   Combo box

Figure 1-10:
The General tab of the Options dialog box contains standard text boxes, text boxes with spinner buttons, along with a couple of combo boxes.

Standard text box

Table 1-4	The Parts of a Dialog Box
Button or Box in Question	*What It's Good For*
Tab	Provides a means of displaying a certain set of options in a complex dialog box like the Options dialog box (shown in Figure 1-11), bringing together a whole mess of different types of program settings that you can change.
Text box (or Edit box)	Provides a place for typing a new entry. Many edit boxes contain default entries that you can alter or replace entirely.

Button or Box in Question	What It's Good For
List box	Provides a list of options from which you choose. If the list box contains more options than can be displayed in its box, the list box contains a scroll bar that you can use to bring new options into view. Some list boxes are attached to a text box, enabling you to make a new entry in the text box either by typing it or by selecting it in the related list box.
Combo box (or drop-down list box)	Provides a condensed version of a standard list box that, instead of displaying several options in its list, shows only the current option (which originally is also the default option). To open the combo box and display the other options, you click the drop-down button that accompanies the box. After the list is displayed, you can select a new option from it as you would in any standard list box.
Check box	Presents a dialog box option that you can turn on or off. When the check box has a check mark in it, you know that its option is selected. When a check box is blank, you know that its option is not selected.
Radio (or Option) button	Presents items that have mutually exclusive options. The radio or option button consists of a circle followed by the named option. These buttons are always arranged in groups, and only one of the buttons in the group can be selected at one time. Excel lets you know which option is currently selected by placing a dot in the middle of its circle. (When an option button is selected, it looks like a knob on an old-fashioned radio, thus the name *radio button*.)
Spinner buttons	Spinner buttons appear as a pair of small boxes one atop the other. The spinner button on the top has an upward-pointing arrowhead on it, whereas the spinner button on the bottom has a downward-pointing arrowhead on it. You use the spinner buttons to scroll up and down through a series of preset options as you select the one you want.
Command button	Initiates an action. The command button is rectangular in shape, and the name of the command displays within the button. If a name in a command button is followed by an ellipsis (.), Excel displays another dialog box containing even more options when you select the button.

Radio or Option button

Check box

Drop-down list box   Command button

Note: Although you can move a dialog box out of the way of some data in your worksheet, you cannot change the box's size or shape — these dimensions are permanently fixed by the program.

Many dialog boxes contain default options or entries that are automatically selected unless you make new choices before you close the dialog box.

- ✔ To close a dialog box and put your selections into effect, click the OK button or the Close button (some boxes lack an OK button).

- ✔ If the OK button is surrounded by a dark border, which is very often the case, you can also press Enter to put your selections into effect.

- ✔ To close a dialog box without putting your selections into effect, you can either click the Cancel or Close button (the one with the X) in the dialog box, or simply press Esc.

Most dialog boxes group related options together as an item. (Often, this is done by placing a box around the options.) When making selections in a dialog box with the mouse, you simply click the selection that you want to use or, in the case of text entries, click the pointer in the entry to set the insertion point and then modify the entry.

When making selections with the keyboard, however, you must sometimes first activate the item before you can select any of its options.

- ✔ Press the Tab key until you activate one of the options in the item. (Shift+Tab activates the previous item.)

- ✔ When you press Tab (or Shift+Tab), Excel indicates which option is activated either by highlighting the default entry or by placing a dotted line around the name of the option.

- ✔ After activating an option, you can change its setting either by pressing ↑ or ↓ (this works with sets of radio buttons or options in a list or drop-down list boxes), pressing the space bar (this works to select and deselect check boxes), or by typing a new entry (used in text boxes).

You can also select an option by pressing Alt and then typing the underlined (command) letter in the option or item name.

- ✔ By pressing Alt and typing the command letter of a text box option, you select the entry in that text box (which you can then replace by typing the new entry).

- ✔ By pressing Alt and typing the command letter of a check box option, you can select or deselect the option (by adding or removing its check mark).

- ✔ By pressing Alt and typing the command letter of a radio button, you can select the option while at the same time deselecting whatever radio button was previously current.

- ✔ By pressing Alt and typing the command letter of a command button, you either initiate the command or display another dialog box.

In addition to the more elaborate dialog boxes shown in Figures 1-10 and 1-11, you also encounter a simpler type of dialog box used to display messages and warnings. These dialog boxes are appropriately known as *alert boxes*. Many dialog boxes of this type contain just an OK button that you must click to close the dialog box after reading the message.

Ogling the Online Help

You can get online help with Excel 2003 anytime that you need it while using the program. The only problem with the traditional online Help system is that it is only truly helpful when you are familiar with the Excel jargon. If you don't know what Excel calls a particular feature, you'll have trouble locating it in the Help topics (just like trying to look up in a dictionary a word that you have no idea how to spell). To help alleviate this problem, Excel makes use of the Answer Wizard to enable you to search for information on Microsoft's Web site. In your own words, you can type in a question about how to do something in Excel. The Answer Wizard then attempts to translate your question, phrased in perfectly good English, into its horrible Excel techno-babble so that it can then display the Help topics that give you the information you need.

Ask Mr. Answer Wizard

The Answer Wizard enables you to ask questions in plain English about using Excel. You can access the Answer Wizard in the Ask a Question combo box on the right side of the menu bar or in the Search text box in the Microsoft Excel Help task pane (opened by pressing F1).

For example, to search for information on printing a worksheet, you can type the question **How do I print a worksheet?** in the Search text box in the Microsoft Excel Help task pane and then click the Start Searching button (the green button with the right arrow to the immediate right) as shown in Figure 1-12. The Answer Wizard responds by displaying a list of printing-related topics similar to those shown in Figure 1-13.

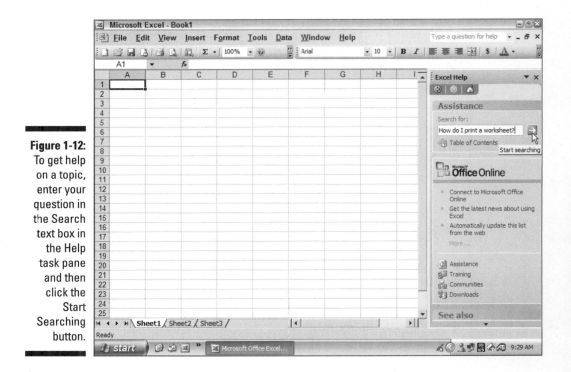

Figure 1-12: To get help on a topic, enter your question in the Search text box in the Help task pane and then click the Start Searching button.

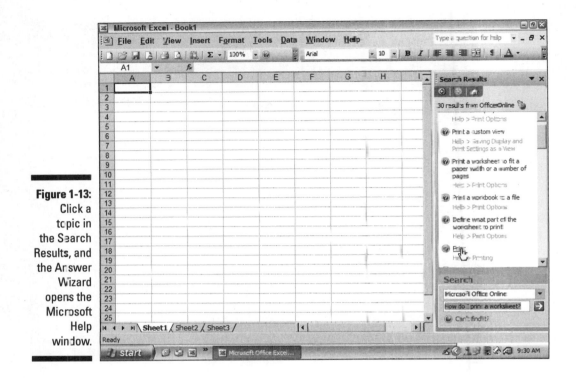

Figure 1-13:
Click a topic in the Search Results, and the Answer Wizard opens the Microsoft Help window.

To explore one of the listed topics, click its Page-with-a-Question-Mark icon or its descriptive text (note that it becomes underlined, like a Web hyperlink, as soon as you position the mouse pointer anywhere over its text). The Answer Wizard then opens the Microsoft Excel Help window similar to the one shown in Figure 1-14. This Help window contains a number of bulleted headings related to the topic that you select (the bullets appearing in the form of right-pointing triangles). You can expand each heading to displays its information by clicking the topic heading or its triangular bullet.

As soon as you click a heading or its bullet, its information displays below the heading (and the triangular bullet that precedes the heading points downward instead of to the right). As you read through the help text, you may come across other bulleted subheadings. To expand these and display their information, click their bullets or their heading text.

To expand all headings with a particular help topic, click the Show All link near the top of the Microsoft Excel Help window. To display all the text displayed beneath expanded headings across the entire computer screen click the Microsoft Excel Help window's Maximize button. To obtain a printout of the help information that you're viewing, click the Print button (the one bearing the printer icon) beneath the window's title bar.

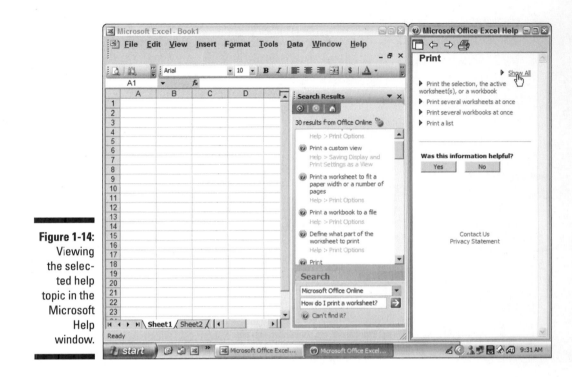

Figure 1-14:
Viewing
the selec-
ted help
topic in the
Microsoft
Help
window.

After you're done exploring the help topics in the Microsoft Excel Help window, click the Help window's Close button. As soon as you close the Help window, Excel 2003 automatically expands to fill up the space previously taken by this window. You can then close the Microsoft Excel Help task pane by pressing Ctrl+F1.

Talking to Clippit

You can personalize the Answer Wizard in the form of Clippit, the animated paperclip. To make Clippit appear, choose Help⇨Show the Office Assistant.

Once visible, you can activate Clippit to ask it a question about using Excel by clicking its icon. Doing this displays a cartoon bubble above Clippit's head, containing a text box where you type your question.

You then type your keywords or question in this text box and then press Enter or click his Search button, Excel then opens the Search Results task pane with a list of possibly relevant topics (just like the list that appears when you use the Ask a Question text box on the menu bar or the Search text box in the Microsoft Excel Help task pane). As soon as you click a topic in Search Results list, the Microsoft Help window appears to the immediate right of the Microsoft Excel Help task pane.

Even after you close the Help window after perusing the relevant help topics, Clippit remains on the screen. Note that the biggest problem with using Clippit is that it often obscures the Excel Help task pane and Help window if you keep it anywhere on the right side of the Excel screen, requiring you to drag its sorry paperclip out of the way before you can actually get to the help that you so dearly seek.

To get rid of Clippit, you have to choose Help⊏Hide Office Assistant on the Excel menu bar or right-click his icon and then choose Hide on the shortcut menu. (If I were you, I would stick to the Ask a Question or Search text box and skip Clippit altogether.)

Using the Table of Contents

If you have access to the Internet as you work in Excel, you can also look up help information topically in the Table of Contents. To download this information and make use of it, follow these steps:

1. **Press F1.**

   Excel opens the Microsoft Excel Help task pane.

2. **Click the <u>Table of Contents</u> link immediately below the Search text box.**

   Excel connects you to the Microsoft Web site and downloads the Table of Contents for Excel 2003.

3. **Click the book icon for the main topic you want to explore.**

   Excel expands the topic by downloading pages of information related to the main topic.

4. **Click the link for the page of information you want to view.**

   Excel downloads the help information into the Microsoft Help window that appears to the immediate right of the Microsoft Excel Help task pane.

5. **(Optional) To display all of the information on the selected topic, click the Maximize button in the Help window and, if necessary, the Show All button.**

6. **(Optional) To print the help topic, click the Print button on the Help window's toolbar.**

When you finish reading or printing the information in the Help window, you select another topic in the Excel Help task pane or close the Help window.

7. **To close the Help window, click the Close button in its upper-right corner.**

Excel resizes its own window to take up the missing space. You can then close the Microsoft Excel Help task pane by pressing Ctrl+F1.

When It's Time to Make Your Exit

When you're ready to call it a day and quit Excel, you have several choices for shutting down the program:

- ✔ Click the Close button on the Excel program window.
- ✔ Choose the File⇨Exit command from the pull-down menus.
- ✔ Double-click the Control menu button on the Excel program window (the green icon with the italic *L* crossed to form an X in a box that is the very first thing that appears on the title bar in the very upper-left corner of the screen).
- ✔ Press Alt+F4.

If you try to exit Excel after working on a workbook and you haven't saved your latest changes, the program beeps at you and displays an alert box querying whether you want to save your changes. To save your changes before exiting, click the Yes command button. (For detailed information on saving documents, see Chapter 2.) If you've just been playing around in the worksheet and don't want to save your changes, you can abandon the document by clicking the No button.

Chapter 2

Creating a Spreadsheet from Scratch

After you know how to launch Excel 2003, it's time to find out how not to get yourself into trouble when actually using it! In this chapter, you find out how to put all kinds of information into all those little, blank worksheet cells I describe in Chapter 1. Here you find out about the Excel AutoCorrect and AutoComplete features and how they can help cut down on errors and speed up your work. You also get some basic pointers on other smart ways to minimize the drudgery of data entry, such as filling out a series of entries with the AutoFill feature and entering the same thing in a bunch of cells all at the same time.

And after discovering how to fill up a worksheet with all this raw data, you find out what has to be the most important lesson of all — how to save all that information on disk so that you don't ever have to enter the stuff again!

So What Ya Gonna Put in That New Workbook of Yours?

When you start Excel without specifying a document to open — which is what happens when you start the program by from the Windows XP Start menu (refer to Chapter 1) — you get a blank workbook in a new workbook window. This workbook, temporarily named Book1, contains three blank worksheets (Sheet1, Sheet2, and Sheet3). To begin to work on a new spreadsheet, you simply start entering information in the first sheet of the Book1 workbook window.

The ins and outs of data entry

Here are a few simple guidelines (a kind of data-entry etiquette, if you will) that you should keep in mind when you start creating a spreadsheet in Sheet1 of your new workbook:

✔ Whenever you can, organize your information in tables of data that use adjacent (neighboring) columns and rows. Start the tables in the upper-left corner of the worksheet and work your way down the sheet, rather than across the sheet, whenever possible. When it's practical, separate each table by no more than a single column or row.

✔ When you set up these tables, don't skip columns and rows just to "space out" the information. In Chapter 3, you see how to place as much white space as you want between information in adjacent columns and rows by widening columns, heightening rows, and changing the alignment.

✔ Reserve a single column at the left edge of the table for the table's row headings.

✔ Reserve a single row at the top of the table for the table's column headings.

✔ If your table requires a title, put the title in the row above the column headings. Put the title in the same column as the row headings. You can get information on how to center this title across the columns of the entire table in Chapter 3.

In Chapter 1, I make a big deal about how big each of the worksheets in a workbook is. You may wonder why I'm now on your case about not using that space to spread out the data that you enter into it. After all, given all the real estate that comes with each and every Excel worksheet, you'd think conserving space would be one of the last things you'd have to worry about.

And you'd be 100 percent correct . . . except for one little, itty-bitty thing: Space conservation in the worksheet equals memory conservation. You see, as a table of data grows and expands into columns and rows in new areas of the worksheet, Excel decides that it had better reserve a certain amount of computer memory and hold it open just in case you might go crazy and fill that area full of cell entries. This means that if you skip columns and rows that you really don't need to skip (just to cut down on all that cluttered data), you end up wasting computer memory that could otherwise be used to store more information in the worksheet.

You must remember this . . .

So now you know: It's the amount of computer memory available to Excel that determines the ultimate size of the spreadsheet you can build, not the total number of cells in the worksheets of your workbook. When you run out of memory, you've effectively run out of space — no matter how many columns and rows are still left to fill. To maximize the information you can get into a single worksheet, always adopt the "covered wagon" approach to worksheet design by keeping your data close together.

Doing the Data-Entry Thing

Begin by reciting (in unison) the basic rule of worksheet data entry. All together now:

> To enter data in a worksheet, position the cell pointer in the cell where you want the data, and then begin typing the entry.

Note that before you can position the cell pointer in the cell where you want the entry, Excel must be in Ready mode (look for Ready as the Program indicator at the beginning of the status bar). When you start typing the entry, however, Excel goes through a mode change from Ready to Enter mode (and *Enter* replaces *Ready* as the Program indicator)

If you're not in Ready mode, try pressing Esc.

As soon as you begin typing in Enter mode, the characters that you type appear both in a cell in the worksheet area and on the formula bar near the top of the screen. Starting to type something that's ultimately destined to go into the current cell also triggers a change to the Formula bar because two new boxes, Cancel and Enter, appear in between the Name Box drop-down button and the Insert Function button.

As you continue to type, Excel displays your progress both on the formula bar and in the active cell in the worksheet (see Figure 2-1). However, the insertion point (the flashing vertical bar that acts as your cursor) is displayed only at the end of the characters displayed in the cell.

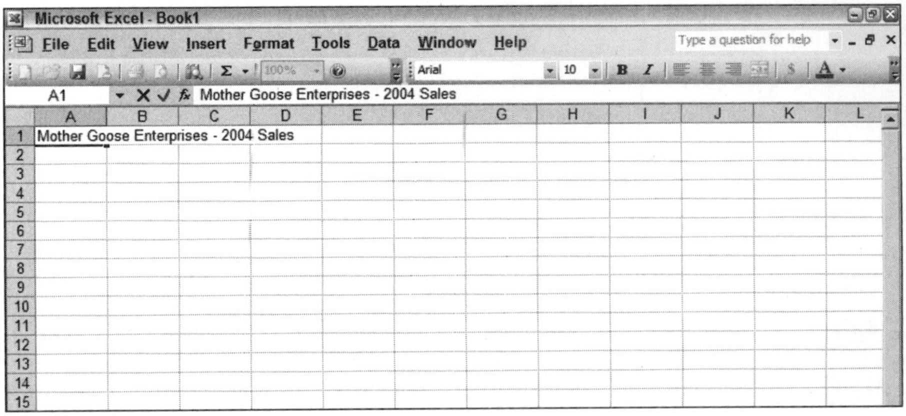

Figure 2-1: What you type appears both in the current cell and on the Formula bar.

After you finish typing your cell entry, you still have to get it into the cell so that it stays put. When you do this, you also change the program from Enter mode back to Ready mode so that you can move the cell pointer to another cell and, perhaps, enter or edit the data there.

To complete your cell entry and, at the same time, get Excel out of Enter mode and back into Ready mode, you can click the Enter box on the Formula bar, press the Enter key, or press one of the arrow keys (↓, ↑, →, or ←) to move to another cell. You can also press the Tab or Shift+Tab keys to complete a cell entry.

Now, even though each of these alternatives gets your text into the cell, each does something a little different afterwards, so please take note:

- If you click the Enter box (the one with the check mark) on the Formula bar, the text goes into the cell, and the cell pointer just stays in the cell containing the brand-new entry.

- If you press the Enter key on your keyboard, the text goes into the cell, and the cell pointer moves down to the cell below in the next row.

- If you press one of the arrow keys, the text goes into the cell, and the cell pointer moves to the next cell in the direction of the arrow. Press ↓, and the cell pointer moves below in the next row just as when you finish off a cell entry with the Enter key. Press → to move the cell pointer right to the cell in the next column; press ← to move the cell pointer left to the cell in the previous column; and or press ↑ to move the cell pointer up to the cell in the next row above.

✔ If you press Tab, the text goes into the cell, and the cell pointer moves to the adjacent cell in the column on the immediate right (the same as pressing the → key). If you press Shift+Tab, the cell pointer moves to the adjacent cell in the column on the immediate left (the same as pressing the ← key) after putting in the text.

No matter which of the methods you choose when putting an entry in its place, as soon as you complete your entry in the current cell, Excel deactivates the Formula bar by removing the Cancel and Enter boxes. Thereafter, the data you entered continues to appear in the cell in the worksheet (with certain exceptions that I discuss later in this chapter), and every time you put the cell pointer into that cell, the data will reappear on the Formula bar as well.

If, while still typing an entry or after finishing typing but prior to completing the entry, you realize that you're just about to stick it in the wrong cell, you can clear and deactivate the Formula bar by clicking the Cancel box (the one with the X in it) or by pressing Esc. If, however, you don't realize that you had the wrong cell current until after you've entered your data there, you have to either move the entry to the correct cell (something you find out how to do in Chapter 4) or delete the entry (see Chapter 4) and then reenter the data in the correct cell.

It Takes All Types

Unbeknownst to you as you go about happily entering data in your spreadsheet, Excel constantly analyzes the stuff you type and classifies it into one of three possible data types: a piece of *text*, a *value*, or a *formula*.

If Excel finds that the entry is a formula, the program automatically calculates the formula and displays the computed result in the worksheet cell (you continue to see the formula itself, however, on the Formula bar). If Excel is satisfied that the entry does not qualify as a formula (I give you the qualifications for an honest-to-goodness formula a little later in this chapter), the program then determines whether the entry should be classified as text or as a value.

Excel makes this distinction between text and values so that it knows how to align the entry in the worksheet. It aligns text entries with the left edge of the cell and values with the right edge. Also, because most formulas work properly only when they are fed values, by differentiating text from values, the program knows which will and will not work in the formulas that you build. Suffice to say that you can foul up your formulas but good if they refer to any cells containing text where Excel expects values to be.

Getting the Enter key to put the cell pointer where you want it

Excel automatically advances the cell pointer to the next cell down in the column every time that you press Enter to complete the cell entry. If you want to customize Excel so that pressing Enter doesn't move the cell pointer as the program enters your data, or to have it move the cell pointer to the next cell up, left, or right, choose Tools➪Options from the menu bar, and then click the Edit tab in the Options dialog box to select it.

To prevent the cell pointer from moving at all, select the Move Selection after Enter check box to remove its check mark. To have the cell pointer move in another direction, click the Direction pop-up list box right below and then select the new direction you want to use (Right, Up, or Left). When you're finished changing the settings, click OK or press Enter.

The telltale signs of text

A text entry is simply an entry that Excel can't pigeonhole as either a formula or value. This makes text the catchall category of Excel data types. As a practical rule, most text entries (also known as *labels*) are a combination of letters and punctuation or letters and numbers. Text is used mostly for titles, headings, and notes in the worksheet.

You can tell right away whether Excel has accepted a cell entry as text because text entries are automatically aligned at the left edge of their cells. If the text entry is wider than the cell can display, the data spills over into the neighboring cell or cells on the right, *as long as those cells remain blank* (see Figure 2-2).

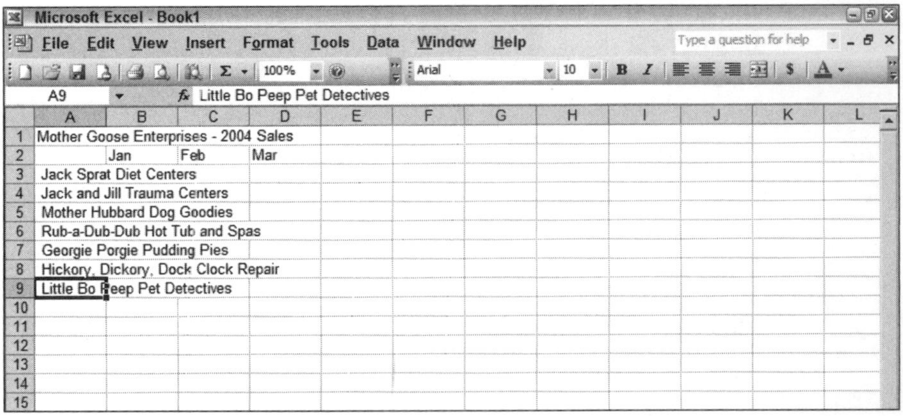

Figure 2-2:
Long text
entries spill
over into
neighboring
blank cells.

	A	B	C	D	E	F	G	H	I	J	K	L
1	Mother Goose Enterprises - 2004 Sales											
2		Jan	Feb	Mar								
3	Jack Sprat Diet Centers											
4	Jack and Jill Trauma Centers											
5	Mother Hubbard Dog Goodies											
6	Rub-a-Dub-Dub Hot Tub and Spas											
7	Georgie Porgie Pudding Pies											
8	Hickory, Dickory, Dock Clock Repair											
9	Little Bo Peep Pet Detectives											
10												
11												
12												
13												
14												
15												

If, sometime later, you enter information in a cell that contains spillover text from a cell to its left, Excel cuts off the spillover of the long text entry (see Figure 2-3). Not to worry: Excel doesn't actually lop these characters off the cell entry — it simply shaves the display to make room for the new entry. To redisplay the seemingly missing portion of the long text entry, you have to widen the column that contains the cell where the text is entered. (To find out how to do this, skip ahead to Chapter 3.)

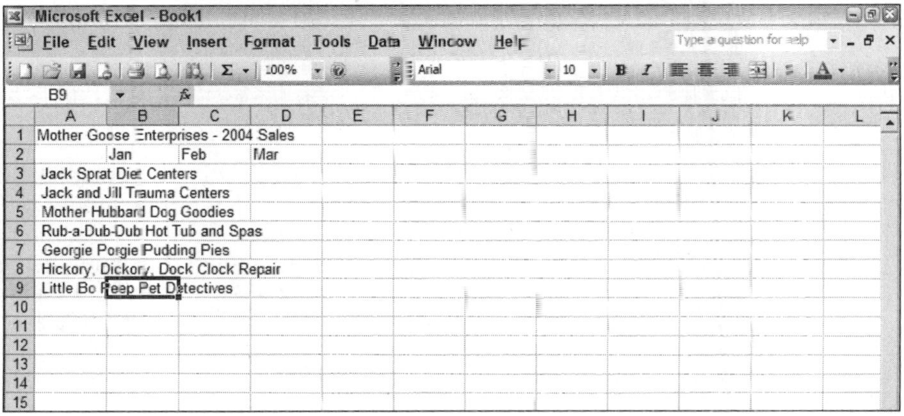

Figure 2-3:
Entries in cells to the right cut off the spillover text in cells on the left.

How Excel evaluates its values

Values are the building blocks of most of the formulas that you create in Excel. As such, values come in two flavors: numbers that represent quantities (*14* stores or *$140,000* dollars) and numbers that represent dates (*July 30, 1995*) or times (*2* pm).

You can tell whether Excel has accepted your entry as a value because values are aligned at the right edge of their cells. If the value that you enter is wider than the column containing the cell can display, Excel automatically converts the value to (of all things) *scientific notation*. For example, 6E+08 indicates that the 6 is followed by eight zeros for a grand total of 600 million! To restore a value that's been converted into that weird scientific notation stuff back to a regular number, simply widen the column for that cell. (Read how in Chapter 3.)

Making sure that Excel's got your number

When building a new worksheet, you'll probably spend a lot of your time entering numbers, representing all types of quantities from money that you made (or lost) to the percentage of the office budget that went to coffee and donuts. (You mean you don't get donuts?)

To Excel, text is nothing but a big zero

Use the AutoCalculate indicator to prove to yourself that Excel gives all text entries the value of 0 (zero). As an example, enter the number **10** in one cell and then some stupid piece of text, such as **Excel is like a box of chocolates**, in the cell directly below. Then drag up so that both cells (the one with 10 and the one with the text) are highlighted. Take a gander at the AutoCalculate indicator on the status bar, and you see that it reads SUM=10, proving that the text adds nothing to the total value of these two cells.

To enter a numeric value that represents a positive quantity, like the amount of money you made last year, just select a cell, type the numbers — for example, **459600** — and complete the entry in the cell by clicking the Enter box, pressing the Enter key, and so on. To enter a numeric value that represents a negative quantity, like the amount of money the office spent on coffee and donuts last year, begin the entry with the minus sign or hyphen (–) before typing the numbers — for example, **–175** (that's not too much to spend on coffee and donuts when you just made $459,600) — and then complete the entry.

If you're trained in accounting, you can enclose the negative number (that's *expense* to you) in parentheses. You'd enter it like this: **(175)**. Just note that if you go to all the trouble to use parentheses for your negatives (expenses), Excel goes ahead and automatically converts the number so that it begins with a minus sign; if you enter **(175)** in the Coffee and Donut expense cell, Excel spits back **–175**. (Relax, you can find out how to get your beloved parentheses back for the expenses in your spreadsheet in Chapter 3.)

With numeric values that represent dollar amounts, like the amount of money you made last year, you can include dollar signs ($) and commas (,) just as they appear in the printed or handwritten numbers you're working from. Just be aware that when you enter a number with commas, Excel assigns a number format to the value that matches your use of commas. (For more information on number formats and how they are used, see Chapter 3.) Likewise, when you preface a financial figure with a dollar sign, Excel assigns an appropriate dollar-number format to the value (one that automatically inserts commas between the thousands).

When entering numeric values with decimal places, use the period as the decimal point. When you enter decimal values, the program automatically adds a zero before the decimal point (Excel inserts 0.34 in a cell when you enter **.34**) and drops trailing zeros entered after the decimal point (Excel inserts 12.5 in a cell when you enter **12.50**).

If you don't know the decimal equivalent for a value that contains a fraction, you can just go ahead and enter the value with its fraction. For example, if you don't know that 2.1875 is the decimal equivalent for 2³⁄₁₆, just type **2 ³⁄₁₆** (making sure to add a space between the 2 and 3) in the cell. After completing the entry, when you put the cell pointer in that cell, you see 2³⁄₁₆ in the cell of the worksheet, but 2.1875 appears on the formula bar. As you see in Chapter 3, it's then a simple trick to format the display of 2³⁄₁₆ in the cell so that it matches the 2.1875 on the Formula bar.

Note: If you need to enter simple fractions, such as ¾ or ⅝, you must enter them as a mixed number preceded by zero; for example, enter **0 ¾** or **0 ⅝** (be sure to include a space between the zero and the fraction). Otherwise, Excel gets mixed up and thinks that you're entering the dates March 4 (3/4) and May 8 (5/8).

When entering in a cell a numeric value that represents a percentage (so much out of a hundred), you have this choice:

- ✔ You can either divide the number by 100 and enter the decimal equivalent (by moving the decimal point two places to the left like your teacher taught you; for example, enter **.12** for 12 percent).

- ✔ You can enter the number with the percent sign (for example, enter **12%**).

Either way, Excel stores the decimal value in the cell (0.12 in this example). If you use the percent sign, Excel assigns a percentage-number format to the value in the worksheet so that it appears as 12%.

How to fix your decimal places (when you don't even know they're broken)

If you find that you need to enter a whole slew of numbers that use the same number of decimal places, you can turn on Excel's Fixed Decimal setting and have the program enter the decimals for you. This feature really comes in handy when you have to enter hundreds of financial figures that all use two decimal places (for example, for the number of cents).

To *fix* the number of decimal places in a numeric entry, follow these steps:

1. **Choose Tools⇨Options on the menu bar.**

   The Options dialog box opens.

2. **Click the Edit tab in the Options dialog box**

3. **Click the Fixed Decimal check box to fill it with a check mark.**

   By default, Excel fixes the decimal place two places to the left of the last number you type. To change the default Places setting, go to Step 4; otherwise move to Step 5.

4. **Type a new number in the Places text box or use the spinner buttons to change the value.**

   For example, you could change the Places setting to 3 to enter numbers with the following decimal placement: 00.000.

5. **Click OK or press Enter.**

   Excel displays the FIX status indicator on the status bar to let you know that the Fixed Decimal feature is active.

After fixing the decimal place in numeric values, Excel automatically adds the decimal point to any numeric value that you enter — all you do is type the digits and complete the entry in the cell. For example, to enter the numeric value 100.99 in a cell after fixing the decimal point to two places, type the digits **10099** without adding any period for a decimal point. When you complete the cell entry, Excel automatically inserts a decimal point two places from the right in the number you typed, leaving 100.99 in the cell.

When you're ready to return to normal data entry for numerical values (where you enter any decimal points yourself), open the Options dialog box, choose the Edit tab again, click the Fixed Decimal check box again, this time to clear it, and then click OK or press Enter. Excel removes the FIX indicator from the status bar.

Tapping on the old ten-key

You can make the Fixed Decimal feature work even better by selecting the block of the cells where you want to enter the numbers (see "Entries all around the block," later in this chapter) and then pressing Num Lock so that you can do all the data entry for this cell selection from the numeric keypad (à la ten-key adding machine).

Don't get in a fix over your decimal places!

While the Fixed Decimal setting is turned on, Excel adds a decimal point to all the numeric values that you enter. However, if you want to enter a number without a decimal point, or one with a decimal point in a position different from the one called for by this feature, you have to remember to type the decimal point (period) yourself. For example, to enter the number 1099 instead of 10.99 when the decimal point is fixed at two places, type **1099** followed immediately by a period (.) in the cell.

And, for heaven's sake, please don't forget to turn off the Fixed Decimal feature before you start work on another worksheet or exit Excel. Otherwise, when you intend to enter values, such as 20, you'll end up with 0.2 instead, and you won't have a clue what's going on!

Using this approach, all you have to do to enter the range of values in each cell is type the number's digits and press Enter or the numeric keypad — Excel inserts the decimal point in the proper place as it moves the cell pointer down to the next cell. Even better, when you finish entering the last value in a column, pressing Enter automatically moves the cell pointer to the cell at the top of the next column in the selection.

Look at Figures 2-4 and 2-5 to see how you can make the ten-key method work for you. In Figure 2-4, the Fixed Decimal feature is turned on (using the default of two decimal places), and the block of cells from B3 through D9 are selected. You also see that six entries have already been made in cells B3 through B8 and a seventh, 30834.63, is about to be completed in cell B9. To make this entry when the Fixed Decimal feature is turned on, you simply type **3083463** from the numeric keypad.

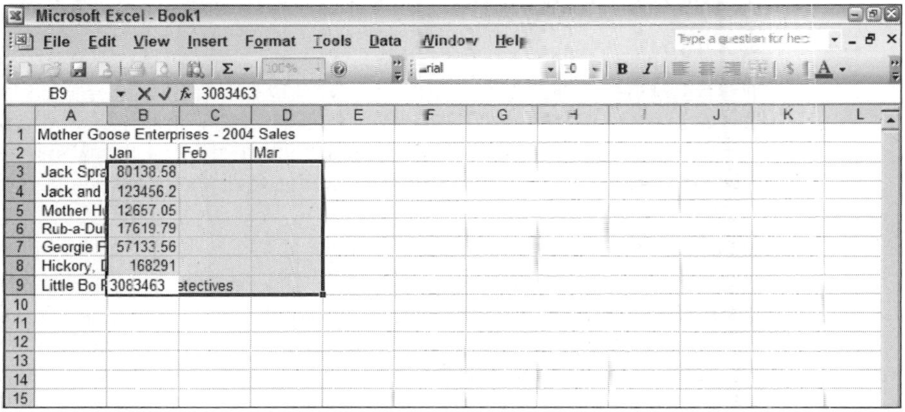

Figure 2-4:
To enter the value 30834.63 in cell B9, type **3083463** and press Enter.

In Figure 2-5, check out what happens when you press Enter (either on the regular keyboard or the numeric keypad). Not only does Excel automatically add the decimal point to the value in cell B9, but it also moves the cell pointer up and over to cell C3 where you can continue entering the values for this column.

Entering dates with no debate

At first look, it may strike you as a bit odd that dates and times are entered as values in the cells of a worksheet rather than as text. The reason for this is simple, really: Dates and times entered as values can be used in formula calculations, whereas dates and times entered as text cannot. For example, if you enter two dates as values, you can then set up a formula that subtracts the more recent date from the older date and returns the number of days between them. This kind of thing just couldn't happen if you were to enter the two dates as text entries.

Excel determines whether the date or time that you type is entered as a value or as text by the format you follow. If you follow one of Excel's built-in date and time formats, the program recognizes the date or time as a value. If you don't follow one of the built-in formats, the program enters the date or time as a text entry — it's as simple as that.

Excel recognizes the following time formats:

3	AM or PM
3	A or P (for AM and PM)
3:21	AM or PM
3:21:04	AM or PM
15:21	
15:21:04	

Excel knows the following date formats. (Note that month abbreviations always use the first three letters of the name of the month: Jan, Feb, Mar, and so forth.)

November 6, 2003 or November 6, 03

11/6/03 or 11-6-03

6-Nov-04 or 6/Nov/04 or even 6Nov04

11/6 or 6-Nov or 6/Nov or 6Nov

Nov-04 or Nov/04 or Nov04

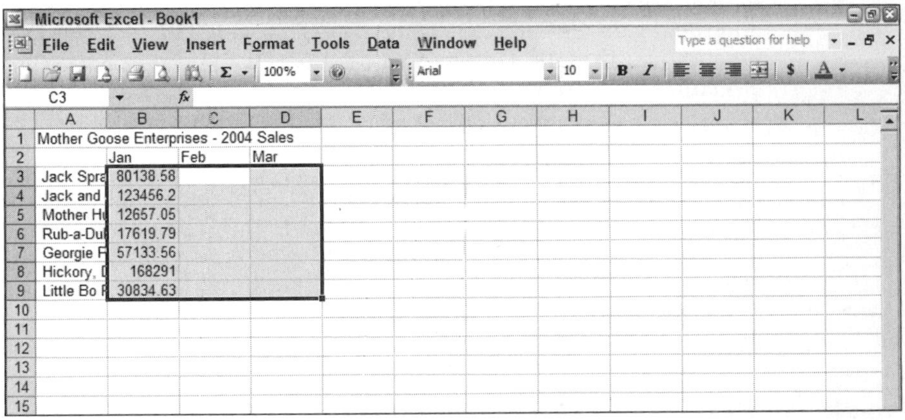

Figure 2-5: Press Enter to complete the 30834.63 entry in cell B9; Excel automatically moves the cell pointer up and over to cell C3.

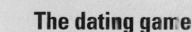

The dating game

Dates are stored as serial numbers that indicate how many days have elapsed from a particular starting date; times are stored as decimal fractions indicating the elapsed part of the 24-hour period. Excel supports two date systems: the 1900 date system used by Excel in Windows, where January 1, 1900 is the starting date (serial number 1) and the 1904 system used by Excel for the Macintosh, where January 2, 1904 is the starting date.

If you ever get a hold of a workbook created with Excel for the Macintosh that contains dates that seem all screwed up when you open the file, you can rectify this problem by choosing Tools⇨Options on the menu bar, selecting the Calculation tab in the Options dialog box, and then clicking the 1904 Date System check box under Workbook options before you click OK.

Make it a date in the 21st century

Contrary to what you might think, when entering dates in the twenty-first century, you need to enter only the last two digits of the year. So, for example, to enter the date January 6, 2004, in a worksheet, I enter **1/6/04** in the target cell. Likewise, to put the date February 15, 2010, in a worksheet, I enter **2/15/10** in the target cell.

Note that this system of having to put in only the last two digits of dates in the twenty-first century works only for dates in the first three decades of the new century (2000 through 2029). To enter dates for the years 2030 on, you need to input all four digits of the year.

This also means, however, that to put in dates in the first three decades of the twentieth century (1900 through 1929), you must enter all four digits of the year. For instance, to put in the date July 21, 1925, you have to enter **7/30/1925** in the target cell. Otherwise, if you enter just the last two digits (**25**) for the year part of the date, Excel enters a date for the year 2025 and not 1925!

Excel 2003 always displays all four digits of the year in the cell and on the Formula bar even when you only enter the last two. So, for instance, if you enter **11/06/04** in a cell, Excel automatically displays 11/06/2004 in the worksheet cell (and on the Formula bar when that cell is current).

That way, you can always tell when you enter a twentieth rather than a twenty-first century date even if you can't keep the stupid rules for when to enter just the last two digits and when to enter all four. (Read through Chapter 3 for information on how to format your date entries so that only the last digits are displayed in the worksheet.)

For information on how to perform simple arithmetic operations between the dates and time you enter in a worksheet and have the results make sense, see the information about dates in Chapter 3.

Fabricating those fabulous formulas!

As entries go in Excel, formulas are the real workhorses of the worksheet. If you set up a formula properly, it computes the right answer when you first enter it into a cell. From then on, it keeps itself up-to-date, recalculating the results whenever you change any of the values that the formula uses.

You let Excel know that you're about to enter a formula (rather than some text or a value), in the current cell by starting the formula with the equal sign (=). Most simple formulas follow the equal sign with a built-in function such as SUM or AVERAGE. (See the section "Inserting a function into a formula with the Insert Function button," later in this chapter, for more information on using functions in formulas.) Other simple formulas use a series of values or cell references that contain values separated by one or more of the following mathematical operators:

+ (plus sign) for addition

– (minus sign or hyphen) for subtraction

* (asterisk) for multiplication

/ (slash) for division

^ (caret) for raising a number to an exponential power

For example, to create a formula in cell C2 that multiplies a value entered in cell A2 by a value in cell B2, enter the following formula in cell C2: **=A2*B2**.

To enter this formula in cell C2, follow these steps:

1. **Select cell C2.**

2. **Type the entire formula** =A2*B2 **in the cell.**

3. **Press Enter.**

Or

1. **Select Cell C2.**

2. **Type** = **(equal sign).**

3. **Select cell A2 in the worksheet by using the mouse or the keyboard.**

   This action places the cell reference A2 in the formula in the cell (as shown in Figure 2-6).

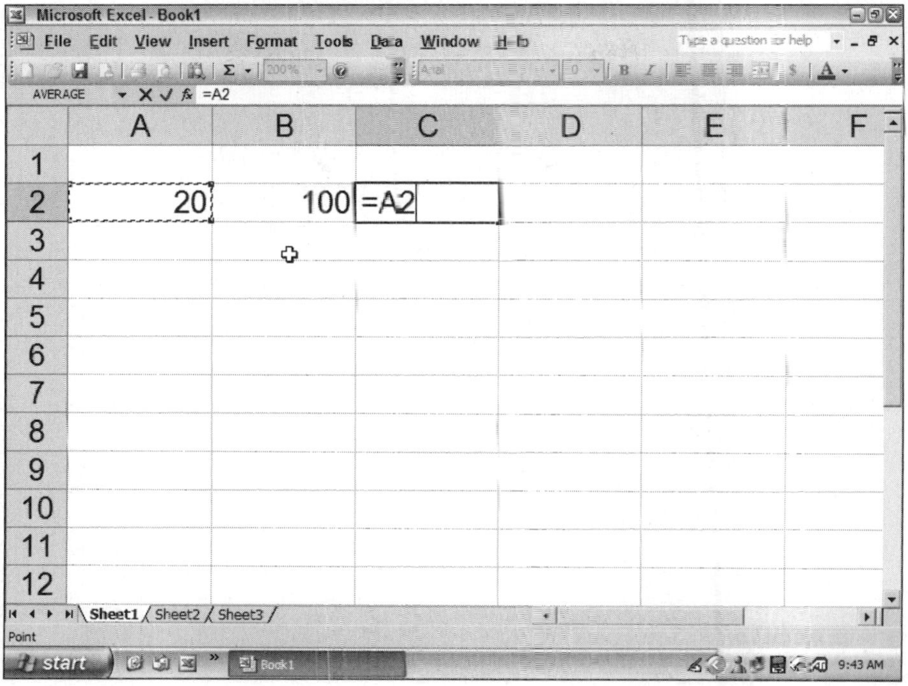

Figure 2-6:
To start the
formula,
type = and
then select
cell A2.

4. **Type * (Shift+8 on the top row of the keyboard).**

   The asterisk is used for multiplication rather than the x symbol you used in school.

5. **Select cell B2 in the worksheet by using the mouse or the keyboard.**

   This action places the cell reference B2 in the formula (as shown in Figure 2-7).

6. **Click the Enter box to complete the formula entry, while at the same time keeping the cell pointer in cell C2.**

   Excel displays the calculated answer in cell C2 and the formula =A2*B2 in the Formula bar (as shown in Figure 2-8).

When you finish entering the formula =**A2*B2** in cell C2 of the worksheet, Excel displays the calculated result, depending on the values currently entered in cells A2 and B2. The major strength of the electronic spreadsheet is the capability of formulas to automatically change their calculated results to match changes in the cells referenced by the formulas.

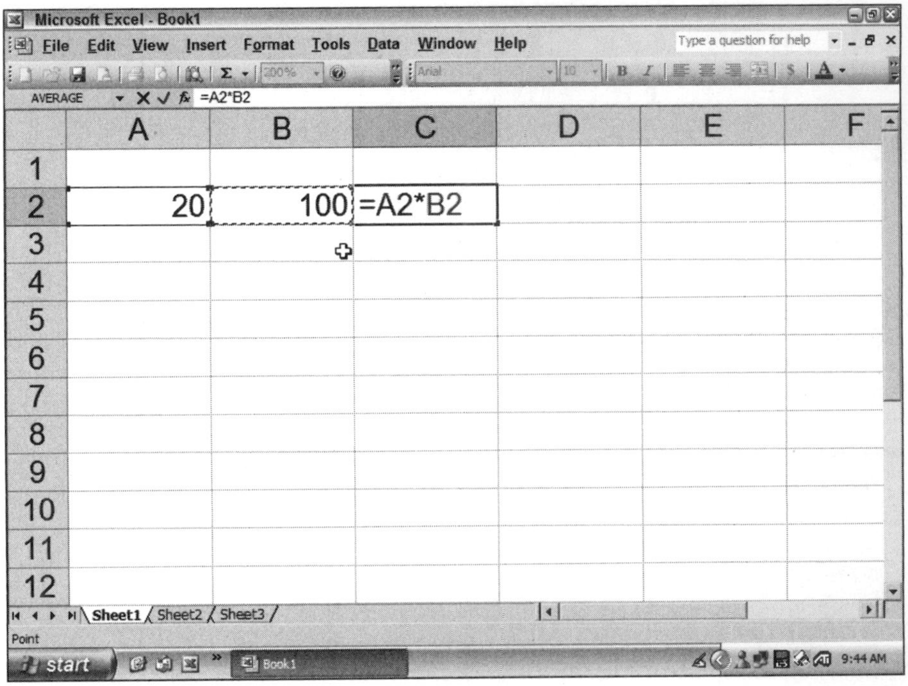

	Microsoft Excel - Book1						
	File Edit View Insert Format Tools Data Window Help					Type a question for help	
	AVERAGE	▼ X ✓ ƒx	=A2*B2				
	A	**B**	**C**	**D**	**E**	**F**
1						
2	20	100	=A2*B2			
3		⊹				
4						
5						
6						
7						
8						
9						
10						
11						
12						

Figure 2-7:
To complete the second part of the formula, type * and select cell B2.

Now comes the fun part: After creating a formula like the preceding one that refers to the values in certain cells (rather than containing those values itself), you can change the values in those cells, and Excel automatically recalculates the formula, using these new values and displaying the updated answer in the worksheet! Using the example shown in Figure 2-8, say that you change the value in cell B2 from 100 to 50. The moment that you complete this change in cell B2, Excel recalculates the formula and displays the new answer, 1000, in cell C2.

If you want it, just point it out

The method of selecting the cells you use in a formula, rather than typing their cell references, is known as *pointing*. Pointing is not only quicker than typing cell references, it also reduces the risk that you might type the wrong cell reference. When you type a cell reference, you can easily type the wrong column letter or row number and not realize your mistake just by looking at the calculated result returned in the cell.

If you select the cell you want to use in a formula, either by clicking it or moving the cell pointer to it, you have less chance of entering the wrong cell reference.

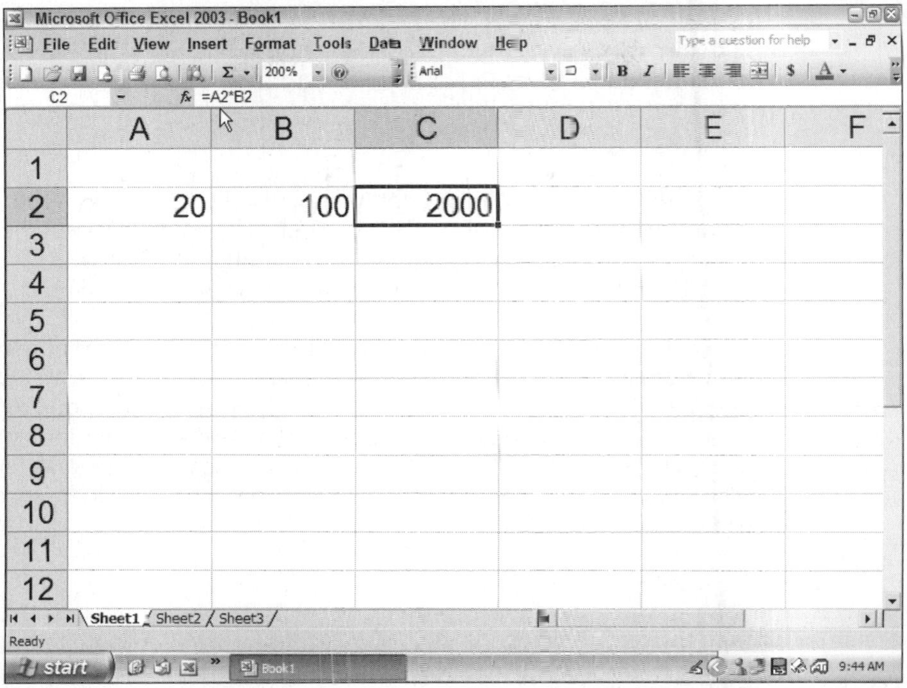

Figure 2-8:
Click the
Enter box,
and Excel
displays the
answer in
cell C2 while
the formula
appears in
the Formula
bar above.

Altering the natural order of operations

Many formulas that you create perform more than one mathematical operation. Excel performs each operation, moving from left to right, according to a strict pecking order (the natural order of arithmetic operations). In this order, multiplication and division pull more weight than addition and subtraction and, therefore, are performed first, even if these operations don't come first in the formula (when reading from left to right).

Consider the series of operations in the following formula:

    =A2+B2*C2

If cell A2 contains the number 5, B2 contains the number 10, and C2 contains the number 2, Excel evaluates the following formula:

    =5+10*2

In this formula, Excel multiplies 10 times 2 to equal 20 and then adds this result to 5 to produce the result 25.

If you want Excel to perform the addition between the values in cells A2 and B2 before the program multiplies the result by the value in cell C2, enclose the addition operation in parentheses as follows:

=(A2+B2)*C2

The parentheses around the addition tell Excel that you want this operation performed before the multiplication. If cell A2 contains the number 5, B2 contains the number 10, and C2 contains the number 2, Excel adds 5 and 10 to equal 15 and then multiplies this result by 2 to produce the result 30.

In fancier formulas, you may need to add more than one set of parentheses, one within another (like the wooden Russian dolls that nest within each other) to indicate the order in which you want the calculations to take place. When nesting parentheses, Excel first performs the calculation contained in the most inside pair of parentheses and then uses that result in further calculations as the program works its way outward. For example, consider the following formula:

=(A4+(B4–C4))*D4

Excel first subtracts the value in cell C4 from the value in cell B4, adds the difference to the value in cell A4, and then finally multiplies that sum by the value in D4.

Without the additions of the two sets of nested parentheses, left to its own devices, Excel would first multiply the value in cell C4 by that in D4, add the value in A4 to that in B4, and then perform the subtraction.

Don't worry too much when nesting parentheses in a formula if you don't pair them properly so that you have a right parenthesis for every left parenthesis in the formula. If you do not include a right parenthesis for every left one, Excel displays an alert dialog box that suggests the correction that needs to be made to balance the pairs. If you agree with the program's suggested correction, you simply click the Yes button. However, be sure that you only use parentheses: ( ). Excel balks at the use of brackets — [ ] — or braces — { } — in a formula by giving you an Error alert box.

Formula flub-ups

Under certain circumstances, even the best formulas can appear to have freaked out after you get them in your worksheet. You can tell right away that a formula's gone haywire because instead of the nice calculated value you expected to see in the cell, you get a strange, incomprehensible message in all uppercase letters beginning with the number sign (#) and ending with an exclamation point (!) or, in one case, a question mark (?). This weirdness is known, in the parlance of spreadsheets, as an *error value*. Its purpose is to let you know that some element — either in the formula itself or in a cell referred to by the formula — is preventing Excel from returning the antici-pated calculated value.

When one of your formulas returns one of these error values, an alert indica-tor (in the form of an exclamation point in a diamond) appears to the left of the cell when it contains the cell pointer, and the upper-left corner of cell contains a tiny green triangle. When you position the mouse pointer on this alert indicator, Excel displays a brief description of the formula error and adds a drop-down button to the immediate right of its box. When you click this button, a pop-up menu appears with a number of related options. To access online help on this formula error, including suggestions on how to get rid of the error, click the Help on This Error item on this pop-up menu.

The worst thing about error values is that they can contaminate other formu-las in the worksheet. If a formula returns an error value to a cell and a second formula in another cell refers to the value calculated by the first formula, the second formula returns the same error value, and so on down the line.

After an error value shows up in a cell, you have to discover what caused the error and edit the formula in the worksheet. In Table 2-1, I list some error values that you might run into in a worksheet and then explain the most common causes.

Table 2-1	Error Values That You Can Encounter from Faulty Formulas
What Shows Up in the Cell	**What's Going On Here?**
#DIV/0!	Appears when the formula calls for division by a cell that either contains the value 0 or, as is more often the case, is empty. Division by zero is a no-no in mathematics.
#NAME?	Appears when the formula refers to a *range name* (see Chapter 6 for info on naming ranges) that doesn't exist in the worksheet. This error value appears when you type the wrong range name or fail to enclose in quotation marks some text used in the formula, causing Excel to think that the text refers to a range name.
#NULL!	Appears most often when you insert a space (where you should have used a comma) to separate cell references used as arguments for functions.

(continued)

Table 2-1 *(continued)*

What Shows Up in the Cell	What's Going On Here?
#NUM!	Appears when Excel encounters a problem with a number in the formula, such as the wrong type of argument in an Excel function or a calculation that produces a number too large or too small to be represented in the worksheet.
#REF!	Appears when Excel encounters an invalid cell reference, such as when you delete a cell referred to in a formula or paste cells over the cells referred to in a formula.
#VALUE!	Appears when you use the wrong type of argument or operator in a function, or when you call for a mathematical operation that refers to cells that contain text entries.

Fixing Up Those Data Entry Flub-Ups

We all wish we were perfect, but alas, because so few of us are, we are best off preparing for those inevitable times when we mess up. When entering vast quantities of data, it's really easy for those nasty little typos to creep into your work. In your pursuit of the perfect spreadsheet, here are things you can do. First, get Excel to automatically correct certain data entry typos right as they happen with its AutoCorrect feature. Second, manually correct any disgusting little errors that get through, either while you're still in the process of making the entry in the cell or after the entry has gone in.

You really AutoCorrect that for me

The AutoCorrect feature is a godsend for those of us who tend to make the same stupid typos over and over again. With AutoCorrect, you can alert Excel 2003 to your own particular typing gaffes and tell the program how it should automatically fix them for you.

When you first install Excel, the AutoCorrect feature already knows to automatically correct two initial capital letters in an entry (by lowercasing the second capital letter), to capitalize the name of the days of the week, and to replace a set number of text entries and typos with particular substitute text.

You can add to the list of text replacements at any time when using Excel. These text replacements can be of two types: typos that you routinely make along with the correct spellings, and abbreviations or acronyms that you type all the time along with their full forms.

To add to the replacements:

1. **Choose Tools⇨AutoCorrect Options on the menu bar to open the AutoCorrect dialog box.**

2. **On the AutoCorrect tab in this dialog box, enter the typo or abbreviation in the Replace text box.**

3. **Enter the correction or full form in the With text box.**

4. **Click the Add button or press Enter to add the new typo or abbreviation to the AutoCorrect list.**

5. **Click the OK button to close the AutoCorrect dialog box.**

Cell editing etiquette

Despite the help of AutoCorrect, some mistakes are bound to get you. How you correct them really depends upon whether you notice before or after you complete the cell entry.

- ✔ If you catch the mistake before you complete an entry, you can delete it by pressing your Backspace key until you remove all the incorrect characters from the cell. Then you can retype the rest of the entry or the formula before you complete the entry in the cell.

- ✔ If you don't discover the mistake until after you've completed the cell entry, you have a choice of replacing the whole thing or editing just the mistakes.

- ✔ When dealing with short entries, you'll probably want to take the replacement route. To replace a cell entry, you have only to position the cell pointer in that cell, type your replacement entry, and then complete the replacement entry by clicking the Enter box or pressing Enter or one of the arrow keys.

- ✔ When the error in an entry is relatively easy to fix and the entry is on the long side, you'll probably want to edit the cell entry rather than replace it. To edit the entry in the cell, simply double-click the cell or select the cell and then press F2.

- ✔ Doing either one reactivates the Formula bar by once again displaying the Enter and Cancel boxes, while at the same time placing the insertion point in the cell entry in the worksheet. (If you double-click, the insertion point is positioned wherever you click; press F2, and the insertion point is positioned after the last character in the entry.)

✔ Notice also that the mode indicator changes to Edit. While in this mode, you can use the mouse or the arrow keys to position the insertion point at the place in the cell entry that needs fixing.

In Table 2-2, I list the keystrokes that you can use to reposition the insertion point in the cell entry and delete unwanted characters. If you want to insert new characters at the insertion point, simply start typing. If you want to delete existing characters at the insertion point as you type new ones, press the Insert key on your keyboard to switch from the normal insert mode to overtype mode. To return to normal insert mode, press Insert a second time. When you finish making corrections to the cell entry, you must complete the edits by pressing Enter before Excel updates the contents of the cell.

While Excel is in Edit mode, you must reenter the edited cell contents by either clicking the Enter box or pressing Enter. You can use the arrow keys as a way to complete an entry only when the program is in Enter mode. When the program is in Edit mode, the arrow keys move the insertion point only through the entry that you're editing, not to a new cell.

Table 2-2	Keystrokes for Fixing Those Cell Entry Flub-Ups
Keystroke	**What the Keystroke Does**
Delete	Deletes the character to the right of the insertion point
Backspace	Deletes the character to the left of the insertion point
→	Positions the insertion point one character to the right
←	Positions the insertion point one character to the left
↑	Positions the insertion point, when it is at the end of the cell entry, to its preceding position to the left
End or ↓	Moves the insertion point after the last character in the cell entry
Home	Moves the insertion point in front of the first character of the cell entry
Ctrl+→	Positions the insertion point in front of the next word in the cell entry
Ctrl+←	Positions the insertion point in front of the preceding word in the cell entry
Insert	Switches between insert and overtype mode

TECHNICAL STUFF

The Tale of Two Edits: Cell versus Formula bar editing

Excel gives you a choice between editing a cell's contents either in the cell or on the Formula bar. Whereas most of the time, editing right in the cell is just fine, when dealing with really, really long entries (like humongous formulas that seem to go on forever or text entries that take up paragraphs and paragraphs), you may prefer to do your editing on the Formula bar. This is because Excel expands the Formula bar to as many rows as necessary to display the entire cell contents; in the worksheet display, however, the cell contents may be running right off the screen.

To edit the contents in the Formula bar rather than in the cell itself, you must position the cell pointer in the cell and then double-click somewhere (probably the first place that needs changing) in the cell contents on the Formula bar.

Taking the Drudgery out of Data Entry

Before leaving the topic of data entry, I feel duty-bound to cover some of the shortcuts that really help to cut down on the drudgery of this task. These data-entry tips include using the Speech Recognition capabilities (including voice dictation and commands), AutoComplete and AutoFill features, as well as doing data entry in a preselected block of cells and entering the same things in a bunch of cells all at the same time.

Listening to his master's voice

Speech Recognition has got to be one of Excel 2003's coolest features. With it, you can have Excel take dictation or follow your voice commands. When you use Speech Recognition in dictation mode, Excel enters the text or values that you speak into the cells of your worksheets. When you use Speech Recognition in command mode, Excel selects the menu commands, toolbars, and dialog box options as you say them.

The only tricks to using the new Speech Recognition are that your computer must be equipped with a fast enough processor and the proper sound equipment, and that you must not only install the Speech Recognition but also train it to recognize your voice. According to Microsoft, the minimum computer configuration needed to run Speech Recognition is a Pentium II running at a minimum speed of 300 MHz with a minimum of 128 MB of random-access memory (RAM). If you have a somewhat more antiquated PC, you're going to have to forego the fun of speaking to Excel and stick to the good old keyboard.

If the speed of your machine is up to the challenge, you still have to have a quality microphone, preferably one attached to a headset (like the reception-ist in your office might use). These cost between $40 and $80 and are readily available at all the electronics and computer supply stores. Cheap microphones that come with today's PCs are just not sensitive enough for this kind of work and, unlike a headset microphone, don't lie close enough to your mouth to prevent them from picking up stray sounds.

Stray sounds are a big concern when using the Speech Recognition feature. If you work in a bullpen-type office environment where you are routinely both-ered by the voices of your co-workers, chances are good that the Office 11 Speech Recognition will pick up stray sounds no matter what quality your microphone. You may find the Speech Recognition feature in Excel 2003 more trouble than it's worth — your neighbors' chattering may make weird, incom-prehensible words and symbols appear in your worksheets at the times when you're not even dictating in a worksheet!

The Speech Recognition feature is not installed during a standard installation of Office 11, although it is set up to be installed the first time that you try to use it in any Office program. Thus, you can install the Speech Recognition from within Excel 2003: Choose Tools⇨Speech⇨Speech Recognition from the Excel menu bar. The program responds by starting the Speech Recognition installation process (which, by the way, requires the use of your Office 11 CD-ROM disc to complete).

After you successfully install the Speech Recognition feature on your computer, the Language bar appears, floating over the middle of your Excel worksheet window. (If it doesn't, simply choose Tools⇨Speech⇨Speech Recognition on the Excel menu bar.) Note that unlike Excel's other floating toolbars, which you can permanently put out of the way by docking them on one of the sides of the program window (see the section about toolbar docking maneuvers in Chapter 3 for details), the Language bar always remains a floater that obscures some part of the Excel screen.

The only way around this is to minimize the Language bar so that its tools appear on the Windows XP taskbar to the immediate left of the Notification area — the last area on the right that contains the current time (Figures 2-9 and 2-10 show the Language bar minimized on the Windows taskbar). That way, you don't have to fool with moving the Language bar as you work, which could actually cause speech recognition errors to crop up if try to do this while you're in the midst of dictating or issuing voice commands.

To minimize the floating Language bar, click the Minimize button (the one with a minus sign icon above the downward-pointing triangle at the very end of the floating toolbar). The first time you click Minimize, Excel displays an alert dialog box indicating that, when the Language bar is minimized, you can restore it by clicking it and then choosing Show the Language Bar from its pop-up menu. Disregard this notice (you can even click the Don't Show Me This Message Again check box) and then click OK to close this alert dialog box and place to have the icons on the Language toolbar appear on the Windows XP taskbar, as shown in Figure 2-9.

The Language bar appears in two forms: the full Language bar, with all the buttons displayed (Microphone, Dictation, Voice Command, Current Mode, Speech Tools, Handwriting, and On-Screen Keyboard), as shown in Figure 2-9; and the condensed Language bar, with all buttons displayed but the Dictation, Voice Command, and Current Mode buttons, as shown in Figure 2-10.

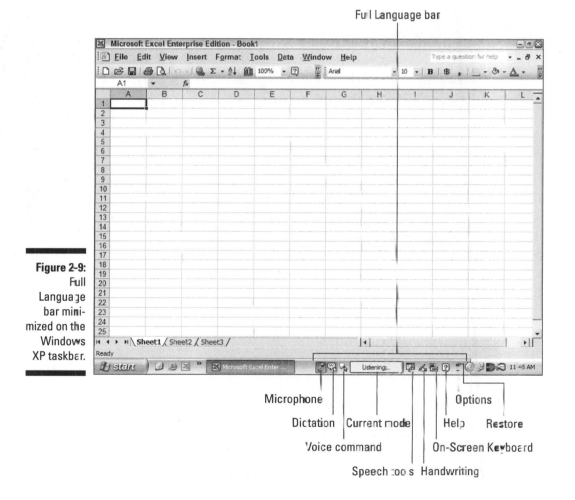

Full Language bar

Figure 2-9:
Full Language bar minimized on the Windows XP taskbar.

Microphone

Dictation | Current mode

Voice command

Options

Help   Restore

On-Screen Keyboard

Speech tools Handwriting

Condensed Language bar

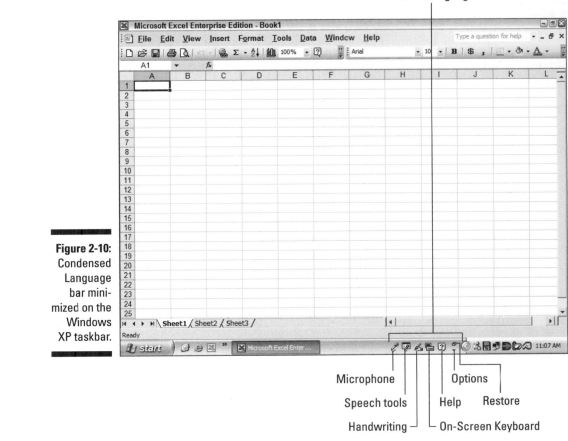

Figure 2-10:
Condensed
Language
bar mini-
mized on the
Windows
XP taskbar.

Microphone

Speech tools

Handwriting

Options

Help

Restore

On-Screen Keyboard

To condense the full Language bar, you click the Microphone button. Doing this not only shortens the bar by hiding the Dictation, Voice Command, and Current Mode buttons but also turns off the Speech Recognition feature. (This feature only works in the full Language bar.)

To expand the condensed Language bar to full, you click the Microphone button. Doing this not only displays all the Language bar buttons but also turns on the Speech Recognition feature in Dictation mode (as indicated by the word "Listening" in the Current Mode button — the one with cartoon-type balloon around it). You can then switch from Dictation to Voice Command mode by clicking the Voice Command button (which changes the text in the Current Mode button from Dictation to Voice Command).

Doing your voice training

Before trying to use the Speech Recognition feature — barking your Excel commands to fill in worksheet data — you need to train it to recognize your manner of speaking. The training procedure is simple although somewhat time consuming and, at times, tedious. To initiate this training, follow these steps:

1. **Choose Tools⇨Speech⇨Speech Recognition to display the Language toolbar.**

2. **Click the Speech Tools button on the Language bar, and then click Training on its pop-up menu (refer to Figure 2-10).**

   The first dialog box of the Voice Training Wizard opens so you can choose the training lesson that you want to do. The wizard includes several different lessons; the more lessons you do, the better the Speech Recognition feature performs.

3. **In the Introduction to Microsoft Speech Recognition training dialog box of the Voice Training Wizard, click the Next button.**

   The second dialog box of the Voice Training Wizard appears, prompting you to indicate your gender and your relative age (12 yrs or less, or 13 yrs and up).

4. **Select the Male or the Female radio button and then select the 13 yrs and Up or the 12 yrs or Less radio button before you click the Next button.**

5. **Click the Sample button in the next dialog box to check the position of your microphone, and then click the Next button.**

   The microphone must be right in front of your lips when you read the training text, and, after training begins, you should make no further adjustments to it.

6. **Read aloud the text "This papaya tastes perfect" and listen to the playback. If need be, readjust the distance of the microphone in front of your lips until it no longer sounds in the playback like you are blowing into the microphone. With your microphone in proper position, click the Finish button to begin the introductory voice training.**

   During the course of the voice training, you read the text that appears in the list box area of the Voice Training dialog box. While you read the text, the Speech Recognition facility highlights the words as it recognizes them.

   Read the text in a natural voice, making sure that you don't stop to enunciate each word; rather, read the words as phrases.

7. **Read the text as it appears in the list box of the next dialog box of the Voice Training Wizard.**

If you find that the training wizard is just not able to understand a particular word, click the Skip Word button to continue (skipping a few words won't adversely affect the training session). You can tell when the training wizard has trouble understanding because it pauses at undecipherable words, refusing to continue to highlight any further text. If you need to take a break or are interrupted, click the Pause button. After pausing the training lesson, you resume the training by clicking the Resume button.

When you finish speaking all the training text, the wizard displays a dialog box in which it updates your profile (created at the time when you installed the Speech Recognition software) with the results of the training session. When this updating is complete, the last dialog box of the Voice Training Wizard appears. From this final dialog box you can choose between more voice training or to close the wizard and return to Excel, where you can begin using the software to dictate cell entries or to select Excel commands.

 8. **Click the More Training button for more voice training (the more training, the better the recognition accuracy).**

    or

    If you want to try out the Speech Recognition software before doing any more training, click the Finish button instead.

Click the Finish button, and the Voice Training Wizard closes, returning you to Excel 2003. You are now ready to try out the Speech Recognition software in the program.

Getting Excel to take dictation!

You can use the Speech Recognition software in Excel in Dictation mode to enter data into your worksheets. To do this, you need to activate the Speech Recognition software in Excel and then make sure that the Dictation mode is selected on the Language bar before you begin dictating.

 1. **Launch Excel.**

 2. **Put on your headset and position your microphone before you put the cell pointer in the cell of the worksheet where you want to start entering data.**

 3. **Choose Tools⇨Speech⇨Speech Recognition on the Excel menu bar to open the Language bar up for business.**

    To place the Language bar tools out of the way on the Windows XP taskbar, click the Minimize button (the one with the minus sign) at the far right of the Language toolbar.

 4. **Make sure that the word Dictation or Listening appears in the Current Mode button (the one with cartoon-type balloon around it (refer to**

Figure 2-9). If your Language bar is condensed (refer to Figure 2-10), click the Microphone button to expand the bar and display this button along with the Dictation and Voice Command buttons.

5. **Click the Dictation button on the Language bar to select Dictation mode.**

6. **Begin dictating the data (text or values) that you want to enter in the current cell.**

   When dictating your data entry, speak the entire number, heading, or phrase you want to enter in the cell (see Table 2-3 for hints on what to say to get the Speech Recognition to enter particular punctuation and symbols, such as commas and dollar signs). When speaking the cell entry, don't be concerned if the values or words don't appear in the cell and on the Formula bar right as you say them — your computer does not display your text until it finishes processing your voice input. Keep your eye on the balloon button to the immediate right of Voice Command on the Language bar to get hints on how to modify your speech if your words aren't recognized. If your data entry is not recognized and appears as garbled text, press the Esc key and re-speak the value or text.

7. **To turn off the dictation, click the Microphone button on the Language bar or choose Tools⇨Speech⇨Speech Recognition on the menu bar. (Clicking the Microphone button is effectively the same thing as choosing this command on the Excel menu bar.)**

In Table 2-3, you can see the word or, in some cases, the words that you can speak for common punctuation and symbols that you may need to include in your dictation.

Table 2-3   Words for Dictating Common Punctuation and Symbols

Word(s) You Say	What Speech Recognition Enters
Ampersand	&
Asterisk	*
At	@
At sign	@
Bracket, Left bracket, or Open bracket	[
Backslash	\
Caret	^
Close bracket, Right bracket, or End bracket	]

(continued)

Table 2-3 *(continued)*

Word(s) You Say	What Speech Recognition Enters
Close parenthesis or Right paren	)
Close quote	"
Close single quote	'
Colon	:
Comma	,
Curly brace, Left brace, or Open brace	{
Dollar sign	$
Dot	.
Double dash	--
Ellipsis	...
End curly brace, Right brace, or Close brace	}
Equals	=
Exclamation point	!
Greater than	>
Hyphen or Dash	–
Less than	<
Open brace	{
Open bracket	[
Open quote or Quote	"
Open single quote or Single quote	'
Paren	(
Percent	%
Percent sign	%
Period	.
Plus or Plus sign	+
Pound sign	#
Question mark	?

Word(s) You Say	What Speech Recognition Enters
Quote or Open quote	"
Right bracket	]
Semicolon	;
Slash	/
Tilde	~
Underscore	_
Vertical bar	|

When dictating numbers into a cell, keep the following things in mind:

✔ Numbers 20 and less are spelled out when Speech Recognition inserts them in a cell. (You say "Four," and the insertion reads four.)

✔ Numbers above 21 are inserted as Arabic numerals. (You say "Twenty-two," and the insertion reads 22.)

When dictating values (such as $4,524.56) into a cell, say "Four thousand five hundred twenty-four dollars fifty-six cents," more or less as you would when talking to a co-worker. Just avoid adding the word *and*, as in "Three hundred fifty dollars *and* twenty-five cents." Adding the *and* to your dictation causes the Speech Recognition software to attempt to spell out the value much as it appears in this tip!

Getting Excel to obey your every command!

As exciting as the dictation part of Speech Recognition is, I really find the Voice Command mode to be the best part. I guess this is because I don't mind entering worksheet values and text from the keyboard as much as I mind selecting Excel commands with the mouse. I really appreciate substituting my mouth for my mouse when it comes to bossing Excel around.

Getting Excel to obey your voice commands is simply a matter of switching from Dictation mode to Command mode. With the Language bar displayed, switch by clicking the Voice Command button. If the bar isn't yet displayed, follow these steps to get into Command mode and speak your command:

1. **Choose Tools⇨Speech⇨Speech Recognition on the Excel menu bar to display it on your screen.**

2. **Click the Voice Command button on the Language bar to select Voice Command mode (indicated by the appearance of the text Voice**

Command **in the Current Mode button — the one with the cartoon-type balloon around it). If the Language bar is condensed so that this button is hidden, click the Microphone button to expand the bar to full and add this button to its display.**

3. **Begin dictating your Excel menu command, toolbar command, or command to move the cell pointer.**

4. **When you finish saying your command (assuming that Excel does what you want), click the Microphone button on the Language bar to turn off the microphone.**

When dictating commands to Excel, keep the following guidelines in mind. (In the following examples, I put quotes around what I literally want you to say. Remember that these are only examples, and not what you do every time.)

✔ To select an Excel menu command, say the name of the menu ("Format") and then say the name of the menu item ("Column"). If the command that you select has submenu items, say the name of the submenu item ("AutoFit Selection"). To escape from the menus, say "Cancel" or "Escape" until the menu bar is no longer selected.

✔ To select a tool from any of the displayed toolbars (of which, only the Standard and Formatting are normally displayed), say the name of the tool ("Bold," "Align Right," "Print Preview," or "Save"). Refer to Tables 1-2 and 1-3 for the names of all the tools on the Standard and Formatting toolbars. To display other toolbars by voice, say the menu command "View" and then say "Toolbars" followed by the name of the toolbar you want to open.

✔ To select options in a dialog box that you've opened by saying either a menu or toolbar command, say the name of the tab you want to display ("General") and then say the name of the option that you want to select or change ("Sheets in Workbook"). If the option requires an input, type it in or select with the mouse. When you finish changing the options in the dialog box, say "OK" to close the box and make your changes. Say "Cancel" to close the box and abandon your changes.

✔ To move the cell pointer by voice command, say the keystrokes for moving the cell pointer (refer to Table 1-4). To move the equivalent of pressing an arrow key, say "Arrow" followed by the direction ("Left," "Right," "Up," or "Down"), as in "Arrow Left" to move one column to the left or "Arrow Up" to move one row up.

You can say "Tab" instead of "Arrow Right" and "Shift Tab" instead of "Arrow Left" to move one cell right and left, respectively.

To move the cell pointer to column A of the current row, say "Home." To scroll up or down, say "Page Up" or "Page Down." Note that the Speech Recognition does not recognize keystroke combinations that use the Ctrl key — so if you want to move the cell pointer in great jumps as I outline in Table 1-4, you need to say "End," followed by the name of the direction arrow. For example, if you say "End, Right Arrow," Excel moves the cell pointer right to the first occupied cell in that row that is either preceded or followed by a blank cell. Should all the cells to the right be blank, the cell pointer goes to all the way to the last column of the worksheet: that is, column IV.

Closing the Language bar

When you finish using the Language bar to dictate cell entries and issue Excel commands with your voice, you can close the Language bar. To do this, right-click somewhere on the bar and then click Close the Language Bar on the shortcut menu. An alert dialog box telling you that you've closed the Language bar then appears. Click the OK button in this dialog box to put the bar away. (You can also click the Do Not Show Me This Message Again check box so that you can close the Language bar in the future without having to deal with this alert.)

When you next need the Language bar to dictate text or commands in Excel, you can reopen it by choosing Tools⇨Speech⇨Speech Recognition from the Excel menu bar.

Having your handwriting analyzed

Voice is not the only new way to make entries in the cells of your worksheet. Excel 2003 also supports a Handwriting recognition feature that can turn your handwritten text and values into typed text. Note that although Handwriting recognition does support the use of a special input device, such as a graphics tablet that you can attach to computer, you can also hand write cell entries with the mouse (which is kind of like writing with a bar of soap, actually).

The Handwriting recognition feature is available from the Language bar (although it must be installed separately) that you display in Excel by choosing Tools⇨Speech⇨Speech Recognition from the menu bar. When you click the Handwriting button on the Language bar (refer to Figure 2-10), a pop-up menu with the following options appears:

✔ **Click the Writing Pad** item to open the Writing Pad dialog box in which you can handwrite your cell entry. The Writing Pad dialog box contains a line that you can use as the baseline for the entry that you write.

✔ **Click the Write Anywhere** item to open the Write Anywhere tool palette. When this palette is displayed, you can use the entire screen as your writing pad.

✔ **Click the On-Screen Standard Keyboard** item to display a mini-standard keyboard, which you can tap (if you're using a graphics tablet) or click (if you're using a mouse) to supplement your handwriting or use instead.

✔ **Click the On-Screen Symbol Keyboard** item to open a mini-keyboard displaying keys for entering accented letters commonly used in European languages such as French, Spanish, and German. As with the on-screen standard keyboard, you enter accented letters and special characters from this keyboard by tapping (if you're using a graphics tablet) or clicking (if you're using a mouse) its keys.

The handwriting that you make with the Writing Pad or Write Anywhere options is automatically recognized and inserted into the current cell under any of the following conditions:

✔ You write enough text that the Handwriting feature accurately recognizes.

✔ You pause your writing for a time.

✔ You reach the end of the line in the Writing Pad dialog box.

✔ You click the Recognize Now button (the one showing the T being inserted into a page).

If the Handwriting recognition feature converts your writing incorrectly — consequently inserting a mistake into the cell entry — press the Backspace key to wipe out all the erroneous characters, and then try rewriting them.

Both the Writing Pad dialog box and Write Anywhere palette contain the following editing buttons that you can click with the tablet stylus or click with the mouse (instead of having to press them from your regular keyboard):

✔ **Enter:** Complete the entry and move the cell pointer down one row

✔ **Backspace:** Delete characters to the left of the cursor

✔ **Space:** Insert a space in the entry

✔ **Tab:** Complete the entry and move the cell pointer right one column

✔ **Clear:** Delete characters to the right of the cursor

In addition, you can expand both the dialog box and tool palette to include more tools. Click the >> button to expand either so that they display additional tools, including a four-directional cursor keypad with buttons you can use to complete the cell entry and move to the next cell in the direction of its arrow.

I'm just not complete without you

The AutoComplete feature in Excel 2003 is not something you can do anything about, just something to be aware of as you enter your data. In an attempt to cut down on your typing load, our friendly software engineers at Microsoft came up with the AutoComplete feature.

AutoComplete is kinda like a moronic mind reader who anticipates what you might want to enter next based upon what you just entered. This feature comes into play only when you're entering a column of text entries. (It does not come into play when entering values or formulas or when entering a row of text entries.) When entering a column of text entries, AutoComplete looks at the kinds of entries that you make in that column and automatically duplicates them in subsequent rows whenever you start a new entry that begins with the same letter as an existing entry.

For example, suppose that I enter **Jack Sprat Diet Centers** (one of the companies owned and operated by Mother Goose Enterprises) in cell A3 and then move the cell pointer down to cell A4 in the row below and press J (lowercase or uppercase, it doesn't matter). AutoComplete immediately inserts the remainder of the familiar entry — *ack Sprat Diet Centers* — in this cell after the J, as shown in Figure 2-11.

Now this is great if I happen to need Jack Sprat Diet Centers as the row heading in both cells A3 and A4. Anticipating that I might be typing a different entry that just happens to start with the same letter as the one above, AutoComplete automatically selects everything after the first letter in the duplicated entry it inserted (from *ack* on, in this example). This enables me to replace the duplicate supplied by AutoComplete just by continuing to type. This is what I did after capturing the Excel screen that you see in Figure 2-11 because I needed to enter Jack and Jill Trauma Centers — another of Mother's companies — in cell A4.

If you override a duplicate supplied by AutoComplete in a column by typing one of your own (as in my example with changing Jack Sprat Diet Centers to Jack and Jill Trauma Centers in cell A4), you effectively shut down its ability to supply any more duplicates for that particular letter. So, for instance, in my example, after changing Jack Sprat Diet Centers to Jack and Jill Trauma Centers in cell A4, AutoComplete doesn't do anything if I then type J in cell A5. In other words, you're on your own if you don't continue to accept AutoComplete's typing suggestions.

TIP

If you find that the AutoComplete feature is really making it hard for you to enter a series of cell entries that all start with the same letter but are otherwise not alike, you can turn off the AutoComplete feature. Choose Tools⇨ Options and select the Edit tab. Then, select the Enable AutoComplete for Cell Values check box to remove its check mark before clicking OK.

Figure 2-11:
Auto-
Complete
duplicates
a previous
entry if you
start a new
entry in
the same
column that
begins with
the same
letter.

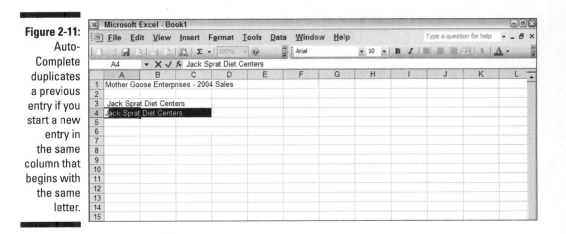

Figure 2-11:
Auto-Complete duplicates a previous entry if you start a new entry in the same column that begins with the same letter.

Fill 'er up with AutoFill

Many of the worksheets that you create with Excel require the entry of a series of sequential dates or numbers. For example, a worksheet may require you to title the columns with the 12 months, from January through December or to number the rows from 1 to 100.

Excel's AutoFill feature makes short work of this kind of repetitive task. All you have to enter is the starting value for the series. In most cases, AutoFill is smart enough to figure out how to fill out the series for you when you drag the fill handle to the right (to take the series across columns to the right) or down (to extend the series to the rows below).

Remember that the AutoFill handle looks like this — + — and appears only when you position the mouse pointer on the lower-right corner of the cell (or the last cell, when you've selected a block of cells). Keep in mind that if you drag a cell selection with the white-cross mouse pointer rather than the AutoFill handle, Excel simply extends the cell selection to those cells you drag through (see Chapter 3). If you drag a cell selection with the arrowhead pointer, Excel moves the cell selection (see Chapter 4).

When creating a series with the fill handle, you can drag in only one direction at a time. For example, you can fill the series or copy the entry to the range to the left or right of the cell that contains the initial values, or you can fill the series or copy to the range above or below the cell that contains the initial values. You can't, however, fill or copy the series to two directions at the same time (such as down and to the right by dragging the fill handle diagonally).

As you drag the mouse, the program keeps you informed of whatever entry would be entered into the last cell selected in the range by displaying that entry next to the mouse pointer (as a kind of AutoFill tips, if you will). When you release the mouse button after extending the range with the fill handle, Excel either creates a series in all of the cells that you select or copies the entire range with the initial value. To the right of the last entry in the filled or copied series, Excel also displays a drop-down button that contains a shortcut menu of options. You can use this shortcut menu to override Excel's default filling or copying. For example, when you use the fill handle, Excel copies an initial value into a range of cells. But, if you want a sequential series, you could do this by selecting the Fill Series command on the AutoFill Options shortcut menu.

In Figures 2-12 and 2-13, I illustrate how to use AutoFill to enter a row of months, starting with January in cell B2 and ending with June in cell G2. To do this, you simply enter **January** in cell B2 and then position the mouse pointer on the fill handle in the lower-right corner of this cell before you drag through to cell G2 on the right (as shown in Figure 2-12). When you release the mouse button, Excel fills in the names of the rest of the months (February through June) in the selected cells (as shown in Figure 2-13). Note that Excel keeps the cells with the series of months selected, giving you another chance to modify the series. (If you went too far, you can drag the fill handle to the left to cut back on the list of months; if you didn't go far enough, you can drag it to the right to extend the list of months further.)

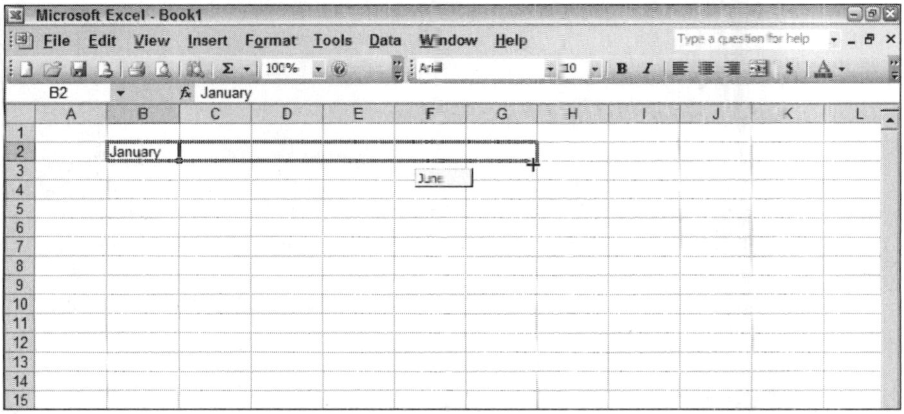

Figure 2-12:
To fill in a series of months, type **January** in the first cell, then drag the fill handle to select the cell range for the rest of the months.

Also, you can use the options on the AutoFill Options shortcut menu (opened by clicking the drop-down button that appears on the fill handle to the right of June) to override the series created by default. To have Excel copy January into each of the selected cells, choose Copy Cells on this menu. To have the program fill the selected cells with the formatting used in cell B2 (in this case, the cell has had bold and italics applied to it — see Chapter 3 for details on formatting cells), you select Fill Formatting only on this menu. To have Excel fill in the series of months in the selected cells without copying the formatting used in cell B2, you select the Fill Without Formatting command from this shortcut menu.

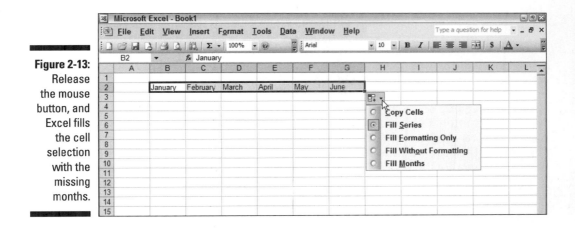

Figure 2-13:
Release the mouse button, and Excel fills the cell selection with the missing months.

See Table 2-4 in the following section to see some of the different initial values that AutoFill can use and the types of series that Excel can create from them.

Working with a spaced series

AutoFill uses the initial value that you select (date, time, day, year, and so on) to design the series. All the sample series I show in Table 2-4 change by a factor of one (one day, one month, or one number). You can tell AutoFill to create a series that changes by some other value: Enter two sample values in neighboring cells that describe the amount of change you want between each value in the series. Make these two values the initial selection that you extend with the fill handle.

For example, to start a series with Saturday and enter every other day across a row, enter **Saturday** in the first cell and **Monday** in the cell next door. After selecting both cells, drag the fill handle across the cells to the right as far you need to fill out a series based on these two initial values. When you release the mouse button, Excel follows the example set in the first two cells by entering every other day (Wednesday to the right of Monday, Friday to the right of Wednesday, and so on).

Table 2-4	Samples of Series You Can Create with AutoFill
Value Entered in First Cell	Extended Series Created by AutoFill in the Next Three Cells
June	July, August, September
Jun	Jul, Aug, Sep
Tuesday	Wednesday, Thursday, Friday
Tue	Wed, Thu, Fr
4/1/99	4/2/99, 4/3/99, 4/4/99
Jan-00	Feb-00, Mar-00, Apr-00
15-Feb	16-Feb, 17-Feb, 18-Feb
10:00 PM	11:00 PM, 12:00 AM, 1:00 AM
8:01	9:01, 10:01, 11:01
Quarter 1	Quarter 2, Quarter 3, Quarter 4
Qtr2	Qtr3, Qtr4, Qtr
Q3	Q4, Q1, Q2
Product 1	Product 2, Product 3, Product 4
1st Product	2nd Product, 3rd Product, 4th Product

Copying with AutoFill

You can use AutoFill to copy a text entry throughout a cell range (rather than fill in a series of related entries). To copy a text entry to a cell range, hold down the Ctrl key as you click and drag the fill handle. When you hold down the Ctrl key as you click the fill handle, a plus sign appears to the right of the fill handle — your sign that AutoFill will *copy* the entry in the active cell instead of creating a series using it. You can also tell because the entry that appears as the AutoFill tip next to the mouse pointer as you drag contains the same text as the original cell. If you decide, after copying an initial label or value to a range, that you should have used it to fill in a series, all you have to do is click the drop-down button that appears on the fill handle at cell with the last copied entry and select the Fill Series command on the AutoFill Options shortcut menu that then appears.

Although holding down Ctrl as you drag the fill handle copies a text entry, just the opposite is true when it comes to values! Suppose that you enter the number **17** in a cell and then drag the fill handle across the row — Excel just copies the number 17 in all the cells that you select. If, however, you hold down Ctrl as you drag the fill handle, Excel then fills out the series (17, 18, 19, and so on). If you forget and create a series of numbers when you only need the value copied, rectify this situation by selecting the Copy Cells command on the AutoFill Options shortcut menu.

Creating custom lists for AutoFill

In addition to varying the increment in a series created with AutoFill, you can also create your own custom series. For example, in the bosom of Mother Goose Enterprises, you will find the following companies:

- Jack Sprat Diet Centers
- Jack and Jill Trauma Centers
- Mother Hubbard Dog Goodies
- Rub-a-Dub-Dub Hot Tubs and Spas
- Georgie Porgie Pudding Pies
- Hickory, Dickory, Dock Clock Repair
- Little Bo Peep Pet Detectives

Rather than having to type this list of companies in the cells of each new worksheet (or even copy them from an existing worksheet), you can create a custom series that produces the whole list of companies simply by entering Jack Sprat Diet Centers in the first cell and then dragging the fill handle to the blank cells where the rest of the companies should appear.

To create this kind of custom series, follow these steps:

1. **Choose Tools⇨Options on the menu bar to open the Options dialog box (as shown in Figure 2-14).**

2. **From the Options dialog box, click the Custom Lists tab to display the Custom Lists and List Entries list boxes.**

   When you do this, NEW LIST is automatically selected in the Custom Lists box.

   If you've already gone to the time and trouble of typing the custom list in a range of cells, go to Step 3. If you haven't yet typed the series in an open worksheet, go to Step 6 instead.

3. **Click inside the Import List from Cells text box and click the Minimize Dialog Box button (the one with the picture of the tiny grid to the right of the Import List from Cells text box) so that you can see your list and drag through the range of cells to select them (see Chapter 3 for details).**

4. After selecting the cells in the worksheet, click the Maximize Dialog box button.

This button automatically replaces the Minimize Dialog box button to the right of the Import List from Cells text box.

5. Then click the Import button to copy this list into the List Entries list box.

Skip to Step 8.

6. Choose the List Entries list box and then type each entry (in the desired order), being sure to press Enter after typing each one.

When all the entries in the custom list appear in the List Entries list box in the order you want them, proceed to Step 7.

7. Click the Add button to add the list of entries to the Custom lists box.

Finish creating all the custom lists you need, using the preceding steps. When you are done, move on to Step 8.

8. Click OK or press Enter to close the Options dialog box and return to the current worksheet in the active workbook.

After adding a custom list to Excel, from then on you need only enter the first entry in a cell and then use the fill handle to extend it to the cells below or to the right.

If you don't even want to bother with typing the first entry, use the AutoCorrect feature — refer to the section "You really AutoCorrect that for me," earlier in this chapter — to create an entry that will fill in as soon as you type your favorite acronym for it (such as *jsdc* for *Jack Sprat Diet Centers*).

Inserting special symbols

Excel 2003 makes it easy to enter special symbols, such as foreign currency indicators, as well as special characters, such as the Trademark and Copyright symbols, into your cell entries. To insert a special symbol or character in a cell entry, choose Insert⇨Symbol on the Excel menu bar.

When you choose this command, the Symbol dialog box (similar to the one shown in Figure 2-15) appears. As you can see in this figure, this dialog box contains two tabs: Symbols and Special characters. To insert a mathematical or foreign currency symbol on the Symbols tab, click its symbol in the list box and then click the Insert button. (You can also do this by double-clicking the symbol.) To insert characters, such as foreign language or accented characters from other character sets, click the Subset drop-down button, then click the name of the set in the drop-down list, and then click the desired characters in the list box below. You can also insert commonly used currency and mathematical symbols, such as the Pound or plus-or-minus symbol, by clicking them in the Recently Used Symbols section at the bottom of this tab of the Symbol dialog box.

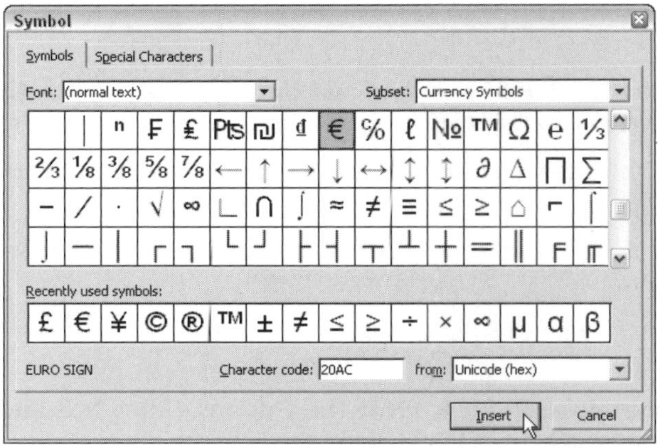

Figure 2-15:
Use the
Symbol
dialog box
to insert
special
symbols and
characters
into your
cell entries.

To insert special characters, such as the Registered trademark, paragraph symbol, and ellipsis, click the Special Characters tab of the Symbol dialog box, locate the symbol in the scrolling list, click it, and then click the Insert button. (You can also insert one of these special characters by double-clicking as well.)

When you finish inserting special symbols and characters, close the Symbol dialog box by clicking its Close button in its upper-right corner.

Entries all around the block

When you want to enter a table of information in a new worksheet, you can simplify the job of entering the data if you select all the empty cells in which you want to make entries before you begin entering any information. Just position the cell pointer in the first cell of what is to become the data table and then select all the cells in the subsequent columns and rows. (For information on the ways to select a range of cells, see Chapter 3.) After you select the block of cells, you can begin entering the first entry.

When you select a block of cells (also known as a *range*) before you start entering information, Excel restricts data entry to that range as follows:

- ✔ The program automatically advances the cell pointer to the next cell in the range when you click the Enter box or press Enter to complete each cell entry.

- ✔ In a cell range that contains several different rows and columns, Excel advances the cell pointer down each row of the column as you make your entries. When the cell pointer reaches the cell in the last row of the column, the cell pointer advances to the first selected row in the next column to the right. If the cell range uses only one row, Excel advances the cell pointer from left to right across the row.

- ✔ When you finish entering information in the last cell in the selected range, Excel positions the cell pointer in the first cell of the now-completed data table. To deselect the cell range, click the mouse pointer on one of the cells in the worksheet (inside or outside the selected range — it doesn't matter) or press one of the arrow keys.

WARNING!

Be sure that you don't press one of the arrow keys to complete a cell entry within a preselected cell range instead of clicking the Enter box or pressing Enter. Pressing an arrow key deselects the range of cells when Excel moves the cell pointer. To move the cell pointer around a cell range without deselecting the range, try these methods:

- ✔ Press Enter to advance to the next cell down each row and then across each column in the range. Press Shift+Enter to move up to the previous cell.

- ✔ Press Tab to advance to the next cell in the column on the right and then down each row of the range. Press Shift+Tab to move left to the previous cell.

- ✔ Press Ctrl+. (period) to move from one corner of the range to another.

Data entry express

You can save a lot of time and energy when you want the same entry (text, value, or formula) to appear in many cells of the worksheet; you can enter the information in all the cells in one operation. You first select the cell ranges to hold the information. (Excel lets you select more than one cell range for this kind of thing — see Chapter 3 for details.) Then you construct the entry on the formula bar and press Ctrl+Enter to put the entry into all the selected ranges.

The key to making this operation a success is to hold the Ctrl key as you press Enter so that Excel inserts the entry on the formula bar into all the selected cells. If you forget to hold Ctrl and you just press Enter, Excel places the entry in the first cell only of the selected cell range.

You can also speed up data entry in a list that includes formulas by making sure that the Extend List Formats and Formulas check box is selected on the Edit tab in the Options dialog box. (Open this by choosing Tools⊏>Options on the menu bar.) When this check box is selected, Excel automatically formats new data that you type in the last row of a list to match that of like data in earlier rows and copies down formulas that appear in the preceding rows. Note, however, that for this new feature to kick in, you must manually enter the formulas and format the data entries in at least three rows preceding the new row.

How to Make Your Formulas Function Even Better

Earlier in this chapter, I show you how to create formulas that perform a series of simple mathematical operations, such as addition, subtraction, multiplication, and division. (See the section "Fabricating those fabulous formulas!") Instead of creating more-complex formulas from scratch out of an intricate combination of these operations, you can find an Excel function to get the job done.

A *function* is a predefined formula that performs a particular type of computation. All you have to do to use a function is supply the values that the function uses when performing its calculations. (In the parlance of the Spreadsheet Guru, such values are known as the *arguments of the function.*) As with simple formulas, you can enter the arguments for most functions either as a numerical value (for example, **22** or **–4.56**) or, as is more common, as a cell reference (**B10**) or as a cell range (**C3:F3**).

Just as with a formula you build yourself, each function you use must start with an equal sign (=) so that Excel knows to enter the function as a formula rather than as text. Following the equal sign, you enter the name of the function (in uppercase or lowercase — it doesn't matter, as long as you don't misspell the name). Following the name of the function, you enter the arguments required to perform the calculations. All function arguments are enclosed in a pair of parentheses.

If you type the function directly in a cell, remember not to insert spaces between the equal sign, function name, and the arguments enclosed in parentheses. Some functions use more than one value when performing their designated calculations. When this is the case, you separate each function with a comma (not a space).

After you type the equal sign, function name, and the left parenthesis (( ) that marks the beginning of the arguments for the function, you can point to any cell or cell range that you want to use as the first argument instead of typing the cell references. When the function uses more than one argument, you can point to the cells or cell ranges you want to use for the second argument right after you enter a comma (,) to complete the first argument.

After you finish entering the last argument, type a right parenthesis ( )) to mark the end of the argument list. Then click the Enter box or press Enter or the appropriate arrow key to insert the function in the cell and have Excel calculate the answer.

Inserting a function into a formula with the Insert Function button

Although you can enter a function by typing it directly in a cell, Excel provides an Insert Function button on the Formula bar you can use to select any of Excel's functions. When you click this button, Excel opens the Insert Function dialog box (shown in Figure 2-16) where you can select the function you want to use. After you select your function, Excel opens the Function Arguments dialog box. In this dialog box, you can specify the function arguments. The real boon comes when you're fooling with an unfamiliar function or one that's kind of complex (some of these puppies can be really hairy). You can get loads of help in completing the argument text boxes in the Function Arguments dialog box by clicking the <u>Help on this Function</u> hyperlink in the lower-left corner of this dialog box.

To open the Insert Function dialog box, you select the cell that needs the formula and then click the Insert Function button (the one marked *fx*) on the Formula bar. When you click the Insert Function button, an Insert Function dialog box, similar to the one shown in Figure 2-16, appears.

The Insert Function dialog box contains three boxes: a Search for a Function text box, a Select a Category drop-down list box, and a Select a Function list box. When you open the Insert Function dialog box, Excel automatically selects Most Recently Used as the category in the Select a Category drop-down list box and displays the functions you usually use in the Select a Function list box.

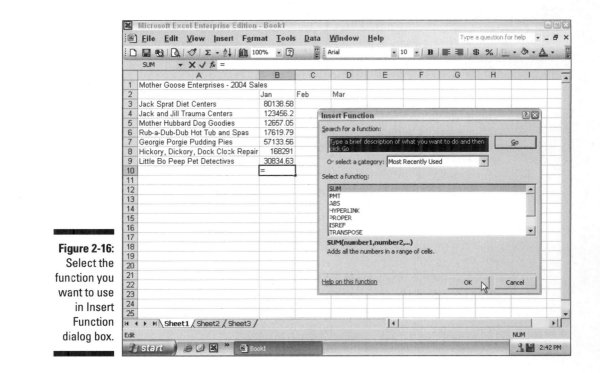

Figure 2-16:
Select the function you want to use in Insert Function dialog box.

If your function isn't among the most recently used, you must then select the appropriate category of your function in the Select a Category drop-down list box. If you don't know the category, you must search for the function by typing a description of its purpose in the Search for a Function text box and then pressing Enter or clicking the Go button. For example, to locate all the Excel functions that total values, you enter the word **total** in the Search for Function list box and click the Go button. Excel then displays its list of recommended totaling functions in the Select a Function list box. You can peruse the recommended functions by selecting each one. As you select each function in this list, the Insert Function dialog box shows you the required arguments followed by a description, at the bottom of the dialog box, of what the function does.

After you locate and select the function you want to use, click the OK button to insert the function into the current cell and open the Function Arguments dialog box. This dialog box displays the required arguments for the function along with any that are optional. For example, suppose that you select the Sum function (the crown jewel of the Most Recently Used function category) in the Select a Function list box and then click OK. As soon as you do, the program inserts

```
SUM( )
```

in the current cell and on the Formula bar (following the equal sign), and the Function Arguments dialog box showing the SUM arguments appears on the screen (as shown in Figure 2-17). This is where you add the arguments for the Sum function.

As you can read in the Function Arguments dialog box shown in Figure 2-17, you can select up to 30 numbers to be summed. What's not obvious, however (there's always some trick, huh?), is that these numbers don't have to be in single cells. In fact, most of the time you'll be selecting a whole slew of numbers in nearby cells (in a multiple cell selection — that range thing) that you want to total.

To select your first number argument in the dialog box, you click the cell (or drag through the block of cells) in the worksheet while the insertion point is in the Number1 text box. Excel then displays the cell address (or range address) in the Number1 text box while, at the same time, showing the value in the cell (or values, if you select a bunch of cells) in the box to the right. Excel displays the total so far near the bottom of the Function Arguments dialog box after the words Formula result=.

Keep in mind that when selecting cells, you can minimize this arguments dialog box down to just the contents of the Number1 text box by clicking the

Minimize Dialog box button on the right of the Number1 text box. After mini-mizing the arguments dialog box so that you can select the cells to be used as the first argument, you can expand it again by clicking the Maximize Dialog box button (the only button displayed on the far right) or by pressing the Esc key. Instead of minimizing the dialog box, you can also temporarily move it out of the way by clicking on any part and then dragging the dialog box to its new destination on the screen.

If you're adding more than one cell (or bunch of cells) in a worksheet, press the Tab key or click the Number2 text box to move the insertion point that text box. (Excel responds by extending the argument list with a Number3 text box.) Here is where you specify the second cell (or cell range) that is to be added to the one now showing in the Number1 text box. After you click the cell or drag through the second cell range, the program displays the cell address(es), with the numbers in the cell(s) to the right and the running total near the bottom of the Function Arguments dialog box after the words `Formula result=` (as shown in Figure 2-17). Note that you can minimize the entire arguments dialog box down to just the contents of the argument text box you're dealing with (Number2, Number3, and so on) by clicking its partic-ular Minimize Dialog box button if the dialog box obscures the cells that you need to select.

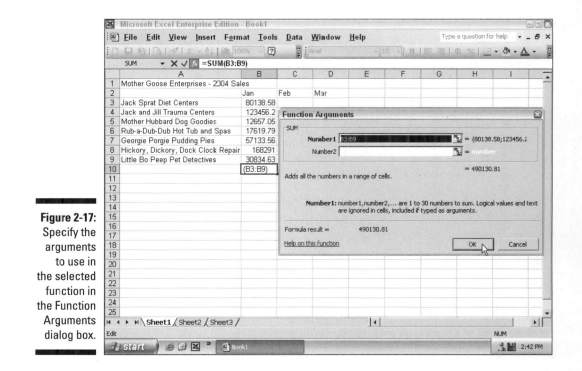

Figure 2-17: Specify the arguments to use in the selected function in the Function Arguments dialog box.

When you finish pointing out the cells or bunches of cells to be summed, click the OK button to close the Function Arguments dialog box and put the SUM function in the current cell.

Editing a function with the Insert Function button

Use the Excel Insert Function button to edit formulas that contain functions right from the Formula bar. Select the cell with the formula with the function to be edited before you click the Insert Function button (the one sporting the *fx* that appears immediately in front of the current cell entry on the Formula bar).

As soon as you click the Insert Function button, Excel opens the Function Arguments dialog box where you can edit its arguments. To edit just the arguments of a function, select the cell references in the appropriate argument's text box (marked Number1, Number2, Number3, and so on) and then make whatever changes are required to the cell addresses or select a new range of cells. Keep in mind that Excel automatically adds any cell or cell range that you highlight in the worksheet to the current argument. If you want to replace the current argument, you need to highlight it and then get rid of its cell addresses by pressing the Delete key before you highlight the new cell or cell range to be used as the argument. (Remember that you can always minimize this dialog box or move it to a new location if it obscures the cells you need to select.)

When you finish editing the function, press Enter or click the OK button in the Function Arguments dialog box to put it away and update the formula in the worksheet.

I'd be totally lost without AutoSum

Before leaving this fascinating discussion on entering functions, I want you to get to the AutoSum tool on the Standard toolbar. Look for the Greek sigma Σ symbol. This little tool is worth its weight in gold. In addition to entering the Sum, Average, Count, Max, or Min functions, it also selects the most likely range of cells in the current column or row that you want to use as the function's argument and then automatically enters them as the function's argument. And nine times out of ten, Excel selects (by highlighting) the correct cell range to be totaled, averaged, counted, and so forth. For that tenth case, you can manually correct the range by simply dragging the cell pointer through the block of cells that need to be summed.

By default, clicking the AutoSum button (as its name implies), inserts the Sum function into the current cell. If you want to use this button to insert another function, such as Average, Count, Max, or Min, you need to click its drop-down button and select the name of the desired function on its pop-up menu. Note that if you select the More Functions command on this menu, Excel opens the Insert Function dialog box as though you had clicked the *fx* button on the Formula bar.

In Figure 2-18, check out how to use the AutoSum tool to total the sales of Jack Sprat Diet Centers in row 3. Position the cell pointer in cell E3, where the first-quarter total is to appear, and click the AutoSum tool. Excel inserts SUM (equal sign and all) onto the Formula bar; places a *marquee* (the moving dotted line) around the cells B3, C3, and D3; and uses the cell range B3:D3 as the argument of Sum function.

Now look at the worksheet after you insert the function in cell E3 (see Figure 2-19). The calculated total appears in cell E3 while the following Sum function formula appears in the Formula bar:

```
=SUM(B3:D3)
```

After entering the function to total the sales of Jack Sprat Diet Centers, you can copy this formula to total sales for the rest of the companies by dragging the fill handle down column E until the cell range E3:E9 is highlighted.

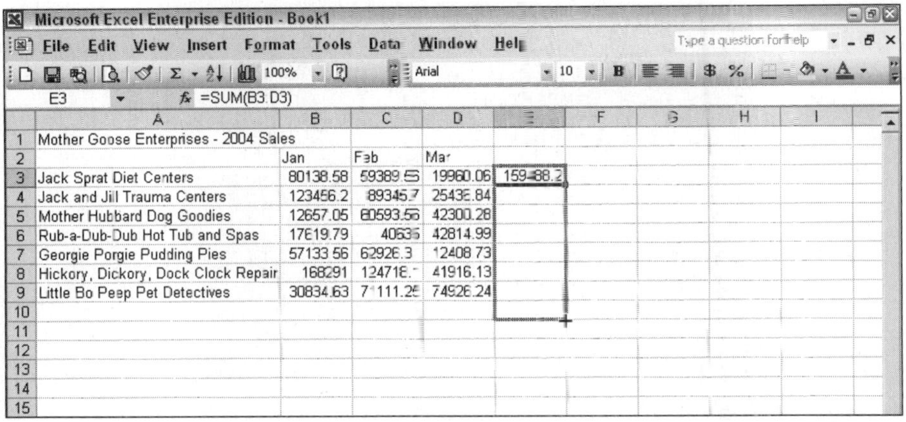

Figure 2-19:
The work-
sheet with
the first
quarter
totals
calcula-
ted with
AutoSum.

Look at Figure 2-20 to see how you can use the AutoSum tool to total the January sales for all the Mother Goose Enterprises in column B. Position the cell pointer in cell B10 where you want the total to appear. Click the AutoSum tool, and Excel places the marquee around cells B3 through B9 and correctly enters the cell range B3:B9 as the argument of the SUM function.

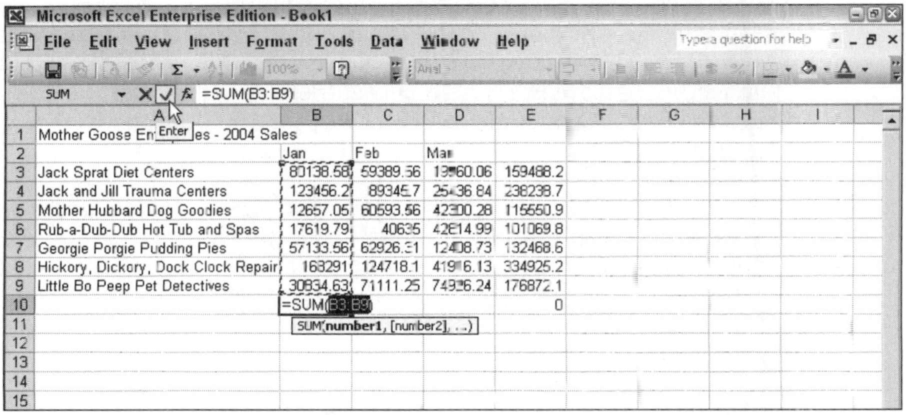

Figure 2-20:
Click the
AutoSum
button in
cell B10 and
press Enter
to total the
January
sales for all
companies
in column B.

In Figure 2-21, you see the worksheet after inserting the function in cell B10 and using the AutoFill feature to copy the formula to cells C10, D10, and E10 to the right. (To use AutoFill, drag the fill handle through the cells to the right until you reach cell E10 before you release the mouse button.)

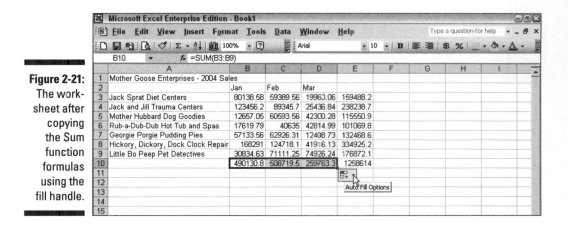

Making Sure That the Data Is Safe and Sound

All the work you do in any of the worksheets in your workbook is at risk until you save the workbook as a disk file (either to a disk or to your hard drive). Should you lose power or should your computer crash for any reason before you save the workbook, you're out of luck. You have to re-create each and every keystroke — a painful task, made all the worse because it's so unnecessary. To avoid this unpleasantness altogether, adopt this motto: Save your work anytime you enter more information than you could possibly bear to lose.

To encourage frequent saving on your part, Excel even provides you with a Save button on the Standard toolbar (the one with the picture of a 3¼" floppy disk, third from the left). You don't even have to take the time and trouble to choose the Save command from the File menu (or even press Ctrl+S); you can simply click this tool whenever you want to save new work on disk.

When you click the Save tool for the first time you, Excel displays the Save As dialog box. Use this dialog box to replace the temporary document name (Book1, Book2, and so forth) with a more descriptive filename and to select a new drive and folder before you save the workbook as a disk file. It's just this easy:

   ✔ To rename the workbook, type the filename in the File Name text field. When you first open the Save As dialog box, the suggested Book1-type filename is selected; you can just start typing the new filename to replace it.

✔ To change the drive on which the workbook is stored, click the Save In drop-down list button and then click the appropriate drive name, such as Hard disk (C:) or 3½ Floppy (A:), in the drop-down list box.

✔ To change the folder in which the workbook is saved, select the drive if necessary (as I describe in the preceding bullet) and then click the desired folder. If you want to save the workbook in a folder that's inside one of the folders shown in the list box, just double-click that folder. When all is said and done, the name of the folder where the workbook file will be saved should appear in the Save In text field.

To save the file in a brand-new folder, click the Create New Folder button (refer to Figure 2-21). The New Folder dialog box opens. Enter the folder name in the Name text field and then click OK or press Enter.

The Excel 2003 Save As dialog box contains a bunch of large buttons that appear on the left side of the dialog box: My Recent Documents, Desktop, My Documents, My Computer, and My Network Places. Use these buttons to select the following folders in which to save your new workbook file:

✔ Click the My Recent Documents button to save your workbook in the Recent folder. The Recent folder resides in this hierarchy: Windows folder (on your hard drive)\Application Data folder\Microsoft folder\Office folder\Recent folder.

✔ Click the Desktop button to save your workbook on your computer's desktop.

✔ Click the My Documents button to save your workbook in the My Documents folder.

✔ Click the My Computer button to save your workbook on one of the disks on your computer or in your own or a shared documents folder on your hard drive.

✔ Click the My Network Places button to save your workbook in one of the folders on your company's network.

Under Windows XP, your filenames can contain spaces and be a maximum of 255 characters long. (You do want to name your file with an entire paragraph, don't you?) This is great news, especially if you were once a DOS or Windows 3.1 user who suffered under that eight-dot-three filename restriction for so long. Just be aware when naming your workbook that if you transfer it to a machine that doesn't use Windows XP, 98, the Millennium Edition, or Windows 2000, the Excel filenames will appear severely abbreviated (truncated). Also, they will all be followed with the .xls Excel filename extension (which, by the way, is stuck onto workbook files created in Excel 2003 — Windows XP has enough sense to hide this filename extension from you).

When you finish making changes in the Save As dialog box, click the Save button or press Enter to have Excel 2003 save your work. When Excel saves your workbook file, the program saves all the information in every worksheet in your workbook (including the last position of the cell pointer) in the designated folder and drive. You don't have to fool with the Save As dialog box again unless you want to rename the workbook or save a copy of it in a different directory. If you want to do either of these things, you must choose the Save As command from the File menu rather than click the Save button or press Ctrl+S.

Document Recovery to the Rescue

Excel 2003 offers a document recovery feature that can help you in the event of a computer crash because of a power failure or some sort of operating system freeze or shutdown. The AutoRecover feature saves your workbooks at regular intervals. In the event of a computer crash, Excel displays a Document Recovery task pane the next time you start Excel after rebooting the computer.

When you first start using Excel 2003, the AutoRecover feature is set to automatically save changes to your workbook (provided that the file has already been saved) every ten minutes. You can shorten or lengthen this interval as you see fit. Choose Tools⇨Options, and then click the Save tab. Use the spinner buttons or enter a new automatic save interval into the text box marked `Save AutoRecover Info Every 10 Minutes` before clicking OK.

The Document Recovery task pane shows the available versions of the workbook files that were open at the time of the computer crash. It identifies the original version of the workbook file and when it was saved along with the recovered version of the file and when it was saved. To open the recovered version of a workbook (to see how much of the work it contains that was unsaved at the time of the crash), position the mouse pointer over the AutoRecover version. Then click its drop-down menu button and click Open on its pop-up menu. After you open the recovered version, you can (if you choose) then save its changes by choosing File⇨Save on the Excel menu bar.

To save the recovered version of a workbook without bothering to first open it up, place your mouse over the recovered version, click its drop-down button, and choose the Save As option on the pop-up menu. To permanently abandon the recovered version (leaving you with *only* the data in the original version), click the Close button at the bottom of the Document Recovery task pane. When you click the Close button, an alert dialog box appears, giving you the chance to retain the recovered versions of the file for later viewing. To retain the files for later viewing, select the Yes (I want to view these files later) radio button before clicking OK. To retain only the original versions of the files shown in the task pane, select the No (remove these files. I have saved the files I need) radio button instead.

Note that the AutoRecover features only works or Excel workbooks that you have saved at least one time (as explained in the earlier section "Making Sure That the Data Is Safe and Sound"). In other words, if you build a new workbook and don't bother to save and rename it prior to experiencing a computer crash, the AutoRecover feature will not bring back any part of it. For this reason, it is very, very important that you get into the habit of saving new workbooks with File⇨Save very shortly after beginning to work on one its worksheets. Or you can use the trusty keyboard shortcut Ctrl+S.

Part II
Editing Without Tears

The 5th Wave   By Rich Tennant

"NIFTY CHART, FRANK, BUT NOT ENTIRELY NECESSARY."

In this part . . .

The business world wouldn't be half bad if it weren't for the fact that right around the time you master your job, somebody goes and changes it on you. When your life must always be flexible, changing gears and "going with the flow" can really grate on a person! The sad truth is that a big part of the work that you do with Excel 2003 is changing the stuff you slaved so hard to enter into the spreadsheet in the first place.

In Part II, I break this editing stuff down into three phases: formatting the raw data; rearranging the formatting data and/or in some cases deleting it; and, finally, spitting out the final formatted and edited data in printed form. Take it from me, after you know your way around editing your spreadsheets (as presented in this part of the book), you're more than halfway home with Excel 2003.

Chapter 3

Making It All Look Pretty

*I*n spreadsheet programs like Excel, you normally don't worry about how the stuff looks until after you enter all the data in the worksheets of your workbook and save it all safe and sound (see Chapters 1 and 2). Only then do you pretty up the information so that it's clearer and easy to read.

After you decide on the types of formatting that you want to apply to a portion of the worksheet, select all the cells to be beautified and then click the appropriate tool or choose the menu command to apply those formats to the cells. But before you discover all the fabulous formatting features you can use to dress up cells, you first need to know how to pick out the group of cells that you want to apply the formatting to — *selecting the cells* or alternately, *making a cell selection.*

Be aware, also, that entering data into a cell and formatting that data are two completely different things in Excel. Because they're separate, you can change the entry in a formatted cell, and new entries assume the cell's formatting. This enables you to format blank cells in a worksheet, knowing that when you get around to making entries in those cells, those entries automatically assume the formatting you assign to those cells.

Choosing a Select Group of Cells

Given the monotonously rectangular nature of the worksheet and its components, it shouldn't come as a surprise to find that all the cell selections you make in the worksheet have the same kind of cubist feel to them. After all, worksheets are just blocks of cells of varying numbers of columns and rows.

A *cell selection* (or *cell range*) is whatever collection of neighboring cells you choose to format or edit. The smallest possible cell selection in a worksheet is just one cell: the so-called *active cell*. The cell with the cell pointer is really just a single cell selection. The largest possible cell selection in a worksheet is all the cells in that worksheet (the whole enchilada, so to speak). Most of the cell selections you need for formatting a worksheet will probably fall somewhere in between, consisting of cells in several adjacent columns and rows.

Excel shows a cell selection in the worksheet by highlighting the block. (Look at Figure 3-1 to see several cell selections of different sizes and shapes.)

In Excel, you can select more than one cell range at a time (a phenomenon somewhat ingloriously called a *noncontiguous* or *nonadjacent selection*). In fact, although Figure 3-1 appears to contain several cell selections, it's really just one big, nonadjacent cell selection with cell D12 (the active one) as the cell that was selected last.

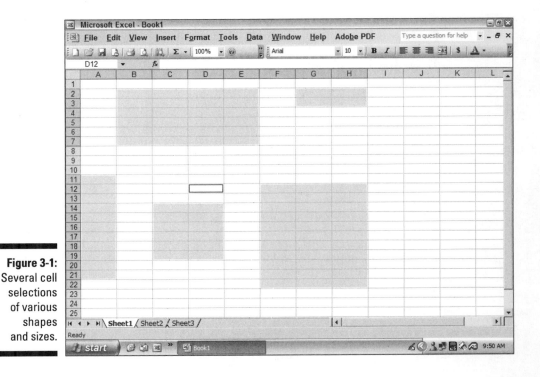

Figure 3-1:
Several cell
selections
of various
shapes
and sizes.

Point-and-click cell selections

The mouse is a natural for selecting a range of cells. Just position the mouse pointer (in its thick, white-cross form) on the first cell and drag in the direction that you want to extend the select on.

- ✔ To extend the cell selection to columns to the right, drag your mouse to the right, highlighting neighboring cells as you go.

- ✔ To extend the selection to rows to the bottom, drag your mouse down.

- ✔ To extend the selection down and to the right at the same time, drag your mouse diagonally toward the cell in the lower-right corner of the block you're highlighting.

Shifty cell selections

To speed up the old cell-selection procedure, you can use the old Shift+click method, which goes as follows:

1. **Click the first cell in the selection.**

   This selects that cell.

2. **Position the mouse pointer in the last cell in the selection.**

   This is kitty-corner from the first cell in your selected rectangular block.

3. **Press the Shift key and hold it down while you click the mouse button again.**

   When you click the mouse button the second time, Excel selects all the cells in the columns and rows between the first cell and last cell.

The Shift key works with the mouse like an *extend* key to extend a selection from the first object you select through to, and including, the second object you select. See the section "Extend that cell selection," later in this chapter. Using the Shift key enables you to select the first and last cells. as well as all the intervening cells in a worksheet or all the document names in a dialog list box.

If, when making a cell selection with the mouse, you notice that you include the wrong cells before you release the mouse button, you can deselect the cells and resize the selection by moving the pointer in the opposite direction. If you already released the mouse button, click the first cell in the highlighted range to select just that cell (and deselect all the others) and then start the whole selection process again.

Nonadjacent cell selections

To select a nonadjacent cell selection made up of more than one noncontiguous (that is, not touching) block of cells, drag through the first cell range and then hold down the Ctrl key while you click the first cell of the second range and drag the pointer through the cells in this range. As long as you hold down Ctrl while you select the subsequent ranges, Excel doesn't deselect any of the previously selected cell ranges.

The Ctrl key works with the mouse like an *add* key to include non-neighboring objects in Excel. See the section "Nonadjacent cell selections with the keyboard," later in this chapter. By using the Ctrl key, you can add to the selection of cells in a worksheet or to the document names in a dialog list box without having to deselect those already selected.

Going for the "big" cell selections

You can select the cells in entire columns or rows or even all the cells in the worksheet by applying the following clicking-and-dragging techniques to the worksheet frame:

- ✔ To select every single cell in a particular column, click its column letter on the frame at the top of the worksheet document window.
- ✔ To select every cell in a particular row, click its row number on the frame at the left edge of the document window.
- ✔ To select a range of entire columns or rows, drag through the column letters or row numbers on the frame surrounding the workbook.
- ✔ To select more than entire columns or rows that are not right next to each other (that old noncontiguous stuff, again), press and hold down the Ctrl key while you click the column letters or row numbers of the columns and rows that you want to add to the selection.

- ✔ To select each and every cell in the worksheet, press Ctrl+A or click the Select All button, which is the unmarked button in the upper-left corner of the workbook frame, formed by the intersection of the row with the column letters and the column with the row numbers.

Selecting the cells in a table of data, courtesy of AutoSelect

Excel provides a really quick way (called AutoSelect) to select all the cells in a table of data entered as a solid block. To use AutoSelect, simply follow these steps:

1. **Click the first cell of the table to select it.**

   This is the cell in the table's upper-left corner.

2. **Hold down the Shift key while you double-click either the right or bottom edge of the selected cell with the arrowhead mouse pointer. (See Figure 3-2.)**

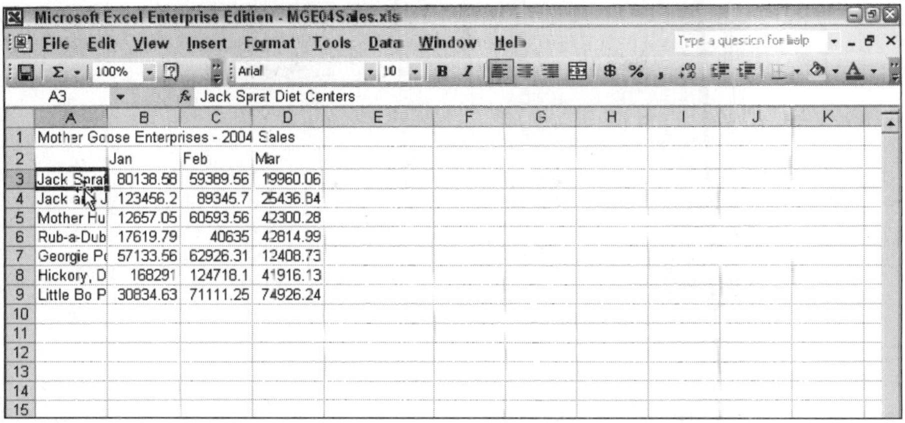

Figure 3-2:
Position
the mouse
pointer on
the first
cell's bottom
edge to
select all
cells of the
first table
column.

Double-clicking the *bottom* edge of the cell causes the cell selection to expand to the cell in the last row of the first column (as shown in Figure 3-3). If you double-click the *right edge* of the cell, the cell selection expands to the cell in the last column of the first row.

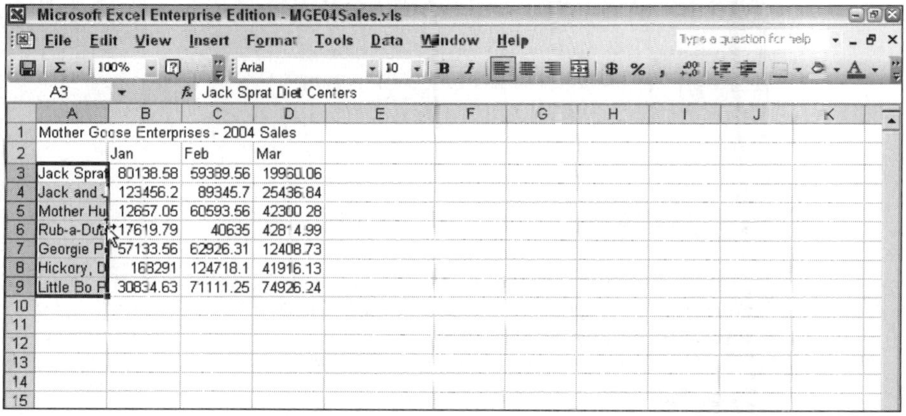

Figure 3-3:
Hold down
Shift while
you double-
click the
bottom
edge of the
first cell to
extend the
selection
down the
column.

3a. Double-click somewhere on the right edge of the cell selection (refer to Figure 3-3) if the cell selection now consists of the first column of the table.

This selects all the remaining rows of the table of data (as shown in Figure 3-4).

3b. Double-click somewhere on the bottom edge of the current cell selection if the cell selection now consists of the first row of the table.

This selects all the remaining rows in the table.

Figure 3-4:
Hold down
Shift as you
double-click
the right
edge of the
current
selection
to extend
it across
the rows of
the table.

	A	B	C	D	E	F	G	H	I	J	K
1	Mother Goose Enterprises - 2004 Sales										
2		Jan	Feb	Mar							
3	Jack Sprat	80138.58	59389.56	19960.06							
4	Jack and J	123456.2	89345.7	25436.84							
5	Mother Hu	12657.05	60593.56	42300.28							
6	Rub-a-Dub	17619.79	40635	42814.99							
7	Georgie P(	57133.56	62926.31	12408.73							
8	Hickory, D	168291	124718.1	41916.13							
9	Little Bo P	30834.63	71111.25	74926.24							
10											
11											
12											
13											
14											
15											

Although the preceding steps may lead you to believe that you have to select the first cell of the table when you use AutoSelect, you can actually select any of the cells in the four corners of the table. Then when expanding the cell selection in the table with the Shift key depressed, you can choose whatever direction you like (left, by clicking the left edge; right, by clicking the right edge; up, by clicking the top edge; or down, by clicking the bottom edge) to select either the first or last row of the table or the first or last column. After expanding the cell selection to include either the first or last row or first or last column, you need to click whichever edge of that current cell selection will expand it so that it includes all the remaining table rows or columns.

Keyboard cell selections

If you're not really keen on using the mouse, you can use the keyboard to select the cells you want. Sticking with the Shift+click method of selecting cells, the easiest way to select cells with the keyboard is to combine the Shift key with other keystrokes that move the cell pointer. (I list these keystrokes in Chapter 1.)

Start by positioning the cell pointer in the first cell of the selection and then holding the Shift key while you press the appropriate cell-pointer movement keys. When you hold the Shift key as you press direction keys — such as the arrow keys ($\uparrow$, $\rightarrow$, $\downarrow$, $\leftarrow$), PgUp, or PgDn — Excel anchors the selection on the current cell, moves the cell pointer, and also highlights cells as it goes.

When making a cell selection this way, you can continue to alter the size and shape of the cell range with the cell-pointer movement keys as long as you don't release the Shift key. After you release the Shift key, pressing any of the cell-pointer movement keys immediately collapses the selection, reducing it to just the cell with the cell pointer.

Extend that cell selection

If holding the Shift key as you move the cell pointer is too tiring, you can place Excel in Extend mode by pressing (and promptly releasing) F8 before you press any cell-pointer movement key. Excel displays the EXT (for extend) indicator on the status bar — when you see this, the program will select all the cells that you move the cell pointer through (just as though you were holding down the Shift key).

Look for the EXT indicator in the lower-right corner of the screen, near the NUM (NUM lock indicator).

After you highlight all the cells you want in the cell range, press F8 again to turn off Extend mode. The EXT indicator disappears from the status bar, and then you can once again move the cell pointer with the keyboard without highlighting everything in your path. In fact, when you first move the pointer, all previously selected cells are deselected.

AutoSelect keyboard style

For the keyboard equivalent of AutoSelect with the mouse (read this chapter's section "Selecting the cells in a table of data, courtesy of AutoSelect"), you combine the use of the F8 (Extend key) or the Shift key with the Ctrl+arrow keys or End+arrow keys to zip the cell pointer from one end of a block to the other, merrily selecting all the cells in its path as it goes.

To select an entire table of data with a keyboard version of AutoSelect, follow these steps:

1. **Position the cell pointer in the first cell.**

   That's the cell in the upper-left corner of the table.

2. **Press F8 (or hold the Shift key) and then press Ctrl+→ (or End, →) to extend the cell selection to the cells in the columns on the right.**

3. **Then press Ctrl+↓ (or End, ↓) to extend the selection to the cells in the rows below.**

Keep in mind that the directions in the preceding steps are somewhat arbitrary — you can just as well press Ctrl+↓ (or End, ↓) before you press Ctrl+→ (or End, →). Just be sure (if you're using the Shift key instead of F8) that you don't let up on the Shift key until after you finish performing these two directional maneuvers. Also, if you press F8 to get the program into Extend mode, don't forget to press this key again to get out of Extend mode after the table cells are all selected, or you'll end up selecting cells that you don't want included when you next move the cell pointer.

Nonadjacent cell selections with the keyboard

Selecting more than one cell range is a little more complicated with the keyboard than it is with the mouse. When using the keyboard, you alternate between *anchoring* the cell pointer and moving the cell pointer to select the cell range and *unanchoring* the cell pointer and repositioning it at the beginning of the next range. To unanchor the cell pointer so that you can move it into position for selecting another range, press Shift+F8. This puts you in Add mode, in which you can move to the first cell of the next range without selecting any more cells. Excel lets you know that the cell pointer is unanchored by displaying the ADD indicator on the status bar.

To select more than one cell range by using the keyboard, follow these general steps:

1. **Move the cell pointer to the first cell of the first cell range that you want to select.**

2. **Press F8 to get into Extend mode.**

   Move the cell pointer to select all the cells in the first cell range. Alternatively, hold the Shift key as you move the cell pointer.

3. **Press Shift+F8 to switch from Extend mode to Add mode.**

   The ADD indicator appears in the status bar.

4. **Move the cell pointer to the first cell of the next nonadjacent range that you want to select.**

5. **Press F8 again to get back into Extend mode and then move the cell pointer to select all the cells in this new range.**

6. **If you still have other nonadjacent ranges to select, repeat Steps 3, 4, and 5 until you select and add all the cell ranges that you want to use.**

Cell selections à la Go To

If you want to select a really big cell range that would take a long time to select by pressing various cell-pointer movement keys, use the Go To feature to extend the range to a far distant cell. All you gotta do is follow this pair of steps:

1. **Position the cell pointer in the first cell of the range; then press F8 to anchor the cell pointer and get Excel into Extend mode.**

2. **Press F5 or choose Edit⇨Go To on the menu bar to open the Go To dialog box, type the address of the last cell in the range (the cell kitty-corner from the first cell), and then press Enter.**

Because Excel is in Extend mode at the time you use Go To to jump to another cell, the program not only moves the cell pointer to the designated cell address but selects all the intervening cells as well. After selecting the range of cells with the Go To feature, don't forget to press F8 (the Extend key) again to prevent the program from messing up your selection by adding on more cells the next time you move the cell pointer.

Trimming Your Tables with AutoFormat

Here's a formatting technique that doesn't require you to do any prior cell selecting. (Kinda figures, doesn't it?) In fact, the AutoFormat feature is so automatic that to use it, the cell pointer just has to be somewhere within the table of data prior to your choosing the Format➪AutoFormat command on the Excel menu bar.

As soon as you open the AutoFormat dialog box, Excel automatically selects all the cells in the table. (You get a rude message in an alert box if you choose the command when the cell pointer isn't within the confines of the table or in one of the cells directly bordering the table.)

This option is not available when multiple nonadjacent cells are selected.

You can make short work of formatting a table of data by choosing one of the 16 built-in table formats. Here's how:

1. **Choose Format➪AutoFormat to open the AutoFormat dialog box.**

2. **In the AutoFormat dialog box, click the sample table format in the AutoFormat list box to select the format you want to apply to the table of data in your worksheet (see Figure 3-5).**

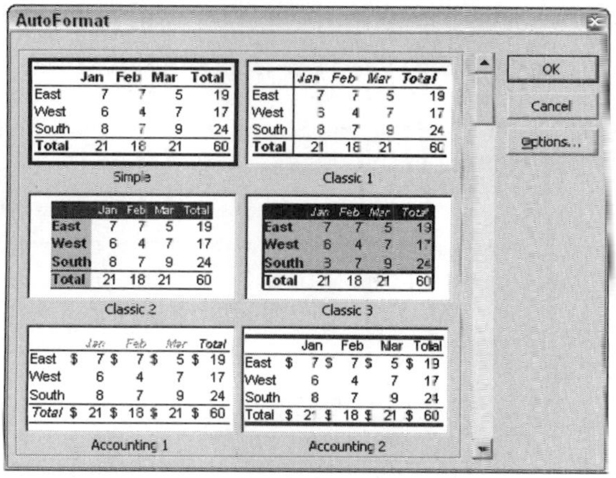

Figure 3-5: Selecting the Simple table format for the Mother Goose first-quarter sales table.

If you need to, scroll through the list to see all the possible table formats. When you click a sample format in the list box, Excel puts a black border around it, indicating that this format is selected.

3. **Click the OK button or press Enter to close the AutoFormat dialog box and apply the selected format to the table of data in your worksheet.**

When you're familiar enough with the table formats to know which one you want to use, save time by double-clicking the desired sample format in the list box in the AutoFormat dialog box to both close the dialog box and apply the formatting to the selected table.

TIP

If you ever goof up and select a table format that you just absolutely hate once you see it in the worksheet, choose Edit⇨Undo AutoFormat on the menu bar (or click the Undo button on the Standard toolbar) before you do anything else; Excel restores the table to its previous state. (For more on getting yourself out of a jam with the Undo feature, see Chapter 4.) If you decide later on that you don't want any of the automatic table formatting, you can get rid of all of it (even when it's too late to use Undo) by opening the AutoFormat dialog box and choosing None in the Table format list box (located at the very bottom of the list) before you click OK or press Enter.

Each of the built-in table formats offered by AutoFormat is nothing more than a particular combination of various kinds of cell and data formatting that Excel applies to the cell selection in a single operation. (Boy, does this ever save time!) Each one enhances the headings and values in the table in a slightly different way.

Refer to Figure 3-5 to see the AutoFormat dialog box with the Simple table format selected just prior to applying its formatting to the first quarter 2004 sales table for Mother Goose Enterprises. (See Chapter 2 for a formal intro-duction to Mother Goose Enterprises.) In Figure 3-6, you can see how the sales table appears with the Simple table format applied to it. Notice that AutoFormat made the worksheet title and headings in rows 1 and 2 bold; it drew borderlines to separate these headings from the rest of the table data; and it also centered the worksheet title over columns A through E and the headings in cells B2 through E2. However, Simple table format does nothing to spruce up the dollar amounts in the table.

Figure 3-6:
Mother's first-quarter sales table in the Simple table format.

Microsoft Excel Enterprise Edition - MGE04Sales.xls

File Edit View Insert Format Tools Data Window Help

A1   fx Mother Goose Enterprises - 2004 Sales

	A	B	C	D	E
1	Mother Goose Enterprises - 2004 Sales				
2		Jan	Feb	Mar	
3	Jack Sprat Diet Centers	80138.58	59389.56	19960.06	159488.2
4	Jack and Jill Trauma Centers	123456.2	89345.7	25436.84	238238.74
5	Mother Hubbard Dog Goodies	12657.05	60593.56	42300.28	115550.89
6	Rub-a-Dub-Dub Hot Tub and Spas	17619.79	40635	42814.99	101069.78
7	Georgie Porgie Pudding Pies	57133.56	62926.31	12408.73	132468.6
8	Hickory, Dickory, Dock Clock Repair	168291	124718.1	41916.13	334925.23
9	Little Bo Peep Pet Detectives	30834.63	71111.25	74926.24	176872.12
10	Total	490130.81	508719.48	259763.27	1258613.56
11					
12					
13					
14					
15					

Want to see a different style of formatting? In Figure 3-7, I chose the Accounting 1 table format for the same cell range. When you select this table format, Excel formats the values in the first and last row with the Currency number format (indicated by the dollar signs) and the rest of the values with the Comma number format (indicated by the commas between the thousands). This type of table format also adds lines to separate the row of column headings and row with the monthly and quarterly totals from the rest of the data.

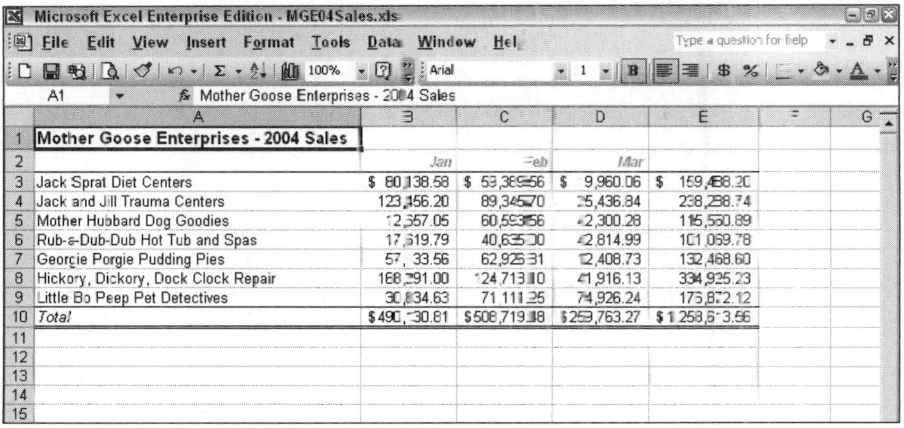

Figure 3-7: Mother's first-quarter sales table in the Accounting 1 table format.

	A	B	C	D	E	F	G
1	Mother Goose Enterprises - 2004 Sales						
2		Jan	Feb	Mar			
3	Jack Sprat Diet Centers	$ 80,138.58	$ 59,389.56	$ 9,960.06	$ 159,488.20		
4	Jack and Jill Trauma Centers	123,456.20	89,345.70	25,436.84	238,238.74		
5	Mother Hubbard Dog Goodies	12,657.05	60,593.56	42,300.28	115,550.89		
6	Rub-a-Dub-Dub Hot Tub and Spas	17,619.79	40,635.00	42,814.99	101,069.78		
7	Georgie Porgie Pudding Pies	57,133.56	62,925.31	12,408.73	132,468.60		
8	Hickory, Dickory, Dock Clock Repair	168,291.00	124,713.10	41,916.13	334,925.23		
9	Little Bo Peep Pet Detectives	30,834.63	71,111.25	74,926.24	176,872.12		
10	Total	$490,730.81	$508,719.18	$259,763.27	$1,258,673.56		
11							
12							
13							
14							
15							

If you format a table with a title that has been centered in a cell by using the Merge and Center button on the formatting toolbar, you need to click a table cell other than the one with the merged-and-centered title prior to choosing Format➪AutoFormat. Choosing this command when the cell pointer is in a merged-and-centered cell causes Excel to select only that cell for formatting. To get the program to select all the cells in the table (including the merged-and-centered one), place the cell pointer in any nonmerged-and-centered cell, and then choose Format➪AutoFormat.

Festooning Your Cells with the Formatting Toolbar

Some worksheets require a lighter touch than the AutoFormat feature offers. For example, you may have a table where the only emphasis you want to add is to make the column headings bold at the top of the table and to underline the row of totals at the bottom (done by drawing a borderline along the bottom of the cells).

Floating the menu bar

Toolbars, like the Standard and Formatting toolbars, are not the only things that float in Excel. You can even float the Excel menu bar containing all the pull-down menus. When you select a menu on a floating menu bar, its commands may appear above the bar next to the menu's name rather than below the bar (as is normal), depending upon how much room there is between the floating bar and the bottom of the screen. To float a toolbar on the screen, position the mouse pointer somewhere on bar that appears at the very front of the toolbar (this bar looks fuzzy because it's made up of tiny, gray horizontal lines), hold down the mouse button, and drag the toolbar where you desire. To restore a floating toolbar to its original docked position on the screen, drag the toolbar's title bar to that location.

With the tools on the Formatting toolbar (which appears right beside the Standard toolbar on the second bar directly below the menu bar), you can accomplish most data and cell formatting without ever venturing into the shortcut menus, let alone (heaven forbid) opening up the pull-down menus.

Use the tools on the Formatting toolbar to assign new fonts and number formats to cells; to change the alignment of their contents; or to add borders, patterns, and colors to them. (Refer to Table 1-3 for a complete rundown on the use of each of these tools.)

Transient toolbars

Normally, the Standard and Formatting toolbars appear side by side on the second bar at the top of the Excel 2003 program in a stationary position politely referred to as being in a *docked* position (*beached* is more like it). Although Excel automatically docks these toolbars together at the top of the screen, you are free to move them (as well as any other toolbars that you open) around by dragging them (kicking and screaming) into new positions. To do this, you position the mouse pointer on the dotted vertical bar at the very beginning of each docked toolbar and then start dragging when the black double-headed arrow mouse pointer appears.

When you drag the Standard or Formatting toolbar down from their perches into the work area containing the open workbook, the toolbar then appears in a separate little window (where you can see all of its buttons) like the one containing the Formatting toolbar (see Figure 3-8). Such toolbars-in-a-window are referred to as *floating toolbars* because they float like clouds above the open workbook below (how poetic!). And not only can you move these little dears, but you can resize them as well:

✔ You can move a floating toolbar into new positions over the worksheet document by dragging it by its tiny title bar.

✔ You can resize a floating toolbar by dragging any one of its sides. Wait until the mouse pointer changes to a double-headed arrow before you start dragging.

✔ As you drag a side of the floating toolbar, the outline of the toolbar assumes a new shape to accommodate the tools in a prescribed tool arrangement. When the toolbar outline assumes the shape you want, release the mouse button, and Excel redraws the toolbar.

✔ To close a floating toolbar when you no longer want it in the document window, click the close box (the small box with a black X in the upper-right corner of the toolbar window).

Toolbar docking maneuvers

Sometimes a floating toolbar can be a real pain because you constantly have to move it out of the way while you add to and edit your worksheet data. To get a toolbar out of the way so that it no longer obscures any of the worksheet cells, you can simply dock it.

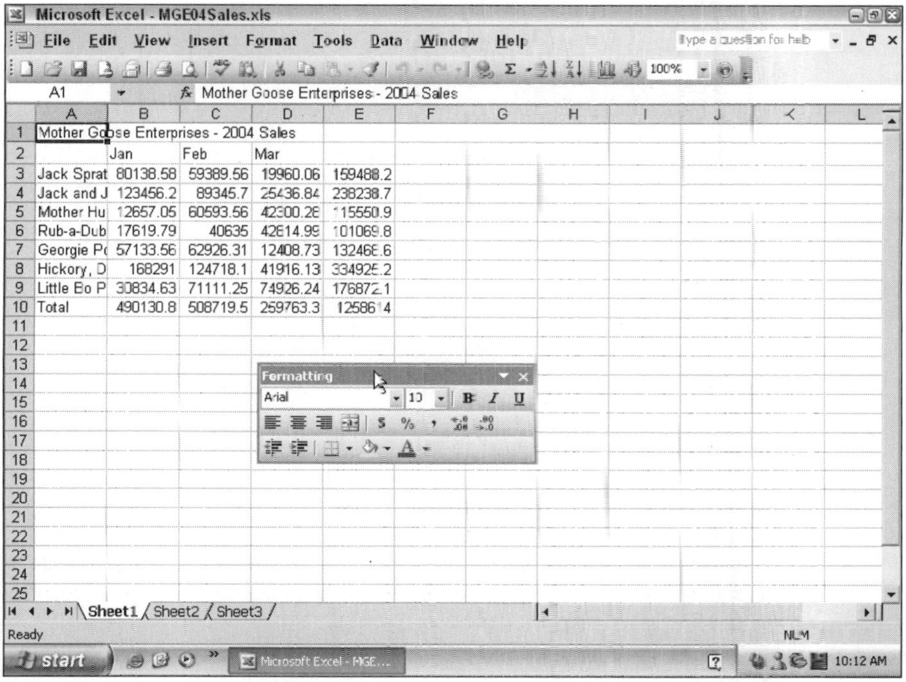

Figure 3-8: The Formatting toolbar floating peacefully over the cells of the worksheet.

Excel has four docking stations: the top of the screen above the Formula bar, the very left edge of the screen, the very right edge of the screen, and the bottom of the screen right above the status bar. See how Excel looks after I dock the Drawing and Text To Speech toolbars side by side at the bottom of the work area in Figure 3-9.

To dock a floating toolbar in one of these four areas, drag it by its title bar as far to the side of the window as possible (holding down with your mouse button while you drag it). Then release the mouse button when the outline of the bar assumes a shape that accommodates a single column (when docking left or right) or a single row (when docking top or bottom). Toolbars that you dock on the left or right of the document window reorient their tools so that they run vertically down the toolbar.

Some toolbars, such as the Standard, Formatting, and Web toolbars, have a button that's attached to a combo box (that is, one that combines a drop-down list box with a text box). Note that when you dock a toolbar with this type of button vertically on the left or right side of the screen, the toolbar no longer displays the button's combo box. To keep the text box, you must dock its toolbar horizontally, either at the top or bottom of the screen.

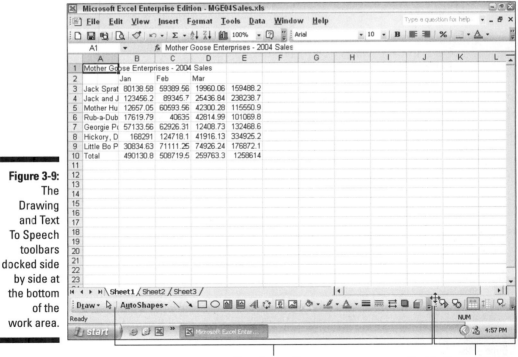

Figure 3-9: The Drawing and Text To Speech toolbars docked side by side at the bottom of the work area.

Drawing toolbar

Text to Speech toolbar

Note, too, that when you dock multiple toolbars side by side on the same bar of the screen, Excel automatically determines how best to size the toolbars, which tools to display on the bar, and which to display on the palette (opened by clicking the Toolbar Options button the one at the very end with >>). If you wish, you can change the relative size of the side-by-side toolbars by dragging the dashed gray vertical bar at the start of a particular toolbar to the left or right (left to make the toolbar bigger and right to make it smaller).

Using the Format Cells Dialog Box

Excel's Format⇨Cells command on the menu bar (Ctrl+1 for short) makes it a snap to apply a whole rash of different kinds of formatting to a cell selection. The Format Cells dialog box that this command calls up contains six tabs: Number, Alignment, Font, Border, Patterns, and Protection. In this chapter, I show you how to use them all except the Protection tab; for information on that tab, see Chapter 6.

The keystroke shortcut that opens the Format Cells dialog box — Ctrl+1 — is one worth knowing. Many of you will be doing almost as much formatting as you do data entry in a worksheet. Just keep in mind that the keyboard shortcut is pressing the Ctrl key plus the *number* 1 key, and not the *function key* F1.

Getting to know the number formats

As I explain in Chapter 2, how you enter values into a worksheet determines the type of number format that they get. Here are some examples:

- ✔ If you enter a financial value complete with the dollar sign and two decimal places, Excel assigns a Currency number format to the cell along with the entry.

- ✔ If you enter a value representing a percentage as a whole number followed by the percent sign without any decimal places, Excel assigns to the cell the Percentage number format that follows this pattern along with the entry.

- ✔ If you enter a date (dates are values, too) that follows one of the built-in Excel number formats, such as 11/06/02 or 06-Nov-02, the program assigns a Date number format that follows the pattern of the date along with a special value representing the date.

Although you can format values in this manner as you go along (which is necessary in the case of dates), you don't have to do it this way. You can always assign a number format to a group of values before or after you enter them. And, in fact, formatting numbers after you enter them is often the most efficient way to go because it's just a two-step procedure:

1. **Select all the cells containing the values that need dressing up.**

2. **Select the number format that you want to use either from the Formatting toolbar or the Format Cells dialog box.**

TIP

Even if you're a really, really good typist and prefer to enter each value exactly as you want it to appear in the worksheet, you still have to resort to using number formats to make the values that are calculated by formulas match the others you enter. This is because Excel applies a General number format (which the Format Cells dialog box defines: "General format cells have no specific number format.") to all the values it calculates as well as any you enter that don't exactly follow one of the other Excel number formats. The biggest problem with the General format is that it has the nasty habit of dropping all leading and trailing zeros from the entries. This makes it very hard to line up numbers in a column on their decimal points.

You can view this sad state of affairs in Figure 3-10, which is a sample worksheet with the first-quarter 2004 sales figures for Mother Goose Enterprises before any of the values have been formatted. Notice how the numbers in the monthly sales figures columns zig and zag because they don't align according to decimal place. This is the fault of Excel's General number format; the only cure is to format the values with another more uniform number format.

Currying your cells with the Currency Style

Given the financial nature of most worksheets, you probably use the Currency format more than any other. This is a really easy format to apply because the Formatting toolbar contains a Currency Style tool that adds a dollar sign, commas between thousands of dollars, and two decimal places to any values in a selected range. If any of the values in the cell selection are negative, this Currency format displays them in parentheses (the way accountants like them).

Figure 3-10:
Numbers
with
decimals
don't align
when you
choose
General
formatting.

Microsoft Excel Enterprise Edition - MGE04Sales.xls

File   Edit   View   Insert   Format   Tools   Data   Window   Help   Type a question for help

Arial   10   B

B10   ƒx   =SUM(B3:B9)

	A	B	C	D	E	F	G	H	I	J	K	L
1	Mother Goose Enterprises - 2004 Sales											
2		Jan	Feb	Mar								
3	Jack Sprat	80138.58	59389.56	19960.06	159488.2							
4	Jack and J	123456.2	89345.7	25436.84	238238.7							
5	Mother Hu	12657.05	60593.56	42300.28	115550.9							
6	Rub-a-Dub	17619.79	40635	42814.99	101069.8							
7	Georgie Po	57133.56	62926.31	12408.73	132468.6							
8	Hickory, D	168291	124718.1	41916.13	334925.2							
9	Little Bo P	30834.63	71111.25	74926.24	176872.1							
10	Total	490130.8	508719.5	259763.3	1258614							
11												
12	Month/Qtr	0.389421	0.40419	0.206388								
13												
14												
15												

You can see in Figure 3-11 that only the cells containing totals are selected for the Currency format (cell ranges E3:E10 and E10:D10). This cell selection was then formatted with the Currency format by simply clicking the Currency Style button on the Formatting toolbar (the one with the $ icon, naturally).

Note: Although you could put all the figures in the table into the Currency format to line up the decimal points, this would result in a superabundance of dollar signs in a fairly small table. In this example, I only formatted the monthly and quarterly totals à la Currency Style.

"Look, Ma, no more format overflow!"

When I apply the Currency Style format to the selection in the cell ranges of E3:E10 and B10:D10 in the sales table shown in Figure 3-11, Excel not only adds dollar signs, commas between the thousands, a decimal point, and two decimal places to the highlighted values, but also, at the same time, automatically widens columns B, C, D, and E just enough to display all this new formatting. In earlier versions of Excel, you would have had to widen these columns yourself, and instead of the perfectly aligned numbers, you would have been confronted with columns of #######s in cell ranges E3:E10 and B10:D10. Such pound signs (where nicely formatted dollar totals should be) serve as overflow indicators, declaring that whatever formatting you added to the value in that cell has added so much to the value's display that Excel can no longer display it within the current column width.

Fortunately, Excel eliminates the format overflow indicators when you're formatting the values in your cells by automatically widening their columns. The only time you'll ever run across these dreaded ######s in your cells is when you take it upon yourself to manually narrow a worksheet column (see the section "Calibrating Columns," later in this chapter) to such an extent that Excel can no longer display all the characters in its cells with formatted values.

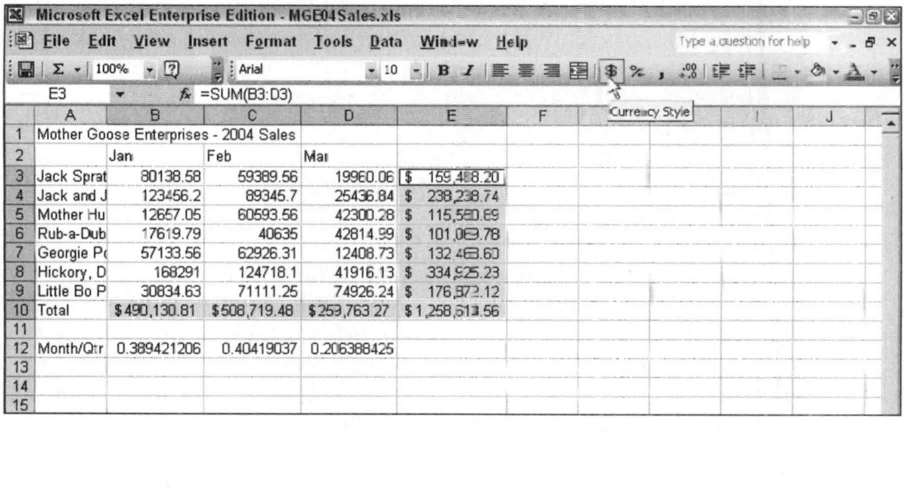

Figure 3-11:
The totals in the Mother Goose sales table after clicking the Currency Style button on the Formatting toolbar.

	A	B	C	D	E	F
1	Mother Goose Enterprises - 2004 Sales					
2		Jan	Feb	Mar		
3	Jack Sprat	80138.58	59389.56	19960.06	$ 159,488.20	
4	Jack and J	123456.2	89345.7	25436.84	$ 238,238.74	
5	Mother Hu	12657.05	60593.56	42300.28	$ 115,550.89	
6	Rub-a-Dub	17619.79	40635	42814.99	$ 101,069.78	
7	Georgie Po	57133.56	62926.31	12408.73	$ 132,468.60	
8	Hickory, D	168291	124718.1	41916.13	$ 334,925.23	
9	Little Bo P	30834.63	71111.25	74926.24	$ 176,872.12	
10	Total	$490,130.81	$508,719.48	$259,763.27	$1,258,613.56	
11						
12	Month/Qtr	0.389421206	0.40419037	0.206388425		
13						
14						
15						

Currying your cells with the Comma Style

The Comma Style format offers a good alternative to the Currency Style format. Like Currency, the Comma format inserts commas in larger numbers to separate thousands, hundred thousands, millions, and . . . well, you get the idea.

This format also displays two decimal places and puts negative values in parentheses. What it doesn't display is dollar signs. This makes it perfect for formatting tables where it's obvious that you're dealing with dollars and cents or for larger values that have nothing to do with money.

The Comma Style format also works well for the bulk of the values in the sample first-quarter sales worksheet. Check out Figure 3-12 to see this table after I format the cells containing the monthly sales for each Mother Goose company with the Comma Style format. To do this, select the cell range B3:D9 and click the Comma Style button — the one with the comma icon (,) — on the Formatting toolbar.

Note how, in Figure 3-12, that the Comma Style format takes care of the earlier decimal alignment problem in the quarterly sales figures. Moreover, Comma Style-formatted monthly sales figures align perfectly with the Currency style-formatted monthly totals in row 10. If you look really closely (you may need a magnifying glass for this one), you see that these formatted values no longer abut the right edges of their cells; they've moved slightly to the left. The gap on the right between the last digit and the cell border accommodates the right parenthesis in negative values, ensuring that they, too, align precisely on the decimal point.

Playing around with the Percent Style

Many worksheets use percentages in the form of interest rates, growth rates, inflation rates, and so on. To insert a percentage in a cell, place the percent sign (%) after the number. To indicate an interest rate of 12 percent, for example, you enter **12%** in the cell. When you do this, Excel assigns a Percent Style number format and, at the same time, divides the value by 100 (that's what makes it a percentage) and places the result in the cell (0.12 in this example).

Not all percentages in a worksheet are entered by hand in this manner. Some may be calculated by a formula and returned to their cells as raw decimal values. In such cases, you should add a Percent format to convert the calculated decimal values to percentages (done by multiplying the decimal value by 100 and adding a percent sign).

The sample first-quarter-sales worksheet just happens to have some percentages calculated by formulas in row 12 that need formatting (these formulas indicate what percentage each monthly total is of the first-quarter total in cell E10). In Figure 3-13, these values reflect Percent Style formatting. To accomplish this feat, you simply select the cells and click the Percent Style button on the Formatting toolbar. (Need I point out that it's the tool with the % symbol?)

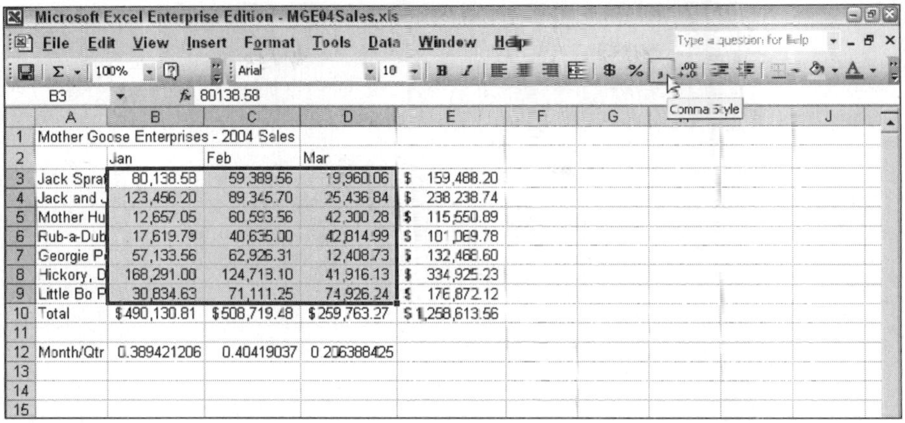

Figure 3-12: Monthly sales figures after formatting their cells with the Comma Style number format.

Deciding how many decimal places

You can increase or decrease the number of decimal places used in a number entered with the Currency Style, Comma Style or Percent Style tool or the Formatting toolbar simply by clicking the Increase Decimal tool or the Decrease Decimal tool. These two tools are also located on the Formatting toolbar, often on the More Buttons palette that opens when you click the Formatting toolbar's More Buttons button.

Each time that you click the Increase Decimal tool (the one with the arrow pointing left), Excel adds another decimal place to the number format you apply. Percentages appear in the cell range B12:D12 (see Figure 3-14) after I increase the number of decimal places in the Percent format from none to two. (Note that the Percent Style doesn't use any decimal places.) I accomplish this by clicking the Increase Decimal tool twice in a row.

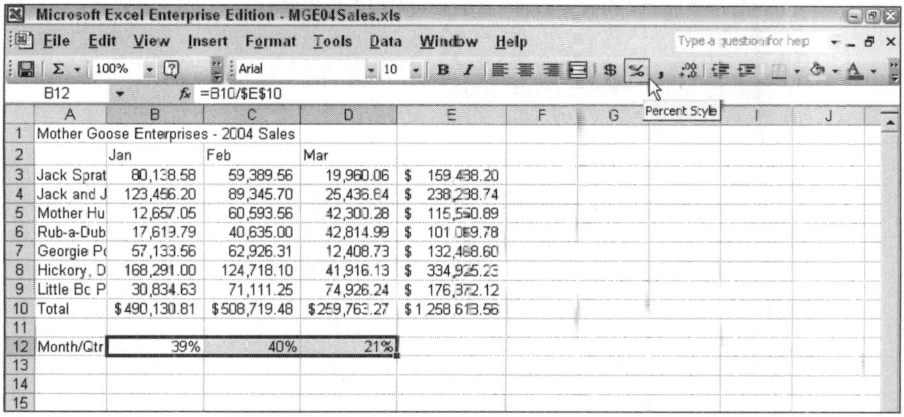

Figure 3-13: Monthly-to-quarterly sales percentages with Percent Style number formatting.

Figure 3-14:
Monthly-to-quarterly
sales
percentages
after adding
two decimal
places to
the Percent
Style
number
format.

```
Microsoft Excel Enterprise Edition - MGE04Sales.xls
File   Edit   View   Insert   Format   Tools   Data   Window   Help          Type a question for help
     Σ ▾  100%  ▾        Arial                 ▾ 10  ▾  B  I  U  ≡ ≡ ≡ ≣  $  %  ,  .00 .00
                                                                              Increase Decimal
   B12        ▾        fx  =B10/$E$10
        A              B          C          D          E          F     G     H     I     J
1  Mother Goose Enterprises - 2004 Sales
2                      Jan        Feb        Mar
3  Jack Sprat      80,138.58   59,389.56   19,960.06   $   159,488.20
4  Jack and J     123,456.20   89,345.70   25,436.84   $   238,238.74
5  Mother Hu       12,657.05   60,593.56   42,300.28   $   115,550.89
6  Rub-a-Dub       17,619.79   40,635.00   42,814.99   $   101,069.78
7  Georgie P       57,133.56   62,926.31   12,408.73   $   132,468.60
8  Hickory, D     168,291.00  124,718.10   41,916.13   $   334,925.23
9  Little Bo P     30,834.63   71,111.25   74,926.24   $   176,872.12
10 Total         $490,130.81 $508,719.48 $259,763.27  $1,258,613.56
11
12 Month/Qtr       38.94%      40.42%      20.64%
13
14
15
```

The values behind the formatting

Make no mistake about it — all that these fancy number formats do is spiff up the presentation of the values in the worksheet. Like a good illusionist, a particular number format sometimes appears to magically transform some entries; but in reality, the entries are the same old numbers you started with. For example, suppose that a formula returns the following value:

```
25.6456
```

Now suppose that you format the cell containing this value with the Currency Style tool. The value now appears as follows:

```
$25.65
```

This change may lead you to believe that Excel rounded the value up to two decimal places. In fact, the program has rounded up only the *display* of the calculated value — the cell still contains the same old value of 25.6456. If you use this cell in another worksheet formula, keep in mind that Excel uses the behind-the-scenes value in its calculation, not the spiffed-up one shown in the cell.

But what if you want the values to match their formatted appearance in the worksheet? Well, Excel can do that in a single step. Be forewarned, however, that this is a one-way trip. You can convert all underlying values to the way they are displayed by selecting a single check box, but you can't return them to their previous state by deselecting this check box.

Well, because you insist on knowing this little trick anyway, here goes (just don't write and try to tell me that you weren't warned):

1. **Make sure that you format all the values in your worksheet with the right number of decimal places.**

   You must do this step before you convert the precision of all values in the worksheet to their displayed form.

2. **Choose Tools⇨Options from the menu bar.**

3. **From the Options dialog box that appears, click the Calculation tab to bring up the calculation options.**

4. **Under the Workbook Options section, click the Precision as Displayed check box (to fill it with a check mark) and click OK.**

   Excel displays the Data Will Permanently Lose Accuracy alert dialog box.

5. **Go ahead (live dangerously) and click the OK button or press Enter to convert all values to match their display.**

After converting all the values in a worksheet by selecting the Precision as Displayed check box, as described in the preceding steps, you may be wise to select the File⇨Save As command and edit the filename in the File Name text box (maybe, by appending **as Displayed** to the current filename) before you click the Save button or press Enter. That way, you'll still have a disk copy of the original workbook file with the values as entered and calculated by Excel that can act as a backup to your new *as Displayed* version.

Make it a date!

In Chapter 2, I mention that you can easily create formulas that calculate the differences between the dates and times that you enter in your worksheets. The only problem is that when Excel subtracts one date from another date or one time from another time, the program automatically formats the calculated result in a corresponding date or time number format as well. So, for example, if you enter 8-15-04 in cell B4 and 4/15/04 in cell C4 and in cell E4 enter the following formula for finding the number of elapsed days between the two dates:

```
=B4-C4
```

Excel returns the result of 122 disguised as 5/1/1900 in cell E4. To reformat the result, you need to assign the General number format to the cell — you can do this quickly by selecting the cell and then pressing Ctrl+Shift+~ (tilde). When you assign the General format to this cell, the value 122 replaces 5/1/1900, indicating that 122 days have elapsed between the two dates.

Likewise, when dealing with formulas that calculate the difference between two times in a worksheet, you also have to reformat the result that appears in a corresponding time format into the General format. For example, suppose that you enter 8:00 AM in cell C8 and 4:00 PM in cell D8 and then create in cell E8 the following formula for calculating the difference in hours between the two times:

```
=D8-C8
```

You still have to convert the result in cell E8 — that automatically appears as 8:00 AM — to the General format. When you do this, the fraction 0.333333 — representing its fraction of the total 24-hour period — replaces 8:00 AM in cell E8. You can then convert this fraction of a total day into the corresponding number of hours by multiplying this cell by 24.

Ogling the other number formats

Excel supports many more number formats than just the Currency, Comma, and Percent style formats. To use them, select the cell range (or ranges) you want to format and select Format Cells on the cell shortcut menu (right-click somewhere in the cell selection to activate this menu), or choose Format⇨ Cells (Ctrl+1 is the keyboard shortcut) to open the Format Cells dialog box.

After the Format Cells dialog box opens, choose the Number tab and select the desired format from the Category list box. Some Number format categories — such as Date, Time, Fraction, and Special — give you further formatting choices in a Type list box. Other number formats, such as Number and Currency, have their own particular boxes that give you options for refining their formats. When you click the different formats in these list boxes, Excel shows what effect this would have on the first of the values in the current cell selection in the Sample area above. When the sample has the format that you want to apply to the current cell selection, you just click OK or press Enter to apply the new number format.

Excel contains a nifty category of number formats called Special. The Special category contains the following four number formats that may interest you:

- **Zip Code:** Retains any leading zeros in the value (important for zip codes and of absolutely no importance in arithmetic computations). Example: 00123.

- **Zip Code + 4:** Automatically separates the last four digits from the first five digits and retains any leading zeros. Example: 00123-5555.

- **Phone Number:** Automatically encloses the first three digits of the number in parentheses and separates the last four digits from the previous three with a dash. Example: (999) 555-1111.

- **Social Security Number:** Automatically puts dashes in the value to separate its digits into groups of three, two, and four. Example: 666-00-9999.

These Special number formats really come in handy when creating databases in Excel, which often deal with stuff like zip codes, telephone numbers, and sometimes even Social Security numbers (see Chapter 9 for more on creating databases).

Calibrating Columns

For those times when Excel 2003 doesn't automatically adjust the width of your columns to your complete satisfaction, the program makes your changing the column widths a breeze. The easiest way to adjust a column is to do a *best-fit,* using the AutoFit feature. With this method, Excel automatically determines how much to widen or narrow the column to fit the longest entry currently in the column.

Here's how to use AutoFit to get the best-fit for a column:

1. **Position the mouse pointer on the right border of the gray frame with the column letter at the top of the worksheet.**

   The mouse pointer changes to a double-headed arrow pointing left and right.

2. **Double-click the mouse button.**

   Excel widens or narrows the column width to suit the longest entry.

You can apply a best-fit to more than one column at a time. Simply select all the columns that need adjusting (if the columns neighbor one another, drag through their column letters on the frame; if they don't, hold down the Ctrl key while you click the individual column letters). After you select the columns, double-click any of the right borders on the frame.

Best-fit à la AutoFit doesn't always produce the expected results. A long title that spills into several columns to the right produces an awfully wide column when you use best-fit.

When AutoFit's best-fit won't do, drag the right border of the column (on the frame) until it's the size you need instead of double-clicking it. This manual technique for calibrating the column width also works when more than one column is selected. Just be aware that all selected columns assume whatever size you make the one that you're actually dragging.

You can also set the widths of columns from the Column Width dialog box. When you use this dialog box, you enter the number of characters that you want for the column width. To open this dialog box, choose the Column Width command from the Column shortcut menu (open this by clicking on any selected column or column letter with the secondary mouse button), or choose Format⇨Column⇨Width on the menu bar.

The Column Width text box in the Column Width dialog box shows how many characters are in the standard column width in the worksheet or in the current column width if you previously adjusted it. To change the widths of all the columns you select in the worksheet (except those already adjusted manually or with AutoFit), enter a new value in the Column Width text box and click OK.

If you want Excel to size the column to best-fit, choose Format⇨Column⇨ AutoFit Selection from the menu bar. Note that you can use this AutoFit Selection command to apply best-fit to a column based on just some of the cell entries. For example, say that you wanted to use best-fit to make a column just wide enough for a range of headings but not including the worksheet title (that spills over several blank columns to the right). All you have to do is select just the cells in that column that contain the headings on which the new column width should be based before you choose Format⇨ Column⇨AutoFit Selection.

To return a column selection to the standard (default) column width, choose Format⇨Column⇨Standard Width on the menu bar. This opens the Standard Width dialog box containing the value 8.43 in the Standard Column Width text box (the default width of all columns in a new worksheet). To return all the selected columns to this standard width, click OK in this dialog box or simply press Enter.

Rambling rows

The story with adjusting the heights of rows is pretty much the same as that with adjusting columns except that you do a lot less row adjusting than you do column adjusting. That's because Excel automatically changes the height of the rows to accommodate changes to their entries, such as selecting a larger font size or wrapping text in a cell. I discuss both of these techniques in the upcoming section "Altering the Alignment." Most row-height adjustments come about when you want to increase the amount of space between a table title and the table or between a row of column headings and the table of information without actually adding a blank row. (See the section "From top to bottom," later in this chapter, for details.)

To increase the height of a row, drag the bottom border of the row frame down until the row is high enough and then release the mouse button. To shorten a row, reverse this process and drag the bottom row-frame border up. To use AutoFit to create a best-fit for the entries in a row, you double-click the bottom row frame border.

As with columns, you can also adjust the height of selected rows with a dialog box. To open the Row Height dialog box, choose the Row Height command from the Row shortcut menu (open this by clicking on a row number with the secondary mouse button) or choose Format⇔Row⇔Height on the menu bar. To set a new row height for the selected row (or rows), enter the number of characters in the Row Height text box and click OK. (The default row height is 12.75 characters, in case you care.) To return to the best-fit for a particular row, choose Format⇔Row⇔AutoFit on the menu bar.

Now you see it, now you don't

A funny thing about narrowing columns and rows: You can get too carried away and make a column so narrow or a row so short that it actually disappears from the worksheet! This can come in handy for those times when you don't want part of the worksheet visible. For example, suppose you have a worksheet that contains a column listing employee salaries — you need these figures to calculate the departmental budget figures, but you would prefer to leave sensitive info off most printed reports. Rather than waste time moving the column of salary figures outside the area to be printed, you can just hide the column until after you print the report.

Hiding columns and rows, courtesy of the pull-down and shortcut menus

Although you can hide worksheet columns and rows by just adjusting them out of existence, Excel does offer an easier method of hiding them, via the Format pull-down menu or column or row shortcut menus. Suppose that you need to hide column B in the worksheet because it contains some irrelevant or sensitive information that you don't want printed. To hide this column, you could follow these steps:

1. **Click anywhere in column B to select the column.**

2. **Choose Format⇔Column⇔Hide on the menu bar.**

That's all there is to it — column B goes *poof!* All the information in the column disappears from the worksheet. When you hide column B, notice that the row of column letters in the frame now reads A, C, D, E, F, and so forth.

You could just as well have hidden column B by clicking its column letter on the frame with the secondary mouse button and then clicking the Hide command on the column's shortcut menu.

So now, suppose that you've printed the worksheet and need to make a change to one of the entries in column B. To unhide the column, follow these steps:

1. **Position the mouse pointer on column letter A in the frame and drag the pointer right to select both columns A and C.**

   You must drag from A to C to include hidden column B as part of the column selection — don't click while holding down the Ctrl key or you won't get B.

2. **Choose Format➪Column➪Unhide on the menu bar.**

Excel brings back the hidden B column, and all three columns (A, B, and C) are selected. You can then click the mouse pointer on any cell in the worksheet to deselect the columns.

You could also unhide column B by selecting columns A and C, clicking either one of them with the secondary mouse button, and then clicking the Unhide command on the column shortcut menu.

Hiding columns and rows with the mouse

I won't lie to you — hiding and redisplaying columns with the mouse can be *very* tricky. It requires a degree of precision that you may not possess (especially if you've just recently started using the rodent). However, if you consider yourself a real mouse master, you can hide and unhide columns solely by dragging the mouse pointer as follows:

- ✔ To hide a column with the mouse, drag the column's right edge to the left until it's on top of the left edge and then release the mouse button.

- ✔ To hide a row with the mouse, drag the row's bottom border up until it's on top of the upper border.

While you drag a border, Excel displays a screen tip with the current column width or row height measurement in a box near the mouse pointer (just like with the screen tips that appear when using the scroll bars or with the fill handle when using AutoFill to extend a series, as I explain in Chapter 1). When this Width or Height indicator reaches 0.00, you know that it's time to release the mouse button.

Unhiding a column or row with the mouse is a reversal of the hiding process. To do this, you drag the column or row border in between the nonsequential columns or rows in the opposite direction (right for columns and down for rows). The only trick to this is that you must position the mouse pointer just right on the column or row border so that the pointer doesn't just change to a double-headed arrow but changes to a double-headed arrow split in the middle. (Contrast the shapes of the split double-headed arrow pointer with the regular, old double-headed arrow pointer in Table 1-1.)

If you ever manually hide a column or row only to find that you just can't get that blasted split-bar pointer to appear so that you can drag it back into existence, don't get frantic. With columns, just drag through the first and last column or row between those that are hidden and then choose the Unhide command on the columns or rows shortcut menu (see the preceding section "Hiding columns and rows, courtesy of the pull-down and shortcut menus").

Futzing with the Fonts

When you start a new worksheet, Excel assigns a uniform font and type size to all the cell entries you make. This font varies according to the printer you use — for a laser printer like the HP LaserJet or Apple LaserWriter, Excel uses the Arial font in a 10-point size. Although this font is fine for normal entries, you may want to use something with a little more zing for titles and headings in the worksheet.

If you don't especially care for the standard font that Excel uses, modify it by choosing Tools➪Options on the menu bar and then selecting the General tab. Look for the Standard Font option called near the bottom of the Options dialog box. Select the new standard font you want from its drop-down list. If you want a different type size, choose the Size option as well and either enter the new point size for the standard font or select it from this option's drop-down list.

With the tools on the Formatting toolbar, you can make most font changes (including selecting a new font style or new font size) without having to resort to changing the settings on the Font tab in the Format Cells dialog box (Ctrl+1).

✔ To select a new font for a cell selection, click the drop-down button next to the Font combo box on the Formatting toolbar; then select the name of the font you want to use from the list box. Note that Excel 2003 now displays the name of each font that appears in this list box in the actual font named (so that the font name becomes an example of what the font looks like — onscreen anyway).

✔ If you want to change the font size, click the drop-down button next to the Font Size combo box on the Formatting toolbar; then select the new font size.

You can also add the attributes of **bold**, *italics*, <u>underlining</u>, or s t r i k e t h r o u g h to the font you use. The Formatting toolbar contains the Bold, Italic, and Underline buttons, which not only add these attributes to a cell selection but remove them as well. After you click any of these attribute tools, notice that the tool becomes shaded whenever you position the cell pointer in the cell or cells that contain that attribute. When you click an outlined format button to remove an attribute, Excel no longer shades the attribute button when you select the cell.

Although you'll probably make most font changes with the toolbars, on rare occasions you may find it more convenient to make these changes from the Font tab in the Format Cells dialog box (Ctrl+1).

As you can see in Figure 3-15, this Font tab in the Format Cells dialog box brings together under one roof fonts, font styles (bold and italics), effects (underlining and strikethrough), and color changes. When you want to make a lot of font-related changes to a cell selection, working in the Font tab may be your best bet. One of the nice things about using this tab is that it contains a Preview box that shows you how your font changes appear (on-screen at least).

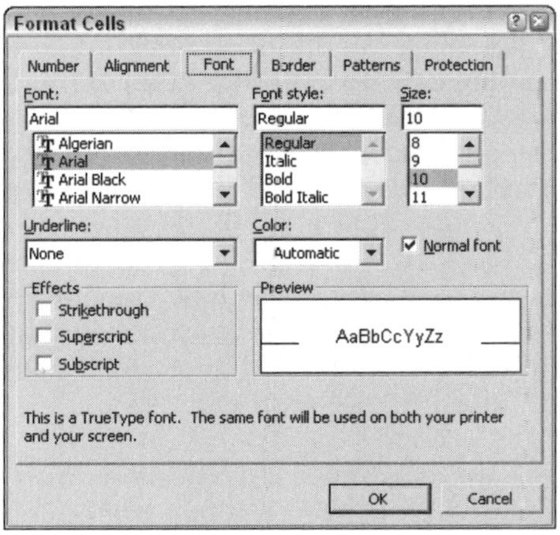

Figure 3-15:
Use the Font tab on the Format Cells dialog box to make lots of font changes at one time.

If you change font colors with the Color option on the Font tab in the Format Cells dialog box or with the Font Color button on the Formatting toolbar (the very last button) and then print the worksheet with a black-and-white printer, Excel renders the colors as shades of gray. The Automatic choice in the Font tab Color drop-down list box picks up the color assigned in Windows as the window text color. This color is black unless you change it on the Advanced Appearance tab of the Display Properties dialog box in Windows XP and 2000. (For help on this subject, please see *Microsoft Windows XP For Dummies* by Andy Rathbone, from Wiley Publishing, Inc. — and be sure to tell Andy that Greg sent ya!)

Altering the Alignment

The alignment assigned to cell entries when you first make them is simply a function of the type of entry it is: All text entries are left-aligned, and all values are right-aligned. You can, however, alter this standard arrangement anytime it suits you.

The Formatting toolbar contains three normal alignment tools: the Align Left, Center, and Align Right buttons. These buttons align the current cell selection exactly as you expect them to. To the immediate right of the Right Align button, you usually find the special alignment button called Merge and Center.

Despite its rather strange name, you'll want to get to know this button. You can use it to center a worksheet title across the entire width of a table in seconds (or faster, depending upon your machine). I show you in Figures 3-16 and 3-17 how you can use this tool. In Figure 3-16, notice that the worksheet title Mother Goose Enterprises – 2004 Sales is in cell A1. Because it's a long text entry, it spills over to the empty cell to the right (B1). To center this title over the table (which extends from column A through E), select the cell range A1:E1 (the width of the table) and then click the Merge and Center button on the Formatting toolbar.

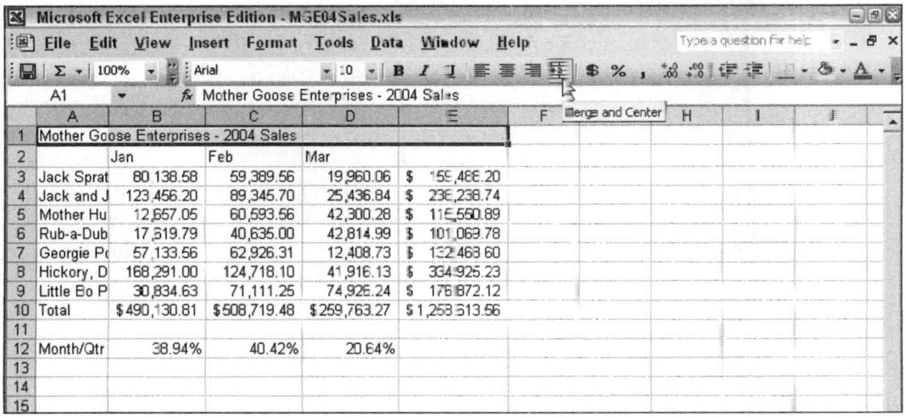

Figure 3-16:
A work-
sheet title
before
merging and
centering.

Look at Figure 3-17 to see the result: The cells in row 1 of columns A through E are merged into one cell, and now the title is properly centered in this supercell and consequently over the entire table.

Microsoft Excel Enterprise Edition - MGE04Sales.xls

File　Edit　View　Insert　Format　Tools　Data　Window　Help

Type a question for help

A1　　　　fx　Mother Goose Enterprises - 2004 Sales

	A	B	C	D	E	F	G	H	I	J
1	Mother Goose Enterprises - 2004 Sales									
2		Jan	Feb	Mar						
3	Jack Sprat	80,138.58	59,389.56	19,960.06	$ 159,488.20					
4	Jack and J	123,456.20	89,345.70	25,436.84	$ 238,238.74					
5	Mother Hu	12,657.05	60,593.56	42,300.28	$ 115,550.89					
6	Rub-a-Dub	17,619.79	40,635.00	42,814.99	$ 101,069.78					
7	Georgie Po	57,133.56	62,926.31	12,408.73	$ 132,468.60					
8	Hickory, D	168,291.00	124,718.10	41,916.13	$ 334,925.23					
9	Little Bo P	30,834.63	71,111.25	74,926.24	$ 175,872.12					
10	Total	$ 490,130.81	$ 508,719.48	$ 259,763.27	$ 1,258,613.56					
11										
12	Month/Qtr	38.94%	40.42%	20.64%						
13										
14										
15										

Figure 3-17:
A work-
sheet title
after
centering
it across
columns A
through E.

If you ever need to split up a supercell that you've merged with the Merge and Center back into its original, individual cells, select the cell, and then simply click the Merge and Center button again. You can also do this by opening the Format Cells dialog box (Ctrl+1),clicking the Alignment tab, and deselecting the Merge Cells check box before you click OK or press Enter (a few more steps, I'd say!).

Intent on indents

In Excel 2003, you can indent the entries in a cell selection by clicking the Increase Indent button on the Formatting toolbar. The Increase Indent button is normally located immediately to the left of the Borders button, and it sports a picture of an arrow pushing the lines of text to the right. Each time you click this button, Excel indents the entries in the current cell selection to the right by one character width of the standard font. (See the section "Futzing with the Fonts," earlier in this chapter, if you don't know what a standard font is or how to change it.)

You can remove an indent by clicking the Decrease Indent button on the Formatting toolbar; it's the button normally immediately to the left of the Increase Indent button with the picture of the arrow pushing the lines of text to the left. Also, you can change how many characters an entry is indented with the Increase Indent button or outdented with the Decrease Indent button. Open the Format Cells dialog box (choose Format⇔Cells, or use the keyboard shortcut Ctrl+1). Select the Alignment tab, and then alter the value in the Indent text box (by typing a new value in this text box or by dialing up a new value with its spinner buttons).

From top to bottom

Left, right, and *center* alignment all refer to the placement of a text entry in relation to the left and right cell borders (that is, horizontally). You can also align entries in relation to the top and bottom borders of their cells (that is, vertically). Normally, all entries are vertically aligned with the bottom of the cells (as though they were resting on the very bottom of the cell). You can also vertically center an entry in its cell or align it with the top of its cell.

To change the vertical alignment of a cell range that you've selected, open the Format Cells dialog box (Ctrl+1) and then choose the Alignment tab (shown in Figure 3-18) and select Top, Center, Bottom, or Justify in the Vertical drop-down list box.

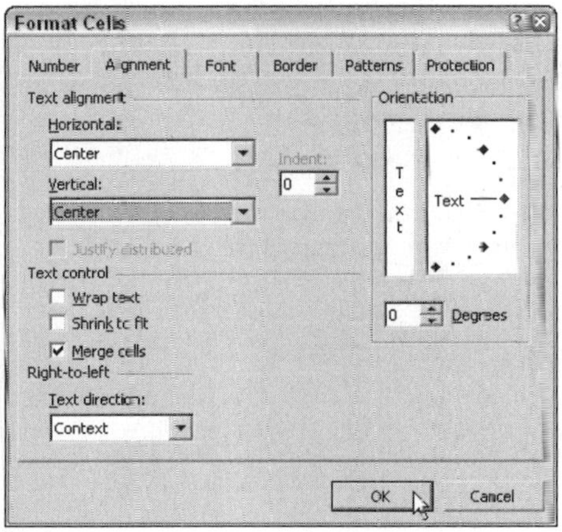

Figure 3-18:
Select
Center on
the Vertical
text
alignment
drop-down
list box to
change the
vertical
alignment.

Figure 3-19 shows the title for the 2004 Mother Goose Enterprises sales worksheet after it's centered vertically in its cell. (This text entry was previously centered across the cell range A1:E1; the height of row 1 is increased from the normal 12.75 characters to 32.25 characters.)

Tampering with how the text wraps

Traditionally, column headings in worksheet tables have been a problem — you either had to keep them really short or abbreviate them if you wanted to avoid widening all the columns more than the data warranted. You can avoid this problem in Excel by using the Wrap Text feature. In Figure 3-20, I show a new worksheet in which the column headings containing the various Mother Goose companies use the Wrap Text feature to avoid widening the columns as much as these long company names would otherwise require.

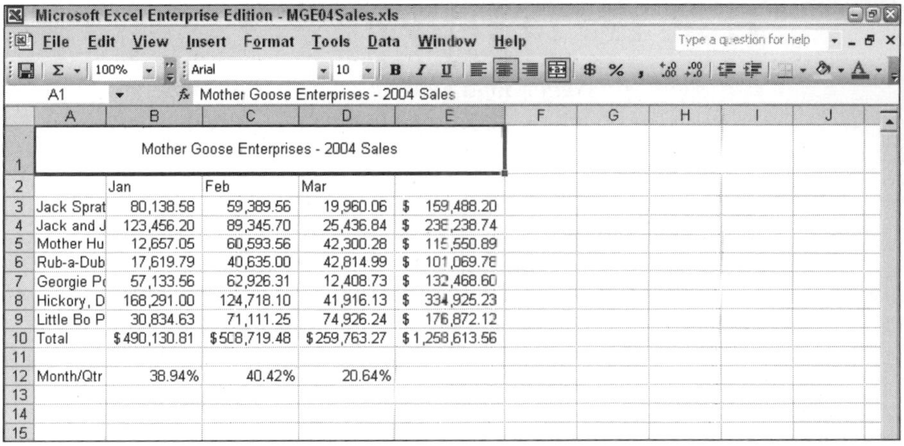

Figure 3-19:
The work-
sheet title
after
centering it
vertically
between the
top and
bottom
edges of
row 1.

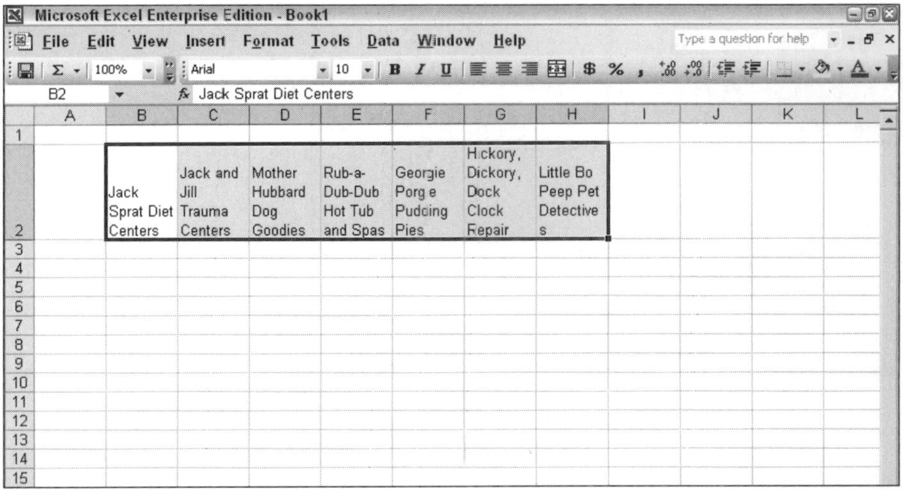

Figure 3-20:
A new
worksheet
with the
column
headings
formatted
with the
Wrap Text
option.

To create the effect shown in Figure 3-20, select the cells with the column headings (the cell range B2:H2). Choose Format⇨Cells (Ctrl+1), and select the Alignment tab of the Format Cells dialog box that opens. Then select the Wrap Text check box to activate text wrapping. (You can see this check box in Figure 3-18.)

Selecting Wrap Text breaks up the long text entries in the selection (that either spill over or are cut off) into separate lines. To accommodate more than one line in a cell, the program automatically expands the row height so that the entire wrapped-text entry is visible.

When you select Wrap Text, Excel continues to use the horizontal and vertical alignment you specify for the cell. Note that you can use any of the Horizontal alignment options including Left (Indent), Center, Right, Justify, or Center Across Selection. You can't, however, use the Fill option. Select the Fill option on the Horizontal drop-down list box only when you want Excel to repeat the entry across the entire width of the cell.

If you want to wrap a text entry in its cell and have Excel justify the text with both the left and right borders of the cell select the Justify Fill option from the Horizontal pop-up menu in the Alignment tab in the Format Cells dialog box.

You can break a long text entry into separate lines by positioning the insertion point in the cell entry (or on the Formula bar) at the place where you want the new line to start and pressing Alt+Enter. Excel expands the row containing the cell (and the Formula bar above) when it starts a new line. When you press Enter to complete the entry or edit, Excel automatically wraps the text in the cell, according to the cell's column width and the position of the line break.

Rotating cell entries

Instead of wrapping text entries in cells, you may find it more beneficial to change the orientation of the text by rotating the text up (in a counterclockwise direction) or down (in a clockwise direction). Peruse Figure 3-21 for a situation where changing the orientation of the wrapped column headings works much better than just wrapping them in their normal orientation in the cells.

This example shows the same column headings for the sample order form I introduce in Figure 3-20 after rotating them 90 degrees counterclockwise. Notice that switching the rotating the text up into this orientation allows their columns to be narrower than when displayed in the normal orientation.

To make this switch, first select the cell range B2:H2. Choose Format⇨Cells (or press Ctrl+1), and click the Alignment tab of the Format cells dialog box that appears. In the Text Orientation section (upper-right side of the dialog box), click the diamond at the top (at twelve o'clock, so to speak, in the diagram) so that the word Text points to the top of the page (you're turning it 90° counterclockwise). Check your results by looking at the Degrees text box below — the number 90 should appear there.

You can also rotate the entries in your cell selection by entering the number of degrees in the Degree box if you don't want to fool around with the diamonds in the diagram. Or, you can use the spinner arrows to increase or decrease the rotation of your text. Leave the Wrap Text box selected so that the text is both rotated and wrapped (thus avoiding really long, skinny columns). When you're satisfied with your choice, press Enter or click OK.

You're not limited to movements of 90°. After selecting the text you want to rotate, click any of the diamonds to turn your selection how you want it to appear. To create what you see in Figure 3-22, the same company headings have been rotated 45° counterclockwise from their horizontal orientation. To accomplish this, I click the diamond in between the one at the top of the diagram (at twelve o'clock) and the one in the middle of the diagram (at three o'clock). Note that I could have done the same thing just as well by entering **45** in the Degrees text box below the diagram in the Orientation section.

You can set any amount of text rotation from 90 degrees up (counterclockwise) from horizontal (90 in the Degrees text box) all the way to 90 degrees down (clockwise) from horizontal (–90 in the Degrees text box). You can do this either by entering the number of degrees in the Degrees text box, clicking the appropriate place on the semicircular diagram, or by dragging the line extending from the word Text in the diagram to the desired angle. To set the text vertically so that each letter is above the other in a single column, click the area of the diagram that shows the word Text arranged in this manner (to the immediate left of the diagram that enables you to rotate the text up or down from normal horizontal).

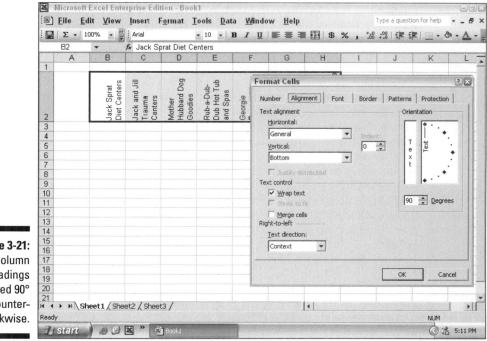

Figure 3-21:
Column headings rotated 90° counter-clockwise.

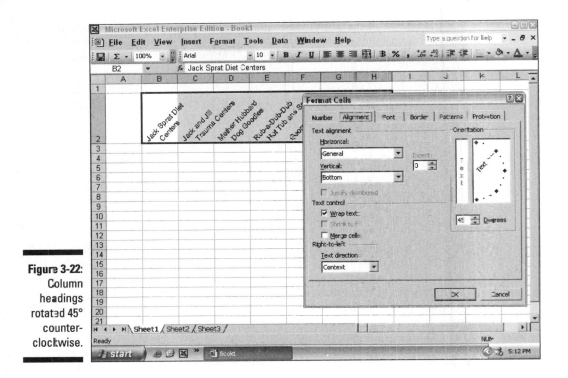

Shrink to fit

For those times when you need to prevent Excel from widening the column to fit its cell entries (as might be the case when you need to display an entire table of data on a single screen or printed page), use the Shrink to Fit text control. Choose Format⇨Cells, and click the Alignment tab of the Format Cells dialog box that appears. Then select the Shrink to Fit check box in Text Control section. Excel reduces the font size of the entries to the selected cells so that they don't require changing the current column width. Just be aware when using this Text Control option that, depending the length of the entries and width of the column, you can end up with some text entries so small that they're completely illegible to the human eye! Also note that you can't use the Text Wrap and Shrink to Fit at the same time. (Selecting one automatically deselects the other.)

Bring on the borders!

The gridlines you normally see in the worksheet to separate the columns and rows are just guidelines to help you keep your place as you build your spreadsheet. You can choose to print them with your data or not. To emphasize sections of the worksheet or parts of a particular table, you can add borderlines or shading to certain cells. Don't confuse the *borderlines* that you add to accent a particular cell selection with the *gridlines* normally used to define cell borders in the worksheet — borders that you add are printed whether or not you print the worksheet gridlines.

To better see the borders that you add to the cells in a worksheet, remove the gridlines normally displayed in the worksheet as follows:

1. **Choose the Tools⇨Options command on the menu bar and then select the View tab from the Options dialog box that appears.**

2. **From the Window Options section, click the Gridlines check box to remove its check mark.**

3. **Click OK or press Enter.**

Note that the Gridlines check box in the Options dialog box determines whether gridlines display in the worksheet on your screen. To determine whether gridlines print as part of the worksheet printout, choose the File⇨Page Setup command. Click the Sheet tab from the Page Setup dialog box that appears, and select the Gridlines check box to print or deselect this check box to prevent them from printing.

To add borders to a cell selection, choose Format⇨Cells (or press Ctrl+1). Click the Border tab from the Format Cells dialog box that opens (shown in Figure 3-23). Select the type of line you want to use in the Style area of the dialog box (such as thick, thin, bold, or hash marks) and then select from the Border section of the dialog box the edge or edges you want this line applied to.

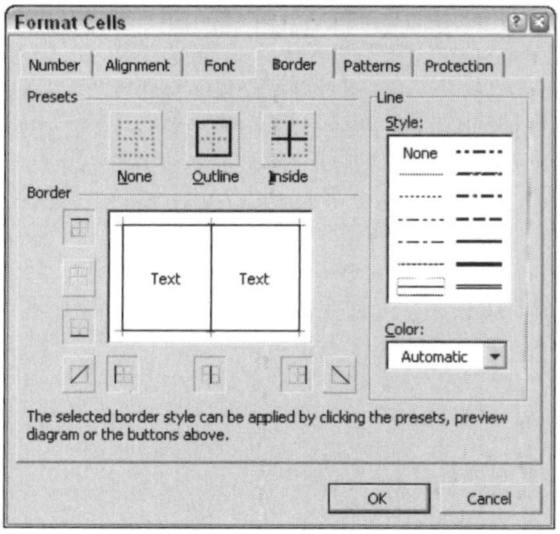

Figure 3-23:
Select borders for a cell selection with the Border tab on the Format Cells dialog box.

When selecting where you want the borderlines drawn, keep these things in mind:

✔ To have Excel draw borders around only the outside edges of the entire selection, click the Outline button in the Presets section of the Border tab.

✔ If you want borderlines to appear around all four edges of each cell in the selection (like a paned window), select the Inside button in the Presets section instead.

When you want to add borderlines to a single cell or around the outer edge of a cell selection, you don't even have to open the Border dialog box; you can simply select the cell or cell range and then click the Borders button drop-down list button on the Formatting toolbar and select which type of border-lines to use in the border palette that appears.

To get rid of borders, you must select the cell or cells that presently contain them, open the Format Cells dialog box (Ctrl+), and click the None button in the Presets section. Note that you can also do the same thing by clicking the first button in the Borders pop-up menu (the one showing only dotted lines around and within the rectangle).

In Excel 2003, you can have cell borders without having to fool around with the options on the Borders tab on Format Cells dialog box or attached to the Borders button on Formatting toolbar. Instead, you simply draw your borders right on cells of the worksheet. To do this, click the Borders pop-up button on the Formatting toolbar and then choose the Draw Borders option at the bottom of the menu. Excel responds by displaying the floating Borders tool-bar shown in Figure 3-24.

When you first open the Borders toolbar, the Pencil tool is selected on this toolbar, and you can use its Pencil mouse pointer to outline the cell range that you select by dragging through its cells. If you want to put borders around each cell in the range that you select with Pencil pointer, click the drop-down button attached to the Draw Border tool and select the Draw Border Grid option on its pop-up menu before you drag through the cell range.

To change the type of line or line thickness of the border you draw, click the drop-down button on the Line Style tool and select the desired line type and thickness on its pop-menu. To change the color of the border you draw, click the Line Color tool on the Border toolbar and choose the desired color on its pop-up color palette.

To erase borders that you've drawn in your worksheet, click the Erase Border tool and then drag through the bordered cell range with the Eraser pointer. Note that you can also erase borders around cells of the worksheet by draw-ing over them with the Pencil pointer after having selected the No Border option on Line Style pop-up menu and either the Draw Border or Draw Border Grid on the Draw Border pop-up menu.

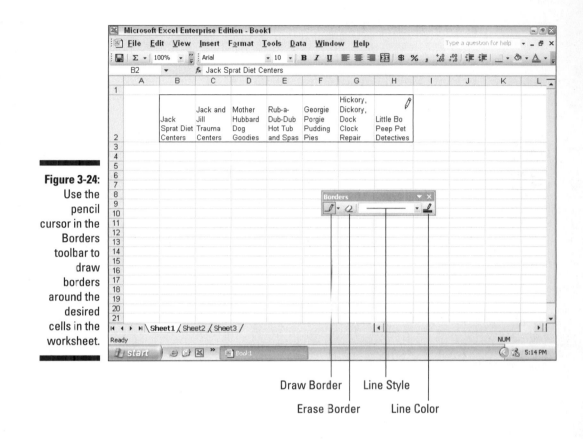

Figure 3-24:
Use the
pencil
cursor in the
Borders
toolbar to
draw
borders
around the
desired
cells in the
worksheet.

Draw Border | Line Style

Erase Border | Line Color

Putting on new patterns

You can also add emphasis to particular sections of the worksheet or one of its tables by changing the color and/or pattern of its cells. If you're using a black-and-white printer (as all but a fortunate few of us are), you will want to restrict your color choices to light gray in the color palette. Also, you will want to restrict your use of patterns to only the very open ones with few dots when enhancing a cell selection that contains any kind of entries (otherwise, the entries will be almost impossible to read when printed).

To choose a new color and/or pattern for part of the worksheet, select the cells you want to pretty up, open the Format Cells dialog box (Ctrl+1), and then choose the Patterns tab (shown in Figure 3-25). To change the color of the cells, click the desired color in the Color palette shown under the Cell shading heading. To change the pattern of the cells (in addition or instead), click the Pattern's pop-up button to open an expanded color palette that contains a number of black-and-white patterns to choose from. Click the desired pattern in this expanded palette. Excel shows what your creation will look like in the worksheet in the Sample box of the Patterns tab of the Format Cells dialog box.

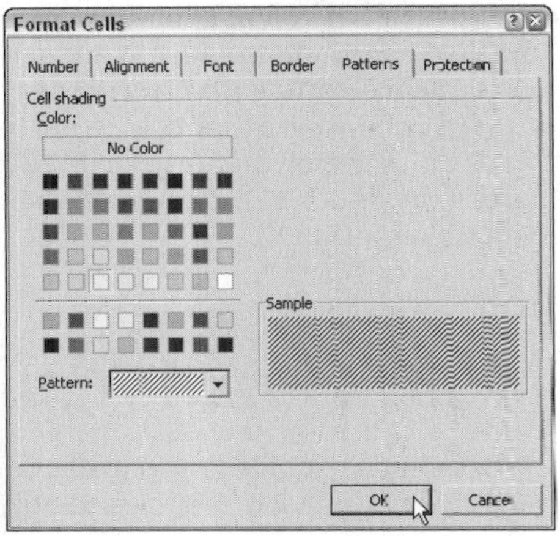

Figure 3-25:
Select new
colors and
patterns
with the
Patterns
tab on the
Format Cells
dialog box.

To remove a color or shading pattern from cells, select the cell range, open the Format Cells dialog box (Ctrl+1), and select the Patterns tab; then click the No Color option at the top of the Color palette.

You can assign new colors (but not new patterns) to your cell selection from the Fill Color palette opened with the Fill Color button (the button with the paint bucket, second from the end) on the Formatting toolbar. Simply select the cells to be colored, click the Fill Color tool's drop-down list button, and choose the desired color in the color palette that appears. (Remember, too, that the Fill Color palette is one of those toolbars that you can tear off and float in the worksheet area.)

Although you can't select new patterns (only colors) with the Fill Color tool, you can remove both colors and patterns assigned to a cell selection by selecting the cells and then clicking on the Fill Color tool's button and choosing No Fill at the top of the Fill Color palette that appears.

Using those fantastic floating palettes

You can float the Borders palette (like the Fill Color and Font Color palettes) by tearing it off the Formatting toolbar. Click its pop-up menu, and then drag it by the dashed gray bar at top of the pop-menu menu until its title bar appears at the top of the palette, indicating that its is completely free of the toolbar. It's now a floating palette. Note that floating palettes remain open while you work. To close the floating palette later on, you simply click its Close button in the upper-right corner of its little-bitty window. You don't have to drag a floating palette back to the Formatting toolbar because the original Borders, Fill Color, or Font Color button remains on this toolbar, even after creating a floating palette for it.

If you want the text in a cell range to be a different color from the background you assign, you can change the text color from the Font Color palette by clicking the Font Color button on the Formatting toolbar (the very last one). Change the color of the cells' text by choosing a new color from the Font Color palette by clicking the Font Color button on the Formatting toolbar. To return the text to black in a cell range, select the cells and then choose Automatic at the top of the Font Color palette.

Fooling Around with the Format Painter

Using styles to format worksheet cells is certainly the way to go when you have to apply the formatting over and over again in the workbooks you create. However, there may be times when you simply want to reuse a particular cell format and apply it to particular groups of cells in a single workbook without ever bothering to create an actual style for it.

For those occasions when you feel the urge to format on the fly (so to speak), use the Format Painter tool (the paintbrush icon) on the Standard toolbar. This wonderful little tool enables you to take the formatting from a particular cell that you fancy up and apply its formatting to other cells in the worksheet simply by selecting those cells.

To use the Format Painter to copy a cell's formatting to other worksheet cells, just follow these easy steps:

1. **Format an example cell or cell range in your workbook, selecting whatever fonts, alignment, borders, patterns, and color you want it to have.**

2. **With the cell pointer in one of the cells you just fancied up, click the Format Painter button in the Standard toolbar.**

   The mouse pointer changes from the standard thick, white cross to a thick, white cross with an animated paintbrush by its side, and you see a marquee around the selected cell with the formatting to be used by the Format Painter.

3. **Drag the white-cross-plus-animated-paintbrush pointer (the Format Painter pointer) through all the cells you want to format in the same manner as the example cell you first selected.**

   As soon as you release the mouse button, Excel applies all the formatting used in the example cell to all the cells you just selected!

To keep the Format Painter selected so that you can format a bunch of differ-ent cell ranges with the Format Painter pointer, double-click the Format Painter button after you select the sample cell with the desired formatting. To stop formatting cells with the Format Painter pointer, you simply click the Format Painter button (it remains selected when you double-click it) again to restore the button to its unselected state and return the mouse pointer to its normal thick, white-cross shape.

Note that you can use the Format Painter to restore a cell range that you gussied all up back to its boring default (General) cell format. To do this, click an empty, previously unformatted cell in the worksheet before you click the Format Painter button and then use the Format Painter pointer to drag through the cells you want returned to the default General format.

Chapter 4

Going Through Changes

*P*icture this: You just finished creating, formatting, and printing a major project with Excel — a workbook with your department's budget for the next fiscal year. Because you finally understand a little bit about how the Excel thing works, you finish the job in crack time. You're actually ahead of schedule.

You turn the workbook over to your boss so that she can check the numbers. With plenty of time for making those inevitable last-minute corrections, you're feeling on top of this situation.

Then comes the reality check — your boss brings the document back, and she's plainly agitated. "We forgot to include the estimates for the temps and our overtime hours. They've got to go right here. While you're adding them, can you move these rows of figures up and those columns over?"

As she continues to suggest improvements, your heart begins to sink. These modifications are in a different league from, "Let's change these column headings from bold to italics and add shading to that row of totals." Clearly, you're looking at a lot more work on this baby than you had contemplated. Even worse, you're looking at making structural changes that threaten to unravel the very fabric of your beautiful worksheet.

As the preceding fable points out, editing a worksheet in a workbook can occur on different levels:

- ✔ You can make changes that affect the contents of the cells, such as copying a row of column headings or moving a table to a new area in a particular worksheet.

- ✔ You can make changes that affect the structure of a worksheet itself, such as inserting new columns or rows (so that you can enter new data originally left out) or deleting unnecessary columns or rows from an existing table so that you don't leave any gaps.

- ✔ You can even make changes to the number of worksheets in a workbook (either by adding or deleting sheets).

In this chapter, you discover how to safely make all these types of changes to a workbook. As you see, the mechanics of copying and moving data or inserting and deleting rows are simple to master. It's the impact that such actions have on the worksheet that takes a little more effort to understand. Not to worry! You always have the Undo feature to fall back on for those (hopefully rare) times when you make a little tiny change that throws an entire worksheet into complete and utter chaos.

In the final section of this chapter ("Stamping Out Errors with Text to Speech"), find out to use the new Text to Speech feature to check out and confirm the accuracy of the data entries you make in your worksheets. With Text to Speech, you can listen as you computer reads back a series of cell entries as you visually corroborate their accuracy from the original source document. Text to Speech can make this sort of routine and otherwise labor-intensive editing much easier and greatly increase the accuracy of your spreadsheets.

Opening the Darned Thing Up for Editing

Before you can do any damage — I mean, make any changes — in a workbook, you have to open it up in Excel. To open a workbook, you can click the Open button on the Standard toolbar (normally the one second from the left, with the picture of a file folder opening up), or you can choose File➪Open from the menu bar, or use the keyboard shortcuts Ctrl+O or Ctrl+F12.

However you open it, Excel displays the Open dialog box similar to the one shown in Figure 4-1. Then you select the workbook file you want to work on from the list box in the middle of the Open dialog box. After clicking the filename to highlight it in this list box, you can open it by clicking the Open button or pressing Enter. If you're handy with the mouse, double-click the workbook's filename in the list box to open it.

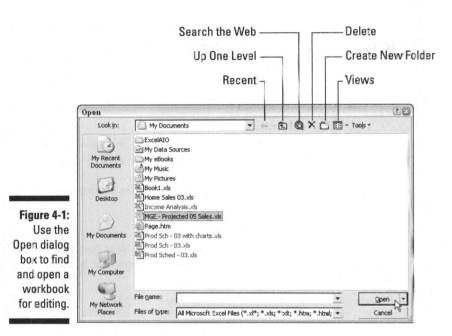

Search the Web ——————| |—— Delete

Up One Level ——| |—— Create New Folder

Recent ¬   ┌ Views

Figure 4-1:
Use the
Open dialog
box to find
and open a
workbook
for editing.

Opening more than one workbook at a time

If you know that you're going to edit more than one of the workbook files'
sheets shown in the list box of the Open dialog box, you can select multiple
files in the list box and Excel will then open all of them (in the order they're
listed) when you click the Open button or press Enter.

Remember that in order to select multiple files all listed sequentially in the
list box, you click the first filename and then hold down the Shift key while
you click the last filename. To select files that are not listed sequentially, you
need to hold down the Ctrl key while you click the various filenames.

After the workbook files are open in Excel, you can then switch documents
by selecting their filenames from the Window pull-down menu. (See Chapter 7
for detailed information on working on more than one worksheet at a time.)

Opening recently edited workbooks

If you know that the workbook you need to edit is one of those that you had
open recently, you don't even have to fool around with the Open dialog box.
Just click the link to the file in the Open section of the Home Task pane

(Ctrl+F1) or choose the File pull-down menu and select the filename from the bottom of the File menu. (Excel keeps a running list of the last four files you opened in the program, and these appear at the top of the Home Task pane and the bottom of the File pull-down menu.) If the workbook you want to work with is one of those shown at the bottom of the File menu, you can open it by clicking its filename in the menu or typing its number (1, 2, 3, or 4).

If you want, you can have Excel list more or fewer files at the top of the New Workbook task pane and the bottom of the File menu. To change the number of files listed at the bottom of the File menu, follow these simple steps:

1. **Choose Tools⇨Options on the menu bar to open the Options dialog box.**

2. **Click the General tab in the Options dialog box.**

3. **Type a new entry (between 1 and 9) in the Entries text box (following the Recently Used File List check box) or use the spinner buttons to increase or decrease this number.**

4. **Click OK or press Enter to close the Options dialog box.**

Note that if you don't want any files listed at the top of the Getting Started task pane and the bottom of the File menu, just remove the check mark from the Recently Used File List check box in the Options dialog box.

When you don't know where to find them

The only problem you can encounter in opening a document from the Open dialog box is locating the filename. Everything's hunky-dory as long as you can see the workbook filename listed in its list box. But what about those times when a file seems to have mysteriously migrated and is now nowhere to be found in the list?

Searching the wide disk over

When you can't find the filename you're looking for in the list box, the first thing you need to do is check to make sure that you're looking in the right folder — because if you're not, you're never going to find the missing file. To tell which folder is currently open, check the Look In drop-down list box at the top of the Open dialog box (refer to Figure 4-1).

If the folder that is currently open is not the one that has the workbook file you need to use, you then need to open the folder that does contain the file. In Excel, you can use the Up One Level button (refer to Figure 4-1) in the Open dialog box to change levels until you see the folder you want to open in the list box. To open the new folder, click its icon in the list box and then click the Open button or press Enter (or you can just double-click its icon).

If the workbook file you want is on another drive, click the Up One Level button until the C: drive icon appears in the Look In drop-down list box. You can then switch drives by clicking the drive icon in the list box and then choosing the Open button or pressing Enter (or you can just double-click the drive icon).

When you locate the file you want to use in the list box in the Open dialog box, open it by clicking its file icon and then clicking the Open button or pressing Enter (or by double-clicking the file icon).

Use the buttons displayed in the My Places panel on the left side of the Open dialog box (My Recent Documents, Desktop, My Documents, My Computer, and My Network Places) to easily open any folders associated with these buttons that contain workbook files:

- **My Recent Documents:** Click this button to open workbook files you save in the Recent folder (located inside the Office folder within the Microsoft folder).

- **Desktop:** Click this folder to open workbook files you save directly on the desktop of your computer.

- **My Documents:** Click this button to open workbook files you save in the Personal folder inside the Windows folder. (In fact, on some computers, the My Documents button in the Excel 200X Open dialog box appears as the Personal button.)

- **My Computer:** Click this button to open workbook files you save in folders on the local disks on your computer.

- **My Network Places:** Click this button to open workbook files you save in folders on the disks attached to your company's network.

Adding folders to the My Places panel

Assuming that you are successful in locating your file by going up and down the drive hierarchy as I describe in the preceding section, you can save yourself all this work the next time you need to open this folder to find a workbook by adding a button for the folder to the My Places panel on the left side of the Open dialog box.

To add a folder to the buttons displayed in the My Places panel (below My Network Places), follow these steps:

1. **Select the folder icon (as I describe in the previous section) in the Open dialog box.**

   2. Select Tools⇨Add to "My Places" in the Open dialog box (refer to Figure 4-1).

   This adds a button for the folder that's selected to the left panel in the Open dialog list box.

After you add a folder to the Open dialog box, you can open it by clicking the Continuation button (the one with triangle pointing downward) to locate and click it in the panel on the left side of the Open dialog box.

You can make the folder buttons that you add to the My Places panel more prominent and easier to select by moving them up in the panel. To do this, right-click the button and then click Move Up on its shortcut menu. To rename a button, right-click its button, click Rename on its shortcut menu, and then enter the new name in the Rename Place dialog box before you click OK. To remove a folder button that's no longer needed on the My Places panel, right-click its button and then click Remove on its shortcut menu.

You can display more buttons in the My Places panel in the Open dialog box by switching from large to small icons. To do this, right-click any one of the buttons in the My Places panel and then click Small Icons on its shortcut menu.

File hide-and-seek from the Open dialog box

The Open dialog box has a Search feature built into it that you can always use to locate a particular file within the open folder. This feature enables you to reduce your search in the Open dialog list box to just those files that fall into a specific category (such as those files you modified today or sometime this week) or just those files that contain a certain phrase or property (for example, those done by a particular author or containing a particular keyword).

When using the Search feature in the Open dialog box, you can tell Excel exactly how you want it to conduct its search including such criteria as:

   ✔ Workbook files with filenames containing certain text

   ✔ Files of a type different from Microsoft Excel files

   ✔ Workbook files that contain a certain text or property such as title, author, or keywords entered into a file summary

   ✔ Workbook files created or modified on a particular date or within a particular range of dates

To open the File Search dialog box where you specify the criteria upon which you want the search conducted choose Tools⇨Search from the Open dialog box. Figure 4-2 shows you the File Search dialog box where you define your search criteria.

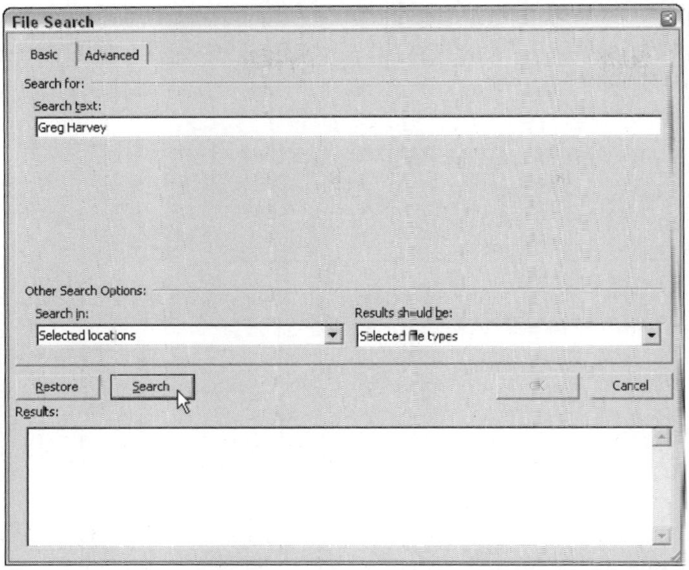

Figure 4-2:
Begin with
the Basic
tab of the
File Search
dialog box
to find a
workbook.

The File Search dialog box contains two tabs: Basic and Advanced. The Basic tab enables you to control three criteria when searching for workbook files:

✔ **Search Text:** Use this text box to specify the keywords or identifying values, words, or phrases. The Search Text feature searches for the text that you enter here in three places when you begin the search: the names of the files, the contents of the files and the properties of the files.

✔ **Search In:** Use this drop-down list box to specify which drives and folders to include in the search. To search all drives and folders on your computer, select the Everywhere check box in the Search In drop-down list (which then changes the option from Selected Locations to Everywhere). To narrow the search to particular disks and/or folders on a drive, click the + sign in front of the My Computer check box on the Search In drop-down list and make sure that only the check boxes for the drives or folders (if you are restricting the search to a single drive) that you want search are selected in the listings beneath My Computer.

✔ **Results Should Be:** Use this drop-down list box to specify which types of files to include in the search. To narrow the search to Excel workbook files only, deselect (clear) all check boxes in the Results Should Be drop-down list except for the one for Excel Files. To locate this check box on the Results Should Be drop-down menu, click the + sign button in front of Office Files to expand this listing.

After you specify these three criteria on the Basic tab, click the Search button (immediately above the Results list box) to initiate your search.

To refine your search criteria, click the Advanced tab. Now the Search Text box of the Basic tab is replaced by three new boxes: Property, Condition, and Value (see Figure 4-3).

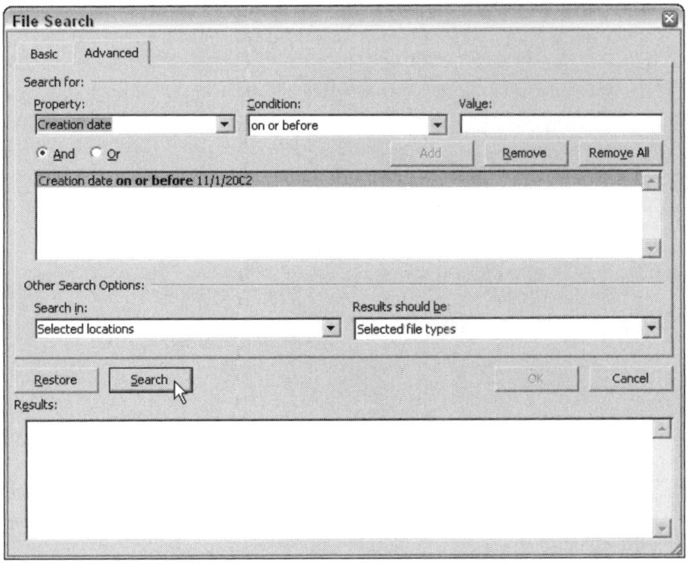

Figure 4-3:
Use the
Advanced
tab of the
File Search
dialog box
to refine
your
workbook
search.

To specify the search criteria, select the aspect to be searched in the Property drop-down list, the type of condition in the Condition drop-down list, and the value to be equaled, included, or exceeded (depending upon the type of condition chosen).

After specifying these three criteria, click the Add button to add this search condition to the Search For list box below (refer to Figure 4-3). When specifying your search criteria with the options on the Advanced tab of the Search dialog box, keep the following things in mind:

✔ Normally, all search criteria that you add to the Search For list box on the Advanced tab are cumulative, meaning that *all* of them must be true in order for Excel to match a file (because the And radio button is selected). If, instead, you want Excel to match a file if it meets *any* of the criteria specified in the Search For list box, click the Or radio button.

✔ By default, Excel searches the text or property and makes its matches according to the contents you specify in the Value text box. If you want to have Excel match other properties (such as Author, Contents, Creation Date, and so on), open the Property drop-down list box and then choose the desired property in its list box.

✔ In general, Excel just looks to see whether a certain value or piece of text is included in the designated Property (whether you choose File name, or Author, and so forth). When you select some properties (such as Company or Location), you are also able to have the program match files only when their property contains exactly that value or text. To do this, you open the Condition drop-down list box and select the Is (Exactly) option.

✔ Enter the value or text that should be matched in the Value text box. For example, if you want to find all the files in which the Contents include the text *Jack Sprat*, you enter **Jack Sprat** in this text box. If, on the other hand, you want to find all the files in which the Contents include the number *1,250,750*, you enter **1250750** in the Value text box.

After you add all the criteria you want for your search (in either the Basic or the Advanced tab), click the Search button to set Excel off hunting for the files that match all your conditions. When the program completes the file search, it displays the matching files (hopefully including the workbook files you want to use) in the Results list box at the very bottom of the Search dialog box.

If the workbook file that you want to open appears in this list box, you can stop Excel from continuing the search by clicking the Stop button. If your search includes a lot of folders (all the folders on the hard drive, or something like that), you may even have to scroll to go through all the file icons that are displayed. If loads and loads of files are found, click the Next 20 Results hyperlink at the bottom of list to display the next 20 matching files. You can continue to do this until you locate the workbook file you want to edit or come to the end of the listings.

If you see the name of a workbook file in the Results list that you want to open, double-click its file icon with the Hand mouse pointer to close the Search dialog box and open the Open dialog box with this file displayed in its list box. To open the selected file from the Open dialog box, double-click its file icon again or just click the icon once before you select the Open button.

File hide-and-seek from the Search task pane

You can perform the same basic and advanced file searches in the Basic File Search and Advanced File Search task panes as you can from the Open dialog box (as I describe in the previous section "File hide-and-seek from the Open dialog box"). To search for a file from the Basic File Search or Advanced File Search task pane, follow these steps:

1. **Choose File➪File Search on the Excel menu bar.**

   Excel opens the Basic File Search Task pane on the right side of the Excel worksheet window.

2. **To perform a basic search, enter the text to search for in the Search Text box.**

   Then specify the location(s) and types of files to find in the Search In and Results Should Be drop-down list boxes, respectively (read the earlier section "File hide-and-seek from the Open dialog box" for help on selecting these basic search criteria).

3. **To perform a more-narrow search, open the Advanced File Search Task pane (shown in Figure 4-4) by clicking the <u>Advanced File Search</u> hyperlink near the bottom of the Basic File Search pane.**

   When you're in the Basic File Search mode, the <u>Advanced File Search</u> hyperlink appears at the bottom of this task pane; when you're in the Advanced File Search mode, the <u>Basic File Search</u> hyperlink appears at the bottom of this task pane.

4. **Then specify the criteria in the Property, Condition, and Value boxes, setting these parameters one-by-one when you click the Add button.**

   (Read the earlier section "File hide-and-seek from the Open dialog box" for help on selecting these advanced search criteria.)

5. **To initiate the search after you specify the search criteria in either the Basic File Search (Step 3) or Advanced File Search pane (Step 4), click the Go button.**

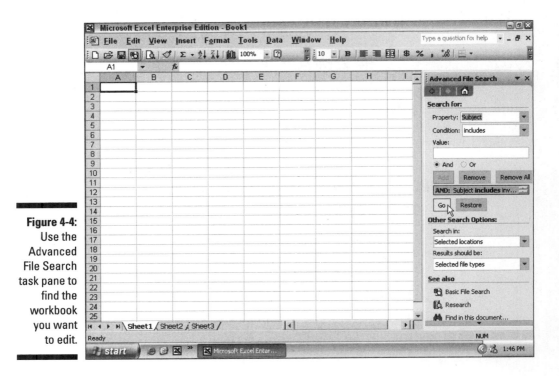

Figure 4-4:
Use the Advanced File Search task pane to find the workbook you want to edit.

Installing Fast Searching

To make file searching faster and more accurate, you need to install the Microsoft Fast Searching feature if you've not already done so. To install Fast Searching, click the Install hyperlink in Basic Search pane. (If this feature is already installed, this link won't appear.) Then click the Yes button in the alert dialog box that appears. (It tells you that Fast Searching is not currently installed and queries whether you want to install it now.) Insert the Office CD-ROM in your CD drive when prompted and click OK to complete the installation.

After Fast Searching installs, you need to enable it. To do this, click the Search Options hyperlink (which replaces the Install hyperlink) in the Basic Search task pane. Then select the Yes, Enable Indexing Service and Run When My Computer Is Idle radio button and click OK in the Indexing Service Settings dialog box.

When you click Go to launch a file search, Excel changes either the Basic File Search or Advanced File Search task pane (depending upon which you used) into a Search Results pane. Excel lists all of the files that meet your search criteria in this task pane. Just like when performing a search from the Open dialog box, you can open a particular workbook file in the Search Results task pane by clicking its filename to select it or by clicking its drop-down button and then clicking the Edit with Microsoft Excel option on its pop-up list.

If the Edit with Microsoft Excel option is unavailable because the file you select is not one that Excel 2002 recognizes specifically as a workbook, try opening it by selecting the Copy Link to Clipboard option on the pop-up menu. Next, open the Open dialog box (Ctrl+O) and paste the path and filename link (Ctrl+V) into its File Name text box before you choose the Open button.

Making a positive ID

Normally, Excel displays the folders and files in the Open dialog box's list box as a simple list showing the folder or file icon.

To switch the way the files display in the Open dialog box's list box, you simply select any of the following options that appear on a pop-up menu when you click the Views button in the Open dialog box (refer to Figure 4-1):

   ✔ Select Details to display the file size in kilobytes, the type of file, and the date the file was last modified, along with the file icon and filename (as shown in Figure 4-5).

✔ Select Properties to display the file summary information next to the file icon and filename when you select each file in the list (as shown in Figure 4-6). (To view the file summary for a file, select the file in the Open dialog box, choose Tools⇔Properties, and then click the Summary tab in the Properties dialog box that opens.)

✔ Select Preview to display a miniature preview showing the upper-left corner of the first worksheet in the workbook file next to the file icon and filename when you select each file in the list (as shown in Figure 4-7).

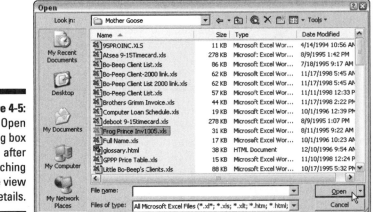

Figure 4-5: The Open dialog box after switching the file view to Details.

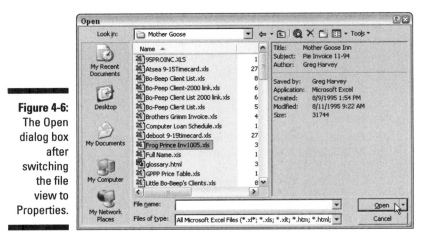

Figure 4-6: The Open dialog box after switching the file view to Properties.

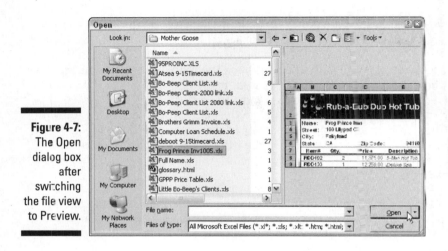

Figure 4-7:
The Open
dialog box
after
switching
the file view
to Preview.

Opening files with a twist

The pop-up menu attached to the Open button in the Open dialog box
enables you to open the selected workbook file(s) in special ways. These
ways include

- **Open Read Only:** This command opens the files you select in the Open
  dialog box's list box in a read-only state, which means that you can look
  but you can't touch. (Actually, you can touch; you just can't save your
  changes.) To save changes in a read-only file you must use the File⇒
  Save As command from the Excel menu bar and give the workbook file
  a new filename. (Refer to Chapter 2.)

- **Open as Copy:** This command opens a copy of the files you select in the
  Open dialog box. Use this method of file-opening as a safety net: If you
  mess up the copies, you always have the originals to fall back on.

- **Open in Browser:** This command opens workbook files you save as Web
  pages (as I describe in Chapter 10) in your favorite Web browser (which
  would normally be the Microsoft Internet Explorer). Note that this command is not available unless the program identifies that the selected file
  or files were saved as Web pages rather than plain old Excel worksheet
  files.

- **Open and Repair:** This command attempts to repair corrupted workbook files before opening them in Excel. When you select this command,
  a dialog box appears giving you a choice between attempting to repair
  the corrupted file and opening the recovered version and extracting the
  data out of the corrupted file and placing it in a new workbook (which
  you can save with the File⇒Save command). Click the Repair button to
  attempt to recover and open the file. Click the Extract Data button if you
  previously tried unsuccessfully to have Excel repair the file.

Much Ado about Undo

Before you start tearing into the workbook that you just opened, get to know the Undo feature and how it can put right many of the things that you could inadvertently mess up. The Undo command on the Edit menu is a regular chameleon command. When you delete the contents of a cell selection with the Clear command on this same menu, Undo changes to Undo Clear. If you move some entries to a new part of the worksheet with the Cut and Paste commands (again, found on the Edit menu), the Undo command changes to Undo Paste.

In addition to choosing Undo (in whatever guise it appears) from the Edit menu, you can also choose this command by pressing Ctrl+Z (perhaps for *unZap*), or you can click the Undo button on the Standard toolbar (the one with the arrow curving to the left).

The Undo command on the Edit menu changes in response to whatever action you just took; it keeps changing after each action. If you forget to strike when the iron is hot, so to speak — by using the Undo feature to restore the worksheet to its previous state *before* you choose another command — you then need to consult the pop-up menu on the Undo button on the Standard toolbar to select the previous action that you want undone. To open this menu, click the drop-down button that appears to the right of the Undo icon (the curved arrow pointing to the left). After the Undo drop-down menu is open, click the action on this menu that you want undone. Excel will then undo this action and all actions that precede it in the list (which are automatically selected).

Undo is Redo the second time around

After choosing the Undo command (by whatever means you find most convenient), Excel 2003 adds a new Redo command to the Edit menu. If you delete an entry from a cell by choosing Edit⇨Clear⇨All from the menu bar and then choose Edit⇨Undo Clear (or press Ctrl+Z, or click the Undo tool on the toolbar), you see the following command at the top of the menu beneath Undo the next time you open the Edit menu:

```
Redo Clear Ctrl+Y
```

When you choose the Redo command, Excel redoes the thing you just undid. Actually, this sounds more complicated than it is. It simply means that you use Undo to switch back and forth between the result of an action and the state of the worksheet just before that action until you decide how you want the worksheet (or until the cleaning crew turns off the lights and locks up the building).

You may find it a heck of a lot easier to just click the Undo and the Redo buttons on the Standard toolbar rather than go through all the rigmarole of choosing their respective commands on the Edit pull-down menu. The Undo button is the one with the picture of the arrow curving to the left; the Redo button is the one with the picture of the arrow curving to the right. Note, however, that the Redo button may not appear on the Standard toolbar the first time you go to use it. If you see only the Undo button on this toolbar, you need to select the Redo button on the More Buttons palette opened by clicking the More Buttons button (the one with the >> symbol).

You can redo multiple actions in a workbook by clicking the drop-down button to the right of the Redo button's icon (the curved arrow pointing to the right) and clicking the action on the menu that you want redone. Excel then redoes the action that you select as well as all the actions that precede it on the menu.

What ya gonna do when you can't Undo?

Just when you think it is safe to begin gutting the company's most important workbook, I really feel that I've got to tell you that (yikes!) Undo doesn't work all the time! Although you can undo your latest erroneous cell deletion, bad move, or unwise copy, you can't undo your latest imprudent save. (You know, like when you meant to choose Save As from the File menu to save the edited worksheet under a different document name but instead chose Save and ended up saving the changes as part of the current document.)

Unfortunately, Excel doesn't let you know when you are about to take a step from which there is no return — until it's too late. After you've gone and done the un-undoable and you open the Edit menu right where you expect the Undo *blah, blah* command to be, it now reads Can't Undo.

To add insult to injury, this extremely unhelpful command appears dimmed to indicate that you can't choose it — as though being able to choose it would change anything!

One exception to this rule is when the program gives you advance warning (which you should heed). When you choose a command that is normally undoable but currently — because you're low on memory, or the change will affect so much of the worksheet, or both — Excel knows that it can't undo the change if it goes through with it, the program displays an alert box telling you that there isn't enough memory to undo this action and asking whether you want to go ahead anyway. If you click the Yes button and complete the edit, just realize that you do so without any possibility of pardon. If you find out, too late, that you deleted a row of essential formulas (that you forgot about because you couldn't see them), you can't bring them back with Undo. In such a case, you would have to close the file (File⇨Close) and *NOT save your changes.*

Doing the Old Drag-and-Drop Thing

The first editing technique you need to learn is called *drag and drop*. As the name implies, it's a mouse technique that you can use to pick up a cell selection and drop it into a new place on the worksheet. Although drag and drop is primarily a technique for moving cell entries around a worksheet, you can adapt it to copy a cell selection, as well.

To use drag and drop to move a range of cell entries (you can only move one cell range at a time), follow these steps:

1. **Select a cell range.**

2. **Position the mouse pointer on one edge of the selected range.**

   Your signal that you can start dragging the cell range to its new position in the worksheet is when the pointer changes to the arrowhead.

3. **Drag your selection to its destination.**

   Drag your selection by depressing and holding down the primary mouse button — usually the left one — while moving the mouse.

   While you drag your selection, you actually move only the outline of the cell range, and Excel keeps you informed of what the new cell range address would be (as a kind of drag-and-drop tool tip) if you were to release the mouse button at that location.

   Drag the outline until it's positioned on the new cells in the worksheet where you want the entries to appear (as evidenced by the cell range in the drag-and-drop tool tip).

4. **Release the mouse button.**

   The cell entries within that range reappear in the new location as soon as you release the mouse button.

In Figures 4-8 and 4-9, I show how you can drag and drop to move a cell range. In Figure 4-8, I select the cell range A10:E10 (containing the quarterly totals) to move it to row 12 to make room for sales figures for two new companies (Simple Simon Pie Shoppes and Jack Be Nimble Candlesticks, which hadn't been acquired when this workbook was first created). In Figure 4-9, you see the Mother Goose Enterprises 2000 sales worksheet right after completing this move.

Notice in Figure 4-9 that the argument for the SUM function in cell B12 has not kept pace with the change — it continues to sum only the range B3:B9. Eventually, this range must be expanded to include cells B10 and B11, the first-quarter sales figures for the new Simple Simon Pie Shoppes and Jack Be Nimble Candlesticks. (You can find out how to do this in the upcoming section, "Formulas on AutoFill.")

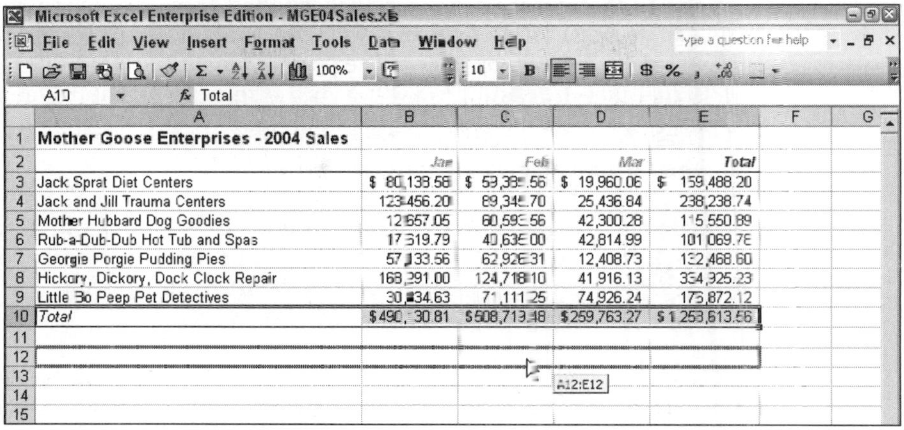

Figure 4-8: Dragging a cell selection to its new position in a worksheet.

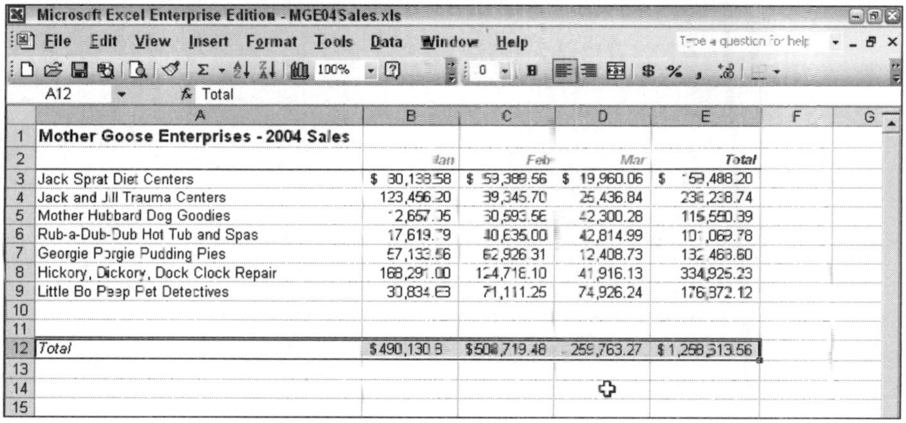

Microsoft Excel Enterprise Edition - MGE04Sales.xls				
A	B (Jan)	C (Feb)	D (Mar)	E (Total)
Mother Goose Enterprises - 2004 Sales				
	Jan	Feb	Mar	Total
Jack Sprat Diet Centers	$ 80,138.58	$ 59,389.56	$ 19,960.06	$ 159,488.20
Jack and Jill Trauma Centers	123,456.20	89,345.70	25,436.84	238,238.74
Mother Hubbard Dog Goodies	12,657.05	60,593.56	42,300.28	115,550.89
Rub-a-Dub-Dub Hot Tub and Spas	17,619.79	40,635.00	42,814.99	101,069.78
Georgie Porgie Pudding Pies	57,133.56	62,926.31	12,408.73	132,468.60
Hickory, Dickory, Dock Clock Repair	168,291.00	124,718.10	41,916.13	334,925.23
Little Bo Peep Pet Detectives	30,834.63	71,111.25	74,926.24	176,872.12
Total	$490,130.81	$508,713.48	$259,763.27	$1,258,613.56

A12:E12

Figure 4-9: A worksheet after dropping the cell selection into its new place.

Microsoft Excel Enterprise Edition - MGE04Sales.xls				
A	B (Jan)	C (Feb)	D (Mar)	E (Total)
Mother Goose Enterprises - 2004 Sales				
	Jan	Feb	Mar	Total
Jack Sprat Diet Centers	$ 80,138.58	$ 59,389.56	$ 19,960.06	$ 159,488.20
Jack and Jill Trauma Centers	123,456.20	89,345.70	25,436.84	238,238.74
Mother Hubbard Dog Goodies	12,657.05	60,593.56	42,300.28	115,550.89
Rub-a-Dub-Dub Hot Tub and Spas	17,619.79	40,635.00	42,814.99	101,069.78
Georgie Porgie Pudding Pies	57,133.56	62,926.31	12,408.73	132,468.60
Hickory, Dickory, Dock Clock Repair	168,291.00	124,718.10	41,916.13	334,925.23
Little Bo Peep Pet Detectives	30,834.63	71,111.25	74,926.24	176,872.12
Total	$490,130.81	$508,719.48	259,763.27	$1,258,613.56

Copies, drag-and-drop style

What if you want to copy a cell range instead of dragging and dropping one? Suppose that you need to start a new table in rows further down the worksheet, and you want to copy the cell range with the formatted title and column headings for the new table. To copy the formatted title range in the sample worksheet, follow these steps:

1. **Select the cell range.**

   In the case of Figures 4-8 and 4-9, that's cell range B2:E2.

2. **Hold the Ctrl key down while you position the mouse pointer on an edge of the selection.**

The pointer changes from a thick, shaded cross to an arrowhead with a + (plus sign) to the right of it with the drag-and-drop screen tips right beside it. Keep in mind that the plus sign next to the pointer is your signal that drag and drop will *copy* the selection rather than *move* it.

3. **Drag the cell-selection outline to the place where you want the copy to appear and release the mouse button.**

If, when using drag and drop to move or copy cells, you position the outline of the selection so that it overlaps any part of cells that already contain entries, Excel displays an alert box with the following question: Do you want to replace contents of the destination cells?

To avoid replacing existing entries and to abort the entire drag-and-drop mission, click the Cancel button in this alert box. To go ahead and exterminate the little darlings, click OK or press Enter.

Insertions courtesy of drag and drop

Like the Klingons of *Star Trek* fame, spreadsheets, such as Excel, never take prisoners. When you place or move a new entry into an occupied cell, the new entry completely replaces the old as though the old entry never existed in that cell.

To insert the cell range you're moving or copying within a populated region of the worksheet without wiping out existing entries, hold the Shift key while you drag the selection. (If you're copying, you have to get really ambitious and hold down both the Shift and Ctrl keys at the same time!) With the Shift key depressed as you drag, instead of a rectangular outline of the cell range, you get an I-beam shape that shows where the selection will be inserted along with the address of the cell range (as a kind of Insertion screen tip) indicating where it would be inserted if you release the mouse button. As you move the I-beam shape, notice that it gloms on to the column and row borders as you move it. When you position the I-beam shape at the column or row border where you want the cell range to be inserted, release the mouse button. Excel inserts the cell range, moving the existing entries to neighboring blank cells (out of harm's way).

When inserting cells with drag and drop, it may be helpful to think of the I-beam shape as a pry bar that pulls apart the columns or rows along the axis of the I. Also, keep in mind that sometimes after moving a range to a new place in the worksheet, instead of the data appearing, you see only #######s in the cells. (Excel 2003 doesn't automatically widen the new columns for the incoming data as it does when formatting the data.) Remember that the way to get rid of the #######s in the cells is by widening those troublesome columns enough to display all the data-plus-formatting, and the easiest way to do this kind of widening is by double-clicking the right border of the column.

TIP

But I held down the Shift key just like you said . . .

Drag and drop in Insert mode is one of Excel's most finicky features. Sometimes you can do everything just right and still get the alert box warning you that Excel is about to replace existing entries instead of pushing them aside. When you see this alert box, always click the Cancel button! Fortunately, you can insert things with the Cut and Insert Paste commands (see the section "Cut and paste, digital style," later in this chapter) without worrying about which way the I-beam selection goes.

Formulas on AutoFill

Copying with drag and drop (by holding down the Ctrl key) is useful when you need to copy a bunch of neighboring cells to a new part of the worksheet. Frequently, however, you just need to copy a single formula that you just created to a bunch of neighboring cells that need to perform the same type of calculation (such as totaling columns of figures). This type of formula copy, although quite common, can't be done with drag and drop. Instead, use the AutoFill feature (read about this in Chapter 2) or the Copy and Paste commands. (See the section "Cut and paste, digital style" later in this chapter.)

Here's how you can use AutoFill to copy one formula to a range of cells. In Figure 4-10, you can see the Mother Goose Enterprises – 2001 Sales worksheet after I add the Simple Simon Pie Shoppes and Jack Be Nimble Candlesticks to the list. Remember that these companies were missing from the original worksheet, so I made room for them by moving the Totals down to row 12 (you can see this back in Figure 4-9).

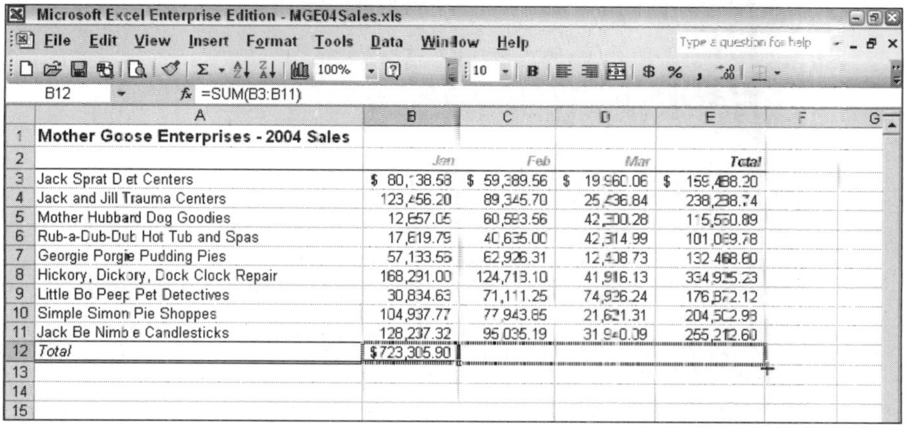

Figure 4-10: Copying a formula to a cell range with AutoFill.

Look at row 12, cell range C12:E12, in Figure 4-11: The Feb and Mar sales totals are now calculated, as is the Total cell for all Mother Goose Enterprises – 2001 quarterly sales.

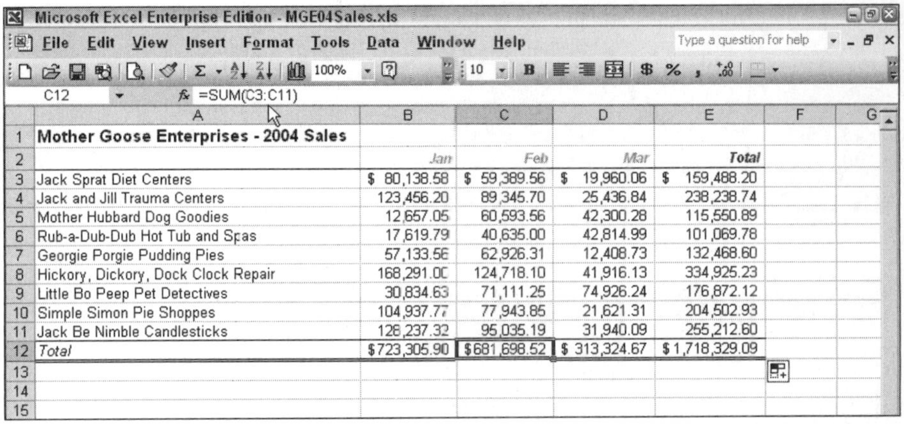

Figure 4-11: The worksheet after copying the formula totaling the monthly sales.

Unfortunately, Excel doesn't update the sum formulas to include the new rows (the Sum function still uses B3:B9 when it should be extended to include rows 10 and 11). To make the Sum function include all the rows, position the cell pointer in cell B12 and click the AutoSum tool on the Standard toolbar. Excel suggests the new range B3:B11 for the Sum function.

Refer to Figure 4-10: You can see the worksheet after I re-create the Sum formula in cell B12 with the AutoSum tool to include the expanded range. I drag the fill handle to select the cell range C12:E12 (where this formula should be copied). Notice that I deleted the original formulas from the cell range C12:E12 in this figure to make it easier to see what's going on; normally, you just copy over the original outdated formulas and replace them with new correct copies.

Relatively speaking

Refer to Figure 4-11 to see the worksheet after the formula in a cell is copied to the cell range C12:E12 and cell C12 is active. Notice how Excel handles the copying of formulas. The original formula in cell B12 is as follows:

```
=SUM(B3:B11)
```

When the original formula is copied next door to cell C12, Excel changes the formula slightly so that it looks like this:

```
=SUM(C3:C11)
```

Excel adjusts the column reference, changing t from B to C, because I copied from left to right across the rows.

When you copy a formula to a cell range that extends down the rows, Excel adjusts the row numbers in the copied formulas rather than the column letters to suit the position of each copy. For example, cell E3 in the Mother Goose Enterprises – 2004 Sales worksheet contains the following formula:

```
=SUM(B3:D3)
```

When you copy this formula down to cell E4, Excel changes the copy of the formula to the following:

```
=SUM(B4:D4)
```

Excel adjusts the row reference to keep current with the new row 4 position. Because Excel adjusts the cell references in copies of a formula relative to the direction of the copying, the cell references are known as *relative cell references*.

Some things are absolutes!

All new formulas you create naturally contain relative cell references unless you say otherwise. Because most copies you make of formulas require adjustments of their cell references, you rarely have to give this arrangement a second thought. Then, every once in a while, you come across an exception that calls for limiting when and how cell references are adjusted in copies.

One of the most common of these exceptions is when you want to compare a range of different values with a single value. This happens most often when you want to compute what percentage each part is to the total. For example, in the Mother Goose Enterprises – 2004 Sales worksheet, you encounter this situation in creating and copying a formula that calculates what percentage each monthly total (in the cell range B14:D14) is of the quarterly total in cell E12.

Suppose that you want to enter these formulas in row 14 of the Mother Goose Enterprises – 2004 Sales worksheet, starting in cell B14. The formula in cell B14 for calculating the percentage of the January-sales-to-first-quarter-total is very straightforward:

```
=B12/E12
```

This formula divides the January sales total in cell B12 by the quarterly total in E12 (what could be easier?). Look, however, at what would happen if you dragged the fill handle one cell to the right to copy this formula to cell C14:

```
=C12/F12
```

The adjustment of the first cell reference from B12 to C12 is just what the doctor ordered. However, the adjustment of the second cell reference from E12 to F12 is a disaster. Not only do you not calculate what percentage the February sales in cell C12 are of the first quarter sales in E12, but you also end up with one of those horrible #DIV/0! error things in cell C14.

To stop Excel from adjusting a cell reference in a formula in any copies you make, convert the cell reference from relative to absolute. You can do this by pressing the function key F4. Excel indicates that you make the cell reference absolute by placing dollar signs in front of the column letter and row number. For example, look at Figure 4-12. Cell B14 in this figure contains the correct formula to copy to the cell range C14:D14:

```
=B12/$E$12
```

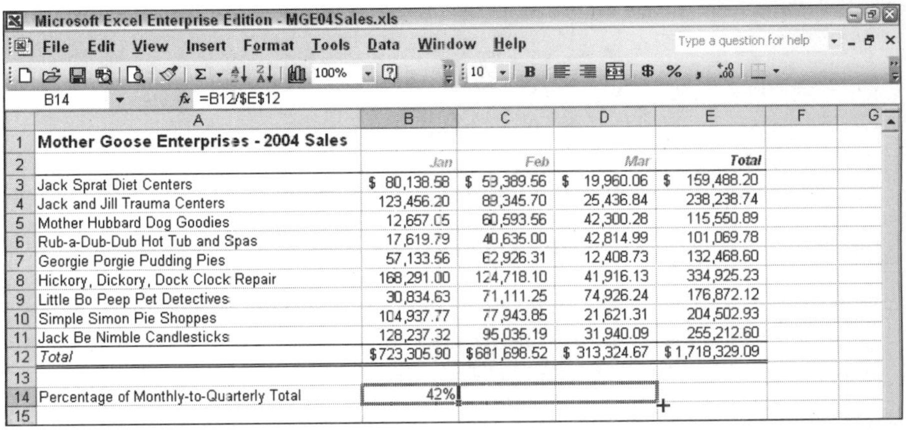

Figure 4-12:
Copying the formula for computing the ratio of monthly to quarterly sales with an absolute cell reference.

Look at the worksheet after this formula is copied to the range C14:D14 with the fill handle and cell C14 selected (see Figure 4-13). Notice that the formula bar shows that this cell contains the following formula:

```
=C12/$E$12
```

Figure 4-13:
The work-sheet after copying the formula with the absolute cell reference.

	Microsoft Excel Enterprise Edition - MGE04Sales.xls						
	File Edit View Insert Format Tools Data Window Help						

C14	▼	fx =C12/$E$12					
	A	B	C	D	E	F	G
1	Mother Goose Enterprises - 2004 Sales						
2		Jan	Feb	Mar	Total		
3	Jack Sprat Diet Centers	$ 80,138.58	$ 59,389.56	$ 19,960.06	$ 159,488.20		
4	Jack and Jill Trauma Centers	123,456.20	89,345.70	25,436.84	238,238.74		
5	Mother Hubbard Dog Goodies	12,657.05	60,593.56	42,300.28	115,550.89		
6	Rub-a-Dub-Dub Hot Tub and Spas	17,619.79	40,635.00	42,814.99	101,069.78		
7	Georgie Porgie Pudding Pies	57, 33.56	62,926.11	2,408.73	132,468.60		
8	Hickory, Dickory, Dock Clock Repair	168,291.00	124,713.10	41,916.13	334,925.23		
9	Little Bo Peep Pet Detectives	30,834.63	71,111.25	74,926.24	176,872.12		
10	Simple Simon Pie Shoppes	104,937.77	77,943.15	21,621.31	204,602.93		
11	Jack Be Nimble Candlesticks	128,237.32	95,035.19	31,940.09	255,212.60		
12	Total	$723,305.90	$681,698.02	$303,324.67	$1,718,329.09		
13							
14	Percentage of Monthly-to-Quarterly Total	42%	40%	18%			
15							
16							

Because E12 was changed to $E$12 in the original formula, all the copies have this same absolute (nonchanging) reference.

TIP

If you goof up and copy a formula where one or more of the cell references should have been absolute but you left them all relative, edit the original formula as follows:

1. **Double-click the cell with the formula and click the Edit Formula button on the formula bar or press F2 to edit it.**

2. **Position the insertion point somewhere on the reference you want to convert to absolute.**

3. **Press F4.**

4. **When you finish editing, click the Enter button on the Formula bar and then copy the formula to the messed-up cell range with the fill handle.**

WARNING!

Be sure to press F4 only to change a cell reference to completely absolute as I describe earlier. If you press the F4 function key a second time, you end up with a so-called mixed reference, where only the row part is absolute and the column part is relative (as in E$12). If you then press F4 again, Excel comes up with another type of mixed reference, where the column part is absolute and the row part is relative (as in $E12). If you go on and press F4 yet again, Excel changes the cell reference back to completely relative (as in E12). After you're back where you started, you can continue to use F4 to cycle through this same set of cell reference changes all over again

Cut and paste, digital style

Instead of using drag and drop or AutoFill, you can use the old standby Cut, Copy, and Paste commands to move or copy information in a worksheet. These commands use the Clipboard as a kind of electronic halfway house where the information you cut or copy remains until you decide to paste it somewhere. Because of this Clipboard arrangement, you can use these commands to move or copy information to any other worksheet open in Excel or even to other programs running in Windows (such as a Word document).

To move a cell selection with Cut and Paste, follow these steps:

1. **Select the cells you want to move.**

2. **Click the Cut button on the Standard toolbar (the button with the scissors icon).**

   Or, if you prefer, you can choose Cut from the cell shortcut menu or Edit⇨Cut from the menu bar.

   You can cut out all of this button-and-menu stuff and just press Ctrl+X. Whenever you choose the Cut command in Excel, the program surrounds the cell selection with a *marquee* (a dotted line that travels around the cells' outline) and displays the following message on the status bar:

   Select destination and press ENTER or choose Paste

3. **Move the cell pointer to, or select, the cell in the upper-left corner of the new range to which you want the information moved.**

4. **Press Enter to complete the move operation.**

   Or, if you're feeling really ambitious, click the Paste button on the Standard toolbar, or choose Paste from the cell shortcut menu, or choose Edit⇨Paste from the menu bar, or press Ctrl+V. (Do you think that there are enough pasting alternatives in Excel?)

Notice that when you indicate the destination range, you don't have to select a range of blank cells that matches the shape and size of the cell selection you're moving. Excel only needs to know the location of the cell in the upper-left corner of the destination range to figure out where to put the rest of the cells.

Copying a cell selection with the Copy and Paste commands follows an identical procedure to the one you use with the Cut and Paste commands. After selecting the range to copy, you have even more choices about how to get the information into the Clipboard. Instead of clicking the Copy button on the Standard toolbar or choosing Copy from the cell shortcut menu or Copy from the Edit menu, you can press Ctrl+C.

Paste it again, Sam . . .

An advantage to copying a selection with the Copy and Paste commands and the Clipboard is that you can paste the information multiple times. Just make sure that, instead of pressing Enter to complete the first copy operation, you click the Paste button on the Standard toolbar or choose the Paste command (from the cell shortcut menu or the Edit menu) or press Ctrl+V.

When you use the Paste command to complete a copy operation, Excel copies the selection to the range you designate without removing the marquee from the original selection. This is your signal that you can select another destination range (either in the same or a different document).

After selecting the first cell of the next range where you want the selection copied, choose the Paste command again. You can continue in this manner, pasting the same selection to your heart's content. When you make the last copy, press Enter instead of choosing the Paste command. If you forget and choose Paste, get rid of the marquee around the original cell range by pressing the Esc key.

Keeping pace with the Paste Options

Right after you click the Paste button on the Standard toolbar or choose the Edit➪Paste command from the menu bar to paste cell entries that you copy (not cut) to the Clipboard, Excel displays a Paste Options button with its own drop-down button at the end of the pasted range. You can use the options available when you click the drop-down button to modify the paste operation in the following ways:

- **Keep Source Formatting:** When you select this option, Excel copies the formatting from the original cells and pastes this into the destination cells (along with the copied entries).

- **Match Destination Formatting:** When you select this option, Excel formats the copied entries according to the formatting assigned to the destination cell range.

- **Values Only:** When you select this option, Excel copies only the calculated results from any formulas in the source range into the destination range. This means that the destination range will consist of entirely of labels and values regardless of how many formulas exist in the source range.

- **Values and Number Formatting:** When you select this option, Excel copies the calculated results of any formulas along with the number formatting assigned to both the values and formulas in the source cell range to the destination range. This means that labels copied from the source range take on the formatting of the destination range, while the values retain the number format given to them in the source range.

✔ **Values and Source Formatting:** When you select this option, Excel copies the calculated results of any formulas along with all the formatting assigned to the labels, values, and formulas in the source cell range to the destination range. This means that all the labels and values in the destination range appear formatted just like the source range even though all the original formulas are lost and only the calculated values are retained.

✔ **Keep Source Column Widths:** When you select this option, Excel makes the width of the columns in the destination range the same as those in the source range when it copies their cell entries.

✔ **Formatting Only:** When you select this option, Excel copies only the formatting (and not the entries) from the source cell range to the destination range.

✔ **Link Cells:** When you select his option, Excel creates linking formulas in the destination range so that any changes that you make to the entries in cells in the source range are immediately brought forward and reflected in the corresponding cells of the destination range.

Paste it from the Clipboard task pane

Excel 2003 can store multiple cuts and copies in the Clipboard (up to the last 24 that you make). This means that you can continue to paste stuff from the Clipboard into a workbook even after finishing a move or copy operation (even when you do so by pressing the Enter key rather than using the Paste command). As soon as you cut or copy more than one cell selection to the Clipboard, Excel 2003 automatically opens the Clipboard task pane showing the items it now contains (see Figure 4-14).

To paste an item from the Clipboard into a worksheet other than the one with the data last cut or copied there, click the item in the Clipboard task pane to paste it into the worksheet starting at the current position of the cell pointer.

Note that you can paste all the items stored in the Clipboard into the current worksheet by clicking the Paste All button at the top of the Clipboard task pane. To clear the Clipboard of all the current items, click the Clear All button. To delete only a particular item from the Clipboard, position the mouse pointer over the item in the Clipboard task pane until its drop-down button appears. Click this drop-down button, and then choose Delete from the pop-up menu.

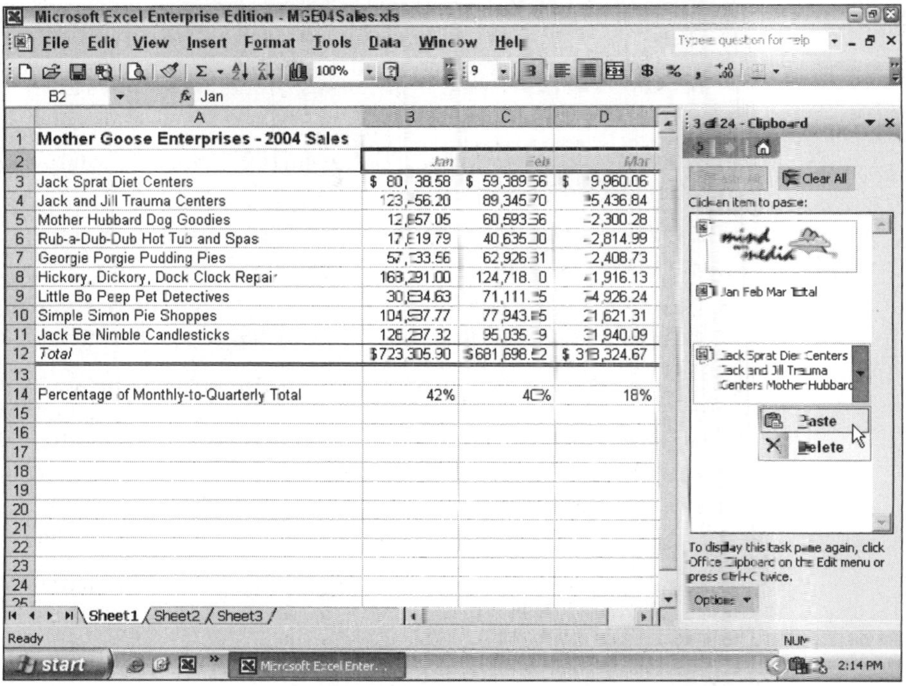

Figure 4-14:
The Clipboard task pane appears as soon as you cut or copy more than one item in to the Windows Clipboard.

So what's so special about Paste Special?

Normally, unless you fool around with the Paste Options (see the section "Keeping Pace with the Paste Options" earlier in this chapter), Excel copies all the information in the range of cells you selected: formatting as well the formulas, text, and other values you enter. If you want, use the Paste Special command to specify that only the entries be copied (without the formatting) or that just the formatting be copied (without the entries). You can also use this command to have Excel copy only values in a cell selection, which means that Excel copies all text entries and values entered in a cell selection but does *not* include formulas or formatting (just like selecting the Values Only Paste option as I describe in a previous section). When you paste values, Excel discards all formulas in the cell selection and retains only the calculated values — these values appear in the new cell range just as though you had entered them manually.

To paste particular parts of a cell selection while discarding others, choose Edit⇨Paste Special from the menu bar. When you choose Paste Special over the regular Paste command, Excel displays the Paste Special dialog box. Here you can specify which parts of the current cell selection to use by selecting the appropriate Paste Special radio button or check box as follows:

- ✔ **All** to paste all the stuff in the cell selection (formulas, formatting, you name it).

- ✔ **Formulas** to paste all the text, numbers, and formulas in the current cell selection without their formatting.

- ✔ **Values** to convert formulas in the current cell selection to their calculated values.

- ✔ **Formats** to paste only the formatting from the current cell selection, leaving the cell entries in the dust.

- ✔ **Comments** to paste only the notes that you attach to their cells (kinda like electronic self-stick notes — see Chapter 6 for details).

- ✔ **Validation** to paste only the data validation rules into the cell range that you set up with the Data⇨Validation command (which enables you to set what value or range of values is allowed in a particular cell or cell range).

- ✔ **All Except Borders** to paste all the stuff in the cell selection without copying any borders you use there.

- ✔ **Column Widths** to apply the column widths of the cells copied to the Clipboard to the columns where the cells are pasted.

- ✔ **Formulas and Number Formats** to include the number formats assigned to the pasted values and formulas.

- ✔ **Values and Number Formats** to convert formulas to their calculated values and include the number formats you assign to all the pasted values.

- ✔ **None** to have Excel perform no operation between the data entries you cut or copy to the Clipboard and the data entries in the cell range where you paste.

- ✔ **Add** to add the data you cut or copy to the Clipboard and the data entries in the cell range where you paste.

- ✔ **Subtract** to subtract the data you cut or copy to the Clipboard from the data entries in the cell range where you paste.

- ✔ **Multiply** to multiply the data you cut or copy to the Clipboard by the data entries in the cell range where you paste.

- ✔ **Divide** to divide the data you cut or copy to the Clipboard by the data entries in the cell range where you paste.

- ✔ **Skip Blanks** check box when you want Excel to paste everywhere except for any empty cells in the incoming range. In other words, a blank cell cannot overwrite your current cell entries.

- **Transpose** check box when you want Excel to change the orientation of the pasted entries. For example, if the original cells' entries run down the rows of a single column of the worksheet, the transposed pasted entries will run across the columns of a single row.

- **Paste Link** button when you're copying cell entries and you want to establish a link between copies you're pasting and the original entries. That way, changes to the original cells automatically update in the pasted copies.

You can alternatively select the Formulas, Values, No Borders. Transpose, and Paste Link paste options directly from the pop-up menu attached to the Paste button on the Standard toolbar without having to open the Paste Special dialog box. *Note:* The No Borders option (from the Paste button of the Standard toolbar) is the same as the All Except Borders option from the Paste Special dialog box. Simply click the drop-down button attached to the Paste button and select the desired option from its pop-up menu. You can also open the Paste Special dialog box from this pop-up menu by selecting the Paste Special item at the very bottom of the menu.

Let's Be Clear about Deleting Stuff

No discussion about editing in Excel would be complete without a section on getting rid of the stuff you put into cells. You can perform two kinds of deletions in a worksheet:

- **Clearing a cell:** Clearing just deletes or empties the cell's contents without removing the cell from the worksheet, which would alter the layout of the surrounding cells.

- **Deleting a cell:** Deleting gets rid of the whole kit and caboodle — cell structure along with all its contents and formatting. When you delete a cell, Excel has to shuffle the position of entries in the surrounding cells to plug up any gaps made by the demise.

Sounding the all clear!

To get rid of just the contents of a cell selection rather than delete the cells along with their contents, select the range of cells to be cleared and press Delete or choose Edit➪Clear➪Contents from the menu bar.

If you want to get rid of more than just the contents of a cell selection, choose Edit⇨Clear from the menu bar and then choose from among the submenu commands:

- ✔ **All:** Choose this to get rid of all formatting and notes, as well as entries in the cell selection.

- ✔ **Formats:** Choose this to delete only the formatting from the current cell selection without touching anything else.

- ✔ **Comments:** Choose this if you only want to remove the notes in the cell selection but leave everything else behind.

Get these cells outta here!

To delete the cell selection rather than just clear out its contents, select the cell range and choose Delete from the cell shortcut menu or Edit⇨Delete from the menu bar. Excel displays the Delete dialog box. You use the radio button options in this dialog box to indicate how Excel should shift the cells left behind to fill in the gaps when the cells currently selected are blotted out of existence:

- ✔ **Shift Cells Left:** Excel normally selects this radio button. This selection moves entries from neighboring columns on the right to the left to fill in gaps created when you delete the cell selection by clicking OK or pressing Enter.

- ✔ **Cells Up:** Select this to move entries up from neighboring rows below.

- ✔ **Entire Row:** Select this to remove all the rows in the current cell selection.

- ✔ **Entire Columns:** Select this to delete all the columns in the current cell selection.

If you know ahead of time that you want to delete an entire column or row from the worksheet, you can select the column or row on the workbook window frame and then choose Delete from the column or row shortcut menu or choose Edit⇨Delete from the menu. You can remove more than one column or row at a time provided that you select them before you choose this command.

Deleting entire columns and rows from a worksheet is risky business unless you are sure that the columns and rows in question contain nothing of value. Remember, when you delete an entire row from the worksheet, you delete *all information from column A through IV* in that row (and you can see only a very few columns in this row). Likewise, when you delete an entire column from the worksheet, you delete *all information from row 1 through 65,536* in that column.

Kindly Step Aside . . .

For those inevitable times when you need to squeeze new entries into an already populated region of the worksheet, you can insert new cells in the area rather than go through all the trouble of moving and rearranging several individual cell ranges. To insert a new cell range, select the cells (many of which are already occupied) where you want the new cells to appear and then choose Insert on the cell shortcut menu or the Insert⇨Cells command from the menu bar. Doing either of these displays the Insert dialog box with the following radio button options:

- ✔ **Shift Cells Right:** Select this to shift existing cells to the right to make room for the ones you want to add before clicking OK or pressing Enter.

- ✔ **Shift Cells Down:** Use this default to instruct the program to shift existing entries down instead before clicking OK or pressing Enter.

- ✔ **Entire Row** or **Entire Column:** As when you delete cells, when you insert cells with the Insert dialog box, you can insert complete rows or columns in the cell range by selecting either of these radio buttons. You can also select the row number or column letter on the frame before you choose the Insert command.

Note that you can also insert entire columns and rows in a worksheet by choosing the Columns or Rows command from the Insert menu without having to open the Insert dialog box.

Keep in mind that just like when you delete whole columns and rows inserting entire columns and rows affects the entire worksheet, not just the part you see. If you don't know what's out in the hinterlands of the worksheet, you can't be sure how the insertion will impact — perhaps even sabotage — stuff (especially formulas) in the other unseen areas. I suggest that you scroll all the way out in both directions to make sure that nothing's out there.

Stamping Out Your Spelling Errors

If you're as good a speller as I am, you'll be really relieved to learn that Excel 2003 has a built-in spell checker that can catch and get rid of all those embarrassing little spelling errors. With this in mind, you no longer have any excuse for putting out worksheets with typos in the titles or headings.

To check the spelling in a worksheet, choose Tools⇨Spelling from the menu bar or click the Spelling button (the one with a check mark under ABC) on the Standard toolbar or press F7.

Any way you do it, Excel begins checking the spelling of all text entries in the worksheet. When the program comes across an unknown word, it displays the Spelling dialog box, similar to the one shown in Figure 4-15.

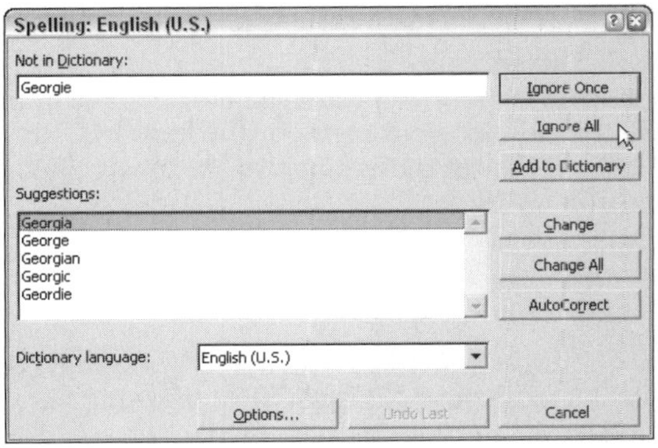

Figure 4-15: Check your spelling from the Spelling dialog box.

Excel suggests replacements for the unknown word shown in the Not in Dictionary text box with a likely replacement in the Suggestions list box of the Spelling dialog box. If that replacement is incorrect, you can scroll through the Suggestions list and click the correct replacement. Use the Spelling dialog box options as follows:

- **Ignore Once and Ignore All:** When Excel's spell check comes across a word its dictionary finds suspicious but you know is viable, click the Ignore Once button. If you don't want the spell checker to bother you querying you about this word again, click the Ignore All button.

- **Add to Dictionary:** Click this button to add the unknown (to Excel) word — such as your name — to a custom dictionary so that Excel won't flag it again when you check the spelling in the worksheet later on.

- **Change:** Click this button to replace the word listed in the Not in Dictionary text box with the word Excel offers in the Suggestions list box.

- **Change All:** Click this button to change all occurrences of this misspelled word in the worksheet to the word Excel displays in the Suggestions list box.

- **AutoCorrect:** Click this button to have Excel automatically correct this spelling error with the suggestion displayed in the Suggestions list box (by adding the misspelling and suggestion to the AutoCorrect dialog box; for more, read through Chapter 2).

- **Dictionary Language:** To switch to another dictionary (such as a United Kingdom English dictionary, or a French dictionary when checking French terms in a multilingual worksheet), click this drop-down button and then select the name of the desired language in the pop-up list.

Notice that the Excel spell checker not only flags words not found in its built-in or custom dictionary but also flags occurrences of double words in a cell entry (such as *total total*) and words with unusual capitalization (such as *NEw York* instead of *New York*). By default, the spell checker ignores all words with numbers and all Internet addresses. If you want it to ignore all words in uppercase letters as well, click the Options button at the bottom of the Spelling dialog box, and then select the Ignore Words in UPPERCASE check box before clicking OK.

Keep in mind that you can check the spelling of just a particular group of entries by selecting the cells before you choose Tools⇨Spelling from the menu bar, click the Spelling button on the Standard toolbar, or press F7.

Stamping Out Errors with Text to Speech

Excel is unique in the Office 2003 suite in its support of the Text to Speech feature, which enables you to have your computer read back any series of cell entries. This feature is perfect for when you need to check the accuracy of a bunch of numbers that you enter from a printed source. By using Text to Speech, you can check your printed source as the computer reads out loud the values and labels that you've actually entered. This new feature provides a real nifty way to catch and correct errors that may otherwise escape unnoticed.

To use the Text to Speech feature to corroborate spreadsheet entries and catch those hard-to-spot errors, follow these steps:

1. **Select the cells in the worksheet that you want to convert to speech.**

2. **Choose Tools⇨Speech⇨Show Text to Speech Toolbar from the Excel menu bar to display the Text to Speech toolbar (shown in Figure 4-16).**

3. **Click the Speak Cells button in the Text to Speech toolbar (the first button, with the arrow pointing right) to have the computer begin reading back the entries in the selected cells.**

   By default, the Text to Speech feature reads the contents of each cell in the current selection by first going across the rows and then down the columns. If you want Text to Speech to read down the columns and then across the rows, click the By Columns button on the toolbar (the fourth button, with the vertical arrow).

4. **To have the Text to Speech feature read back each cell entry as you press the Enter key (at which point the cell pointer moves down to the next cell in the selection), click the Speech on Enter button (the last button on the toolbar, with the curved arrow Enter symbol).**

   After selecting this option, you need to press Enter each time that you want to hear an entry read back to you.

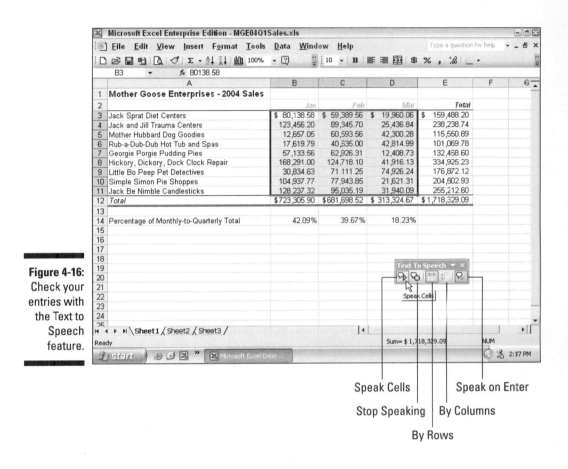

Figure 4-16:
Check your
entries with
the Text to
Speech
feature.

Speak Cells   Speak on Enter

Stop Speaking   By Columns

By Rows

5. **To pause the Text to Speech feature when you're not using the Speech on Enter option (Step 4) and you locate a discrepancy between what you're reading and what you're hearing, click the Stop Speaking button (the second button on the toolbar, with the x).**

6. **When you're finished checking all the entries in the current cell selection, click the Close box (the one with the X) in the upper-right corner of the Text to Speech toolbar to close it.**

Note that unlike when using Excel's Speech Recognition feature (which I outline in Chapter 2), the Text to Speech translation feature requires no prior training or special microphones. All that's required is a pair of speakers or headphones connected to your computer.

If you click the Speak on Enter button in the Text to Speech toolbar, the computer will speak each new cell entry that you make in a worksheet even after you close the Text to Speech toolbar. Just remember that you must complete the new cell entry by pressing the Enter key and not by some other method, such as clicking the Enter button on the formula bar or pressing the ↓ key in order to have the Text to Speech feature read what you just entered.

By default, the Text to Speech feature selects the voice called *LH Michelle* (the LH, by the way, stands for Lernout & Houspie the creators of this voice), a somewhat mechanical but definitely female voice that suggests to me a female version of Stephen Hawking's computer-generated voice (perhaps that of his girlfriend?). Stephen Hawking, in case you don't know, is one of the most renowned theoretical physicists of our age. (Some regard him on par with Einstein.) However, because of extreme physical disabilities, he's been forced to use a computer-generated voice in order to communicate his wonderful ideas about the origins of the universe (a mechanical voice, which in time I have come to identify as *his* voice).

If you wish, you can change the voice of the Text to Speech translation feature from LH Michelle (female) to LH Michael (male, which is, in fact, the voice that Stephen Hawking uses) or Microsoft Sam (which sounds to me about as mechanical as any voice could). To do this,

1. **Choose Start⇨Control Panel from the taskbar.**

   The Control Panel window opens in Category view.

2. **From Control Panel, click the Sounds, Speech, and Audio Devices link, and then click the Speech link in the Sounds, Speech, and Audio Devices window.**

   The Speech Properties dialog box opens.

3. **From the Speech Properties dialog box, click the Text to Speech tab.**

   Make your voice selection in this tab. Click the Voice Selection drop-down button and choose LH Michael or Microsoft Sam from the pop-up menu.

4. **To slow down or speed up the speed of this voice, drag the Voice Speed slider left (to slow the voice down) or right (to speed it up).**

   To check the speed of the voice you choose, click the Preview Voice button, located immediately above the Voice Speed slider. Excel plays you a sample voice at the speed you set.

5. **When you're happy with the voice speed, click OK to close the Speech Properties dialog box.**

6. **Click the X in the upper-right corner of the Sounds, Speech, and Audio Devices window to return to Excel.**

Chapter 5

Printing the Masterpiece

• •

• •

*F*or most people, getting the data down on paper is really what spread-sheets are all about (all the talk about a so-called paperless office to the contrary). Everything — all the data entry, all the formatting, all the formula checking, all the things you do to get a spreadsheet ready — is really just preparation for printing its information.

In this chapter, you find out just how easy it is to print reports with Excel 2003. And you discover that by following just a few simple guidelines, you can produce top-notch reports the first time you send the document to the printer (instead of the second or even the third time around).

The only trick to printing a worksheet is getting used to the paging scheme and learning how to control it. Many of the worksheets you create with Excel are not only longer than one printed page but also wider. Word processors, such as Word 2003, page the document only vertically they won't let you create a document wider than the page size you're using. Spreadsheet programs like Excel 2003, however, often have to break up pages both vertically and horizontally to print a worksheet document (a kind of tiling of the print job, if you will).

When breaking a worksheet into pages, Excel first pages the document vertically down the rows in the first columns of the print area (just like a word processor). After paging the first columns, the program pages down the rows of the second set of columns in the print area. Excel pages down and then over until all the document included in the print area (which can include the entire worksheet or just sections) is paged.

When paging the worksheet, keep in mind that Excel does not break up the information within a row or column. If all the information in a row won't fit at the bottom of the page, the program moves the entire row to the following page. If all the information in a column won't fit at the right edge of the page, the program moves the entire column to a new page. (Because Excel pages down and then over, the column may not appear on the next page of the report.)

You can deal with such paging problems in several ways — and, in this chapter, you see all of them! After you have these page problems under control, printing is a proverbial piece of cake.

Starting the Show with Print Preview

Save wasted paper and your sanity by using the Print Preview feature before you print any worksheet, section of worksheet, or entire workbook. Because of the peculiarities in paging worksheet data, check the page breaks for any report that requires more than one page. Use the Print Preview mode to not only see exactly how the worksheet data will be paged when printed but also to modify the margins, change the page settings, and then print the report when everything looks okay.

To switch to Print Preview mode, click the Print Preview button on the Standard toolbar (the one with the magnifying glass on the page, next to the Print button) or choose File⇨Print Preview from the menu bar. Excel displays all the information on the first page of the report in a separate window with its own toolbar. When positioned over the spreadsheet, the mouse pointer becomes a magnifying glass. Look at Figure 5-1 to see a Print Preview window with the first page of a four-page report.

When Excel displays a full page in the Print Preview window, you can barely read its contents; increase the view to actual size if you need to verify some of the information. Zoom up to 100 percent by clicking the previewed page with the magnifying-glass mouse pointer or the Zoom button at the top of the Print Preview window, or by pressing the Enter key. Check out the difference in Figure 5-2 — here you can see what the first page of the three-page report looks like after I zoom in by clicking the Zoom pointer (with the magnifying-glass icon) on the top central portion of the page.

After you enlarge a page to actual size, use the scroll bars to bring new parts of the page into view in the Print Preview window. If you prefer to use the keyboard, press the ↑ and ↓ keys or PgUp and PgDn to scroll up or down the page, respectively; press ← and → or Ctrl+PgUp and Ctrl+PgDn to scroll left and right, respectively.

To return to the full-page view, click the mouse pointer (in its arrowhead form) anywhere on the page or click the Zoom button on the Print Preview toolbar a second time or press the Enter key again.

Excel indicates the number of pages in a report on the status bar of the Print Preview window (at the far-left bottom of your Excel screen). If your report has more than one page, view pages that follow the one you're previewing by clicking the Next command button at the far-left top of the window. To review a page you've already seen, back up a page by clicking the Previous button. (The Previous button is grayed out if you're on the first page.) You can also advance to the next page by pressing the PgDn or ↓ key or move back to the previous page by pressing the PgUp or ↑ key when the page view is full-page rather than actual size.

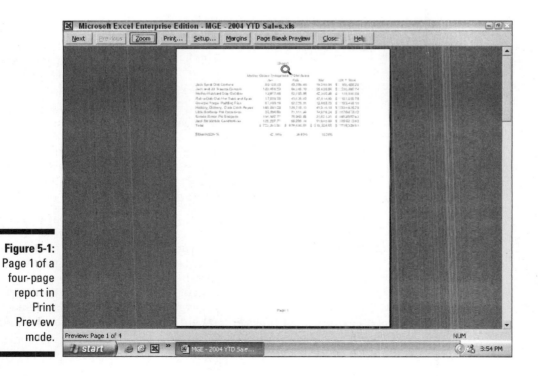

Figure 5-1:
Page 1 of a
four-page
report in
Print
Preview
mode.

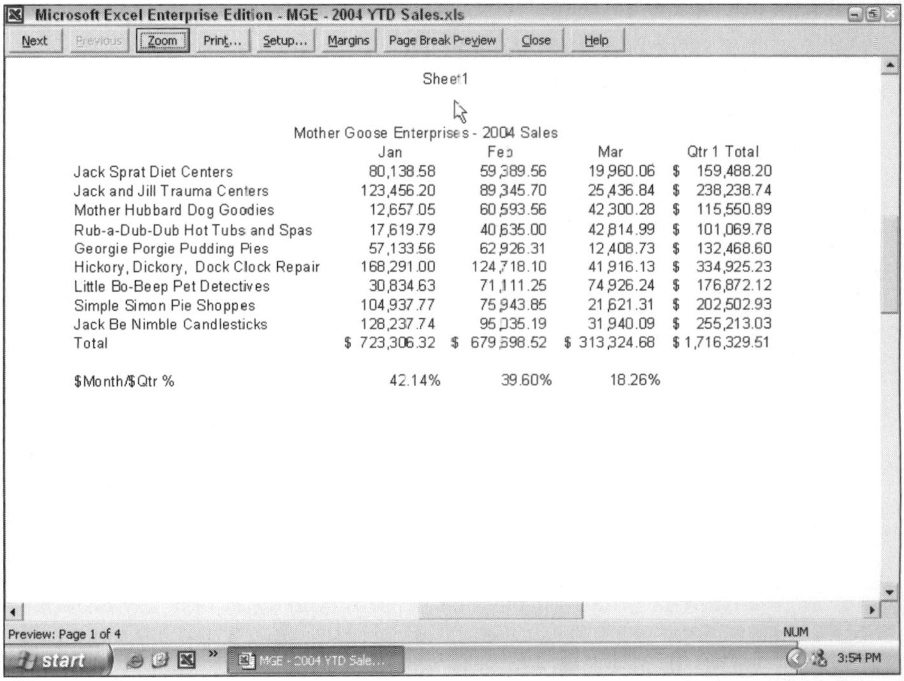

Figure 5-2:
Page 1 of a
four-page
report after
clicking the
top of the
page with
the Zoom
tool.

When you finish previewing the report, you have the following options:

- **Ready to print:** If the pages look okay, click the Print button to display the Print dialog box and print the report from there. (See the section "Printing it your way," later in this chapter.)

- **Page set-up problems:** If you notice some paging problems that you can solve by choosing a new paper size, page order, orientation, or margins, or if you notice a problem with the header or footer (the text you enter in the top or bottom margin of the pages), you can click the Setup button and take care of these problems in the Page Setup dialog box. For more on what printing parameters you can set here, see the upcoming section "My Page Was Set Up!" later in this chapter.

- **Page break problems:** If you notice some paging problems that you can solve by modifying the page breaks, click the Page Break Preview button. This takes you back to the workbook window with a reduced view of the worksheet where you can change the page breaks by dragging the borders with the mouse. After you adjust the borders the way you want them, return to Normal view by choosing View⇨Normal from the Excel menu bar. You can then print the report by choosing File⇨Print from the menu bar or by clicking the Print button on the Standard toolbar. For more details, jump down to the upcoming section "When Ya Gonna Give Your Page a Break?"

- **Margin and column width problems:** If you notice some problems with the margins or with the column widths and you want to adjust them in Print Preview mode, click the Margins button and drag the margin markers that appear into place. (See "Massaging the margins," later in this chapter, for details.)

- **Corrections required:** If you notice any other kind of problem, such as a typo in a heading or a wrong value in a cell, click the Close button to return to the Normal worksheet document window; you cannot make any text-editing changes in the Print Preview window.

- **Corrected and ready to print:** After you make corrections to the worksheet, you can print the report from the Normal document view window by choosing File⇨Print from the menu bar (or pressing Ctrl+P). Alternatively, you can switch back to Print Preview mode to make a last-minute check and click the Print button, or use the Print button on the Standard toolbar (fourth from the left with the printer icon on it).

The Page Stops Here . . .

Excel automatically displays the page breaks in the normal document window after you preview the document. Page breaks appear on-screen as dotted lines between the columns and rows that will print out on different pages.

To get rid of page breaks in the document window, choose Tools⇨Options from the menu bar, choose the View tab, deselect the Page breaks check box (to clear the check mark), and click OK or press Enter.

Printing it right away

As long as you want to use Excel's default print settings to print all the cells in the current worksheet, printing in Excel 2003 is a breeze. Simply click the Print button on the Standard toolbar (the tool with the printer icon). The program then prints one copy of all the information in the current worksheet, including any charts and graphics — but not including comments you add to cells. (See Chapter 6 for details about adding comments to your worksheet and Chapter 8 for details about charts and graphics.)

After you click the Print tool, Excel routes the print job to the Windows print queue, which acts like a middleman to send the job to the printer. While

Excel sends the print job to the print queue, Excel displays a Printing dialog box to inform of its progress (displaying such updates as *Printing Page 2 of 3*). After this dialog box disappears, you are free to go back to work in Excel. (Be aware, however, that Excel will probably move like a slug until the job is actually printed.) To abort the print job while it's being sent to the print queue, click the Cancel button in the Printing dialog box.

If you don't realize that you want to cancel the print job until after Excel finishes shipping it to the print queue (that is, while the Printing dialog box appears on-screen), you must open the dialog box for your printer and cancel printing from there.

To cancel a print job from the printer dialog box, follow these steps:

1. **Click the printer icon in the System tray at the far right of the Windows XP taskbar (to the immediate left of the current time) with the secondary mouse button to open its shortcut menu.**

   This printer icon displays the screen tip 1 document(s) pending for *so-and-so*. For example, when I'm printing, this message reads 1 document(s) pending for Greg when I position the mouse pointer over the printer icon.

2. **Right-click the printer icon and then select the Open Active Printers command from its shortcut menu.**

   This opens the dialog box for the printer with the Excel print job in its queue (as described under the Document heading in the list box).

3. **Select the Excel print job that you want to cancel in the list box of your printer's dialog box.**

4. **Choose Document⇨Cancel Printing from the menu bar.**

5. **Wait for the print job to disappear from the queue in the printer's dialog box and then click the Close button to get rid of it and return to Excel.**

Printing it your way

Printing with the Print tool on the Standard toolbar is fine provided that all you want is a single copy of all the information in the current worksheet. If you want more copies, more or less data (such as all the worksheets in the workbook or just a cell selection within a particular worksheet), or you need to change some of the page settings (such as the size of the page or the orientation of the printing on the page), then you need to print from the Print dialog box (shown in Figure 5-3).

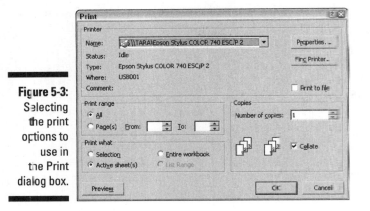

Figure 5-3:
Selecting the print options to use in the Print dialog box.

Excel provides a number of ways to open the Print dialog box

- ✔ Press Ctrl+P.
- ✔ Choose the File➪Print command from the menu bar.
- ✔ Press Ctrl+Shift+F12.

Printing in particular

Within the Print dialog box are the Print Range and Print What areas (from which you can select how much of the information is printed), and the Copies area, from which you can change the number of copies printed. Here's what's in these areas and how you use their options:

- ✔ **All:** When the All radio button is selected, all the pages in your document will print. Because this is the default choice, you would only need to select it if you previously printed a portion of the document by selecting the Page(s) radio button.

- ✔ **Page(s):** Normally, Excel prints all the pages required to produce the information in the areas of the workbook that you want printed. Sometimes, however, you may need to reprint only a page or range of pages that you've modified within this section. To reprint a single page, enter its page number in both the From and To text boxes here or select these page numbers with the spinner buttons. To reprint a range of pages, put the first page number in the From text box and the last page number in the To text box. Excel automatically deselects the All radio button and selects the Page(s) radio button in the Page Range section as soon as you start typing in the From or To text boxes.

- ✔ **Selection:** Select this radio button to have Excel print just the cells that are currently selected in your workbook. (Yes, you must remember to select these cells before opening the Print dialog box and choosing this radio button!)

✔ **Active Sheet(s):** Excel automatically displays and selects this radio button and prints all the information in whatever worksheets are active in your workbook. Normally, this means printing just the data in the current worksheet. To print other worksheets in the workbook when this radio button is selected, hold down Ctrl while you click the sheet's tab. To include all the sheets between two sheet tabs, click the first one and then hold Shift while you click the second tab (Excel selects all the tabs in between).

✔ **Entire Workbook:** Select this radio button to have Excel print all the data in each of the worksheets in your workbook.

✔ **List Range:** If you use Excel to prepare data lists for a SharePoint Team Services (STS) Web site (a special Web site set up for easily sharing different types of documents and information), you can click this radio button to print just the list range on the current worksheet. (See Chapter 9 for more about maintaining list ranges in Excel for STS Web sites.)

✔ **Number of Copies:** To print more than one copy of the report, enter the number of copies you want to print in the Number of Copies text box in the Copies section — or use the spinner buttons to select the required number.

✔ **Collate:** When you collate pages, you simply make separate stacks of each complete report, rather than print all copies of page one, and then all copies of page two, and so on. To have Excel collate each copy of the report for you, select the Collate check box in the Copies section to put a check mark in it.

After you finish choosing new print options, you can send the job to the printer by clicking OK or pressing Enter. To use another printer that's been installed for Windows (Excel lists the current printer in the Name text box and all printers installed for Windows on the Name pop-up list), select the new printer on the Name pop-up menu in the Printer section at the top of the dialog box before you start printing.

Setting and clearing the Print Area

Excel includes a special printing feature called the *Print Area*. You can use the File➪Print Area➪Set Print Area command from the Excel menu to define any cell selection on a worksheet as the Print Area. After you define the Print Area, Excel then prints this cell selection anytime you print the worksheet (either with the Print button on the Standard toolbar or from the Print dialog box or by using the File➪Print command or one of its shortcuts). Whenever you fool with the Print Area, you need to keep in mind that once you define it, its cell range is the only one you can print (regardless of what options you select in the Print dialog box) until you clear the Print Area.

To clear the Print Area (and therefore go back to the printing defaults Excel establishes in the Print dialog box — see the preceding section, "Printing in particular," for details — you just have to select File⇨Print Area⇨Clear Print Area from the menu bar.

You can also define and clear the Print Area from the Sheet tab of the Page Setup dialog box (see the next section "My Page Was Set Up!"). To define the Print Area from this dialog box, insert the cursor in the Print Area text box on the Sheet tab and then select the cell range or ranges in the worksheet (remembering that you can reduce the Page Setup dialog box to just this text box by clicking its minimize box). To clear the Print Area from this dialog box, select the cell addresses in the Print Area text box and press the Delete key.

My Page Was Set Up!

About the only thing the slightest bit complex in printing a worksheet is figuring out how to get the pages right. Fortunately, the options in the Page Setup dialog box give you a great deal of control over what goes on which page. To open the Page Setup dialog box, choose File⇨Page Setup from the menu bar or click the Setup button if the Print Preview window is open. The Page Setup dialog box contains four tabs: Page, Margins, Header/Footer, and Sheet.

The particular options Excel offers in the Page tab of the Page Setup dialog box may vary slightly with the type of printer you use. The settings in Figure 5-4 reflect the Page Setup dialog box when a laser printer (such as an Apple LaserWriter or HP LaserJet printer) is the current printer.

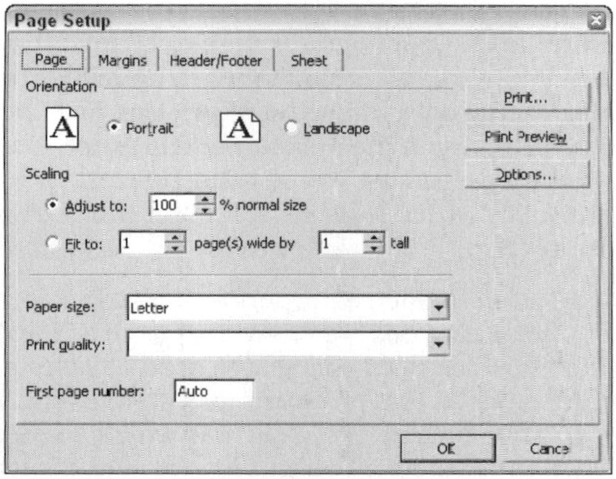

Figure 5-4:
Select print options to apply in the Page Setup dialog box.

For most types of printers, the Page tab of the Page Setup dialog box includes options for changing the orientation, scaling the printing, and choosing paper size and print quality:

✔ **Orientation:** Select the Portrait radio button to position the paper so that the short side is on the top and bottom. Select the Landscape radio button to position the printing with the long side of the paper on top and bottom. (See the upcoming section "Getting the lay of the landscape.")

✔ **Scaling:** In this section of the Page tab are options to enlarge or reduce the printed size of your original or to fit your preset number of workbook pages on the number of printed pages you want.

  • **Adjust To:** Select this radio button to increase or decrease the size of the print by a set percentage (much like using the Zoom feature to zoom in and out on worksheet data on-screen). Setting this option to 100 percent represents normal size; any percentage lower than that reduces the size of the print (and puts more on each page), whereas any percentage above 100 increases the size of the print (and puts less on each page).

  • **Fit To:** Select this radio button to fit all the printing on a single page (by default) or on a set number of pages wide by a set number of pages tall. (See the section "Packing it all on one page" later in this chapter.)

✔ **Paper Size:** Switch to a new paper size from selections in the drop-down list box. This list contains only those paper sizes that your printer can accommodate.

✔ **Print Quality:** Some printers (like dot-matrix printers) let you change the quality of the printing, depending upon whether you're producing a first rough draft or a final printout. Make your selection from the drop-down list here.

✔ **First Page Number:** Choose from options here to change the starting page number when you want the first number to be higher than 1. You use this numbering option only when you're printing page numbers in the header or footer. Excel sets the default here as Auto, which prints the number 1 on page 1 (assuming you're using headers or footers). To change this default, click within this box and enter the starting page you want. (See the section "From header to footer," later in this chapter.)

✔ **Options:** Click this button to open a Properties dialog box for the specific printer you select. This dialog box may have tabs such as Paper, Graphics, Device Options, and PostScript (the language used by laser printers), depending upon the model and type of printer you're using. The options on these tabs let you fine-tune settings, such as which paper tray to use, the graphics quality, the PostScript output format, and the like.

Getting the lay of the landscape

For many printers (including most of the dot-matrix, laser, or ink-jet persuasion), the Page tab of the Page Setup dialog box includes an Orientation section for changing the printing from the more normal Portrait format (the printing runs parallel to the short edge of the paper) to Landscape (the printing runs parallel to the long edge of the paper). With these types of printers, you can usually use the Adjust To or Fit To options (see the upcoming section "Packing it all on one page") to scale the size of the printing, making it possible to enlarge or reduce the printing by a particular percentage or to force all the information on a single page or a set number of pages.

Many worksheets are far wider than they are tall (such as budgets or sales tables that track expenditures over all 12 months). If your printer supports changing the orientation of the page, you may find that such worksheets look better if you switch the orientation from the normal portrait mode (which accommodates fewer columns on a page because the printing runs parallel to the short edge of the page) to landscape mode.

In Figure 5-5, you can see the Print Preview window with the first page of a report in landscape mode. For this report, Excel can fit three more columns of information on this page in landscape mode than it can in portrait mode. However, because this page orientation accommodates fewer rows the total page count for this report increases from two pages in portrait mode to four pages in landscape mode.

Packing it all on one page

If your printer supports scaling options, you're in luck. You can always get a worksheet to fit on a single page simply by selecting the Fit To radio button in the Page Setup dialog box. When you select this radio button, Excel figures out how much to reduce the size of the information you're printing to fit it all on one page.

If you preview this one page and find that the printing is just too small to read comfortably, reopen the Page tab of the Page Setup dialog box (choose File⇨Page Setup) and try changing the number of pages in the Page(s) Wide By and Tall text boxes (to the immediate right of the Fit To radio button).

For example, instead of trying to stuff everything on one page, check out how your worksheet looks if you fit it on two pages across. Try this: Enter **2** in the Page(s) Wide By text box and leave the 1 in the pages Tall text box. Alternatively, see how the worksheet looks on two pages down: Leave the 1 in the Page(s) Wide By text box and enter **2** in the pages Tall text box.

Figure 5-5:
A landscape
mode report
in Print
Preview.

Little Bo-Peep Pet Detectives - Client List

Case No	Last Name	First Name	Street	City	State	Zip	Status	Hours	Rate	Total Due
101-920	Harvey	Scott	12 Elm Street	Scholar	MN	58764	Active	250	75.00	$18,750
101-014	Andersen	Hans	341 The Shadow	Scholar	MN	58764	Closed	175	75.00	$13,125
103-023	Appleseed	Johnny	6789 Fruitree Tr	Along The Way	SD	66017	Active	321	125.00	$40,125
102-013	Baggins	Bingo	99 Hobbithole	Shire	ME	04047	Active	100	125.00	$12,500
103-007	Baum	L. Frank	447 Toto Too Rd	Oz	KS	65432	Closed	421	125.00	$52,625
104-026	Brown	Charles	59 Flat Plains	Saltewater	UT	84001	Active	575	125.00	$71,875
101-001	Bryant	Michael	326 Chef's Lane	Paris	TX	78705	Active	600	100.00	$60,000
101-028	Cassidy	Butch	Sundance Kidde	Hole In Wall	CO	80477	Closed	345.5	75.00	$25,913
102-006	Cinderella	Poore	8 Lucky Maiden Way	Oxford	TN	07557	Closed	800	75.00	$60,000
103-004	Cupid	Eros	97 Mount Olympus	Greece	CT	03331	Active	123.5	75.00	$3,263
103-022	Dragon	Kai	2 Pleistocene Era	Ann's World	ID	00001	Active	450.2	75.00	$33,765
104-031	Eaters	Big	444 Big Pigs Court	Dogtown	AZ	85257	Closed	780	125.00	$97,500
106-022	Foliage	Red	49 Maple Syrup	Waffle	VT	05452	Active	205	125.00	$25,625
102-020	Franklin	Ben	1789 Constitution	Jefferson	WV	20178	Active	113.5	125.00	$14,213
104-019	Fudde	Elmer	8 Warner Way	Hollywood	CA	33461	Active	463.5	125.00	$57,938
102-002	Gearing	Shane	1 Gunfighter's End	LaLa Land	CA	90069	Active	902.5	125.00	$112,813
102-012	Gondor	Aragorn	2956 Gandalf	Midearth	WY	80342	Closed	157	125.00	$19,625
104-005	Gookin	Polly	4 Feathertop Hill	Hawthorne	MA	01824	Active	169.5	125.00	$21,188
105-008	Harvey	Chauncey	60 Lucky Starr Pl	Shetland	IL	60080	Active	226.5	125.00	$28,313
106-021	Horse	Seabisquit	First Place Finish	Raceway	KY	23986	Active	300	125.00	$37,500
101-015	Humperdinck	Engelbert	6 Hansel+Gretel Tr	Gingerbread	MD	20815	Active	705.5	125.00	$88,188
103-017	Jacken	Jill	Up the Hill	Pail of Water	OK	45678	Closed	200	75.00	$15,000
105-027	Laurel	Stan	2 Oliver Hardy	Celluloyde	NM	82128	Closed	352	125.00	$44,000
101-030	Liberty	Statuesque	31 Gotham Centre	Big Apple	NY	10011	Active	236.5	125.00	$29,563
103-016	Oakenshield	Rex	Mines of Goblins	Everest	NJ	07539	Closed	401	125.00	$50,000
103-024	Oakley	Anney	Six Shooter Path	Target	ND	68540	Active	502.5	125.00	$62,813
101-029	Oow	Lu	888 Sandy Beach	Honolulu	HI	98909	Active	732	125.00	$91,500
104-018	Ridinghoode	Crimson	232 Cottage Path	Wulfen	PA	15201	Active	125.5	125.00	$15,688
106-009	Sunnybrook	Rebecca	21 Last Week	Portland	OR	97210	Closed	245	75.00	$18,375

Preview: Page 1 of 4

After using the Fit To option, you may find that you don't want to scale the printing. Cancel scaling by selecting the Adjust To radio button right above the Fit To button and enter **100** in the % Normal Size text box (or select 100 with its spinner buttons).

Massaging the margins

Excel uses a standard top and bottom margin of 1 inch on each page of the report and a standard left and right margin of ¾ inch.

Frequently, you find yourself with a report that takes up a full printed page and then just enough also to spill over onto a second, mostly empty, second page. To squeeze the last column or the last few rows of the worksheet data onto page 1, adjust the margins for the report. To get more columns on a page, try reducing the left and right margins. To get more rows on a page, try reducing the top and bottom margins.

You can change the margins in two ways:

✔ Open the Page Setup dialog box (either by choosing File➪Page Setup from the menu bar or by clicking the Setup button in the Print Preview window) and then select the Margins tab (see Figure 5-6) and enter the new settings in the Top, Bottom, Left, and Right text boxes — or select the new margin settings with their respective spinner buttons.

✔ Open the Print Preview window, click the Margins button, and drag the margin markers to their new positions (see Figure 5-7).

Select one or both Center on Page options in the Margins tab of the Page Setup dialog box (refer to Figure 5-6) to center a selection of data (that takes up less than a full page) between the current margin settings. Select the Horizontally check box to center the data between the left and right margins. Select the Vertically check box to center the data between the top and bottom margins.

If you use the Margins button in the Print Preview window to change the margin settings, you can modify the column widths as well as the margins. (Refer to Figure 5-7.) To change one of the margins, position the mouse pointer on the desired margin marker (the pointer shape changes to a double-headed arrow) and drag the marker with your mouse in the appropriate direction. When you release the mouse button, Excel redraws the page, using the new margin setting. You may gain or lose columns or rows, depending on what kind of adjustment you make. Changing the column widths is the same story: Drag the column marker to the left or right to decrease or increase the width of a particular column.

From header to footer

Headers and footers are simply standard text that appears on every page of the report. A header prints in the top margin of the page, and a footer prints — you guessed it — in the bottom margin. Both are centered vertically in the margins. Unless you specify otherwise, Excel does not automatically add either a header or footer to a new workbook.

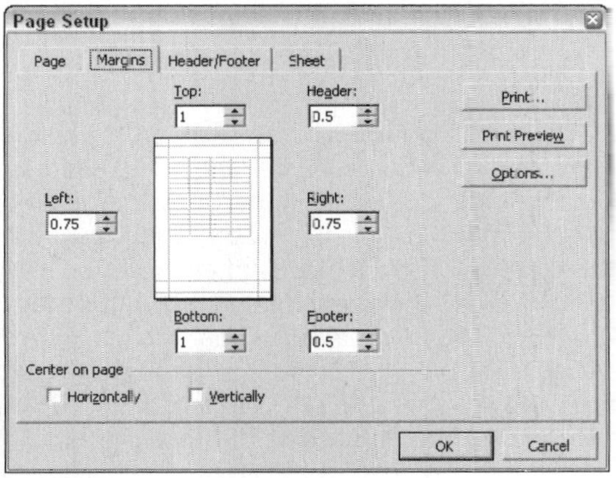

Figure 5-6:
Adjust your report margins from the Margins tab in the Page Setup dialog box.

Header margin marker

Top margin marker

Left margin marker   Column markers   Right margin marker

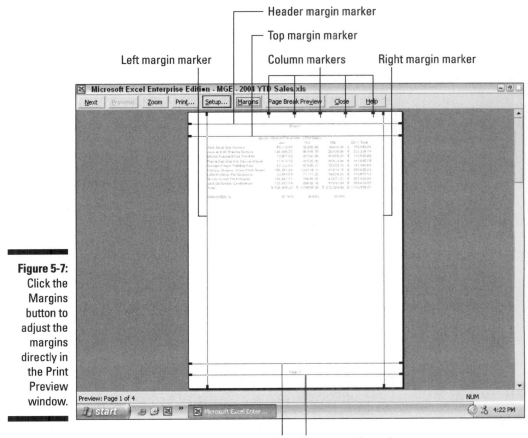

Bottom margin marker   Footer margin marker

Figure 5-7:
Click the
Margins
button to
adjust the
margins
directly in
the Print
Preview
window.

Use headers and footers in a report to identify the document used to produce the report and display the page numbers and the date and time of printing.

Getting a standard job

To add a header and/or footer to your workbook, open the Header/Footer tab in the Page Setup dialog box (choose File⇨Page Setup) and specify your header and footer information in the Header and/or Footer drop-down list boxes (see Figure 5-8). Both the Header and Footer drop-down list boxes in this tab contain a wide number of stock pieces of information for your header and footer, including the name of the worksheet (picked up from the sheet tab — see Chapter 6 to learn how to rename a sheet tab), who prepared the worksheet (picked up from the User Name option in the General tab of the Options dialog box), the page number, the current date, the name of the workbook document, or various combinations of these pieces of information.

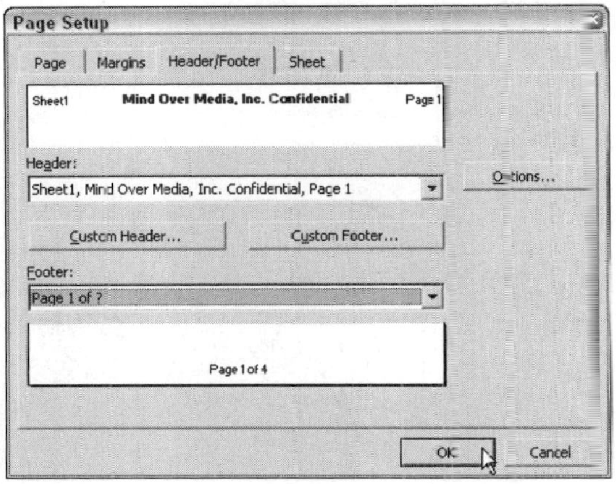

Figure 5-8:
The Header/
Footer tab of
the Page
Setup dialog
box with
a stock
header
and footer.

Look at Figure 5-8 to see the Header/Footer tab of the Page Setup dialog box
after I chose

```
Sheet1, Mind Over Media, Inc. Confidential, Page 1
```

in the Header drop-down list box. Sheet1 is the name of the worksheet; Mind
Over Media, Inc. is the company to which Excel is registered (this name is the
same as the one listed as the registered user in the About Microsoft Excel
dialog box); and Page 1 is, of course, the current page number).

To set up the footer, I chose

```
Page 1 of ?
```

in the Footer drop-down list box (which puts in the current page number,
along with the total number of pages, in the report). You can select this
paging option in either the Header or Footer drop-down list boxes.

Check out the results in Figure 5-9, which is the first page of the report in
Print Preview mode. Here you can see the header and footer as they will
print. (Fortunately, you can verify in the Print Preview window that the
header information won't all print on top of each other as it appears in the
header preview area in the Page Setup dialog box.) You can also see how
choosing Page 1 of ? works in the footer: On the first page, you see the centered footer: Page 1 of 4; on the second page, you would see the centered
footer Page 2 of 4.

If, after selecting some stock header or footer info, you decide that you no
longer need either the header or footer printed in your report, you simply
open the Header/Footer tab in the Page Setup dialog box and then select the
(none) option at the very top of the Header and Footer drop-down list boxes.

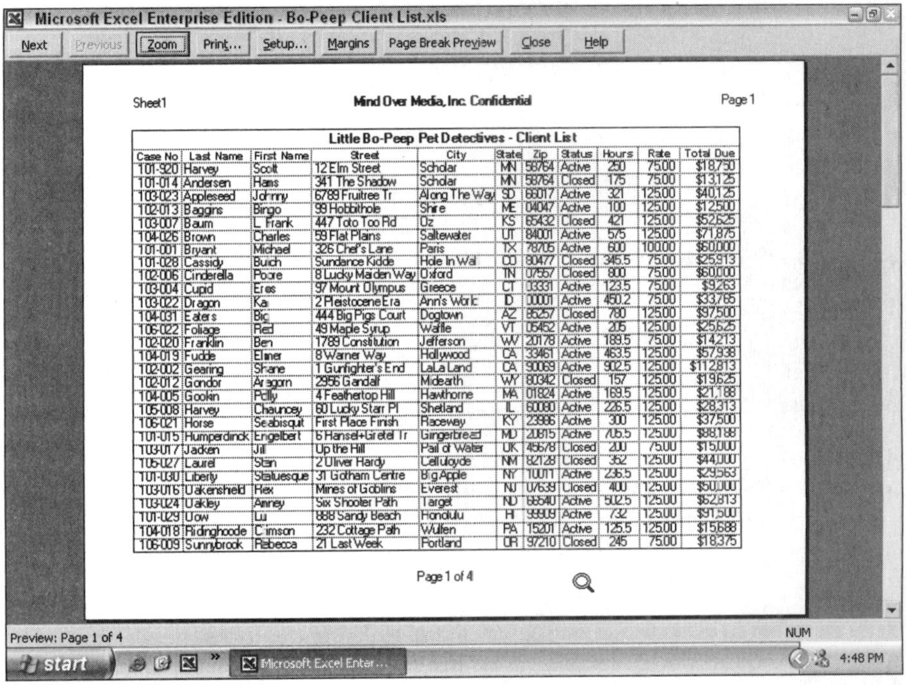

Figure 5-9:
The first page of a report preview shows you how the header and footer will print.

Setting a custom header or footer

Most of the time, the stock headers and footers available in the Header and Footer drop-down list boxes are sufficient for your report printing needs. Every once in a while, however, you may want to insert information not available in these list boxes or in an arrangement Excel doesn't offer in the stock headers and footers.

For those times, you need to turn to the Custom Header and Custom Footer buttons in the Header/Footer tab of the Page Setup dialog box and go about creating your header or footer by inserting your own information.

When you click the Custom Header button after selecting the stock header (refer to Figure 5-8), the Header dialog box appears (shown in Figure 5-10).

Notice that in the custom Header dialog box, the header is divided into three sections: Left Section, Center Section, and Right section. All header text you enter in the Left Section of this dialog box is justified (aligned) with the left margin of the report. All header text you enter in the Center Section box is centered between the left and right margins. And (you guessed it) all text you enter in the Right Section box is justified with the right margin of the report.

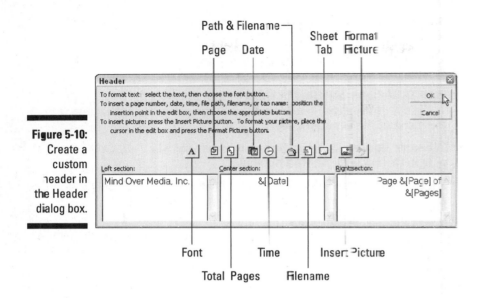

Figure 5-10:
Create a
custom
header in
the Header
dialog box.

Use the Tab key to advance from section to section in the header and to select the contents of that section, or you can press Alt plus the mnemonic letter (Alt+L for the Left Section, Alt+C for the Center Section, and Alt+R for the Right Section). If you want to break the header text in one of the sections, press Enter at the point in the header text where you want to start a new line. To clear the contents of a section, select the items and press Delete.

As you can see in Figure 5-10, Excel puts some pretty weird codes with lots of ampersands (&[Date] and Page &[Page]) in the center and right sections of this stock header. When creating a custom header (or footer), you, too, can mix weird ampersand codes with the standard text (such as *For Your Eyes Only,* for example). To insert the weird ampersand codes in a section of the header (or footer), you click the appropriate button:

- **Page button:** Click this button to insert the &[Page] code that puts in the current page number.

- **Total page button:** Click this button to insert the &[Pages] code that puts in the total number of pages. For example, to have Excel display the Page 1 of 4 kind of format:

    1. Type the word Page **and press the spacebar.**

    2. Click the Page button and press the spacebar again.

    3. Type the word of **and press the spacebar a third time.**

    This inserts Page &[Page] of &[Pages] in the custom header (or footer).

 ✔ **Date button:** Click this button to insert the &[Date] code that puts in the current date.

 ✔ **Time button:** Click this button to insert the &[Time] code that puts in the current time.

 ✔ **Path & Filename button:** Click this button to insert the &[Path]&[Filename] codes that put in the directory path along with the name of the workbook file.

 ✔ **Filename button:** Click this button to insert the &[Filename] code that puts in the name of the workbook file.

 ✔ **Sheet Tab button:** Click this button to insert the &[Tab] code that puts in the name of the worksheet as shown on the sheet tab.

 ✔ **Insert Picture button:** Click this button to insert the &[Picture] code that inserts the image that you select from the Insert Picture dialog box (that shows the contents of the My Pictures folder on your computer by default).

 ✔ **Format Picture button:** Click this button to apply the formatting that you choose from the Format Picture dialog box to the &[Picture] code that you enter with the Insert Picture button without adding any code of its own.

In addition to inserting ampersand codes in the custom header (or footer), you can select a new font, font size, or font attribute for any of its sections by clicking the Font button in the Header dialog box. When you click the Font button, Excel opens the Font dialog box from which you can select a new font, font style, font size, or special effects (such as ~~strikethrough~~, ^{superscript}, or $_{subsubscript}$).

When you've finished creating your custom header (or footer), click OK to close the Header (or Footer) dialog box and return to the Header/Footer tab of the Page Setup dialog box (where you can see the fruits of your labor in the sample boxes).

Sorting out the sheet settings

The Sheet tab of the Page Setup dialog box (similar to the one shown in Figure 5-11) contains a variety of printing options that may come in handy from time to time:

 ✔ **Print Area:** This text box shows you the cell range of the current print area that you selected with the File➪Print Area➪Set Print Area command from the menu bar. Use this text box to make changes to the range of cells that you want to print. To change the print area range, select this text box, and then drag through the cell range in the worksheet or type in the cell references or range names (details appear in Chapter 6). Separate individual cell ranges with a comma (as in A1:G72, K50:M75) when designating nonadjacent areas. If necessary, when you select the cell range, reduce the Page Setup dialog box to just the Print area text box by clicking its Collapse/Expand dialog button.

Use the Print Area option when your workbook contains a section that you routinely need to print so that you don't have to keep selecting the range and then selecting the Selection radio button in the Print dialog box every blasted time you print it.

✓ **Print titles:** Use this section of the Sheet tab to set how rows and columns repeat.

Rows to Repeat at Top: Use this option to designate rows of a worksheet as print titles to be printed across the top of each page of the report (see the upcoming section "Putting out the print titles"). Select this text box and then drag down the rows or enter the row references (such as 2:3). If necessary, when selecting the rows to use as print titles, reduce the Page Setup dialog box to just the Rows to Repeat at Top text box by clicking its Collapse/Expand dialog button.

• **Columns to Repeat at Left:** Use this option to designate columns of a worksheet as print titles to be printed at the left edge of each page of the report. (See the upcoming section "Putting out the print titles.") Select this text box and then drag across the columns or enter the column references (such as A:E). If necessary, when selecting the columns to use as print titles, reduce the Page Setup dialog box to just the Columns to repeat at left text box by clicking its Collapse/Expand dialog button.

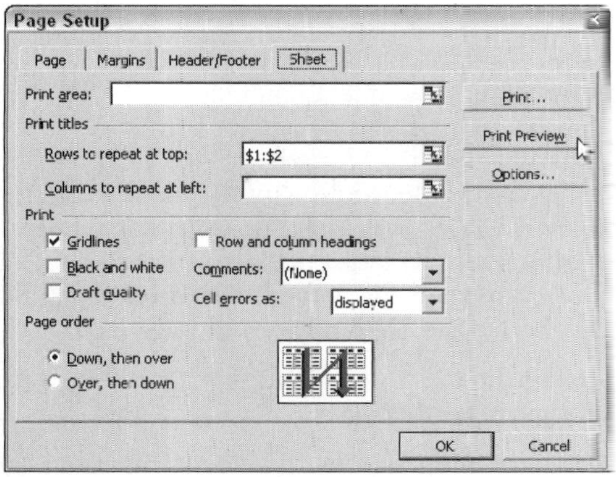

Figure 5-11:
Set a report's print titles in the Sheet tab of the Page Setup dialog box.

Page Setup

Page | Margins | Header/Footer | Sheet

Print area: [＿＿＿＿＿＿＿＿＿＿＿＿] 🔲   Print...

Print titles

Rows to repeat at top: [$1:$2] 🔲   Print Preview

Columns to repeat at left: [＿＿＿＿＿＿＿＿] 🔲   Options...

Print

☑ Gridlines   ☐ Row and column headings

☐ Black and white   Comments: [(None) ▼]

☐ Draft quality   Cell errors as: [displayed ▼]

Page order

⦿ Down, then over

○ Over, then down

[OK]   [Cancel]

✔ **Print:** Select check boxes in this section to set some formatting options, to embed comments, and to set the display of cell errors.

- **Gridlines:** Select this check box to hide or show the cell gridlines in the printed report. (Refer to Figure 5-5 to see the page of a report in Print Preview after removing the check mark from the Gridlines check box.)

- **Black and White:** When you select this check box, Excel prints the different colors assigned to cell ranges in black and white. Select this option when you use colors for text and graphics in a workbook on a color monitor but want to print them in monochrome on a black-and-white printer (otherwise, they become shades of gray on a black-and-white printer).

- **Draft Quality:** When you select this check box, Excel doesn't print cell gridlines (regardless of the status of the Gridlines check box) and omits some graphics from the printout. Select this option when you want to get a fast and dirty copy of the report and you're only concerned with checking the text and numbers.

- **Row and Column Headings:** Select this check box, and Excel includes the worksheet frame with the column letters and row numbers on each page of the report. Select this option when you want to be able to identify the location of the printed information. (See the section "Letting Your Formulas All Hang Out," later in this chapter, for an example.)

- **Comments:** When you select the At End of Sheet or As Displayed on Sheet options on the Comments pop-up menu, Excel prints the text of comments attached to cells that are included in the report. When you select the At End of Sheet option, the program prints the notes in a series all together at the end of the report. When you select the As Displayed on Sheet option, the program prints only the notes that are currently displayed in the worksheet. (See Chapter 6 for details.)

- **Cell Errors As:** When you select <blank>, –, or #N/A in the Cell Errors As pop-up menu, Excel no longer prints out the error values as they are displayed in the worksheet (see Chapter 2 for details on the possible error values and why they show up). Instead, Excel replaces all error values in messed up formulas either as blank cells (if you choose the <blank> option), enters dashes (if you choose the — option), or #N/A symbols, which is itself an error value (if you choose the #N/A option) in these cells.

✔ **Page Order:** Choose from two radio buttons in this section to choose the print order of your report's pages.

- **Down, Then Over:** Normally, Excel selects this radio button, which tells the program to number and paginate a multipage report by proceeding down the rows and then across the columns to be printed.

- **Over, Then Down:** Select this option, and Excel numbers and paginates across the columns and then down the rows to be printed.

Putting out the print titles

Options in the Print titles section of the Sheet tab of the Page Setup dialog box enable you to print particular row and column headings on each page of the report. Excel refers to such row and column headings in a printed report as *print titles*. Don't confuse print titles with the header of a report. Even though both are printed on each page, header information prints in the top margin of the report; print titles always appear in the body of the report — at the top, in the case of rows used as print titles, and on the left, in the case of columns.

To designate print titles for a report, follow these steps:

1. **Open the Page Setup dialog box by choosing File⇨Page Setup from the menu bar.**

   The Page Setup dialog box appears (refer to Figure 5-11).

2. **Select the Sheet tab.**

   To designate worksheet rows as print titles, go to Step 3a. To designate worksheet columns as print titles, go to Step 3b.

3a. **Select the Rows to Repeat at Top text box and then drag through the rows with information you want to appear at the top of each page in the worksheet below. If necessary, reduce the Page Setup dialog box to just the Rows to Repeat at Top text box by clicking the text box's Collapse/Expand dialog button.**

   In the example I show you in Figure 5-11, I click the minimize button associated with the Rows to Repeat at Top text box and then drag through rows 1 and 2 in column A of the Bo Peep Pet Detectives – Client List worksheet, and the program entered the row range $1 $2 in the Rows to Repeat at Top text box.

   Note that Excel indicates the print-title rows in the worksheet by placing a dotted line (that moves like a marquee) on the border between the titles and the information in the body of the report.

3b. **Select the Columns to Repeat at Left text box and then drag through the range of columns with the information you want to appear at the** left edge of each page of the printed report in the worksheet below. If necessary, reduce the Page Setup dialog box to just the Columns to Repeat at Left text box by clicking its Collapse/Expand dialog button.

Note that Excel indicates the print-title columns in the worksheet by placing a dotted line (that moves like a marquee) on the border between the titles and the information in the body of the report.

4. **Click OK or press Enter to close the Page Setup dialog box.**

After you close the Page Setup dialog box, the dotted line showing the border of the row and/or column titles disappears from the worksheet.

In Figure 5-11, rows 1 and 2 containing the worksheet title and column headings for the Bo Peep Pet Detectives clients database are designated as the print titles for the report. In Figure 5-12, you can see the Print Preview window with the second page of the report. Note how these print titles appear on all pages of the report.

To clear print titles from a report if you no longer need them, open the Sheet tab of the Page Setup dialog box and then delete the row and column ranges from the Rows to Repeat at Top and the Columns to Repeat at Left text boxes before you click OK or press Enter.

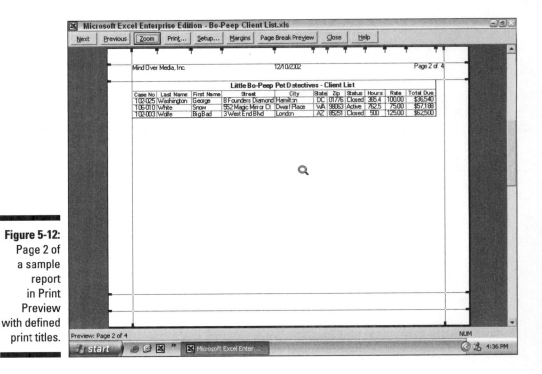

Figure 5-12:
Page 2 of a sample report in Print Preview with defined print titles.

When Ya Gonna Give Your Page a Break?

Sometimes when you print a report, Excel splits onto different pages information that you know should always appear on the same page.

Figure 5-13 shows a worksheet in Page Break Preview with an example of a bad vertical page break that you can remedy by adjusting the location of the page break on Page 1 and 3. Given the page size, orientation, and margin settings for this report, Excel breaks the page between columns K and L. This break separates the Paid column (L) from all the others in the client list, effectively putting this information on its own page 3 and page 4 (not shown in Figure 5-13).

To prevent the data in the Paid column from being printed alone on its own pages, you need to move the page break to a column on the left. In this case, I choose to move the page break back between columns G (with the Zip code data) and H (containing the account Status information) so that the name and address information stays together on Page 1 and 2 and the other client data is printed together on Page 3 and 4. Figure 5-13 shows how you can create the vertical page break in Page Break Preview mode by following these steps:

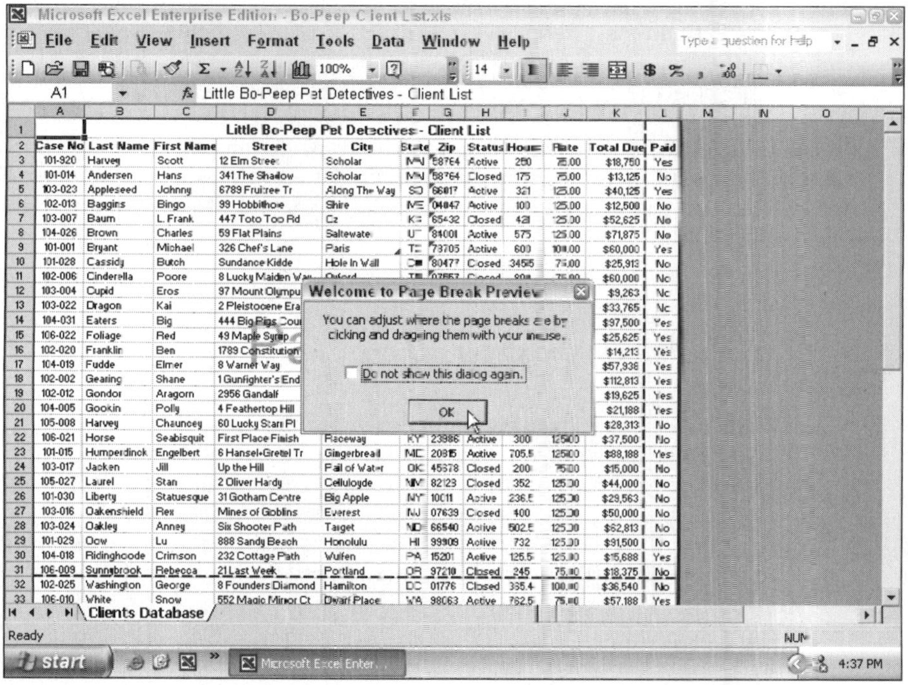

Figure 5-13:
Preview
page breaks
in a report
Page Break
Preview.

1. **Choose View⇨Page Break Preview from the menu bar.**

   This takes you into a page break preview mode that shows your worksheet data at a reduced magnification (60 percent of normal in Figure 5-13) with the page numbers displayed in large light type and the page breaks shown by heavy lines between the columns and rows of the worksheet.

   The first time you choose this command, Excel displays a Welcome to Page Break Preview dialog box (shown in Figure 5-13). To prevent this dialog box from reappearing each time you use Page Break Preview, click the Do Not Show This Dialog Again check box before you close the Welcome to Page Break Preview alert dialog box.

2. **Click OK or press Enter to get rid of the Welcome to Page Break Preview alert dialog box.**

3. **Position the mouse pointer somewhere on the page break indicator (one of the heavy lines surrounding the representation of the page) that you need to adjust; when the pointer changes to a double-headed arrow, drag the page indicator to the desired column or row and release the mouse button.**

   For the example shown in Figure 5-13, I dragged the page break indicator between Page 1 and 3 to the left so that it's between columns G and H. Excel then moved the page break back to this point, which puts all the name and address information together on pages 1 and 2. This new page break then causes all the other columns of client data to print together on pages 3 and 4.

   In Figure 5-14, you can see Page 1 of the report as it then appears in the Print Preview window.

4. **After you finish adjusting the page breaks in Page Break Preview (and, presumably, printing the report), choose View⇨Normal on the menu bar to return the worksheet to its regular view of the data.**

Letting Your Formulas All Hang Out

One more basic printing technique you may need every once in a while is how to print the formulas in a worksheet instead of printing the calculated results of the formulas. You can check over a printout of the formulas in your worksheet to make sure that you haven't done anything stupid (like replace a formula with a number or use the wrong cell references in a formula) before you distribute the worksheet company-wide.

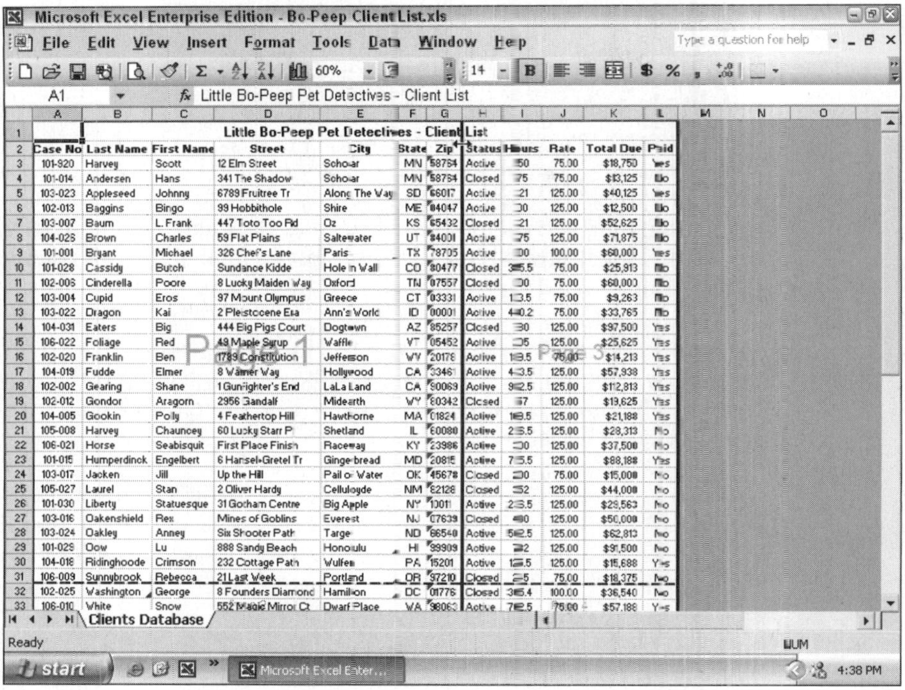

Figure 5-14:
Page 1
of the report
in the Print
Preview
window
after
adjusting
the page
breaks in
Page Break
Preview
mode.

Before you can print a worksheet's formulas, you have to display the formulas, rather than their results, in the cells.

1. **Choose Tools⇨Options on the menu bar.**

2. **Click the View tab.**

3. **Click the Formulas check box, in the Window Options area, to put a check mark in it.**

4. **Click OK or press Enter.**

When you follow these steps, Excel displays the contents of each cell in the worksheet as they normally appear only in the Formula bar or when you're editing them in the cell. Notice that value entries lose their number formatting, formulas appear in their cells (Excel widens the columns with best-fit so that the formulas appear in their entirety) and long text entries no longer spill over into neighboring blank cells.

Excel allows you to toggle between the normal cell display and the formula cell display by pressing Ctrl+`. (That is, press Ctrl and the key with the tilde on top.) This key — usually found in the upper-left corner of your keyboard — does double-duty as a tilde and as a weird backward accent mark: ` (Don't confuse that backward accent mark with the apostrophe that appears on a key below the quotation mark!)

After Excel displays the formulas in the worksheet, you are ready to print it as you would any other report. You can include the worksheet column letters and row numbers as headings in the printout so that if you do spot an error, you can pinpoint the cell reference right away. To include the row and column headings in the printout, click the Row and Column Headings check box in the Sheet tab of the Page Setup dialog box before you send the report to the printer.

After you print the worksheet with the formulas, return the worksheet to normal by opening the Options dialog box and selecting the View tab and then deselecting the Formulas check box before clicking OK, or pressing Enter, or just choosing Ctrl+`.

Part III
Getting Organized and Staying That Way

The 5th Wave   By Rich Tennant

"WELL, SHOOT! THIS EGGPLANT CHART IS JUST AS CONFUSING AS THE BUTTERNUT SQUASH CHART AND THE GOURD CHART. CAN'T YOU JUST MAKE A PIE CHART LIKE EVERYONE ELSE?"

In this part . . .

*I*n today's business world, we all know how vital it is to stay organized — as well as how difficult that can be. Keeping straight the spreadsheets that you create in Excel 2003 is no less important and, in some cases, no less arduous.

In this part, I help you tackle this conundrum by giving you the inside track on how to keep on top of all the stuff in every single worksheet that you create or edit. Not only do you discover in Chapter 6 how to keep track of the information in one worksheet, but also, in Chapter 7, how to juggle the information from one worksheet to another and even from one workbook to another.

Chapter 6

Oh, What a Tangled Worksheet We Weave!

. . . .

In This Chapter

▶ Zooming in and out on a worksheet

▶ Splitting up the workbook window into two or four panes

▶ Freezing columns and rows on-screen for worksheet titles

▶ Attaching comments to cells

▶ Naming your cells

▶ Finding and replacing stuff in your worksheet

▶ Looking up stuff using online resources in the Research Task pane

▶ Controlling when you recalculate a worksheet

▶ Protecting your worksheets

. . . .

*E*ach Excel worksheet offers an awfully big place in which to store information (and each workbook you open offers you three of these babies). But because your computer monitor lets you see only a tiny bit of any of the worksheets in a workbook at any one time, the issue of keeping on top of information is not a small one (pun intended).

Although the Excel worksheet employs a coherent cell-coordinate system that you can use to get anywhere in the great big worksheet, you have to admit that this A1, B2 stuff — although highly logical — remains fairly alien to human thinking. (I mean, saying, "Go to cell IV88," just doesn't have anywhere near the same impact as saying, "Go to the corner of Hollywood and Vine.") Consider for a moment the difficulty of coming up with a meaningful association between the 1998 depreciation schedule and its location in the cell range AC50:AN75 so that you can remember where to find it.

In this chapter, I show you some of the more effective techniques for keeping on top of information. You learn how to change the perspective on a worksheet by zooming in and out on the information, how to split the document window into separate panes so that you can display different sections of the worksheet at the same time, and how to keep particular rows and columns on the screen at all times.

And, as if that weren't enough, you also see how to add comments to cells, assign descriptive, English-type names to cell ranges (like Hollywood_and_ Vine!), and use the Find and Replace commands to locate and, if necessary, replace entries anywhere in the worksheet. Finally, you see how to control when Excel recalculates the worksheet and how to limit where changes can be made.

Zeroing In with Zoom

So what are you gonna do now that the boss won't spring for that 21-inch monitor for your computer? All day long, it seems that you're either straining your eyes to read all the information in those little, tiny cells, or you're scrolling like mad trying to locate a table you can't seem to find. Never fear, the Zoom feature is here. You can use Zoom like a magnifying glass to blow up part of the worksheet or shrink it down to size.

In Figure 6-1, you can see a blowup of worksheet after increasing it to 200-percent magnification (twice normal size). To blow up a worksheet like this, click the 200% option at the top of the Zoom button's pop-up menu — located on the Standard toolbar. (You can also do this by choosing View➪Zoom from the menu bar and then selecting the 200% radio button in the Zoom dialog box, if you really want to go to all that trouble.) One thing's for sure: You don't have to go after your glasses to read the names in those enlarged cells! The only problem with 200-percent magnification is that you can see only a few cells at one time.

In Figure 6-2, check out the same worksheet, this time at 25-percent magnification (roughly one-quarter normal size). To reduce the display to this magnification, you click the 25% setting on the Zoom button's pop-up menu on the Standard toolbar (unless you're just dying to open the Zoom dialog box so that you can accomplish this via its 25% radio button).

Whew! At 25 percent of normal screen size, the only thing you can be sure of is that you can't read a thing! However, notice that with this bird's-eye view, you can see at a glance how far over and down the data in this worksheet extends.

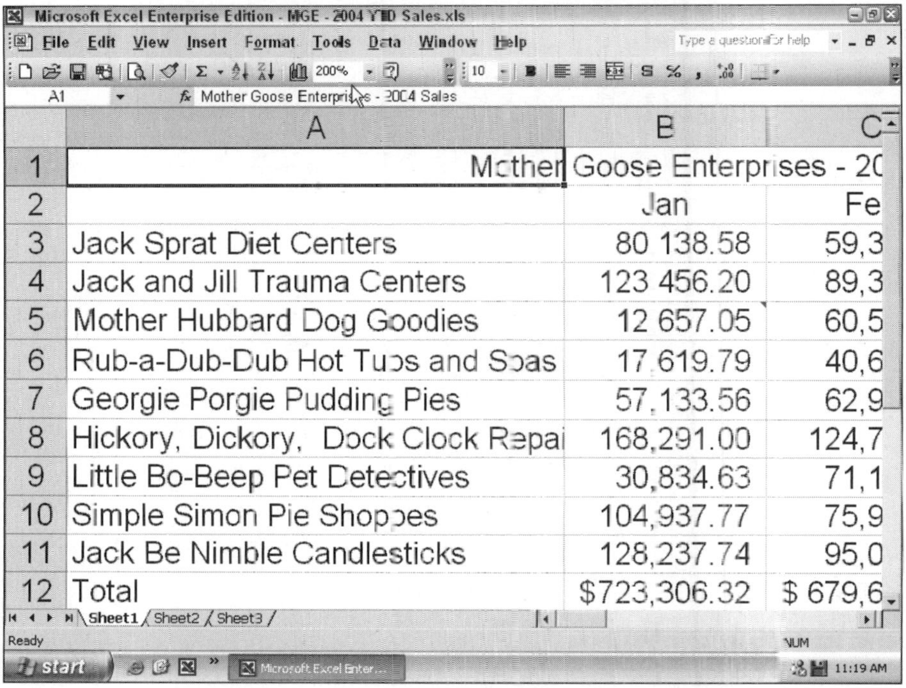

Microsoft Excel Enterprise Edition - MGE - 2004 YTD Sales.xls
File Edit View Insert Format Tools Data Window Help
Type a question for help
200%
A1
Mother Goose Enterprises - 2004 Sales
A
B
C
1 Mother Goose Enterprises - 20
2 Jan Fe
3 Jack Sprat Diet Centers 80,138.58 59,3
4 Jack and Jill Trauma Centers 123,456.20 89,3
5 Mother Hubbard Dog Goodies 12,657.05 60,5
6 Rub-a-Dub-Dub Hot Tubs and Spas 17,619.79 40,6
7 Georgie Porgie Pudding Pies 57,133.56 62,9
8 Hickory, Dickory, Dock Clock Repai 168,291.00 124,7
9 Little Bo-Beep Pet Detectives 30,834.63 71,1
10 Simple Simon Pie Shoppes 104,937.77 75,9
11 Jack Be Nimble Candlesticks 128,237.74 95,0
12 Total $723,306.32 $ 679,6
Sheet1 Sheet2 Sheet3
Ready
NUM
start
Microsoft Excel Enter...
11:19 AM

Figure 6-1: Zooming in: A sample worksheet at 200% magnification.

The Zoom pop-up menu and dialog box offer five precise magnification settings — 200%, 100% (normal screen magnification), 75%, 50%, and 25%. To use other percentages besides these, you have the following options:

- If you want to use other precise percentages in between the five preset percentages (such as 150% or 85%) or settings greater or less than the highest or lowest (such as 400% or 10%), click within the Zoom button's text box on the Standard toolbar, type the new percentage, and press Enter. (You can also do this by opening the Zoom dialog box and entering the percentage in its Custom text box.)
- If you don't know what percentage to enter in order to display a particular cell range on the screen, select the range, choose Selection at the very bottom of the Zoom button's pop-up menu or open the Zoom dialog box, select the Fit Selection radio button, and then click OK or press Enter. Excel figures out the percentage necessary to fill up your screen with just the selected cell range.

TIP

You can use the Zoom feature to locate and move to a new cell range in the worksheet. First, select a small magnification, such as 50%. Then locate the cell range you want to move to and select one of its cells. Finally, use the Zoom feature to return the screen magnification to 100% again. When Excel returns the display to normal size, the cell you select and its surrounding range appear on-screen.

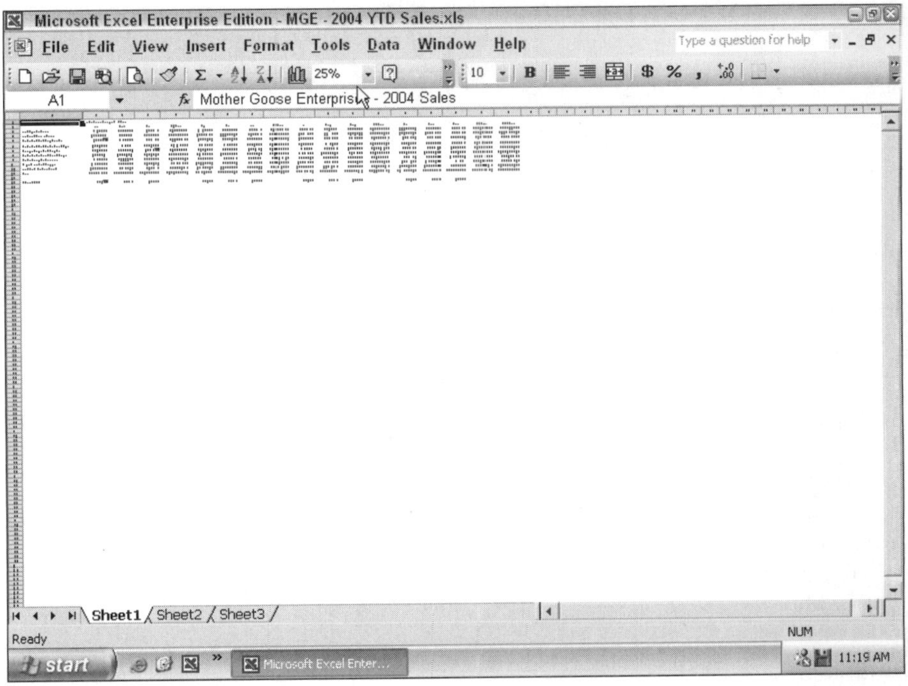

Figure 6-2:
Zooming
out: A
sample
worksheet
at 25%
magnifi-
cation.

Splitting the Difference

Although zooming in and out on the worksheet can help you get your bearings, it can't bring together two separate sections so that you can compare their data on the screen (at least not at a normal size where you can actually read the information). To manage this kind of trick, split the document window into separate panes and then scroll the worksheet in each pane so that they display the parts you want to compare.

Splitting the window is easy. Look at Figure 6-3 to see a projected income statement for the Jack Sprat Diet Centers after splitting its worksheet window horizontally into two panes and scrolling up rows 16 through 28 in the second pane. Each pane has its own vertical scroll bar, which enables you to scroll different parts of the worksheet into view.

To split a worksheet into two (upper and lower) horizontal panes, you can drag the *split bar,* located right above the scroll arrow at the very top of the vertical scroll bar, down until the window divides as you want it. Use the following steps:

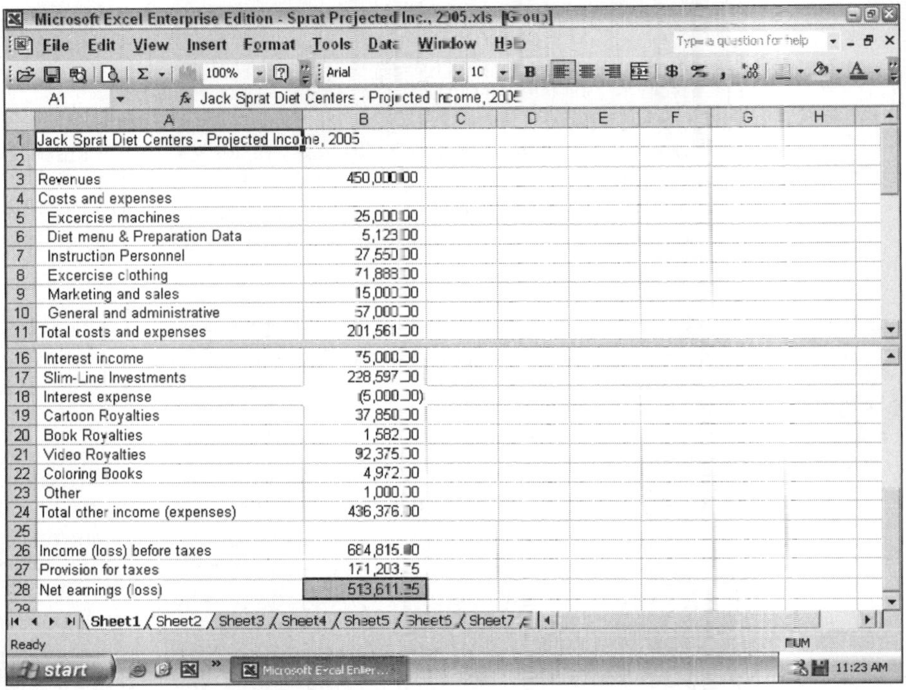

Figure 6-3:
The work-
sheet in
a split
document
window
after
scrolling up
the bottom
rows in the
lower pane.

1. **Click the vertical split bar and hold down the primary mouse button.**

   The mouse pointer changes to a double-headed arrow with a split in its middle (like the one used to display hidden rows).

2. **Drag downward until you reach the row at which you want the document window divided.**

   A gray dividing line appears in the workbook document window as you drag down, indicating where the document window will be split.

3. **Release the mouse button.**

   Excel divides the window into horizontal panes at the pointer's location and adds a vertical scroll bar to the new pane.

You can also split the document window into two vertical (left and right) panes by following these steps:

1. **Click the split bar located at the right edge of the horizontal scroll bar.**

2. **Drag to the left until you reach the column at which you want the document window divided.**

3. Release the mouse button.

Excel splits the window at that column and adds a second horizontal scroll bar to the new pane.

Don't confuse the tab split bar to the left of the horizontal scroll bar with the horizontal split bar at its right. You drag the *tab split bar* to increase or decrease the number of sheet tabs displayed at the bottom of the workbook window; you use the *horizontal split bar* to divide the workbook window into two vertical panes.

Note that you can make the panes in a workbook window disappear by double-clicking anywhere on the split bar that divides the window rather than having to drag the split bar all the way to one of the edges of the window to get rid of it.

Instead of dragging split bars, you can divide a document window with the Window⇨Split command from the menu bar. When you choose this command, Excel uses the position of the cell pointer to determine where to split the window into panes. The program splits the window vertically at the left edge of the pointer and horizontally along the top edge. If you want the workbook window split into just two horizontal panes, do this: Using the top of the cell pointer as the dividing line, position the cell pointer in the first column of the desired row that is displayed on your screen. If you want the workbook window split into just two vertical windows, do this: Using the left edge of the cell pointer as the dividing line, position the cell pointer in the first row of the desired column that's displayed on your screen.

If you position the cell pointer somewhere in the midst of the cells displayed on-screen when you choose the Window⇨Split command, Excel splits the window into four panes along the top and left edge of the cell pointer. For example, if you position the cell pointer in cell C6 of the Little Bo-Peep Pet Detectives Client List worksheet and then choose Window⇨Split, the window splits into four panes: A horizontal split occurs between rows 5 and 6, and a vertical split occurs between columns B and C (as shown in Figure 6-4).

Excel divides whatever portion of the worksheet is displayed onscreen given its current magnification into four equal panes when the cell pointer is in cell A1 at the time you choose Window⇨Split.

After you split the window into panes, you can move the cell pointer into a particular pane either by clicking one of its cells or by pressing Shift+F6 (which moves the pointer to the last occupied cell or the top-left cell in each pane in the workbook window in a counterclockwise direction). To remove the panes from a window, choose Window⇨Remove Split from the menu bar.

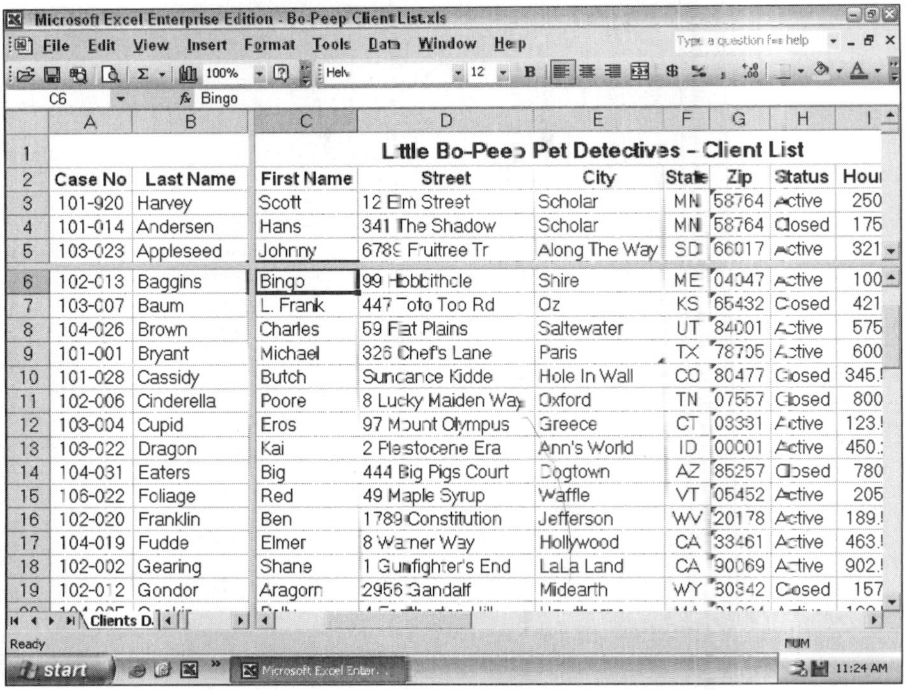

	A	B	C	D	E	F	G	H	I
1				Little Bo-Peep Pet Detectives - Client List					
2	Case No	Last Name	First Name	Street	City	State	Zip	Status	Hour
3	101-920	Harvey	Scott	12 Elm Street	Scholar	MN	58764	Active	250
4	101-014	Andersen	Hans	341 The Shadow	Scholar	MN	58764	Closed	175
5	103-023	Appleseed	Johnny	6789 Fruitree Tr	Along The Way	SD	66017	Active	321
6	102-013	Baggins	Bingo	99 Hobbithole	Shire	ME	04047	Active	100
7	103-007	Baum	L. Frank	447 Toto Too Rd	Oz	KS	65432	Closed	421
8	104-026	Brown	Charles	59 Fat Plains	Saltewater	UT	84001	Active	575
9	101-001	Bryant	Michael	326 Chef's Lane	Paris	TX	78705	Active	600
10	101-028	Cassidy	Butch	Suncance Kidde	Hole In Wall	CO	80477	Closed	345
11	102-006	Cinderella	Poore	8 Lucky Maiden Way	Oxford	TN	07557	Closed	800
12	103-004	Cupid	Eros	97 Mount Olympus	Greece	CT	03331	Active	123
13	103-022	Dragon	Kai	2 Plestocene Era	Ann's World	ID	00001	Active	450
14	104-031	Eaters	Big	444 Big Pigs Court	Dogtown	AZ	85257	Closed	780
15	106-022	Foliage	Red	49 Maple Syrup	Waffle	VT	05452	Active	205
16	102-020	Franklin	Ben	1789 Constitution	Jefferson	WV	20178	Active	189
17	104-019	Fudde	Elmer	8 Warner Way	Hollywood	CA	33461	Active	463
18	102-002	Gearing	Shane	1 Gunfighter's End	LaLa Land	CA	90069	Active	902
19	102-012	Gondor	Aragorn	2956 Gandalf	Midearth	WY	30842	Closed	157

Figure 6-4: The worksheet window split into four panes after placing the cell pointer in cell C6.

Fixed Headings Courtesy of Freeze Panes

Window panes are great for viewing different parts of the same worksheet that normally can't be seen together. You can also use window panes to freeze headings in the top rows and first columns so that the headings stay in view at all times, no matter how you scroll through the worksheet. Frozen headings are especially helpful when you work with a table that contains information that extends beyond the rows and columns shown on-screen.

In Figure 6-5, you can see just such a table. The client-list worksheet contains more rows than you can see at one time (unless you decrease the magnification to 25% with Zoom, which makes the data too small to read). As a matter of fact, this worksheet continues down to row 34.

By splitting the document window into two horizontal panes between rows 2 and 3 and then freezing the top pane, you can keep the column headings in row 2 that identify each column of information on the screen as you scroll the worksheet up and down to review information on different employees. If you further split the window into vertical panes between columns B and C, you can keep the case numbers and last names on the screen as you scroll the worksheet left and right.

Refer to Figure 6-5 to see the employee roster after splitting the window into four panes and freezing them. To create and freeze these panes, follow these steps:

1. **Position the cell pointer in cell C3.**

2. **Choose Window⇨Freeze Panes from the menu bar.**

   In this example, Excel freezes the top and left window pane above row 3 and left of column C.

When Excel sets up the frozen panes, the borders of frozen panes are represented by a single line rather than a thin bar, as is the case with unfrozen panes.

See what happens when you scroll the worksheet up after freezing the window panes (shown in Figure 6-6). In this figure, I scrolled the worksheet up so that rows 18 through 34 appear under rows 1 and 2. Because the vertical pane with the worksheet title and column headings is frozen, it remains on-screen. (Normally, rows 1 and 2 would have been the first to disappear as you scroll the worksheet up.)

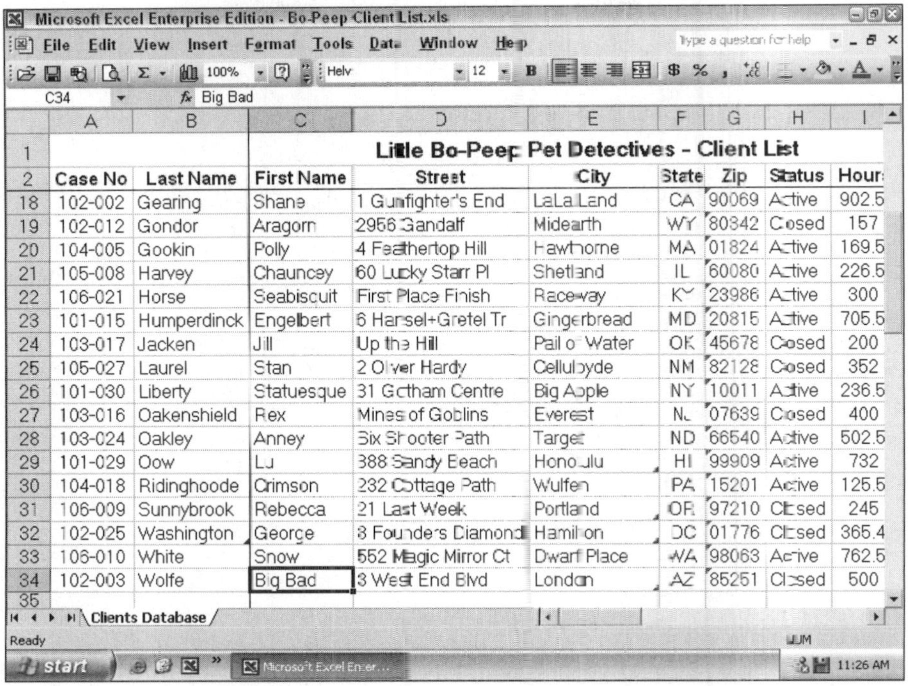

	A	B	C	D	E	F	G	H	I
1			Little Bo-Peep Pet Detectives - Client List						
2	Case No	Last Name	First Name	Street	City	State	Zip	Status	Hours
18	102-002	Gearing	Shane	1 Gunfighter's End	LaLa Land	CA	90069	Active	902.5
19	102-012	Gondor	Aragorn	2956 Gandalf	Midearth	WY	80342	Closed	157
20	104-005	Gookin	Polly	4 Feathertop Hill	Hawthorne	MA	01824	Active	169.5
21	105-008	Harvey	Chauncey	60 Lucky Starr Pl	Shetland	IL	60080	Active	226.5
22	106-021	Horse	Seabiscuit	First Place Finish	Raceway	KY	23986	Active	300
23	101-015	Humperdinck	Engelbert	6 Hansel+Gretel Tr	Gingerbread	MD	20815	Active	705.5
24	103-017	Jacken	Jill	Up the Hill	Pail o' Water	OK	45678	Closed	200
25	105-027	Laurel	Stan	2 Oliver Hardy	Celluloyde	NM	82128	Closed	352
26	101-030	Liberty	Statuesque	31 Gotham Centre	Big Apple	NY	10011	Active	236.5
27	103-016	Oakenshield	Rex	Mines of Goblins	Everest	NJ	07639	Closed	400
28	103-024	Oakley	Anney	Six Shooter Path	Target	ND	66540	Active	502.5
29	101-029	Oow	Lu	388 Sandy Beach	Honolulu	HI	99909	Active	732
30	104-018	Ridinghoode	Crimson	232 Cottage Path	Wulfen	PA	15201	Active	125.5
31	106-009	Sunnybrook	Rebecca	21 Last Week	Portland	OR	97210	Closed	245
32	102-025	Washington	George	8 Founders Diamond	Hamilton	DC	01776	Closed	365.4
33	106-010	White	Snow	552 Magic Mirror Ct	Dwarf Place	WA	98063	Active	762.5
34	102-003	Wolfe	Big Bad	3 West End Blvd	London	AZ	85251	Closed	500
35									

Figure 6-6: The client list after scrolling the rows up to display the final records in this list.

Look to Figure 6-7 to see what happens when you scroll the worksheet to the left. In this figure, I scroll the worksheet so that the data in columns E through L appear after the data in columns A and B. Because the first two columns are frozen, they remain on-screen, helping you identify who belongs to what information.

To unfreeze the window panes in a worksheet, choose Window⇨Unfreeze Panes. Choosing this command removes the window panes, indicating that Excel has unfrozen them.

Electronic Sticky Notes

You can add text comments to particular cells in an Excel worksheet *Comments* act kind of like electronic pop-up versions of sticky notes. For example, you can add a comment to yourself to verify a particular figure before printing the worksheet or to remind yourself that a particular value is only an estimate (or even to remind yourself that it's your anniversary and to pick up a little something special for your spouse on the way home!).

Microsoft Excel Enterprise Edition - Bo-Peep Client List.xls

File   Edit   View   Insert   Format   Tools   Data   Window   Help   Type a question for help

Helv   12   B

L34   fx   Yes

	A	B	E	F	G	H	I	J	K	L
1			**Pet Detectives – Client List**							
2	Case No	Last Name	City	State	Zip	Status	Hours	Rate	Total Due	Paid
18	102-002	Gearing	LaLa Land	CA	90069	Active	902.5	125.00	$112,813	Yes
19	102-012	Gondor	Midearth	WY	80342	Closed	157	125.00	$19,625	Yes
20	104-005	Gookin	Hawthorne	MA	01824	Active	169.5	125.00	$21,188	Yes
21	105-008	Harvey	Shetland	IL	60080	Active	226.5	125.00	$28,313	No
22	106-021	Horse	Raceway	KY	23985	Active	300	125.00	$37,500	No
23	101-015	Humperdinck	Gingerbread	MD	20815	Active	705.5	125.00	$88,188	Yes
24	103-017	Jacken	Pail of Water	OK	45678	Closed	200	75.00	$15,000	No
25	105-027	Laurel	Celluloyde	NM	82128	Closed	352	125.00	$44,000	No
26	101-030	Liberty	Big Apple	NY	10011	Active	236.5	125.00	$29,563	No
27	103-016	Oakenshield	Everest	NJ	07639	Closed	400	125.00	$50,000	No
28	103-024	Oakley	Target	ND	66540	Active	502.5	125.00	$62,813	No
29	101-029	Oow	Honolulu	HI	99909	Active	732	125.00	$91,500	No
30	104-018	Ridinghoode	Wulfen	PA	15201	Active	125.5	125.00	$15,688	Yes
31	106-009	Sunnybrook	Portland	OR	97210	Closed	245	75.00	$18,375	No
32	102-025	Washington	Hamilton	DC	01776	Closed	365.4	100.00	$36,540	No
33	106-010	White	Dwarf Place	WA	98063	Active	762.5	75.00	$57,188	Yes
34	102-003	Wolfe	London	AZ	85251	Closed	500	125.00	$62,500	Yes
35										

Clients Database

Ready   NUM

start   Microsoft Excel Enter...   11:26 AM

Figure 6-7:
The client
list after
scrolling the
columns
left to
display
the last
group
of fields in
this list.

In addition to using notes to remind yourself of something you've done
or that still remains to be done, you can also use a comment to mark your
current place in a large worksheet. You can then use the comment's location
to quickly find your starting place the next time you work with that
worksheet.

Adding a comment to a cell

To add a comment to a cell, follow these steps:

1. **Select the cell to which you want to add the comment.**

2. **Choose Insert⇨Comment from the menu bar.**

   A new text box appears (similar to the one shown in Figure 6-8).
   This text box contains the name of the user as it appears in the User
   name text box (on the General tab of the Options dialog box) and the
   insertion point located at the beginning of a new line right below the
   user name.

3. **Type the text of your comment in the text box that appears.**

4. **When finished entering the comment text, click somewhere outside of the text box.**

   Excel marks the location of a comment in a cell by adding a tiny triangle in the upper-right corner of the cell. (This triangular note indicator appears in red on a color monitor)

5. **To display the comment in a cell, position the thick white-cross mouse pointer somewhere in the cell with the note indicator**

Comments in review

When you have a workbook with sheets that contain a bunch of different comments, you probably won't want to take the time to position the mouse pointer over each of its cells in order to be able to read each one. For those times, you need to choose View⇨Comments on the menu bar. When you choose this command, Excels displays all the comments in the workbook while at the same time displaying the Reviewing toolbar (as shown in Figure 6-9).

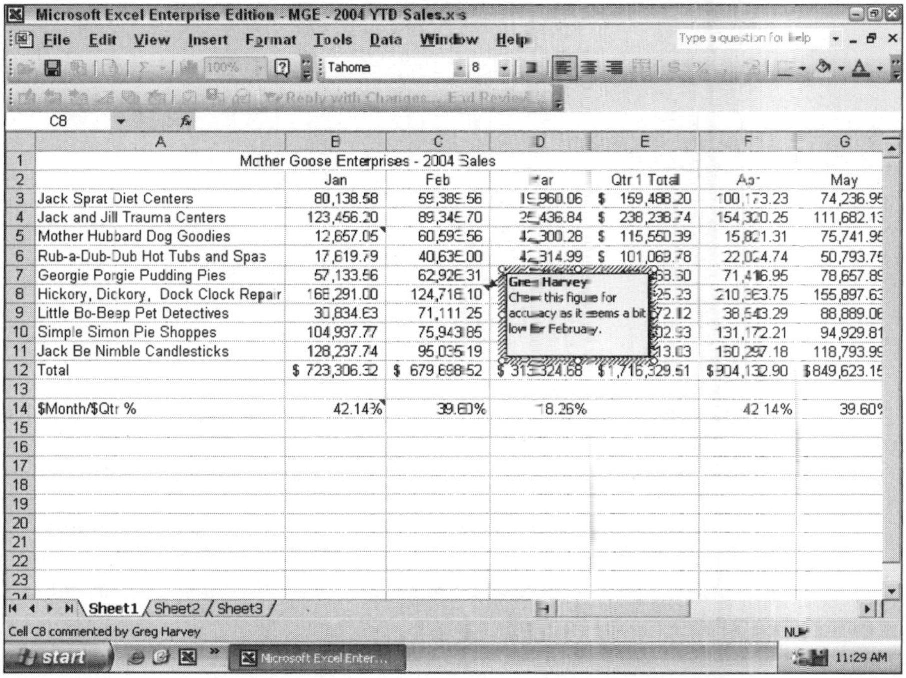

Figure 6-8:
Adding a comment to a cell in a new text box.

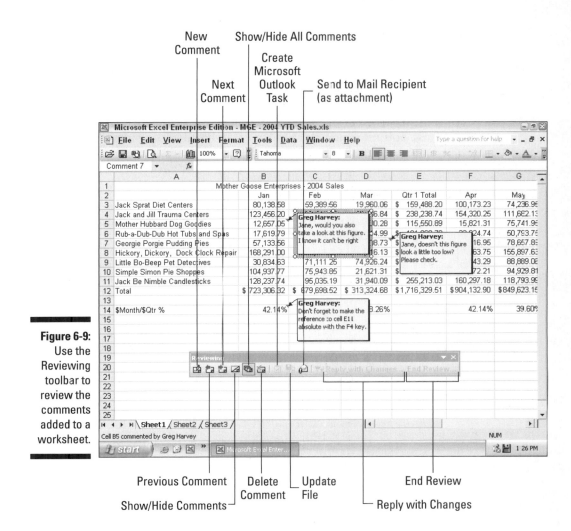

Figure 6-9:
Use the
Reviewing
toolbar to
review the
comments
added to a
worksheet.

With the Reviewing toolbar open, you can then move back and forth
from comment to comment by clicking its Next Comment and Previous
Comment buttons. When you reach the last comment in the workbook,
you receive an alert box asking you whether you want to continue
reviewing the comments from the beginning (which you can do by simply
clicking OK). After you're finished reviewing the comments in your
workbook, you can hide their display by clicking the Show All
Comments buttons on the Reviewing toolbar (or by again choosing
View⇨Comments on the menu bar, if the Reviewing toolbar is no
longer open).

Editing the comments in a worksheet

Excel provides a couple of different methods for editing the contents of a comment, depending upon whether or not the comment is already displayed on the screen. If the comment displays in the worksheet, you can edit its contents by clicking the I-beam mouse pointer in its text box. Clicking the I-beam pointer locates the insertion point, while at the same time selecting the comment's text box (indicated by the appearance of a thick cross-hatched line with sizing handles around the text box). After making your editing changes, just click somewhere outside the comment's text box to deselect the comment.

If the comment doesn't appear in the worksheet, you need to select its cell. After the cell pointer is in the cell with a comment that needs editing, choose Insert⇨Edit Comment on the menu bar or Edit Comment on the cell's shortcut menu (open this by right-clicking the cell).

To change the placement of a comment in relation to its cell, you select the comment by clicking somewhere on it and then positioning the mouse pointer on one of the edges of its text box. When a four-headed arrow appears at the tip of the mouse pointer, you can drag the text box to a new place in the worksheet. Note that when you release the mouse button, Excel redraws the arrow connecting the comment's text box to the note indicator in the upper-right corner of the cell.

To change the size of a comment's text box, you select the comment, position the mouse pointer on one of its sizing handles, and then drag in the appropriate direction (away from the center of the box to increase its size or toward the center to decrease its size). When you release the mouse button, Excel redraws the comment's text box with the new shape and size. When you change the size and shape of a comment's text box, Excel 2003 automatically wraps the text to fit in the new shape and size.

To change the font of the comment text, you need to select the text of the comment (by selecting it for editing and then dragging through the text) and choose Format⇨Comment from the menu bar (or you can press Ctrl+1 like you do to open the Format Cells dialog box). When you do, Excel opens the Format Comment dialog box that contains a lone Font tab (with the same options as the Font tab of the Format Cells dialog box — refer to Figure 3-15). You can then use the options on the Font tab to change the font, font style, font size, or color of the text displayed in the selected comment.

To delete a comment, you need to select its cell in the worksheet and then choose Edit⇨Clear⇨Comments from the menu bar or choose Delete Comment on the cell's shortcut menu. Excel removes the comment along with the note indicator from the selected cell.

Note that you can select a new shape or shading for the text box by using the buttons on the Drawing toolbar. For information on how to identify and use its buttons, peruse Chapter 8.

Getting your comments in print

When printing a worksheet, you can print the comments along with the selected worksheet data by selecting either the At End of Sheet or the As Displayed on Sheet options on Comments pop-up menu in the Sheet tab of the Page Setup dialog box (choose File⇨Page Setup). Refer to Chapter 5 for details.

The Cell Name Game

By assigning descriptive names to cells and cell ranges, you can go a long way toward keeping on top of the location of important information in a worksheet. Rather than try to associate random cell coordinates with specific information, you just have to remember a name. You can also use range names to designate the cell selection that you want to print or use in other Office 2003 programs, such as Word or Access. And, best of all, after you name a cell or cell range, you can use this name with the Go To feature.

If I only had a name . . .

When assigning range names to a cell or cell range, you need to follow a few guidelines:

- ✔ **Range names must begin with a letter of the alphabet, not a number.**

  For example, instead of *01*Profit, use *Profit*01.

- ✔ **Range names cannot contain spaces.**

  Instead of a space, use the underscore (Shift+hyphen) to tie the parts of the name together. For example, instead of Profit 01, use Profit_01.

- ✔ **Range names cannot correspond to cell coordinates in the worksheet.**

  For example, you can't name a cell *Q1* because this is a valid cell coordinate. Instead, use something like Q1_sales.

To name a cell or cell range in a worksheet:

1. **Select the cell or cell range that you want to name.**

2. **Click the cell address for the current cell that appears in the Name Box on the far left of the Formula bar (the fourth row at the top of the screen).**

   Excel selects the cell address in the Name Box.

3. **Type the name for the selected cell or cell range in the Name Box.**

   When typing the range name, you must follow Excel's naming conventions: Refer to the bulleted list of cell-name do's and don'ts earlier in this section for details.

4. **Press Enter.**

To select a named cell or range in a worksheet, click the range name on the Name Box pop-up list. To open this list, click the drop-down arrow button that appears to the right of the cell address on the Formula bar.

Note that you can also accomplish the same thing by pressing F5 or choosing Edit⇨Go To from the menu bar. The Go To dialog box appears (see Figure 6-10). Double-click the desired range name in the Go To list box (alternatively, select the name and click OK or press Enter). Excel moves the cell pointer directly to the named cell. If you selected a cell range, all the cells in that range are selected.

Figure 6-10:
Select a cell
range in a
worksheet.

Name that formula!

Cell names are not only a great way to identify and find cells and cell ranges in your spreadsheet, but they're also a great way to make out the purpose of your formulas. For example, say that you have a simple formula in cell K3 that calculates the total due to you by multiplying the hours you work for a client (in cell I3) by the client's hourly rate (in cell J3). Normally, you would enter this formula in cell K3 as

```
=I3*J3
```

However, if you assign the name *Hours* to cell I3 and the name *Rate* to cell J3, you could then enter the formula as

```
=Hours*Rate
```

in cell K3. I don't think there's anyone who would dispute that the formula =Hours*Rate is much easier to understand than =I3*J3.

To enter a formula using cell names rather than cell references, follow these steps (see Chapter 2 to brush up on how to create formulas):

1. **Name your cells as I describe earlier in this section.**

   For this example, give the name *Hours* to cell I3 and the name *Rate* to Cell J3.

2. **Place the cell pointer in the cell where the formula is to appear.**

   For this example, put the cell pointer in cell K3.

3. **Type = (equal sign) to start the formula.**

4. **Select the first cell referenced in the formula by selecting its cell (either by clicking or moving the cell pointer into it).**

   For this example, you select the Hours cell by selecting cell I3.

5. **Type the arithmetic operator you use in the formula.**

   For this example, you would type * (asterisk) for multiplication. (Refer to Chapter 2 for a list of the other arithmetic operators.)

6. **Select the second cell referenced in the formula by selecting its cell either by clicking or moving the cell pointer as before in Step 4.**

   For this example, you select the Rate cell by selecting cell J3.

7. **Click the Enter box or press Enter to complete the formula.**

   In this example, Excel enters the formula =Hours*Rate in cell K3.

You can't use the fill handle to copy a formula that uses cell names, rather than cell addresses, to other cells in a column or row that perform the same function (see Chapter 4). When you copy an original formula that uses names rather than addresses, Excel copies the original formula without adjusting the cell references to the new rows and columns. See the section "Naming constants," next in this chapter, to find out a way to use your column and row headings to identify the cell references in the copies, as well as the original formula from which the copies are made.

Naming constants

Certain formulas use constant values, such as a 7.5% tax rate or a 10% discount rate. If you don't want to have to enter these constants into a cell of the worksheet in order to use them formulas, you create range names that hold their values and then use their range names in the formulas you create.

For example, to create a constant called *tax_rate* of 7.5%, you follow these steps:

1. **Choose Insert⇨Name⇨Define from the Excel menu bar to open the Define Name dialog box.**

2. **In the Define Name dialog box, type the range name (tax_rate in this example) into the Names in Workbook text box.**

3. **Click within the Refers To text box and replace (enter) the current cell address with the value 7.5%.**

4. **Click the Add button to add this range name to the worksheet.**

5. **Click OK to close the Define Name dialog box.**

After you assign a constant to a range name by using this method, you can apply it to the formulas that you create in the worksheet in one of two ways:

✔ Type the range name to which you assign the constant at the place in the formula where its value is required.

✔ Insert the range name to which you assign the constant value into the formula by selecting the Insert⇨Name⇨Paste command from the menu bar and then double-clicking the range name holding the constant in the Paste Name dialog box.

When you copy a formula that uses a range name containing a constant, its values remain unchanged in all copies of the formula that you create with the Fill handle. (In other words, range names in formulas act like absolute cell addresses in copied formulas — see Chapter 4 for more on copying formulas.)

Also, note that when you update the constant by changing its value in the Define Name dialog box, all of the formulas that use that constant (by referring to the range name) are automatically updated (recalculated) to reflect this change.

Seek and Ye Shall Find . . .

When all else fails, you can use Excel's Find feature to locate specific information in the worksheet. When you choose Edit⇨Find from the menu bar, or press Ctrl+F or Shift+F5, Excel opens the Find and Replace dialog box. In the Find What text box, enter the text or values you want to locate and then click the Find Next button or press Enter to start the search. Choose the Options button in the Find and Replace dialog box to expand the search options (as shown in Figure 6-11).

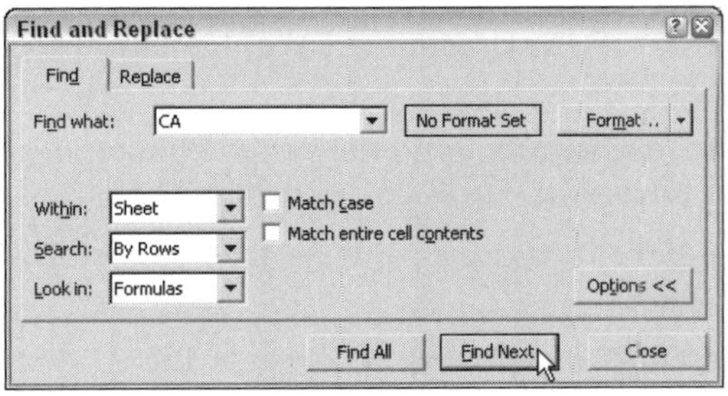

Figure 6-11: Use options in the Find and Replace dialog box to locate cell entries.

You can also open the Find and Replace dialog box from the Basic File Search Task pane by clicking the Find in this Document hyperlink located at the very bottom of the pane. To display the Basic File Search task pane, you click the File Search button on the Standard toolbar or choose File⇨File Search on the menu bar.

When you search for a text entry with the Find and Replace feature, be mindful of whether the text or number you enter in the Find What text box is separate in its cell or occurs as part of another word or value. For example, if you enter the characters **ca** in the Find What text box and you don't select the Match Entire Cell Contents check box Excel finds

- ✔ The field name *Ca* in *Ca*se No cell A2
- ✔ The state code *CA* (for *Ca*lifornia) in cells F8, F9, and F11
- ✔ The *ca* that occurs in Rebec*ca* in cell C31

If you select the Match Entire Cell Contents check box in the Find and Replace dialog box before starting the search, Excel would not consider the *Ca* in *Case No* or the *ca* in *Rebecca* to be a match because both of these cases have other text surrounding the text you're searching for.

When you search for text, you can also specify whether or not you want Excel to match the case you use (uppercase or lowercase) when entering the search text in the Find What text box. By default, Excel ignores case differences between text in cells of your worksheet and the search text you enter in the Find What text box. To conduct a case-sensitive search, you need to select the Match Case check box (available when you click the Options button to expand the Find and Replace dialog box, as shown in Figure 6-12, later in this chapter).

If the text or values that you want to locate in the worksheet have special formatting, you can specify the formatting to match when conducting the search.

To have Excel match the formatting assigned to a particular cell in the worksheet,

1. **Click the drop-down button on the right of the Format button and choose the Choose Format from Cell option on the pop-up menu.**

   The Find and Replace dialog box temporarily disappears, and Excel adds an ink dropper icon to the normal white-cross mouse pointer.

2. **Click this mouse pointer in the cell in the worksheet that contains the formatting you want to match.**

   The Find and Replace dialog box reappears, and the Find and Replace feature picks up cell's formatting.

To select the formatting to match in the search from the options on the Find Format dialog box (which are identical to those of the Format Cells dialog box),

1. **Click the Format button or click its drop-down button and choose Format from its pop-up menu.**

2. **Then, select the formatting options to match from the various tabs (refer to Chapter 3 for help on selecting these options) and click OK.**

When you use either of these methods to select the kinds of formatting to match in your search, the No Format Set button (located between the Find What text box and the Format button) changes to a Preview button. The word *Preview* in this button appears in whatever font and attributes Excel picks up from the sample cell or through your selections on the Font tab of the Find Format dialog box.

When you search for values in the worksheet, be mindful of the difference between formulas and values. For example, cell K24 of the Bo Peep Client List (refer to Figure 6-7) contains the value $15,000. If you type **15000** in the Find What text box and press Enter to search for this value, however, Excel displays an alert box with the following message

```
Cannot find matching data
```

instead of finding the value 15000 in cell K24. This is because the value in this cell is calculated by the following formula,

```
=I24*J24
```

and nowhere in that formula does the value 15000 show up. To have Excel to find any entry matching 15000 in the cells of the worksheet, you need to choose Values in the Look In pop-up menu of the Find and Replace dialog box in place of the normally used Formulas option.

To restrict the search to just the text or values in the text of the comments in the worksheet, choose the Comments option from the Look In pop-up menu.

If you don't know the exact spelling of the word or name or the precise value or formula you're searching for, you can use *wildcards,* which are symbols that stand for missing or unknown text. Use the question mark (?) to stand for a single unknown character; use the asterisk (*) to stand for any number of missing characters. Suppose that you enter the following in the Find What text box and choose the Values option in the Look In pop-up menu:

```
7*4
```

Excel stops at cells that contain the values *74, 704,* and *7,5234,* and even finds the text entry *782 4th Street.*

If you actually want to search for an asterisk in the worksheet rather than use the asterisk as a wildcard, precede it with a tilde (~), as follows:

```
~*4
```

This arrangement enables you to search the formulas in the worksheet for one that multiplies by the number 4 (remember that Excel uses the asterisk as the multiplication sign).

The following entry in the Find What text box finds cells that contain *Jan, January, June, Janet,* and so on.

```
J?n*
```

Normally, Excel searches only the current worksheet for the search text you enter. If you want the program to search all the worksheets in the workbook, you must select the Workbook option from the Within pop-up menu.

When Excel locates a cell in the worksheet that contains the text or values you're searching for, it selects that cell while at the same time leaving the Find and Replace dialog box open. (Remember that you can move the Find and Replace dialog box if it obscures your view of the cell.) To search for the next occurrence of the text or value, click the Find Next button or press Enter.

Excel normally searches down the worksheet by rows. To search across the columns first, choose the By Columns option in the Search pop-up menu. To reverse the search direction and revisit previous occurrences of matching cell entries, press the Shift key while you click the Find Next button in the Find dialog box.

You Can Be Replaced!

If your purpose for finding a cell with a particular entry is so that you can change it, you can automate this process by using the Replace tab on the Find and Replace dialog box. If you choose Edit⇨Replace instead of Edit⇨Find on the menu bar (Ctrl+H), Excel opens the Find and Replace dialog box with the Replace tab (rather than the Find tab) selected. On the Replace tab, enter the text or value you want to replace in the Find What text box and then enter the replacement the text or value in the Replace With text box.

When you enter replacement text, enter it exactly as you want it to appear in the cell. In other words, if you replace all occurrences of *Jan* in the worksheet with *January,* enter the following in the Replace With text box:

```
January
```

Make sure that you use the capital J in the Replace With text box even though you can enter the following in the Find What text box (providing you don't check the Match Case check box that appears only when you choose the Options button to expand the Search and Replace dialog box options):

```
jan
```

After specifying what to replace and what to replace it with (as shown in Figure 6-12), you can have Excel replace occurrences in the worksheet on a case-by-case basis or globally. To replace all occurrences in a single operation, click the Replace All button.

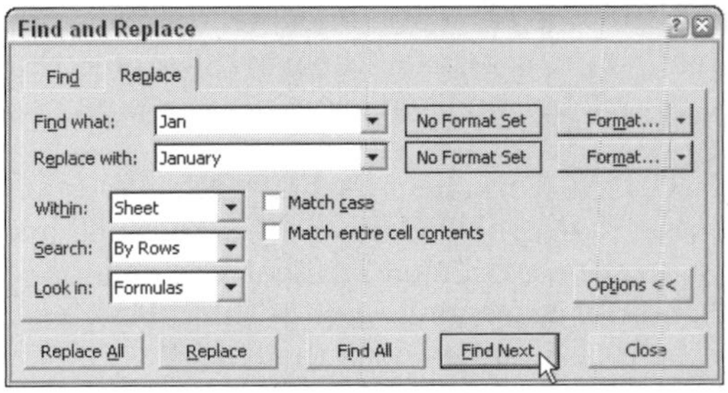

Figure 6-12:
Use Replace
options to
change
particular
cell entries.

Be careful with global search-and-replace operations; they can really mess up a worksheet in a hurry if you inadvertently replace values, parts of formulas, or characters in titles and headings that you hadn't intended to change. With this in mind, always follow one rule:

> Never undertake a global search-and-replace operation on an unsaved worksheet.

Also, verify whether or not the Match Entire Cell Contents check box (displayed only when you click the Options button) is selected before you begin. You can end up with a lot of unwanted replacements if you leave this check box unselected when you really only want to replace entire cell entries (rather than matching parts in cell entries).

If you do make a mess, choose the Edit⇨Undo Replace command (or press Ctrl+Z) to restore the worksheet.

To see each occurrence before you replace it, click the Find Next button or press Enter. Excel selects the next cell with the text or value you enter in the Find What text box. To have the program replace the selected text, click the Replace button. To skip this occurrence, click the Find Next button to continue the search. When you finish replacing occurrences, click the Close button to close the Replace dialog box.

Do Your Research

Excel 2003 includes a new Research Task pane that you can use to search for information using online resources, such as the Encarta World Dictionary, Thesaurus, Stock Quotes, and Encyclopedia. Note that because all of these resources are online, to make use of the Research Task pane, you must have Internet access available.

To open the Research Task pane (similar to the one shown in Figure 6-13), click the Research button on the Standard toolbar or open any one of the other Excel Task panes by pressing Ctrl+F1 or choosing View⇨Task Pane from the Excel menu bar. Then select the Research pane by clicking the drop-down button and clicking Research on the pop-up menu that appears.

To then look up something in the Research pane, you enter the word or phrase you want to locate in the online resources in the Search For text box at the top of the Research pane and then click the type of online reference to be searched in the drop-down menu immediately below this text box:

- ✔ **All Reference Books** to search for the word or phrase in any of the online reference books

- ✔ **Encarta World Dictionary: English (U.S.)** to look up the word or phrase in just this dictionary

- ✔ **A particular thesaurus** (such as Thesaurus English [U.S.] or Thesaurus English [U.K.]) to look for synonyms for the word or phrase

- ✔ **All Research Sites** to look up the word or phrase in any online resource or any Web site on the Internet

- ✔ **MSN Search** to look up the word or phrase just on Web sites on the Internet (in other words, to do a Web search on the word or phrase)

- ✔ **Stock Quotes** to look up stock information about the word or phrase (which should be, of course, the company name or its stock symbol)

- ✔ **Encyclopedia: English (U.S.)** to look up the word or phrase in just this encyclopedia

To start the online search, click the Start Searching button to the immediate right of the Search For text box. Excel then connects you to the designated online resources and displays the search results in the Research Task pane underneath the Show Results From drop-down list box. Figure 6-13, for example, shows the various stock quote figures for Microsoft Corporation for the day and time I did the search.

When you include Web sites in your search, you can visit particular sites by clicking their links in the Research Task pane. When you do, Windows then launches your default Web browser (such as Internet Explorer 6.0) and connects you to the linked page. To return to Excel after visiting a particular Web page, simply click the Close box in the upper-right corner of your Web browser's window.

You can modify which online services are available when you open the Show Results From drop-down menu by clicking the Research Options link that appears at the very bottom of the Research Task pane. When click this link, Excel opens a Research Options dialog box that enables you to add or remove particular reference books and sites.

Start Searching

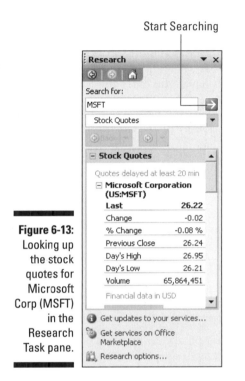

Figure 6-13:
Looking up
the stock
quotes for
Microsoft
Corp (MSFT)
in the
Research
Task pane.

You Can Be So Calculating

Locating information in a worksheet — although admittedly extremely important — is only a part of the story of keeping on top of the information in a worksheet. In really large workbooks that contain many completed worksheets, you may want to switch to manual recalculation so that you can control when the formulas in the worksheet are calculated. You need this kind of control when you find that Excel's recalculation of formulas each time you enter or change information in cells has slowed the program's response to a crawl. By holding off recalculations until you are ready to save or print the workbook, you find that you can work with Excel's worksheets without interminable delays.

To put the workbook on manual recalculation, choose Tools⇨Options from the menu bar and click the Calculation tab (see Figure 6-14). Then select the Manual radio button in the Calculation area. When doing this, you probably won't want to remove (deselect) the check mark from the Recalculate Before Save check box (not generally a very smart idea) so that Excel will still automatically recalculate all formulas before saving the workbook. By keeping this setting active, you are assured of saving only the most up-to-date values.

After switching to manual recalculation, Excel displays the message

> `Calculate`

on the status bar whenever you make a change to the worksheet that somehow affects the current values of its formulas. Whenever you see Calculate on the status bar, this is the signal that you need to bring the formulas up-to-date before saving the workbook (as you would before printing its worksheets).

To recalculate the formulas in a workbook when calculation is on manual, press F9 or Ctrl+= (equal sign) or click the Calc Now (F9) button in the Calculation tab of the Options dialog box.

Excel then recalculates the formulas in all the worksheets in your workbook. If you only made changes to the current worksheet and don't want to wait around for Excel to recalculate every other worksheet in the workbook, you can restrict the recalculation to the current worksheet by clicking the Calc Sheet button on the Calculation tab of the Options dialog box or pressing Shift+F9.

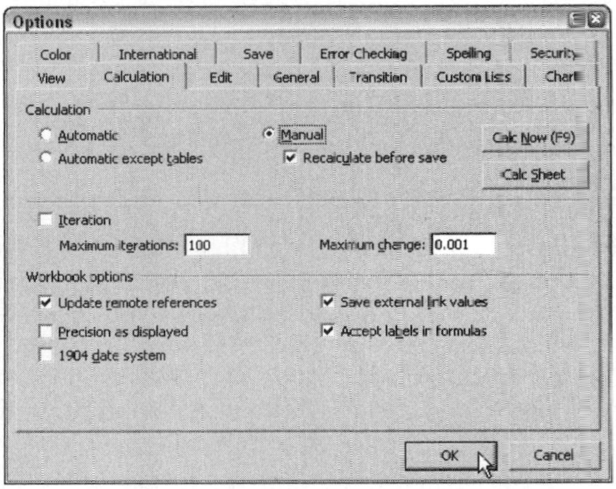

Figure 6-14:
Switch to manual recalculation in the Options dialog box.

Putting on the Protection

After you more or less finalize a worksheet by checking out its formulas and proofing its text, you often want to guard against any unplanned changes by protecting the document.

Each cell in the worksheet can be locked or unlocked. By default, Excel locks all the cells in a worksheet so that, when you follow these steps, Excel locks the whole thing up tighter than a drum.

1. **Choose Tools⊏⟩Protection⊏⟩Protect Sheet from the menu bar.**

   Excel opens the Protect Sheet dialog box (see Figure 6-15) in which you select the check box options you want to be available when the protection is turned on in the worksheet. By default, Excel selects the Protect Worksheet and Contents of Locked Cells check box at the top of the Protect Sheet dialog box. In addition, the program selects both the Select Locked Cells and Select Unlocked Cells check boxes in the Allow All Users of This Worksheet To list box below.

2. **(Optional) Click any of the check box options in the Allow All Users of This Worksheet To list box (such as Format Cells or Insert Columns) that you still want to be functional when the worksheet protection is operational.**

3. **If you want to assign a password that must be supplied before you can remove the protection from the worksheet, type the password in the Password to Unprotect Sheet text box.**

4. **Click OK or press Enter.**

   If you type a password in the Password to Unprotect Sheet text box, Excel opens the Confirm Password dialog box. Reenter the password in the Reenter Password to Proceed text box exactly as you type it in the Password to Unprotect Sheet text box in the Protect Sheet dialog box and then click OK or press Enter.

If you want to go a step further and protect the layout of the worksheets in the workbook, you protect the entire workbook as follows:

1. **Choose Tools⊏⟩Protection⊏⟩Protect Workbook on the menu bar.**

   Excel opens the Protect Workbook dialog box, where the Structure check box is selected and the Windows check box is not selected. With the Structure check box selected, Excel won't let you mess around with the sheets in the workbook (by deleting them or rearranging them). If you want to protect any windows that you set up (as I describe in Chapter 7), you need to select the Windows check box as well.

2. **To assign a password that must be supplied before you can remove the protection from the worksheet, type the password in the Password (optional) text box.**

3. **Click OK or press Enter.**

   If you type a password in the Password (optional) text box, Excel opens the Confirm Password dialog box. Reenter the password in the Reenter Password to Proceed text box exactly as you type it into the Password (optional) text box in the Protect Sheet dialog box, and then click OK or press Enter.

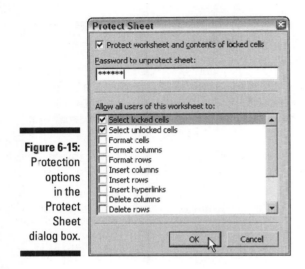

Figure 6-15:
Protection
options
in the
Protect
Sheet
dialog box.

Selecting the Protect Sheet command makes it impossible to make further changes to the contents of any of the locked cells in that worksheet except for those options that you specifically exempt in the Allow All Users of This Worksheet To list box. (See Step 2 in the first set of steps in this section.) Selecting the Protect Workbook command makes it impossible to make further changes to the layout of the worksheets in that workbook.

Excel displays an alert dialog box with the following message when you try to edit or replace an entry in a locked cell:

```
The cell or chart you are trying to change is protected
and therefore read-only.
To modify a protected cell or chart, first remove
protection using the Unprotect Sheet command (Tools menu,
Protection submenu). You may be prompted for a password.
```

Usually, your intention in protecting a worksheet or an entire workbook is not to prevent all changes but to prevent changes in certain areas of the worksheet. For example, in a budget worksheet, you may want to protect all the cells that contain headings and formulas but allow changes in all the cells where you enter the budgeted amounts. That way you can't inadvertently wipe out a title or formula in the worksheet simply by entering a value in the wrong column or row (not an uncommon occurrence). To leave certain cells unlocked so that you can still change them after protecting the worksheet or workbook, follow these steps:

1. **Select the cells that you want to remain unlocked in the protected worksheet or workbook.**

2. **Choose Tools⇨Protection⇨Allow Users to Edit Ranges on the menu bar.**

   The Allow Users to Edit Ranges dialog box appears.

3. **Choose the New button in the Allow Users to Edit Ranges dialog box.**

4. **(Optional) If you want to give a descriptive range name to the range of cells that you want to remain unprotected (other than the Range1 name given by the program), type the new name in the Title text box of the New Range dialog box.**

   When entering a range name in the Title text box, be sure to connect words with an underscore if you enter more than a single word.

5. **Check the cell range in the Refer to Cells text box to make sure that its cell addresses include all of the cells that you want users to be able to edit.**

   If you see that you need to edit this cell range, press Tab to select this text box, and then use the mouse pointer to drag through and select all the cells. As you drag, Excel automatically condenses the dialog box down to the Refers to Cells text box. When you release the mouse button, the program automatically expands the dialog box back to its original size.

6. **(Optional) If you want to password-protect this range (so that only users who have this password can make changes), press Tab until the Range Password text box is selected, and then enter the password there.**

7. **Click OK to close the New Range dialog box and return to the Allow Users to Edit Ranges dialog box.**

   If you enter a range password in Step 6, you need to reproduce the password in the Confirm Password dialog box and then click OK before Excel will return you to the Allow Users to Edit Ranges dialog box.

8. **(Optional) If the worksheet contains other ranges that you want to make available for editing, click the New button and repeat Steps 4–7.**

9. **After you finish defining the ranges that can be edited while protection is turned on, click the Protect Sheet button to open the Protect Sheet dialog box.**

   Here you can specify a password for unprotecting the sheet and designate what features remain operational when protection is turned on. Refer to the first set of four steps at the beginning of this section for details on turning on protection.

To remove protection from the current worksheet or workbook document so that you can once again make changes to its cells (whether locked or unlocked), choose Tools⇔Protection and then choose either the Unprotect Sheet or the Unprotect Workbook command on the cascading menu. If you assign a password when protecting the worksheet or workbook, you must then reproduce the password exactly as you assign it (including any case differences) in the Password text box of the Unprotect Sheet or Unprotect Workbook dialog box.

To protect and share . . .

If you create a workbook with contents to be updated by several different users on your network, you can use the Protect and Share Workbook command from the Tools⇔Protection submenu. This command ensures that Excel tracks all the changes made and that no user can intentionally or inadvertently remove Excel's tracking of changes made to the file. To do this, you simply select the Sharing with Tracked Changes check box in the Protected Shared Workbook dialog box that appears after you choose the command. After you select this check box, you can add a password in the Password (optional) text box below that each user must supply before he or she can open the workbook to make any changes

Chapter 7

Maintaining Multiple Worksheets

. . . .

In This Chapter

▶ Moving from sheet to sheet in your workbook

▶ Adding and deleting sheets in a workbook

▶ Selecting sheets for group editing

▶ Naming sheet tabs descriptively

▶ Rearranging sheets in a workbook

▶ Displaying parts of different sheets

▶ Comparing two worksheets side by side

▶ Copying or moving sheets from one workbook to another

▶ Creating formulas that span different worksheets

. . . .

*W*hen you're brand-new to spreadsheets, you have enough trouble keeping track of a single worksheet — let alone three worksheets — and the very thought of working with more than one may be a little more than you can take. However, after you get a little experience under your belt, you'll find that working with more than one worksheet in a workbook is no more taxing than working with just a single worksheet.

Don't confuse the term *workbook* with *worksheet*. The workbook forms the document (file) that you open and save as you work. Each workbook (file) normally contains three blank worksheets. These worksheets are like the loose-leaf pages in a notebook binder from which you can delete or to which you can add as you need. To help you keep track of the worksheets in your workbook and navigate between them, Excel provides sheet tabs (Sheet1 through Sheet3) that are kinda like tab dividers in a loose-leaf notebook.

Juggling Worksheets

You need to see *how* to work with more than one worksheet in a workbook, but it's also important to know *why* you'd want to do such a crazy thing in the first place. The most common situation is, of course, when you have a bunch of worksheets that are somehow related to each other and, therefore, naturally belong together in the same workbook. For example, take the case of Mother Goose Enterprises with its different companies: Jack Sprat Diet Centers, Jack and Jill Trauma Centers, Mother Hubbard Dog Goodies; Rub-a-Dub-Dub Hot Tubs and Spas; Georgie Porgie Pudding Pies; Hickory, Dickory, Dock Clock Repair; Little Bo Peep Pet Detectives; Simple Simon Pie Shoppes; and Jack Be Nimble Candlesticks. To keep track of the annual sales for all these companies, you could create a workbook containing a worksheet for each of the nine different companies.

By keeping the sales figures for each company in a different sheet of the same workbook, you gain all of the following benefits:

- You can enter the stuff that's needed in all the sales worksheets (if you select those sheet tabs) just by typing it once into the first worksheet (see the section "Editing en masse," later in this chapter).

- In order to help you build the worksheet for the first company's sales, you can attach macros to the current workbook so that they are readily available when you create the worksheets for the other companies. (A *macro* is a sequence of frequently performed, repetitive tasks and calculations that you record for easy playback.)

- You can quickly compare the sales of one company with the sales of another (see the section "Opening Windows on Your Worksheets," later in this chapter).

- You can print all the sales information for each company as a single report in one printing operation. (Read through Chapter 5 for specifics on printing an entire workbook or particular worksheets in a workbook.)

- You can easily create charts that compare certain sales data from different worksheets (see Chapter 8 for details).

- You can easily set up a summary worksheet with formulas that total the quarterly and annual sales for all nine companies (see the section "To Sum Up . . ." later in this chapter).

Sliding between the sheets

Each workbook that you create contains three worksheets, rather predictably named *Sheet1* through *Sheet3*. In typical Excel fashion, these names appear on tabs at the bottom of the workbook window. To go from one worksheet to another, you simply click the tab that contains the name of the sheet you want to see. Excel then brings that worksheet to the top of the stack, displaying its information in the current workbook window. You can always tell which worksheet is current because its name is displayed in bold type on the tab and its tab appears without any dividing line as an extension of the current worksheet.

The only problem with moving to a new sheet by clicking its sheet tab occurs when you add so many worksheets to a workbook (as I describe later in this chapter in the section "Don't Short-Sheet Me!") that not all the sheet tabs are visible at any one time, and the sheet tab you want to click is not visible in the workbook. To deal with this problem, Excel provides tab scrolling buttons (as shown in the lower-left corner of Figure 7-1) that you can use to bring new sheet tabs into view.

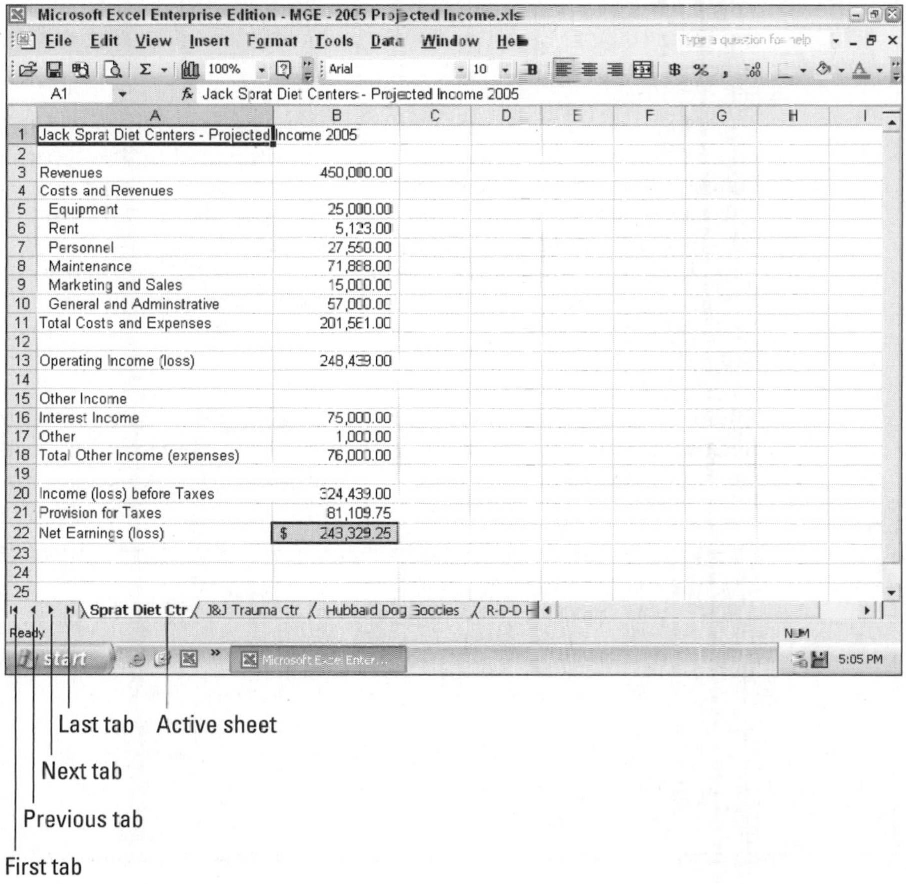

Figure 7-1: Use Tab scrolling buttons to bring new sheet tabs into view.

First tab
Previous tab
Next tab
Last tab Active sheet

✔ Click the Next tab scroll button (with the triangle pointing right) to bring the next unseen tab of the sheet on the right into view. Hold down the Shift key while you click this button to scroll several tabs at a time.

✔ Click the Previous tab scroll button (with the triangle pointing left) to bring the next unseen tab of the sheet on the left into view. Hold down the Shift key while you click this button to scroll several tabs at a time.

✔ Click the Last tab scroll button (with the triangle pointing right to the vertical bar) to bring the last group of sheet tabs, including the very last tab, into view.

✔ Click the First tab scroll button (with the triangle pointing left to the vertical bar) to bring the first group of sheet tabs, including the very first tab, into view.

Just don't forget that scrolling the sheet tab that you want into view is not the same thing as selecting it: You still need to click the tab for the desired sheet to bring it to the front of the stack.

To make it easier to find the sheet tab you want to select without having to do an inordinate amount of tab scrolling, you can drag the tab split bar (see Figure 7-2) to the right to reveal more sheet tabs (consequently making the horizontal scroll bar shorter). If you don't care at all about using the horizontal scroll bar, you can maximize the number of sheet tabs in view by actually getting rid of this scroll bar. To do this, drag the tab split bar to the right until it's smack up against the vertical split bar, which gives you a view of about 12 sheet tabs at a time (on a standard 14-inch monitor with a resolution of 640 x 480 pixels).

When you decide that you then want to restore the horizontal scroll bar to its normal length, you can either manually drag the tab split bar to the left or simply double-click it.

Going sheet to sheet via the keyboard

You can forget all about the darned tab scrolling buttons and sheet tabs and just go back and forth through the sheets in a workbook with your keyboard. To move to the next worksheet in a workbook, press Ctrl+PgDn. To move to the previous worksheet in a workbook, press Ctrl+PgUp. The nice thing about using the keyboard shortcuts Ctrl+PgDn and Ctrl+PgUp is that they work whether or not the next or previous sheet tab is currently displayed in the workbook window!

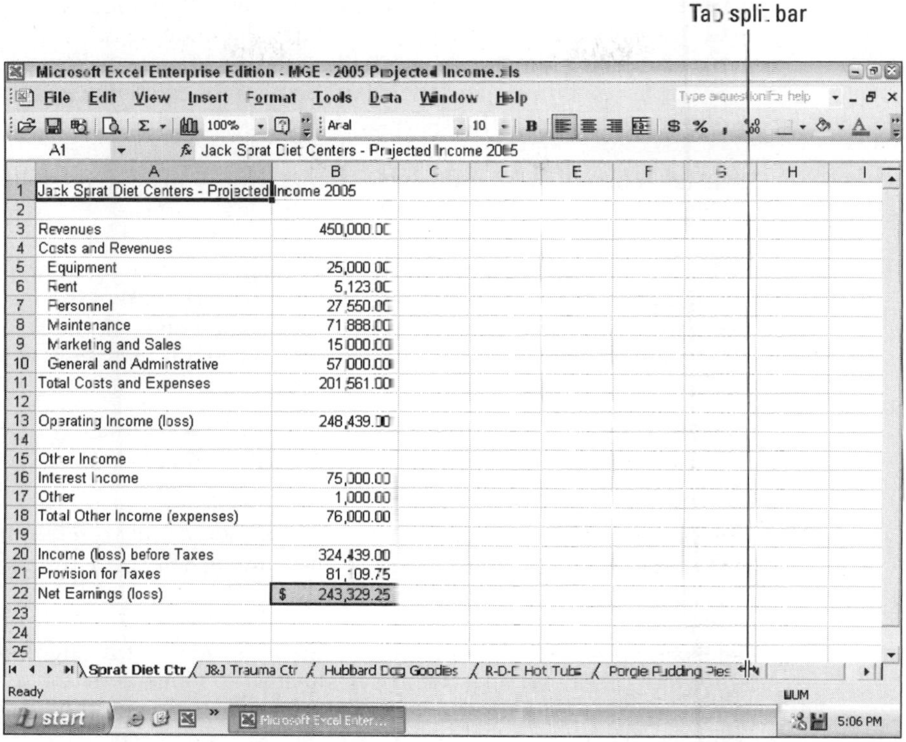

Tab split bar

Figure 7-2:
Use the Tab split bar to display more sheet tabs by making the horizontal scroll bar shorter.

Editing en masse

Each time you click a sheet tab, you select that worksheet and make it active, enabling you to make whatever changes are necessary to its cells. You may encounter times, however, when you want to select bunches of worksheets so that you can make the same editing changes to all of them simultaneously. When you select multiple worksheets, any editing change that you make to the current worksheet — such as entering information in cells or deleting stuff from them — affects the same cells in all the selected sheets in exactly the same way.

In other words, suppose you need to set up three worksheets in a new workbook, all of which contain the names of the 12 months, in row 3 starting in column B. Prior to entering **January** in cell B3 and then using the AutoFill handle (as described in Chapter 2) to fill in the rest of the 11 months across row 3, you would select all three worksheets (say Sheet1, Sheet2, and Sheet3, for argument's sake). Do this, and Excel inserts the names of the 12 months in row 3 of all three selected worksheets when you enter them once in the third row of the first sheet. (Pretty slick, huh?)

Likewise, say you have another workbook in which you need to get rid of Sheet2 and Sheet3. Instead of clicking Sheet2, choosing Edit⇨Delete Sheet, and then clicking Sheet3 and repeating the Edit⇨Delete Sheet command, select both worksheets and then zap them out of existence in one fell swoop by choosing the Edit⇨Delete Sheet command.

To select a bunch of worksheets in a workbook, you have the following choices:

✔ To select a group of neighboring worksheets, click the first sheet tab and then scroll the sheet tabs until you see the tab of the last worksheet you want to select. Hold the Shift key while you click the last sheet tab to select all the tabs in between — the old Shift-click method applied to worksheet tabs.

✔ To select a group of non-neighboring worksheets, click the first sheet tab and then hold down the Ctrl key while you click the tabs of the other sheets you want to select.

✔ To select all the sheets in the workbook, right-click the tab of the worksheet that you want active and choose Select All Sheets from its shortcut menu that appears.

Excel shows you which worksheets that you select by turning their sheet tabs white (although only the active sheet's tab name appears in bold) and displaying [Group] after the filename of the workbook on the Excel window's title bar.

To deselect the group of worksheets when you finish your group editing, you simply click a nonselected (that is, grayed out) worksheet tab. You can also deselect all the selected worksheets other than the one you want active by right-clicking the tab of the sheet you want displayed in the workbook window and then clicking Ungroup Sheets on its shortcut menu.

Don't Short-Sheet Me!

For some of you, the three worksheets automatically put into each new workbook that you start are as many as you would ever, ever need (or want) to use. For others of you, a measly three worksheets might seldom, if ever, be sufficient for the workbooks you create (for instance, say your company operates in 10 locations, or you routinely create budgets for 20 different departments or track expenses for 40 account representatives).

Excel makes it easy to insert additional worksheets in a workbook (up to 255 total) or remove those that you don't need. To insert a new worksheet in the workbook, follow these steps:

1. **Select the tab of the sheet where you want Excel to insert the new worksheet.**

2. **Choose Insert⇨Worksheet from the Excel menu bar or choose Insert from the sheet tab's shortcut menu.**

   If you choose the Insert⇨Worksheet command, Excel inserts a new worksheet and gives its tab the next available number (such as Sheet4).

   If you choose the Insert command on the sheet tab's shortcut menu, Excel opens the Insert dialog box in which you can specify the type of sheet to insert (such as Worksheet, Chart, MS Excel 4.0 Macro, or MS Excel 5.0 dialog), and you need to proceed to Step 3.

3. **Make sure that the Worksheet icon on the General tab of the Insert dialog box is selected and then click OK or press Enter.**

To insert a bunch of new worksheets in a row in the workbook, select a group with the same number of tabs as the number of new worksheets you want to add, starting with the tab where you want to insert the new worksheets. Next, choose Insert⇨Worksheet from the Excel menu bar.

To delete a worksheet from the workbook, follow these steps:

1. **Click the tab of the worksheet that you want to delete.**

2. **Choose Edit⇨Delete Sheet from the Edit menu or right-click the tab and choose Delete from its shortcut menu.**

   Excel then displays a scary message in an alert box about how you're going to permanently delete the selected sheets.

3. **Go ahead and click OK or press Enter if you're really sure that you want to zap the entire sheet.**

   Just keep in mind that this is one of those situations where Undo is powerless to put things right by restoring the deleted sheet to the workbook.

To delete a bunch of worksheets from the workbook, select all the worksheets you want to delete and choose Edit⇨Delete Sheet from the menu bar or choose Delete from the tab's shortcut menu. Then, when you're sure that none of the worksheets will be missed, click OK or press Enter when the alert dialog box appears.

If you find yourself constantly monkeying around with the number of worksheets in a workbook, either by adding a bunch of new worksheets or deleting all but one, you may want to think about changing the default number of worksheets in a workbook so that the next time you open a new workbook, you have a more realistic number of sheets on hand. To change the default number, choose Tools⇨Options to open the Options dialog box, select the General tab, and enter a new number between 1 and 255 in the Sheets in New Workbook text box or select a new number with the spinner buttons before you click OK.

A worksheet by any other name . . .

The sheet names that Excel comes up with for the tabs in a workbook (*Sheet1* through *Sheet3*) are, to put it mildly, not very original — and are certainly not descriptive of their function in life! Luckily, you can easily rename a worksheet tab to whatever helps you remember what you put on the worksheet (provided that this descriptive name is no longer than 31 characters).

To rename a worksheet tab, just follow these steps:

1. **Double-click the sheet tab or right-click the sheet tab and then click Rename on its shortcut menu.**

   This selects the current name on the sheet tab.

2. **Replace the current name on the sheet tab by typing in the new sheet name.**

3. **Press Enter.**

   Excel displays the new sheet name on its tab at the bottom of the workbook window.

A sheet tab by any other color . . .

In Excel 2003, you can assign colors to the different worksheet tabs. This feature enables you to color-code different worksheets. For example, you could assign red to the tabs of those worksheets that need immediate checking and blue to the tabs of those sheets that you've already checked.

To assign a color to a worksheet tab, right-click the tab and choose Tab Color from its shortcut menu to open the Format Tab Color dialog box. Click the color that you want to assign to the selected sheet tab in color palette that appears in the Format Tab Color dialog box, and then click OK. When the Format Tab Color dialog box disappears, the name of the active sheet tab appears underlined in the color you just selected. When you make another sheet tab active, the entire tab takes on the assigned color (and the text of the tab name changes to white if the selected color is sufficiently dark that black lettering is impossible to read).

To remove a color from a tab, open the Format Tab Color dialog box from the tab's shortcut menu and then choose the No Color selection at the very top of the color palette before clicking OK.

Short and sweet (sheet names)

Although Excel allows up to 31 characters (including spaces) for a sheet name, you want to keep your sheet names much briefer for two reasons:

- First, the longer the name, the longer the sheet tab. And the longer the sheet tab, the fewer tabs that can be displayed. And the fewer the tabs, the more tab scrolling you have to do to select the sheets you want to work with.

- Second, should you start creating formulas that use cells in different worksheets (see the section "To Sum Up . . ." later in this

chapter, for an example of this), Excel uses the sheet name as part of the cell reference in the formula. (How else could Excel keep straight the value in cell C1 on Sheet1 from the value in cell C1 on Sheet2?! Therefore, if your sheet names are long, you end up with unwieldy formulas in the cells and on the Formula bar even when you're dealing with simple formulas that only refer to cells in a couple of different worksheets.

So remember: As a general rule, the fewer characters in a sheet name the better. Also remember that each name must be unique — no duplicates allowed.

Getting your sheets in order

Sometimes, you may find that you need to change the order in which the sheets appear in the workbook. Excel makes this possible by letting you drag the tab of the sheet you want to arrange in the workbook to the place where you want to insert it. While you drag the tab, the pointer changes to a sheet icon with an arrowhead on it, and the program marks your progress among the sheet tabs (see Figures 7-3 and 7-4 for examples). When you release the mouse button, Excel reorders the worksheets in the workbook by inserting the sheet at the place where you dropped the tab off.

If you hold down the Ctrl key while you drag the tab, Excel inserts a copy of the worksheet at the place where you release the mouse button. You can tell that Excel is copying the sheet, rather than just moving it in the workbook, because the pointer shows a plus sign (+) on the sheet icon containing the arrowhead. When you release the mouse button, Excel inserts the copy in the workbook, which is designated by the addition of (2) after the tab name. For instance, if you copy Sheet5 to another place in the workbook, the sheet tab of the copy is named *Sheet5 (2)*. You can then rename the tab to something civilized (see the section "A worksheet by any other name . . ." earlier in this chapter, for details).

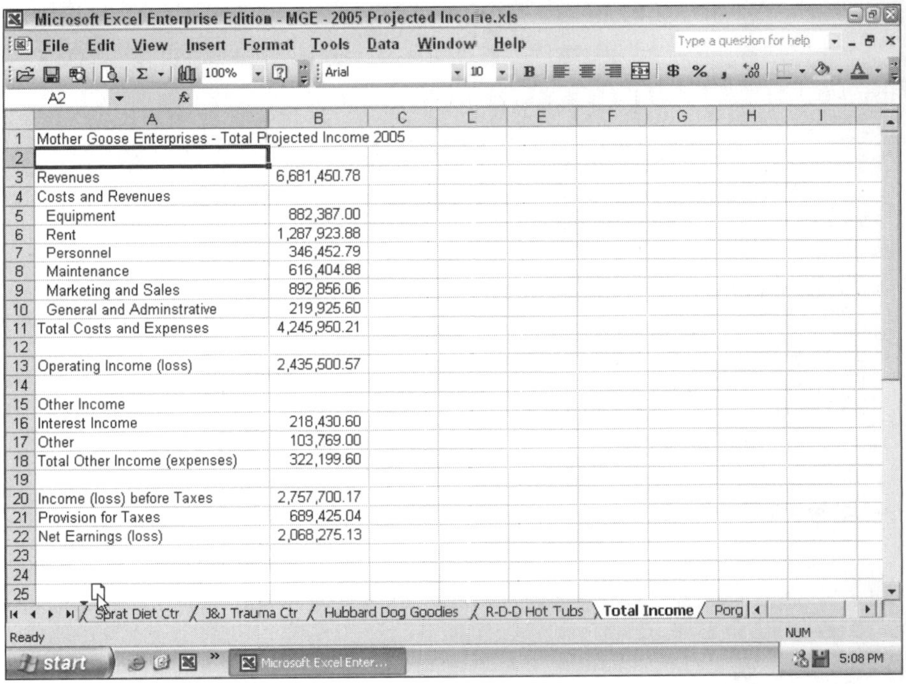

Figure 7-3:
Drag the
Total
Income tab
to the front
to reorder
the sheets
in this
worksheet.

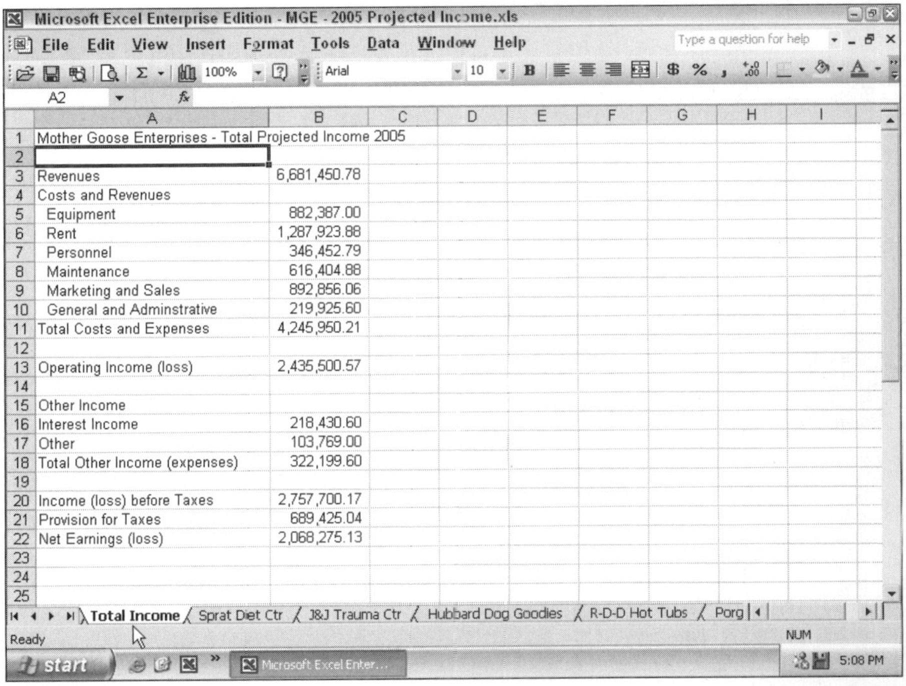

Figure 7-4:
The
relocated
Total
Income
sheet is
now at the
front of the
workbook.

You can also move or copy worksheets from one part of a workbook to another by activating the sheet that you want to move or copy and then choosing Move or Copy on its shortcut menu. In the Before Sheet list box of the Move or Copy dialog box, click the name of the worksheet in front of which you want the active sheet moved or copied.

To move the active sheet immediately ahead of the sheet you select in the Before Sheet list box, simply click OK. To copy the active sheet, be sure to select the Create a Copy check box before you click OK. If you copy a worksheet instead of just moving it, Excel adds a number to the sheet name. For example, if you copy a sheet named *Total Income*, Excel automatically names the copy of the worksheet *Total Income (2)*, and this name appears on its sheet tab.

Opening Windows on Your Worksheets

Just as you can split up a single worksheet into window panes so that you can view and compare different parts of that same sheet on the screen (see Chapter 6), you can split up a single workbook into worksheet windows and then arrange the windows so that you can view different parts of each worksheet on the screen.

To open up the worksheets that you want to compare in different windows, you simply insert new workbook windows (in addition to the one that Excel automatically opens when you open the workbook file itself) and then select the worksheet that you want to display in the new window. You can accomplish this with the following steps:

1. **Choose Window⇨New Window from the menu bar to create a second worksheet window; then click the tab of the worksheet that you want to display in this second window (indicated by the :2 that Excel adds to the end of the filename in the title bar).**

2. **Choose the Window⇨New Window command again to create a third worksheet window; then click the tab of the worksheet that you want to display in this third window (indicated by the :3 that Excel adds to the end of the filename in the title bar).**

3. **Continue in this manner, using the Window⇨New Window command to create a new window and then selecting the tab of the worksheet you want to display in that window for each worksheet you want to compare.**

4. **Choose the Window⇨Arrange command and select one of the Arrange options (as I describe next); then click OK or press Enter.**

When you open the Arrange Windows dialog box, you are presented with the following options:

✓ **Tiled:** Select this radio button to have Excel arrange and size the windows so that they all fit side by side on the screen in the order in which you open them. (Check out Figure 7-5 to see the screen after selecting the Windows of Active Workbook check box and choosing the Tiled radio button, when three worksheet windows are open.)

✓ **Horizontal:** Select this radio button to have Excel size the windows equally and then place them one above the other. (In Figure 7-6, you can see the screen after selecting the Windows of Active Workbook check box and choosing the Horizontal radio button, when four worksheet windows are open.)

✓ **Vertical:** Select this radio button to have Excel size the windows equally and then place them next to each other. (Look at Figure 7-7 to see the screen after selecting the Windows of Active Workbook check box and choosing the Vertical radio button, when four worksheet windows are open.)

✓ **Cascade:** Select this radio button to have Excel arrange and size the windows so that they overlap one another with only their title bars showing. (See Figure 7-8 for the screen after selecting the Windows of Active Workbook check box and choosing the Cascade radio button, when four worksheet windows are open).

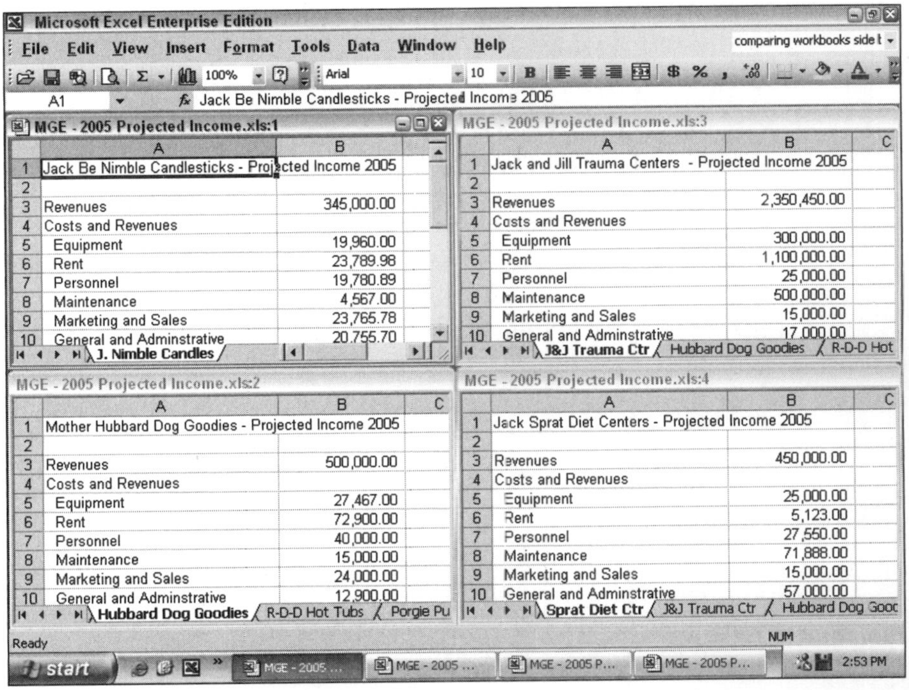

Figure 7-5: Arrange four worksheet windows with the Tiled option.

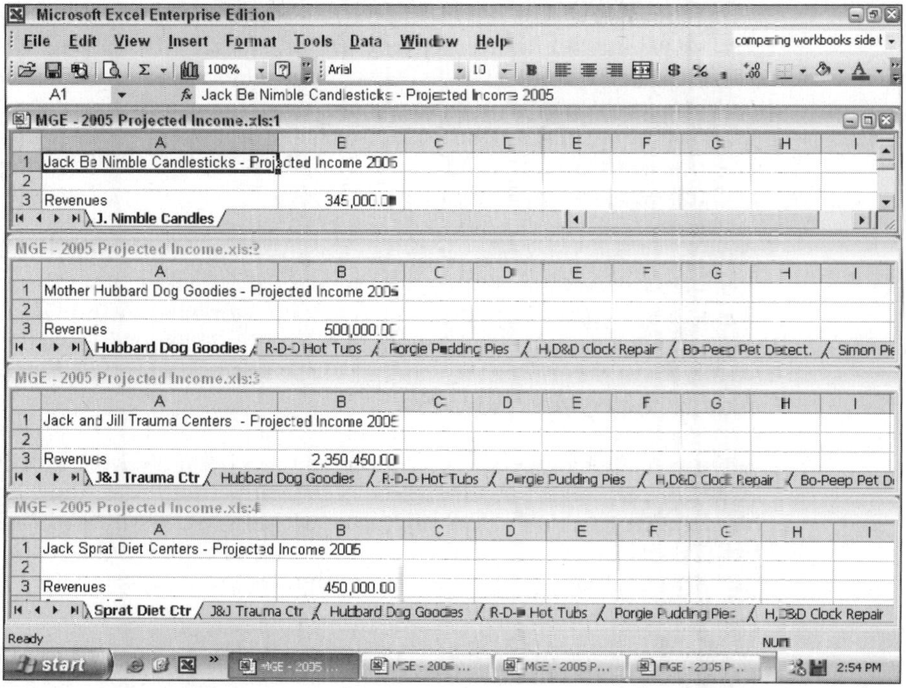

Figure 7-6:
Arrange four worksheet windows with the Horizontal option.

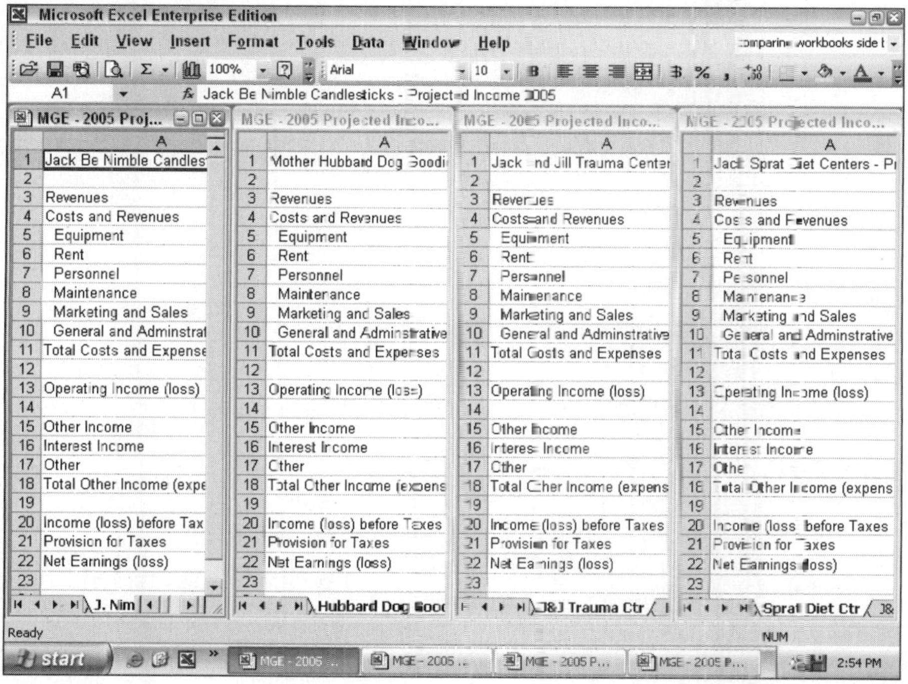

Figure 7-7:
Arrange four worksheet windows with the Vertical option.

✓ **Windows of Active Workbook:** Select this check box to have Excel show only the windows that you have open in the current workbook. Otherwise, Excel also displays all the windows in any other workbooks you have open. Yes, it is possible to open more than one workbook — as well as more than one window within each open workbook — provided that your computer has enough memory and you have enough stamina to keep track of all that information.

After you place the windows in one arrangement or another, activate the one you want to use (if it's not already selected) by clicking it. In the case of the cascade arrangement, you need to click the worksheet window's title bar, or you can click its button on the Windows XP or 2000 taskbar. Use the button's screen tip to determine the number of the window when the buttons are too short to display this information.

When you click a worksheet window that has been tiled or placed in the horizontal or vertical arrangement, Excel indicates that the window is selected by highlighting its title bar and adding scroll bars to the window. When you click the title bar of a worksheet window you place in the cascade arrangement, the program displays the window on the top of the stack, as well as highlighting its title bar and adding scroll bars.

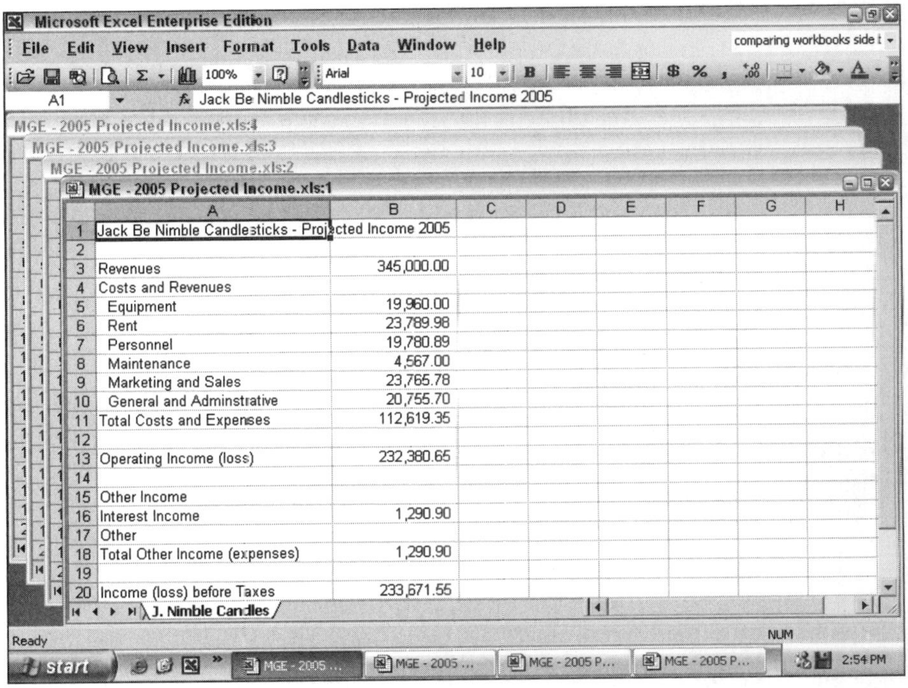

Figure 7-8:
Arrange
four
worksheet
windows
with the
Cascade
option.

You can temporarily zoom the window up to full size by clicking the Maximize button on the window's title bar. When you finish the work you need to do in the full-size worksheet window, return it to its previous arrangement by clicking the window's Restore button.

To select the next tiled, horizontal, or vertical window on the screen or display the next window in a cascade arrangement with the keyboard, press Ctrl+F6. To select the previous tiled, horizontal, or vertical window or to display the previous window in a cascade arrangement, press Ctrl+Shift+F6. Note that these keystrokes work to select the next and previous worksheet window even when the windows are maximized in the Excel program window.

If you close one of the windows you've arranged by its Close button (the one with the X in the upper-right corner) or by pressing Ctrl+W, Excel does not automatically resize the other open windows to fill in the gap. Likewise, if you create another window with the Window➪New Window command, Excel does not automatically arrange it in with the others. (In fact, the new window just sits on top of the other open windows.)

To fill in the gap created by closing a window or to integrate a newly opened window into the current arrangement, choose Windows➪Arrange to open the Arrange Windows dialog box and click OK or press Enter. (The same radio button you selected last time is still selected if you want to choose a new arrangement, select a new radio button before you click OK.)

Don't try to close a particular worksheet window with the File➪Close command on the menu bar, because you'll only succeed in closing the entire workbook file, while at the same time getting rid of all the worksheet windows you created.

When you save your workbook, Excel saves the current window-arrangement as part of the file along with all the rest of the changes. If you don't want to save the current window arrangement, close all but one of the windows (by double-clicking their Control-menu buttons or selecting their windows and then pressing Ctrl+W). Then click that last window's Maximize button and select the tab of the worksheet that you want to display the next time you open the workbook before saving the file.

Comparing Two Worksheets Side by Side

You can use the new Compare Side by Side With command on the Window menu to quickly and easily do a side by side comparison of any two worksheet windows that you have open. When you choose Window➪Compare Side by Side With from the menu bar after opening two windows, Excel automatically tiles them horizontally (as though you had selected the Horizontal option in the Arrange Windows dialog box), while at the same time displaying the Compare Side by Side toolbar (shown in Figure 7-9).

If you have more than two windows open at the time you choose Window⇨ Compare Side by Side With, Excel opens the Compare Side by Side dialog box where you click the name of the window that you want to compare with the one that's active at the time you choose the command. As soon as you click OK in the Compare Side by Side dialog box, Excel horizontally tiles the active window above the one you just selected.

The Compare Side by Side toolbar contains the follow three buttons:

✔ **Synchronous Scrolling:** When you activate this button by first clicking it, any scrolling that you do in the worksheet in the active window is mirrored and synchronized in the worksheet in the inactive window beneath it. To be able to scroll the worksheet in the active window independently of the inactive window, click the Synchronous Scrolling button a second time to deactivate it.

✔ **Reset Window Position:** Click this button after manually resizing the active window (by dragging its size box) to restore the two windows to their previous side-by-side arrangement

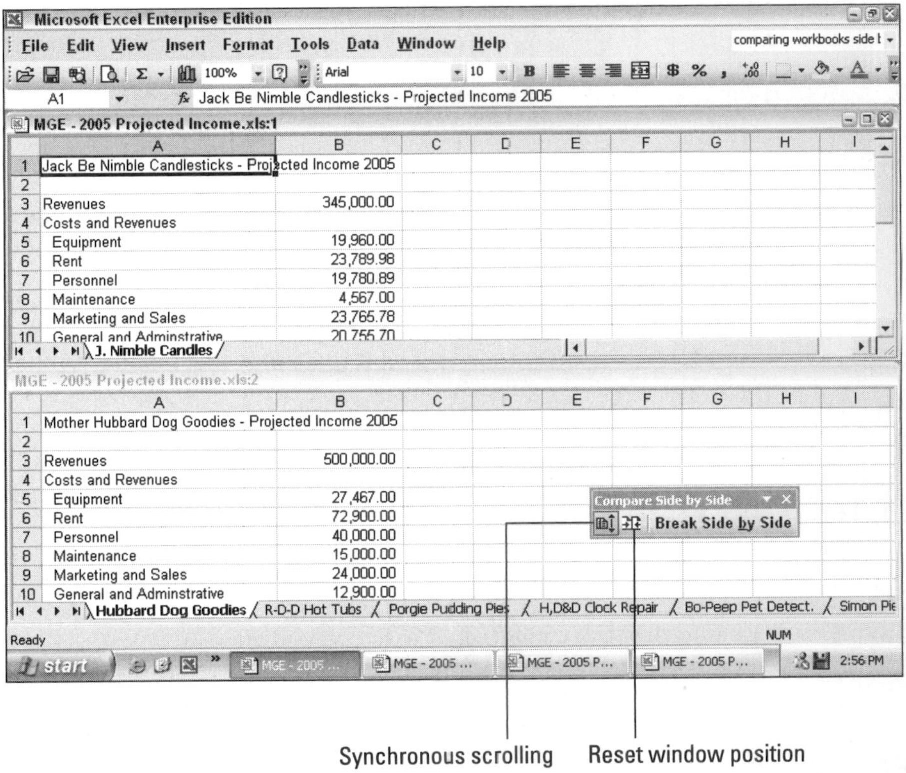

Figure 7-9:
Compar-
ing two
worksheet
windows
side by side.

Synchronous scrolling   Reset window position

✔ **Break Side by Side:** When you click this button, Excel returns the windows to whatever display arrangement you selected before choosing the Window⇨Compare Side by Side With command. If you haven't previously selected a display option in the Arrange Windows dialog box, Excel just displays the active window full size.

Passing Sheets in the Night

In some situations, you need to move a particular worksheet or copy it from one workbook to another. To move or copy worksheets between workbooks, follow these steps:

1. **Open both the workbook with the worksheet(s) that you want to move or copy and the workbook that is to contain the moved or copied worksheet(s).**

   Use the Open tool on the Standard toolbar or choose the File⇨Open command (Ctrl+O) to open the workbooks.

2. **Select the workbook that contains the worksheet(s) that you want to move or copy.**

   To select the workbook with the sheet(s) to be moved or copied, choose its name from the Window pull-down menu.

3. **Select the worksheet(s) that you want to move or copy.**

   To select a single worksheet, click its sheet tab. To select a group of neighboring sheets, click the first tab and then hold down Shift while you click the last tab. To select various nonadjacent sheets, click the first tab and then hold down Ctrl while you click each of the other sheet tabs.

4. **Choose the Edit⇨Move or Copy Sheet command from the menu bar or choose the Move or Copy command from a tab's shortcut menu.**

   Excel opens up the Move or Copy dialog box (similar to the one shown in Figure 7-10) in which you indicate whether you want to move or copy the selected sheet(s) and where to move or copy them to.

5. **In the To Book drop-down list box, select the name of the workbook to which you want to copy or move the worksheets.**

   If you want to move or copy the selected worksheet(s) to a new workbook rather than to an existing one that you have open, select the (new book) option that appears at the very top of the To Book pop-up list.

6. **In the Before Sheet list box, select the name of the sheet that the worksheet(s) you're about to move or copy should precede. If you want the sheet(s) that you're moving or copying to appear at the end of the workbook, choose the (move to end) option.**

7. Select the Create a Copy check box to copy the selected worksheet(s) to the designated workbook (rather than move them).

8. Click OK or press Enter to complete the move or copy operation.

If you prefer a more direct approach, you can move or copy sheets between open workbooks by dragging their sheet tabs from one workbook window to another. Note that this method works with a bunch of sheets as well as with a single sheet; just be sure that you select all their sheet tabs before you begin the drag-and-drop procedure.

To drag a worksheet from one workbook to another, you must open both workbooks. Use the Window⇨Arrange command from the menu bar and then select an arrangement (such as Horizontal or Vertical to put the workbook windows either on top of each other or side by side). Before you close the Arrange Windows dialog box, be sure that the Windows of Active Workbook check box does *not* contain a check mark.

After arranging the workbook windows, drag the worksheet tab from one workbook to another. If you want to copy rather than move the worksheet, hold down the Ctrl key while you drag the sheet icon(s). To locate the worksheet in the new workbook, position the downward-pointing triangle that moves with the sheet icon in front of the worksheet tab where you want to insert it; then release the mouse button.

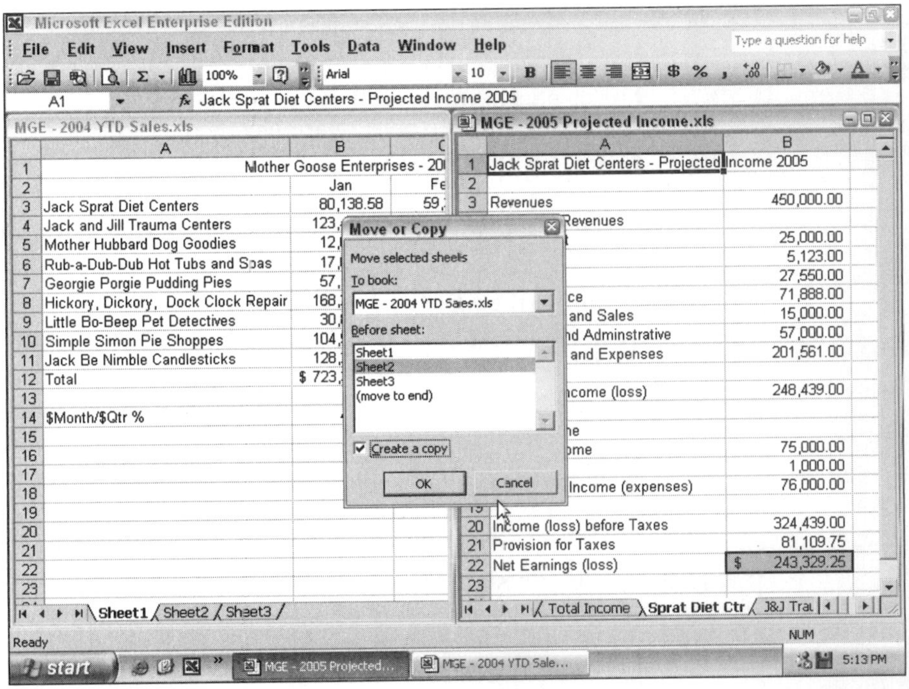

Figure 7-10:
Use the
Move or
Copy dialog
box to move
or copy from
the current
workbook
into a
different
workbook.

This drag-and-drop operation is one of those that you can't reverse by using Excel's Undo feature (see Chapter 4). This means that you if drop the sheet in the wrong workbook, you'll have to go get the wayward sheet yourself and drag it back and drop it into the place where it once belonged!

In Figures 7-11 and 7-12, I illustrate how easy it is to move or copy a worksheet from one workbook to another using this drag-and-drop method.

In Figure 7-11, you see two workbook windows: the MGE – 2004 YTD Sales workbook (left pane) and the MGE – 2005 Projected Income workbook (right pane). I arranged these workbook windows with the Window⇨Compare Side by Side With command. To copy the Sprat Diet Ctr sheet from the MGE – 2005 Projected Income workbook to the MGE – 2004 YTD Sales workbook I simply select the Sprat Diet Ctr sheet tab and then hold down the Ctrl key while I drag the sheet icon to its new position right before Sheet2 of the MGE – 2004 YTD Sales workbook.

Now look at Figure 7-12 to see the workbooks after I release the mouse button. As you can see, Excel inserts the copy of the Sprat Diet Ctr worksheet into the MGE – 2004 YTD Sales workbook at the place indicated by the triangle that accompanies the sheet icon (in between Sheet1 and Sheet2 in this example).

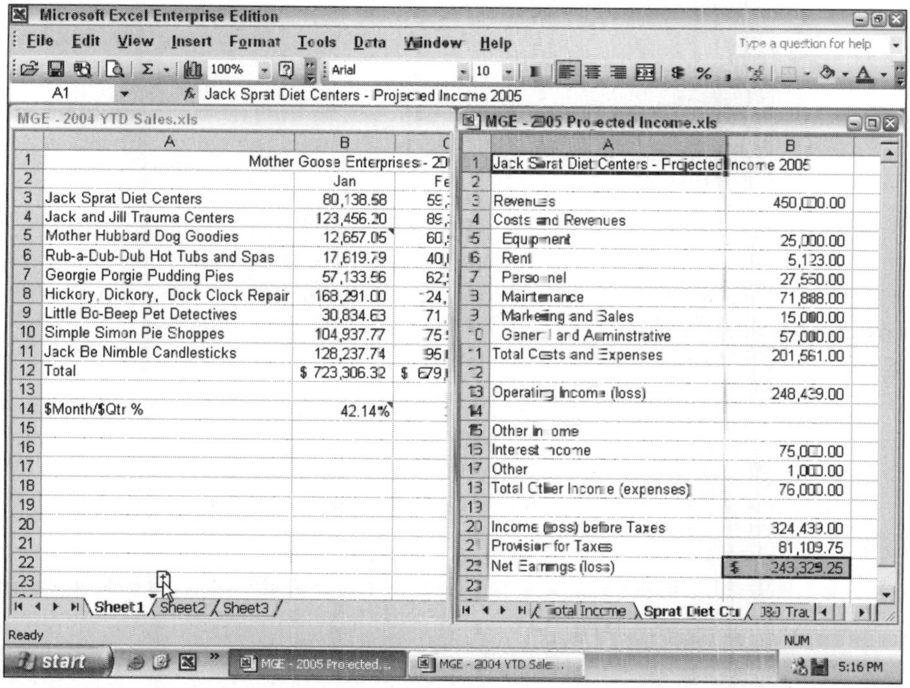

Figure 7-11: Copying the worksheet to the MGE – 2004 YTD Sales workbook via drag-and-drop.

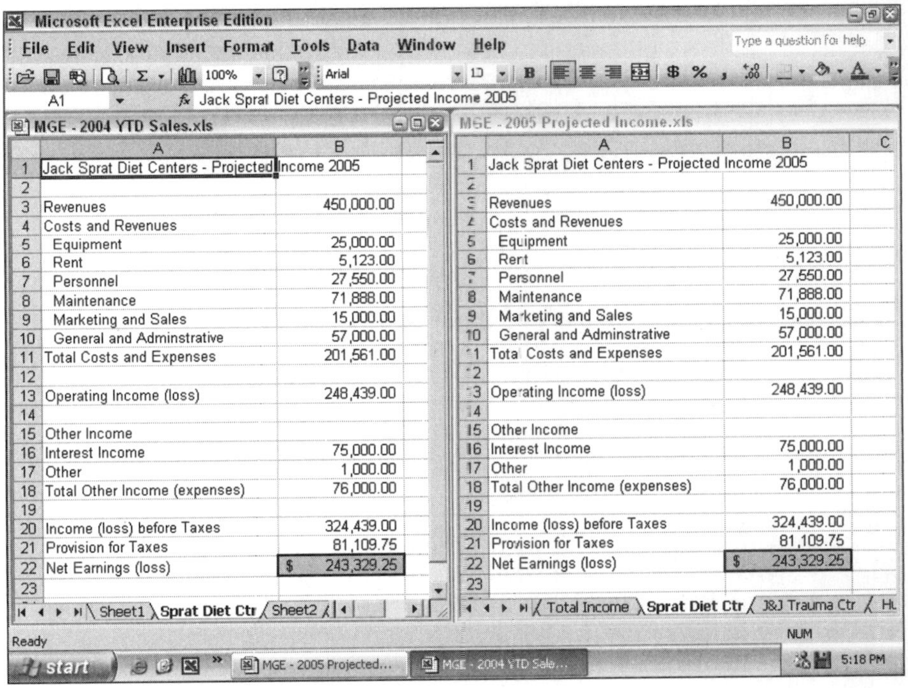

Figure 7-12:
I insert a
copy of the
worksheet
between
Sheet1 and
Sheet2 of
the MGE –
2004 YTD
Sales
workbook.

To Sum Up . . .

I'd be remiss if I didn't introduce you to the fascinating subject of creating a *summary worksheet* that recaps or totals the values stored in a bunch of other worksheets in the workbook.

The best way that I can show you how to create a summary worksheet is to walk you through the procedure of making one (entitled Total Income) for MGE – 2005 Projected Income workbook. This summary worksheet totals the projected revenue and expenses for all the companies that Mother Goose Enterprises owns.

Because the MGE – 2005 Projected Income workbook already contains nine worksheets, each with the 2005 projected revenue and expenses for one of these companies, and because these worksheets are all laid out in the same arrangement, creating this summary worksheet will be a breeze:

1. **I insert a new worksheet in front of the other worksheets in MGE – 2005 Projected Income workbook and rename its sheet tab from *Sheet1* to *Total Income*.**

To find out how to insert a new worksheet, refer to this chapter's section "Don't Short-Sheet Me!" To find out how to rename a sheet tab, read through the earlier section "A worksheet by any other name . . ."

2. **Next, I enter the worksheet title** Mother Goose Enterprises – Projected Income 2005 **in cell A1.**

   Do this by selecting cell A1 and then typing the text.

3. **Finally, I copy the rest of the row headings for column A (containing the revenue and expense descriptions) from the Sprat Diet Ctr worksheet to the Total Income worksheet.**

   To do this, select cell A3 in the Total Income sheet, and then click the Sprat Diet Ctr tab. Select the cell range A3:A22 in this sheet; then press Ctrl+C, click the Total Income tab again, and press Enter.

I am now ready to create the master SUM formula that totals the revenues of all nine companies in cell B3 of the Total Income sheet:

1. **I start by clicking cell B3 and then clicking the AutoSum tool on the Standard toolbar.**

   Excel then puts =SUM( ) in the cell with the insertion point placed between the two parentheses.

2. **I click the Sprat Diet Ctr sheet tab, and then click its cell B3 to select the projected revenues for the Jack Sprat Diet Centers.**

   The Formula bar reads =SUM('Sprat Diet Ctr'!B3) after selecting this cell.

3. **Next I type a comma (,) — the comma starts a new argument. I click the J&J Trauma Ctr sheet tab, and then I click its cell B3 to select projected revenues for the Jack and Jill Trauma Centers.**

   The Formula bar now reads =SUM('Sprat Diet Ctr'!B3,'J&J Trauma Ctr'!B3) after I select this cell.

4. **I continue in this manner, typing a comma (to start a new argument), and then selecting cell B3 with the projected revenues for all the other companies in the following seven sheets.**

   At the end of this procedure, the Formula bar now appears with the whopping SUM formula shown on the Formula bar in Figure 7-13.

5. **To complete the SUM formula in cell B3 of the Total Income worksheet, I then click the Enter box in the Formula bar (I could press Enter on my keyboard, as well).**

In Figure 7-13, note the result after using AutoFit to widen column B. As you can see in the formula bar, the master SUM formula that returns 6,681,450.78 to cell B3 of the Total Income worksheet gets its result by summing the values in B3 in all nine of the supporting worksheets.

All that's left to do now is to use AutoFill to copy the master formula in cell B3 down to row 22 as follows:

1. **With cell B3 still selected, I drag the AutoFill handle in the lower-right corner of cell B3 down to cell B22 to copy the formula for summing the values for the nine companies down this column.**

2. **Then I delete the SUM formulas from cells B4, B12, B14, B15, and B19 (all of which contain zeros because these cells have no income or expenses to be totaled).**

In Figure 7-14, you see the first section of the final summary projected income worksheet after I copy the formula created in cell B3 and after I delete the formulas from the cells that should be blank (all those that came up 0 in column B).

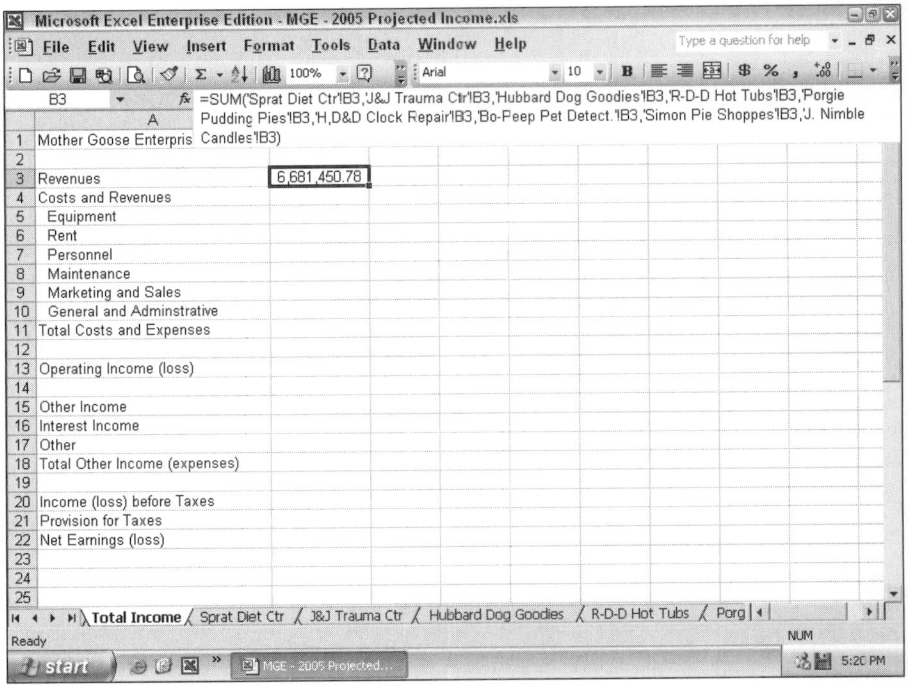

Figure 7-13: The Total Income worksheet after I create a SUM formula to total projected revenues for all nine Mother Goose companies.

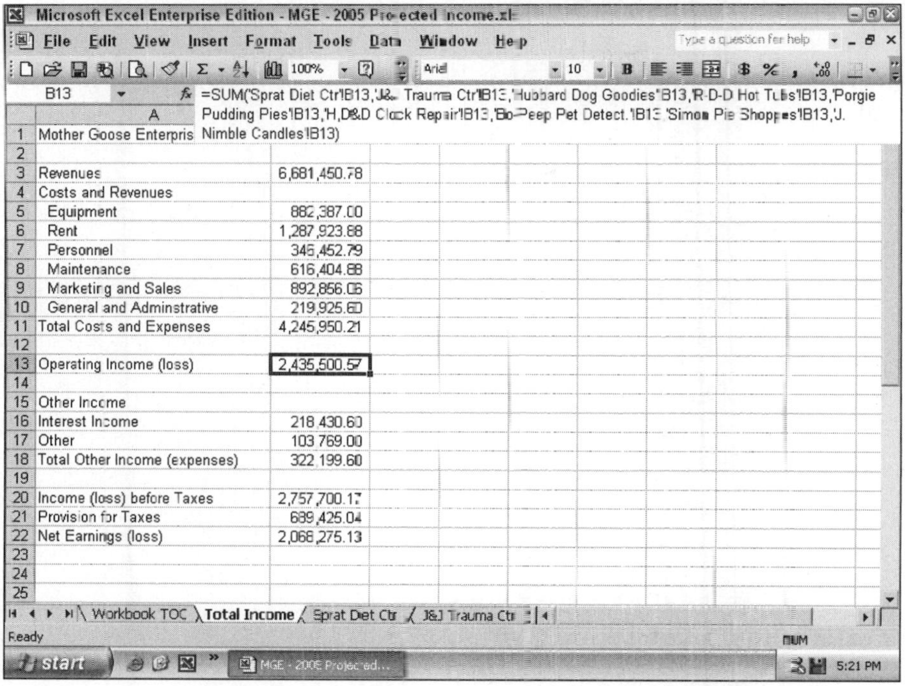

Figure 7-14:
The Total Income worksheet after I copy the SUM formula and delete formulas that return zero values.

Part IV

Life Beyond the Spreadsheet

The 5th Wave   By Rich Tennant

©RICHTENNANT

WELL, OBVIOUSLY ONE OF THE CELLS IN THE NAVIGATIONAL SPREADSHEET IS CORRUPT!

In this part . . .

Don't let anybody kid you: Spreadsheets are the bread
and butter of Excel 2003. And for many of you, creating, editing, and printing spreadsheets is the be-all and
end-all of Excel — "Who could ask for anything more?"
But don't get the wrong impression. Just because Excel is
a whiz at spreadsheets doesn't mean that it's a one-trick
pony. And just because spreadsheets may be the only
thing that you churn out in your present job doesn't mean
that someday you won't be moving into a job where you
need to chart spreadsheet data, create and maintain Excel
databases — and, who knows — even publish your worksheet data on the World Wide Web.

I created this part just in case you need to stray beyond
the confines of the spreadsheet into such exotic areas as
creating charts and adding graphic images, creating, sorting, and filtering databases, and publishing worksheets on
the Internet or company intranet. Between the entertain-
ing information in Chapter 8 about making charts, the fact-
filled information in Chapter 9 on working with Excel
databases, and the tips and tricks on creating hyperlinks
and converting worksheet data into HTML documents in
Chapter 10, you'll be more than ready should the day
arise (or already be here) when you are forced to go
beyond the pale of the good old Excel spreadsheet.

Chapter 8

The Simple Art of Making Charts

. . . .

In This Chapter

▶ Creating great-looking charts with the Chart Wizard

▶ Changing the chart with the Chart toolbar

▶ Formatting the chart's axes

▶ Adding a text box and arrow to a chart

▶ Inserting clip art in your worksheets

▶ Using the drawing tools to add graphics to charts and worksheets

▶ Printing a chart without printing the rest of the worksheet data

. . . .

As Confucius was reported to have said, "A picture is worth a thousand words" (or, in our case, numbers). By adding charts to worksheets, you not only heighten interest in the otherwise boring numbers but also illustrate trends and anomalies that may not be apparent from just looking at the values alone. Because Excel 2003 makes it so easy to chart the numbers in a worksheet, you can also experiment with different types of charts until you find the one that best represents the data — in other words, the picture that best tells the particular story.

Just a word about charts before you discover how to make them in Excel. Remember your high-school algebra teacher valiantly trying to teach you how to graph equations by plotting different values on an x-axis and a y-axis on graph paper? Of course, you were probably too busy with more important things like cool cars and rock 'n' roll to pay too much attention to an old algebra teacher. Besides, you probably told yourself, "I'll never need this junk when I'm out on my own and get a job!"

Well, see, you just never know. It turns out that even though Excel automates almost the entire process of charting worksheet data, you may need to be able to tell the x-axis from the y-axis, just in case Excel doesn't draw the chart the way you had in mind. To refresh your memory and make your algebra teacher proud, the x-axis is the horizontal axis, usually located along the bottom of the chart; the y-axis is the vertical one, usually located on the left side of the chart.

In most charts that use these two axes, Excel plots the categories along the x-axis at the bottom and their relative values along the y-axis on the left. The x-axis is sometimes referred to as the *time axis* because the chart often depicts values along this axis at different time periods, such as months, quarters, years, and so on.

Conjuring Up Charts with the Chart Wizard

Excel makes the process of creating a new chart in a worksheet as painless as possible with the Chart Wizard. The Chart Wizard walks you through a four-step procedure, at the end of which you have a complete and beautiful new chart.

Before you start the Chart Wizard, it's a good idea to first select the cell range that contains the information that you want charted. Keep in mind that to end up with the chart you want, the information should be entered in standard table format. With the information in this format, you can select it all as a single range (see Figure 8-1).

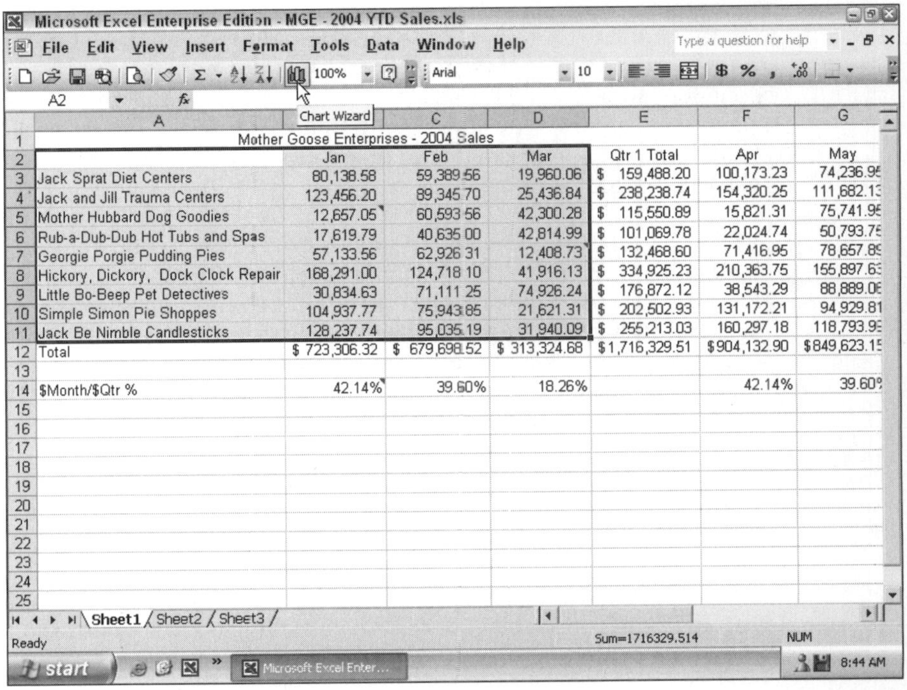

Figure 8-1:
Selecting the information to be charted.

If you create a chart that uses an x-axis and y-axis (as most do), the Chart Wizard naturally uses the row of column headings in the selected table for the category labels along the x-axis. If the table has row headings, the Chart Wizard uses these as the headings in the legend of the chart (if you choose to include one). The *legend* identifies each point, column, or bar in the chart that represents the values in the table.

After you select the information to chart, follow these steps to create the chart:

1. **Click the Chart Wizard button on the Standard toolbar to open the Chart Wizard – Step 1 of 4 – Chart Type dialog box, as shown in Figure 8-2.**

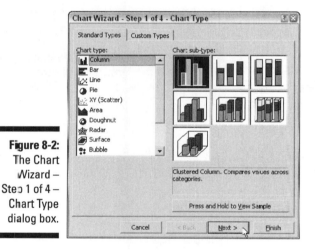

Figure 8-2:
The Chart
Wizard –
Step 1 of 4 –
Chart Type
dialog box.

The Chart Wizard button is the one with the picture of a column chart.

2. **If you want to use a chart other than the default Clustered Column, select a new chart type and/or chart sub-type on the Standard Types or Custom Types tabs in the Chart Wizard – Step 1 of 4 – Chart Type dialog box.**

To select another chart type, click its sample chart in the Chart Type list box. To select a chart sub-type, click its representation in the Chart Sub-Type portion of the dialog box. To see how your data will look using the chart type and chart sub-type you've selected on the Standard Types tab, click and hold down the Press and Hold to View Sample button that's right below the area showing the name of the chart type and chart sub-type.

3. **Click the Next button or press Enter to open the Chart Wizard – Step 2 of 4 – Chart Source Data dialog box.**

   Use options in the Chart Wizard – Step 2 of 4 – Chart Source Data dialog box (similar to the one shown in Figure 8-3) to change the data range that is to be charted (or select it from scratch, if you haven't already done so), as well as to set how the series within that data range is defined. The two tabs of Step 2 of the Chart Wizard are Data Range and Series.

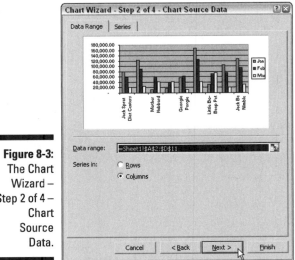

Figure 8-3:
The Chart
Wizard –
Step 2 of 4 –
Chart
Source
Data.

When this dialog box is open with the Data Range tab showing, any cell range selected prior to selecting the Chart Wizard is surrounded by the marquee in your worksheet and specified in formula form (with absolute cell references) in the Data Range text box. To modify this range (perhaps to include the row of column headings or the column of row headings), either reselect the range with the mouse or edit the cell references in the Data Range text box.

If the Chart Wizard – Step 2 of 4 – Chart Source Data dialog box is in the way of the cells you need to select, you can reduce the dialog box to just the text box and title bar by clicking the text box's Collapse/Expand Dialog button. To re-expand the dialog box, click the Expand Dialog button (which replaces the Collapse Dialog button) again. Also, keep in mind that the Source Data dialog box automatically collapses down to the Data Range text box as soon as you start dragging through cells of the worksheet and automatically re-expands the moment you release the mouse button.

4. **Check the cell range shown in the Data Range text box and, if necessary, adjust the range address (either by typing or selecting the cell range in the worksheet itself).**

   Normally, the Chart Wizard makes each column of values in the selected table into a separate *data series* on the chart. The *legend* (the boxed area with samples of the colors or patterns used in the chart) identifies each data series in the chart.

   For the worksheet data selected in Mother Goose Enterprises 2004 first-quarter sales worksheet (refer to Figure 8-1), Excel uses each bar in the column chart to represent a different month's sales and it clusters these sales together by the nine different companies. If you want, you can switch the data series from columns to rows by selecting the Rows radio button. Selecting the Rows radio button in this example makes each bar represent the sales of one of the nine different companies and cluster them together by month.

   When the chart forms the data series by columns, the Chart Wizard uses the entries in the first column (the row headings in cell range A3:A11) to label the x-axis (the *category labels*). The Chart Wizard uses the entries in the first row (the column labels in cell range B2:D2) as the headings in the legend.

5. **If you want the Chart Wizard to use the rows of the selected data range as the data series of the chart (rather than the columns), select the Rows radio button next to the Series In heading on the Date Range tab.**

   If you need to make individual changes to either the names or cells used in the data series, you can do so by clicking the Series tab in the Chart Wizard – Step 2 of 4 – Chart Source Data dialog box.

6. **Click the Next button or press Enter to proceed to the Chart Wizard – Step 3 of 4 – Chart Options dialog box.**

   The Chart Wizard – Step 3 of 4 – Chart Options dialog box (as shown in Figure 8-4) enables you to assign a whole bunch of options, including the titles to appear in the chart, whether to use gridlines, where the legend is displayed, whether data labels appear next to their data series, and whether the Chart Wizard draws a data table showing the values that are being charted right below the data series in the chart.

7. **Select the tab for the options you want to change (Titles, Axes, Gridlines, Legend, Data Labels, or Data Table) and then change the option settings as necessary (see "Changing the Chart Options," later in this chapter, for more information).**

8. **Click the Next button in the dialog box or press Enter to proceed to the Chart Wizard – Step 4 of 4 – Chart Location dialog box.**

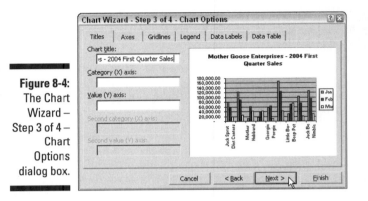

Figure 8-4:
The Chart
Wizard –
Step 3 of 4 –
Chart
Options
dialog box.

Select from two radio buttons in the Chart Wizard – Step 4 of 4 – Chart Location dialog box (see Figure 8-5) to place your new chart either on its own chart sheet in the workbook or as a new graphic object on one of the worksheets in your workbook.

9a. **To place the chart on its own sheet, select the As New Sheet radio button; then, if you wish, enter a new name for the sheet (besides Chart1, Chart2, and so on) in the text box to its right.**

9b. **To place the chart somewhere on one of the worksheets in your workbook, select the As Object In radio button and then select the name of the worksheet in the drop-down list to its right.**

10. **Click the Finish button or press Enter to close the last Chart Wizard dialog box.**

If you select the As New Sheet option, your new chart appears on its own chart sheet, and the Chart toolbar magically appears floating in the workbook document window. Select the As Object In radio button, and your chart appears as a selected graphic — along with the floating Chart toolbar — on the designated worksheet (similar to the one shown in Figure 8-6, which shows the column chart created for the Mother Goose Enterprises 2004 first-quarter sales).

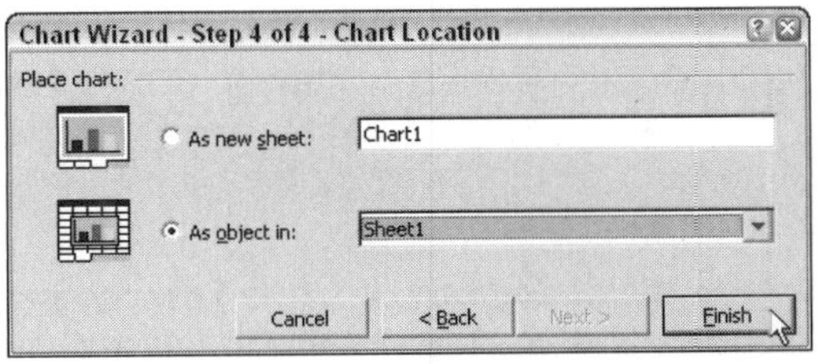

Figure 8-5:
The Chart
Wizard –
Step 4 of 4 –
Chart
Location
dialog box.

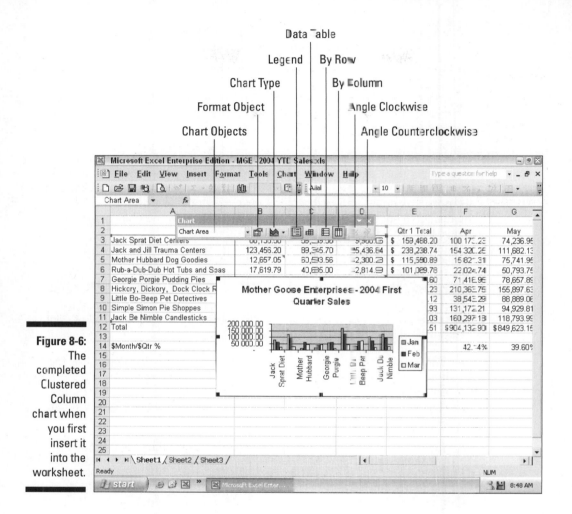

Figure 8-6:
The
completed
Clustered
Column
chart when
you first
insert it
into the
worksheet.

Moving and resizing a chart in a worksheet

After creating a new chart as a graphic object in a worksheet, you can easily move or resize the chart right after creating it because the chart is still selected. (You can always tell when a graphic object, such as a chart, is selected because you see *selection handles* — those tiny squares — around the edges of the object.) Immediately after creating the chart, the Chart toolbar appears floating above in the workbook document window. Excel also outlines each group of cells represented in the selected chart in a different color in the worksheet.

- To move the chart, position the mouse pointer somewhere inside the chart and drag the chart to a new location.

- To resize the chart (you may want to make it bigger if it seems distorted in any way), position the mouse pointer on one of the selection handles. When the pointer changes from the arrowhead to a double-headed arrow, drag the side or corner (depending on which handle you select) to enlarge or reduce the chart.

When the chart is properly sized and positioned in the worksheet, set the chart in place by deselecting it (simply click the mouse pointer in any cell outside the chart). As soon as you deselect the chart, the selection handles disappear, as does the Chart toolbar, from the document window. To reselect the chart (to edit, size, or move it), click anywhere on the chart with the mouse pointer.

Changing the chart with the Chart toolbar

After you create a chart, you can use the buttons on the Chart toolbar (refer to Figure 8-6) to make all kinds of changes to it.

- **Chart Objects:** To select the part of the chart to be changed, click the Chart Objects drop-down button and click the object's name on the pop-up menu or click the object directly in the chart itself with the mouse pointer. When you click a new object in a chart, its name automatically appears in the Chart Objects text box.

- **Format Object:** To change the formatting of the selected chart object (its name is shown in the text box of the Chart Objects button), click the Format Object button to open a dialog box with the formatting options you can modify. Note that the name of this button is shown with screen tips changes to match the chart object that you select, so that if Chart Area appears in the Chart Objects text box, the button is called Format Chart Area. So, too, if Legend appears as the selected chart object in this text box, the button's name changes to Format Legend.

- **Chart Type:** To change the type of chart, click the Chart Type drop-down button and then click the new chart type in the pop-up palette.

- **Legend:** Click the Legend button to hide or display the chart's legend.

- **Data Table:** Click the Data Table button to add or remove a data table that encapsulates the values represented by the chart's graphics. (In Figure 8-7, you can see an example of a data table appended to a Clustered Column chart on its own chart sheet created from the data on the Mother Goose Enterprises – 2004 First Quarter Sales worksheet.)

- **By Row:** Click the By Row button to have the data series in the chart represent the rows of values in the selected data range.

✔ **By Column:** Click the By Column button to have the data series in the chart represent the columns of values in the selected data range.

✔ **Angle Clockwise:** Click the Angle Clockwise button when you want the text of the Category Axis or Value Axis objects labels to slant down 45 degrees (note the downward slant of the *ab* that appears on this button).

✔ **Angle Counterclockwise:** Click the Angle Counterclockwise button when you want the text of the Category Axis or Value Axis objects labels to slant upward 45 degrees (note the upward slant of the *ab* that appears on this button).

Editing the chart directly in the worksheet

At times, you may want to make changes to specific parts of the chart (for example, selecting a new font for titles or repositioning the legend). To make these kinds of changes, you must double-click the particular object (such as the title, legend, plot area, and so on). When you double-click a chart object, Excel selects it and displays a format dialog box specific to the part of the chart you double-clicked. For example, if you double-click somewhere on the legend of a chart, the Format Legend dialog box with its three tabs (Patterns, Font, and Placement), as shown in Figure 8-5, appears. You can then use the options on any of these tabs to spruce up the legend's appearance.

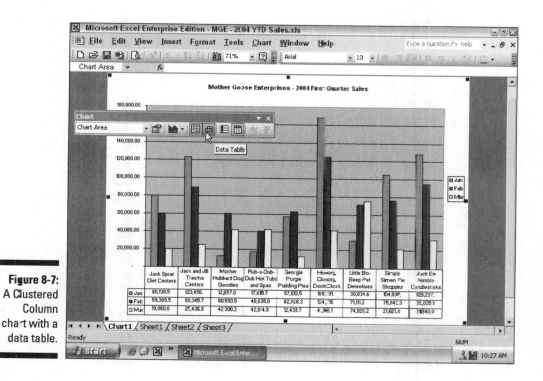

Figure 8-7:
A Clustered Column chart with a data table.

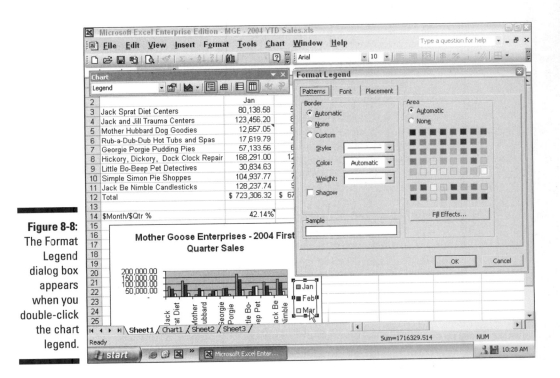

Figure 8-8:
The Format Legend dialog box appears when you double-click the chart legend.

Note that you can also edit a chart by selecting the part you want to change as follows:

- ✔ To select one of these chart objects, simply click it. Use the ScreenTip that appears at the mouse pointer to identify the chart object before you click to select it.

- ✔ You can tell when an object is selected because selection handles appear around it. (You can see the selection handles around the chart legend in Figure 8-8.) With some objects, you can use the selection handles to resize or reorient the object.

- ✔ After selecting some chart objects, you can move them within the chart by positioning the arrowhead pointer in their midst and then dragging their boundary.

- ✔ To display a chart object's shortcut menu, right-click the object and then drag to the desired command on the menu or click it with the primary mouse button.

- ✔ To remove the selected part from the chart, press the Delete key.

After you select one object in the chart by clicking it, you can cycle through and select the other objects in the chart by pressing the ↑ and ↓ keys. Pressing the → key selects the next object; pressing the ← key selects the previous object.

Instant charts

If you just don't have time to complete the Chart Wizard's four-step process, you can create a finished Clustered Column chart-as-graphic-object by selecting the labels and values to be charted, clicking the Chart Wizard button on the Standard toolbar, and then clicking the Finish button in the Chart Wizard – Step 1 of 4 – Chart Type dialog box.

To create a finished chart on its own chart sheet, select the labels and values to be charted and then press F11. Excel then creates a new Clustered Column chart using the selected data on its own chart sheet (Chart1) that precedes all the other sheets in the workbook.

All the parts of the chart that you can select in a chart window have shortcut menus attached to them. If you know that you want to choose a command from the shortcut menu as soon as you select a part of the chart, you can both select the object and open the shortcut menu by right-clicking the chart object. (You don't have to click the object with the left button to select it and then click again with the right to open the menu.)

Note that you can move the chart title by dragging it to a new position within the chart. In addition to moving the title, you can also break up the title on several different lines. Then, if you want, you can use options in the Alignment tab of the Format Chart Title dialog box (Ctrl+1) to change the alignment of the broken-up text.

To force part of the title onto a new line, click the insertion point at the place in the text where the line break is to occur. After the insertion point is positioned in the title, press Enter to start a new line.

In addition to changing the way the titles appear in the chart, you can modify the way the data series, legend, and x- and y-axes appear in the chart by right-clicking them to open their shortcut menus and selecting the appropriate commands from them.

Changing the Chart Options

If you find that you need to make some substantial alterations to your chart, you can open the Chart Options dialog box. (This dialog box contains the same tabs and options as in the Chart Wizard – Step 3 of 4 – Chart Options dialog box when you create a chart — refer to Figure 8-4.) You can open this dialog box by selecting the chart area and choosing Chart⇨Chart Options on the menu bar or choosing Chart Options from the Chart Area's shortcut menu.

The Chart Options dialog box can contain up to six tabs (depending upon the type of chart you select — pie charts, for instance, have only the first three tabs) with options for doing the following:

- **Titles:** Use the options on the Titles tab to add or modify the Chart title (that appears at the top of the chart), the Category title (that appears below the x-axis), or the Value title (that appears to the left of the y-axis).

- **Axes:** Use the options on the Axes tab to hide or display the tick marks and labels along the Category (x) axis or the Value (y) axis.

- **Gridlines:** You can use the options on the Gridlines tab to hide or display the major and minor gridlines that appear from the tick marks along the Category (x) axis or the Value (y) axis.

- **Legend:** Use the options on the Legend tab to hide or display the legend or to change its placement in relation to the chart area (by selecting the Bottom, Corner, Top, Right, or Left radio button).

- **Data Labels:** You can use the options on the Data Labels tab to hide or display labels that identify each data series in the chart.

- **Data Table:** Use the options in the Data Table tab to add or remove a data table that shows the worksheet values being charted. (Refer to Figure 8-7 for an example of a chart with a data table.)

Telling all with a text box

In Figure 8-9, you see an Area chart for the Mother Goose Enterprises – 2004 First Quarter Sales. I added a text box with an arrow that points out how extraordinary the sales were for the Hickory, Dickory, Dock Clock Repair shops in this quarter and formatted the values on the y-axis with the Currency style number format with zero decimal places.

To add a text box to the chart, open the Drawing toolbar (as shown in Figure 8-10) by clicking the Drawing button on the Standard toolbar. As you can see back in Figure 8-9, the Drawing toolbar automatically docks itself at the bottom of the workbook window. Click the Text Box button, and Excel changes the mouse pointer to a narrow vertical line with a short cross near the bottom. Click at the place where you want to draw the text box, or draw the text box either in the chart or the worksheet by dragging its outline. When you click this mouse pointer, Excel draws a square text box. When you release the mouse button after dragging this mouse pointer, Excel draws a text box in the shape and size of the outline.

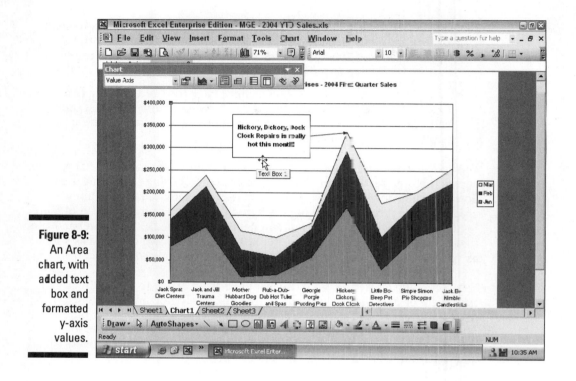

Figure 8-9:
An Area
chart, with
added text
box and
formatted
y-axis
values.

After creating the text box, the program positions the insertion point at the top, and you can then type the text you want to appear within it. The text you type appears in the text box and wraps to a new line when you reach the right edge of the text box. *Remember:* You can press Enter when you want to force text to appear on a new line. When you finish entering the message for your text box, click anywhere outside the box to deselect it.

After adding a text box to an embedded chart (or worksheet), you can edit it as follows:

- You can move the text box to a new location in the chart by dragging it.

- You can resize the text box by dragging the appropriate selection handle.

- Change or remove the border around the text box in the Format Text Box dialog box. To open this dialog box, click the border of the text box to select the box and then press Ctrl+1 to open the Format AutoShape dialog box. Click the Colors and Lines tab in this dialog box and then make all necessary changes to the options in the Line section of the box. For example, to remove all borders from your text box, select No Line on the Color pop-up menu.

✔ To add the drop-shadow effect, click the border of the text box to select it, click the Shadow button on the Drawing toolbar (the one with the picture of a drop shadow behind a rectangle), and then select the type of drop shadow to apply in the pop-up palette.

✔ To make the text box three-dimensional, click the border of the text box to select it, click the 3-D button on the Drawing toolbar (the last one with the 3-D rectangle), and then select the 3-D box shape you want to apply from the pop-up palette.

You can have the text in your text box run vertically down columns that stretch across the box (reading from left to right) instead of using the normal text flow that runs down the lines (that's also read from left to right). Simply create your text box by selecting the Vertical Text Box button instead of the regular Text Box button (located right next to it) on the Drawing toolbar. Note that Excel converts the text you enter so that it runs down columns as soon as you click somewhere in the worksheet off the text box to deselect it.

When creating a text box, you may want to add an arrow to point directly to the object or part of the chart you're referencing. To add an arrow, click the Arrow button on the Drawing toolbar and then drag the crosshair from the place where the end of the arrow (the one *without* the arrowhead) is to appear to the place where the arrow starts (and the arrowhead appears) and release the mouse button.

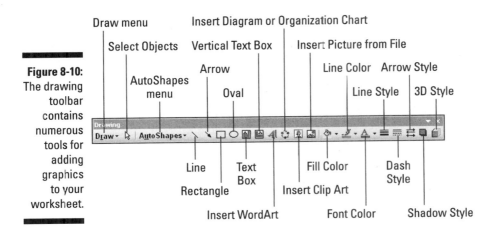

Figure 8-10:
The drawing toolbar contains numerous tools for adding graphics to your worksheet.

Excel then draws a new arrow, which remains selected (with selection handles at the beginning and end of the arrow). You can then modify the arrow as follows:

✔ To move the arrow, drag it into position.

✔ To change the length of the arrow, drag one of the selection handles.

✔ As you change the length, you can also change the direction of the arrow by pivoting the mouse pointer around a stationary selection handle.

✔ If you want to change the shape of the arrowhead or the thickness of the arrow's shaft, select the arrow in the worksheet, click the Arrow Style button on the Drawing toolbar (the one with the three arrows), and then choose the type of arrowhead to apply in the pop-up menu. If you need to change the color of the arrow, the thickness or style of the line, or if you want to create a custom arrowhead, choose the More Arrows command at the bottom of the pop-up menu to open the Format AutoShape dialog box. (You can also open this dialog box by choosing Format⇨Selected Object on the menu bar or by pressing Ctrl+1.)

Formatting the x-axis or y-axis

When charting a bunch of values, Excel isn't too careful how it formats the values that appear on the y-axis (or the x-axis when using some chart types such as the 3-D Column chart or the XY Scatter chart). If you're not happy with the way the values appear on either the x-axis or y-axis, you can change the formatting as follows:

1. **Double-click the x-axis or y-axis in the chart or click the axis and then choose Format⇨Selected Axis on the menu bar (or press Ctrl-1).**

   Excel opens the Format Axis dialog box containing the following tabs: Patterns, Scale, Font, Number and Alignment.

2. **To change the appearance of the tick marks along the axis, change the options on the Patterns tab (which is automatically selected when you first open the Format Axis dialog box) however you desire.**

3. **To change the scale of the selected axis, click the Scale tab and change the Scale options the way you want.**

4. **To change the font of the labels that appear at the tick marks on the selected axis, click the Font tab and change the Font options however you desire.**

5. **To change the formatting of the values that appear at the tick marks on the selected axis, select the Number tab; then click the number format you want to apply in the Category list box followed by the appropriate options associated with that format.**

   For example, to select the Currency format with no decimal places, you select Currency in the Category list box; then enter 0 in the Decimal Places text box or select 0 with the spinner buttons.

6. **To change the formatting of the orientation of the labels that appear at the tick marks on the selected axis, select the Alignment tab. Then**

indicate the new orientation by clicking it in the sample Text box
or by entering the number of degrees (between 90 and –90) in the
Degrees text box (or by selecting this number with the spinner
buttons).

7. **Click OK or press Enter to close the Format Axis dialog box.**

As soon as you close the Format Axis dialog box, Excel redraws the axis of
the chart according to the new settings. For instance, if you choose a new
number format for a chart, Excel immediately formats all the numbers
that appear along the selected axis using that format.

Vacillating values mean changing charts

As soon as you finish modifying the objects in a chart, you can deselect the
chart graphic object, chart labels, and chart values and return to the normal
worksheet and its cells by clicking the pointer anywhere outside the chart.
After a chart is deselected, you can once again move the cell pointer all over
the worksheet. Just keep in mind that if you use the arrow keys to move the
cell pointer, the cell pointer disappears when you move to a cell in the worksheet that's hidden behind the chart. (Of course, if you try to select a cell
covered by a chart by clicking it with the mouse pointer, you'll only succeed
in selecting the chart itself.)

Keep in mind that worksheet values represented graphically in the chart
remain dynamically linked to the chart so that, should you make a change to
one or more of the charted values in the worksheet, Excel will automatically
update the chart to suit.

Picture This!

Charts are not the only kind of graphics you can add to a worksheet. Indeed,
Excel lets you spruce up a worksheet with drawings, text boxes, and even
graphic images imported from other sources, such as scanned images or
drawings created in other graphics programs or downloaded from the Internet.

To bring in a piece of clip art included with Office 2003, you choose the
Insert⇨Picture⇨ClipArt command on the menu bar or click the Insert Clip
Art button on the Drawing toolbar (if this toolbar is displayed). When you do
this, Excel 2003 displays the Clip Art Task pane (similar to the one shown in
Figure 8-11) from which you search for the type of art you want to use. To
locate the clip(s) you want to insert into the current worksheet in the Clip
Art Task pane, you follow these steps:

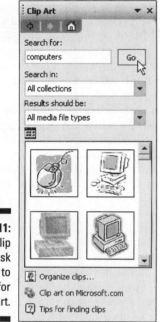

Figure 8-11:
Use the Clip
Art Task
pane to
search for
clip art.

1. **Click the Search For text box at the top and then enter the keyword(s) for the type of clip art you want to find.**

   When entering keywords for finding particular types of clip art, try entering general, descriptive terms such as trees, flowers, people, flying, and the like.

2. **(Optional) Click the Search In drop-down button and remove (deselect) check marks from any clip art collections that you don't want to search.**

   By default, Excel searches all the collections of clip art (including the Media Gallery Online collection on the Web). To limit your search, you need to make sure that only the clip art collections you want to include in the search have check marks before their names.

3. **(Optional) To limit the search to clip art only, click the Results Should Be drop-down button and remove check marks from the All Media Types, Photographs, Movies, and Sounds categories.**

   You can further limit the types of clip art files included in the search by clicking the plus sign in front of Clip Art and then removing check marks from any and all types of clips (such as CorelDraw or Macintosh PICT) that you don't want or need to use.

4. **Click the Go button to the immediate right of the Search For text box to initiate the search.**

When you click the Go button, Excel searches all of the places you specify in the Search In list and displays the search results in the Clip Art Task pane (see Figure 8-12). To insert a particular image into the current worksheet, click it with the mouse. You can also insert an image by positioning the mouse over it to display its drop-down button, and then clicking the drop-down button and choosing Insert at the top of its pop-up menu.

You cannot use the search feature in the Clip Art Task pane until after you index the clips with the Clip Organizer. To do this, click the <u>Organize Clips</u> link near the bottom of the Clip Art Task pane. When you click this link, Excel opens the Add Clips to Organizer window in which you click the Now button to have all your media files indexed by keywords. After the Clip Organizer finishes indexing your clip art, you are ready to search for clips as outlined in the preceding steps.

If you have difficulty finding a piece of clip art, try editing its keywords to make finding it the next time easier. To do this, click the image's drop-down button and then choose the Edit Keywords on its pop-up menu. Doing this opens the Keywords dialog box that shows all the keywords assigned to the image. To add your own keyword to the list, enter it into the Keyword drop-down text box and click the Add button. Also, if you see an image that is close to, but not exactly what, you want, try finding like images by clicking the image's drop-down button, and then choosing Find Similar Style on its pop-up menu.

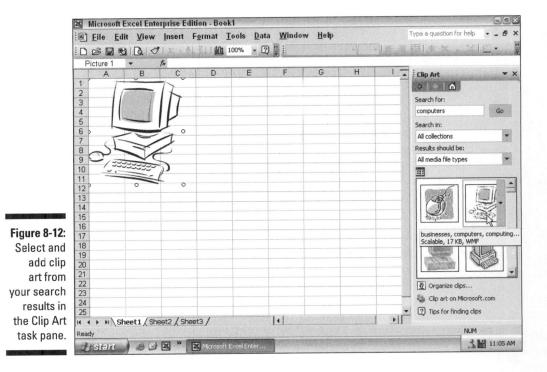

Figure 8-12:
Select and add clip art from your search results in the Clip Art task pane.

Inserting graphic images from files

If you want to bring in a graphic image created in another program and saved in its own graphics file, choose the Insert⇨Picture⇨From File command and then select the graphic file in the Insert Picture dialog box (which works just like opening an Excel workbook file in the Open dialog box).

If you want to bring in a graphic image created in another graphics program that's not saved in its own file, you select the graphic in that program and then copy it to the Clipboard (press Ctrl+C or choose the Edit⇨Copy command on the menu bar) before returning to the Excel worksheet. When you get back to your worksheet, place the cursor where you want the picture to go and then paste the image in place (press Ctrl+V or choose the Edit⇨Paste command).

Drawing your own

In addition to ready-made graphics or images drawn in other graphics programs, you can use the tools on the Drawing toolbar to make your own graphics within Excel. The Drawing toolbar contains all sorts of drawing tools that you can use to draw outlined or filled shapes such as lines, rectangles, squares, and ovals.

As part of these drawing tools, the Drawing toolbar contains an AutoShapes button that gives you access to a whole bunch of ready-made, specialized lines and shapes. To select one of these lines or shapes, you click it on the particular pop-up palette that opens as soon as you highlight the Lines, Connectors, Basics Shapes, Block Arrows, Flowchart, Stars and Banners, or Callouts item on the pop-up menu that appears when you click the AutoShapes button.

Click the More AutoShapes item on the AutoShapes button pop-up menu to open the Clip Art task pane that offers a bunch of additional line drawings, including several different computer shapes, that you can insert into your document by clicking their images.

Working with WordArt

If having the specialized lines and shapes available with the AutoShapes button doesn't provide enough variety for jazzing up your worksheet, you may want to try adding some fancy text with the WordArt button on the Drawing toolbar. You can add this type of text to your worksheet by following these steps:

1. **Select the cell in the area of the worksheet where the WordArt text is to appear.**

   Because WordArt is created as a graphics object on the worksheet, you can size and move the text after you create it just as you could any other worksheet graphic.

2. **Click the WordArt button (the one with the picture of the letter *A* angled downward) on the Drawing toolbar.**

   When you click the WordArt button, Excel displays the WordArt Gallery dialog box, as shown in Figure 8-13.

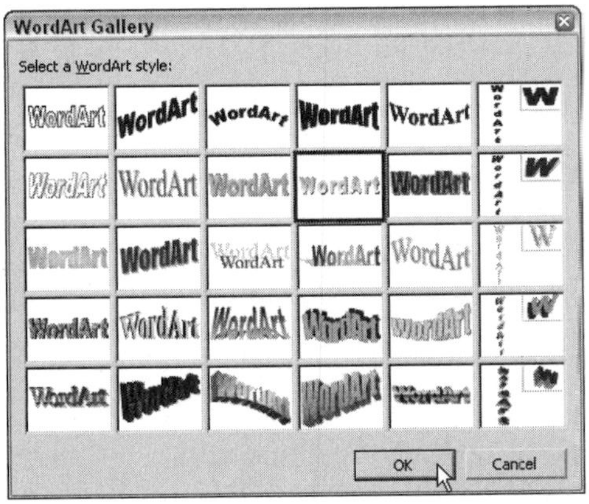

Figure 8-13: Select the type of text from the WordArt Gallery.

3. **Click the picture of the WordArt style you want to use from the WordArt Gallery dialog box and then click OK or press Enter.**

   Excel opens the Edit WordArt Text dialog box where you enter the text you want to appear in the worksheet, and then select its font and font size.

4. **Type the text you want to display in the worksheet in the Text text box.**

   As soon as you start typing, Excel replaces the highlighted `Your Text Here` with the text you want to appear in the worksheet.

5. **Select the font you want to use in the Font drop-down list box and the font size in the Size drop-down list box.**

6. **Click OK.**

   Excel draws your WordArt text in the worksheet at the cell pointer's position, while at the same time displaying the floating WordArt toolbar (as shown in Figure 8-14). You can use the buttons on this toolbar to further format the basic WordArt style or to edit the text.

WordArt Shape

WordArt Gallery   WordArt Vertical Text

Insert WordArt   WordArt Character Spacing

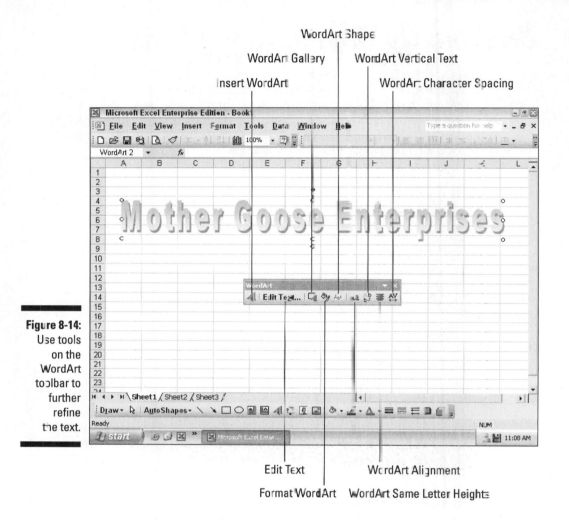

Figure 8-14:
Use tools
on the
WordArt
toolbar to
further
refine
the text.

Edit Text   WordArt Alignment

Format WordArt   WordArt Same Letter Heights

7. **After making any final adjustments to the size, shape, or format of the WordArt text, click a cell somewhere outside of the text to deselect the graphic.**

   When you click outside of the WordArt text, Excel deselects the graphic, and the WordArt toolbar is hidden. (If you ever want the toolbar to reappear, all you have to do is click somewhere on the WordArt text to select the graphic.)

Ordering Up Organization Charts

In Excel 2003, the Drawing toolbar contains an Insert Diagram or Organization Chart button (refer to Figure 8-10) that you can use to quickly and easily add organization charts to your worksheets. Simply click the Insert Diagram or Organization Chart button to display the Diagram Gallery dialog box (shown in Figure 8-15). Select the type of chart to draw by double-clicking its image or clicking the image and then clicking OK.

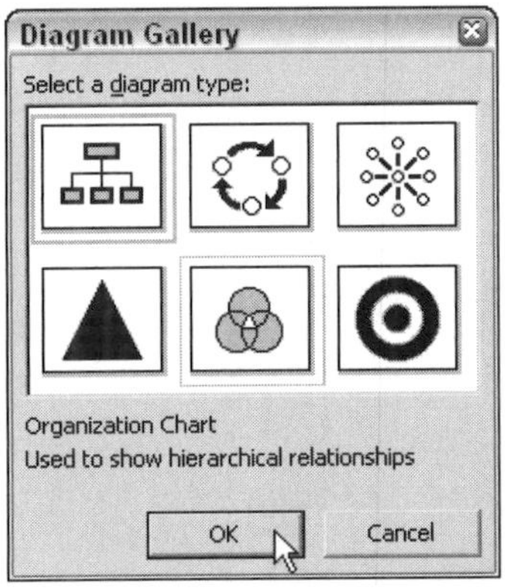

Figure 8-15:
Select an organization chart from the Diagram Gallery.

After Excel inserts the basic structure of the org chart into your worksheet, you can replace the stock text with your own by clicking the Click to Add Text button (what else would Microsoft call it?!) and typing in the name or title of the person or place that inhabits each level of the chart (as shown in Figure 8-16).

To insert an additional shape at the same manager level in the chart, choose the Coworker option on the Insert Shape pop-up menu. To insert a shape for a subordinate managerial level directly below the one that's currently selected, choose the Subordinate option on this pop-up menu. To insert a shape for a subordinate managerial level that is indirectly connected to the shape that's currently selected, choose Assistant on the pop-up menu.

To enhance the look of your org chart, click the AutoFormat button on the Organization Chart toolbar and then select the diagram style you want to apply to the entire org chart from the Organization Chart Style Gallery dialog box. To have Excel size the text you add to the size of the shapes in the chart, choose the Fit Organization Chart to Contents option on the Layout pop-up menu. To increase the size of the shapes and the overall size of the chart to fit the text that you enter in the chart, choose the Expand Organization Chart option on the Layout pop-up menu, instead.

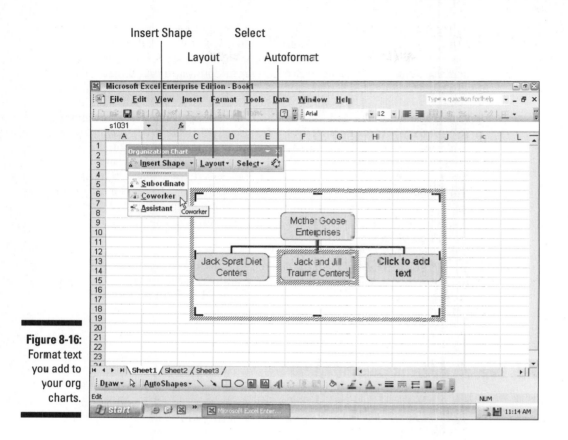

Insert Shape
Select
Layout
Autoformat

Figure 8-16:
Format text
you add to
your org
charts.

One on Top of the Other . . .

In case you haven't noticed, graphic objects float on top of the cells of the worksheet. Most of the objects (including charts) are opaque, meaning that they hide (*without* replacing) information in the cells beneath. If you move one opaque graphic on top of another, the one on top hides the one below, just as putting one sheet of paper over another hides the information on the one below. This means that most of the time, you should make sure that graphic objects don't overlap one another or overlap cells with worksheet information that you want to display.

Sometimes, however, you can create some interesting special effects by placing a transparent graphic object (such as a circle) in front of an opaque one. The only problem you may encounter is if the opaque object gets on top of the transparent one. If this happens, switch their positions by right-clicking the object and then choosing the Order⇨Send to Back command on the object's shortcut menu. If you ever need to bring up a graphic that's underneath another, right-click this underlying graphic and then choose the Order⇨Bring to Front command on the object's shortcut menu.

Sometimes you may find that you need to group several objects together so that they act as one unit (like a text box with its arrow). That way, you can move these objects or size them together in one operation. To group objects together, you need to Shift-click each object to be grouped to select them all, and then right-click the last object to display a shortcut menu where you choose the Grouping⇨Group command. After grouping several objects, whenever you click any part of the mega-object, every part is selected (and selection handles appear only around the perimeter of the combined object).

Should you later decide that you need to independently move or size objects that have been grouped together, you can ungroup them by right-clicking the grouped object and then choosing Grouping⇨Ungroup on the object's short-cut menu.

Nixing the Graphics

Here's something you'll want to know about the graphics you add to a work-sheet: how to hide them. Adding graphics to a worksheet can appreciably slow down the screen response because Excel has to take the time to redraw each and every little picture in the document window whenever you scroll the view even slightly. To keep this sluggishness from driving you crazy, either hide the display of all the graphics (including charts) while you edit other things in the worksheet, or temporarily replace them with gray rectangles that continue to mark their places in the worksheet but don't take nearly as long to redraw.

To hide all the graphics or replace them with gray placeholders, choose the Tools⇨Options command on the menu bar and then select the View tab. Select the Hide All radio button under Objects to get rid of the display of all graphics entirely. Select the Show Placeholders radio button to temporarily replace your charts with shaded rectangles. Note that selecting the Show Placeholders option has no effect on graphics created with the tools on the Drawing toolbar or imported into the worksheet.

Before you print the worksheet, be sure that you redisplay the graphic objects: Open the Options dialog box, select the View tab, and then select the Show All radio button.

Printing Charts Only

Sometimes, you may want to print only a particular chart in the worksheet (independent of the worksheet data it represents or any of the other stuff you've added). To do this, first make sure that hidden or grayed-out charts are displayed in the worksheet. To redisplay hidden charts in a worksheet, you need to select the Show All radio button on the View tab of the Options dialog box. To redisplay charts grayed out with the Show Placeholders option, simply click the chart (Shift-click to display multiple charts). Next, choose the File⇨Print command on the menu bar (or press Ctrl+P) or click the Print tool on the Standard toolbar.

If you choose the File⇨Print command on the menu bar rather than click the Print tool, you see that the Selected Chart radio button under Print What is selected. By default, Excel prints the chart at full size on the page. This may mean that all of the chart cannot be printed on a single page — be sure to click the Preview button to make sure that your entire chart fits on one page.

If you find in Print Preview that you need to change the printed chart size or the orientation of the printing (or both), click the Setup button in the Print Preview window. To change the orientation of the printing (or the paper size), select the Page tab in the Page Setup dialog box and change these options. When everything looks good in the Print Preview window, start printing the chart by choosing the Print button.

Chapter 9

How to Face a Database

The purpose of all the worksheet tables that I discuss elsewhere in this book has been to perform essential calculations (such as to sum monthly or quarterly sales figures) and then present the information in an understandable form. But you can create another kind of worksheet table in Excel: a *database* (or more accurately, a *data list*). The purpose of a database is not so much to calculate new values but rather to store lots and lots of information in a consistent manner. For example, you can create a database that contains the names and addresses of all your clients, or you can create a database that contains all the essential facts about your employees.

Designing the Data Form

Creating a database is much like creating a worksheet table. When setting up a database, you start by entering a row of column headings (technically known as *field names* in database parlance) to identify the different kinds of items you need to keep track of (such as First Name, Last Name, Street, City, State, and so on). After you enter the row of field names, you start entering the information for the database in the appropriate columns of the rows immediately below the field names.

As you proceed, notice that each column of the database contains information for a particular item you want to track in the database, such as the client's company name or an employee's telephone extension. Each column is also known as a *field* in the database. In looking back over your work, you see that each row of the database contains complete information about a particular person or thing you're keeping track of in the database, whether it's a company (such as Do-Rite Drugs) or a particular employee (such as Ida Jones). The individuals or entities described in the rows of the database are also known as the *records* of the database. Each record (row) contains many fields (columns).

Setting up and maintaining a database is easy with Excel's handy, built-in *data form*. You use the data form to add, delete, or edit records in the database. To create a data form for a new database, you first enter the row of column headings used as field names and one sample record in the following row (look at the client database in Figure 9-1). Then you format each field entry just as you want all subsequent entries in that column of the database to appear, including widening the columns so that the column headings and data are completely displayed. Then position the cell pointer in any one of the cells in these two rows and choose the Data⇨Form command from the menu bar.

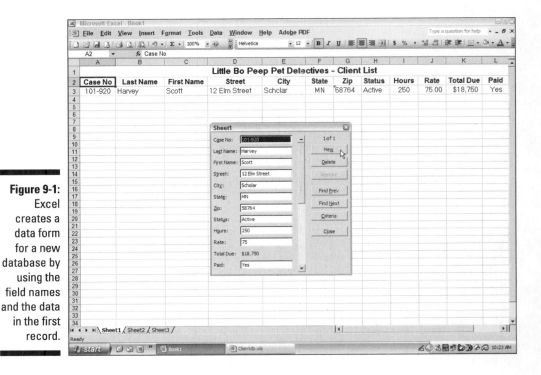

Figure 9-1: Excel creates a data form for a new database by using the field names and the data in the first record.

As soon as you choose the Data⇨Form command on the menu bar, Excel analyzes the row of field names and entries for the first record and creates a data form that lists the field names down the left side of the form with the entries for the first record in the appropriate text boxes next to them. In Figure 9-1, you can see the data form for the new Little Bo Peep Pet Detectives clients' database; it looks kind of like a customized dialog box.

The data form Excel creates includes the entries you made in the first record. The data form also contains a series of buttons (on the right side) that you use to add, delete, or find specific records in the database. Right above the first button (New), the data form lists the number of the record you're looking at followed by the total number of records (1 of 1 when you first create the data form).

Don't forget to format the entries in the fields of the first database record in the second row, as well as the field names in the row above. All the formatting that you assign to the particular entries in the first record is then automatically applied to those fields in subsequent records you enter. For example, if your data list contains a telephone field, simply enter the ten digits of the phone number in the Telephone field of the first record and then format this cell with the Special Phone Number format. (See Chapter 3 for details on sorting number formats.) That way, in the Data Form, you can enter just the digits of the telephone number — **3075550045**, for example. Excel will then apply the Phone Number format to it so that it appears as (307) 555-0045 in the appropriate cell of the data list itself.

Creating a data form from field names alone

You can create a data form for a new database simply by entering a row of field names and then positioning the cell pointer in the first one before you choose Data⇨Form from the menu bar. When you do this, Excel displays the alert dialog box indicating that the program can't determine which row in your list contains the column labels (that is, the field names). To have Excel use the selected row as the field names, click OK or press Enter. Excel will then create a blank data form listing all the fields down the form in the same order as they appear across the selected row.

Creating a blank data form from field names alone is just fine, provided that your database doesn't contain any calculated fields (that is, fields with entries that result from a formula's computation rather than from manual entry). If your new database will contain calculated fields, you need to build the formulas for the fields in the appropriate fields of the first record. Then select both the row of field names and the first database record with the formulas indicating how the entries are calculated before you choose Form on the Data menu. Excel knows which fields are calculated and which are not. (You can tell that a field is a calculated field in the data form because Excel lists its field name but does not provide a text box for you to enter any information for it.)

Adding records to the database

After you create the data form with the first record, you can use the form to add the rest of the records to the database. The process is simple. When you click the New button, Excel displays a blank data form (marked New Record at the right side of the data form), which you get to fill in.

After you enter the information for the first field, press the Tab key to advance to the next field in the record.

Whoa! Don't press the Enter key to advance to the next field in a record. If you do, you'll insert the new, incomplete record into the database.

Continue entering information for each field and pressing Tab to go to the next field in the database.

- ✔ If you notice that you've made an error and want to edit an entry in a field you already passed, press Shift+Tab to return to that field.
- ✔ To replace the entry, just start typing.
- ✔ To edit some of the characters in the field, press → or click the I-beam pointer in the entry to locate the insertion point; then edit the entry from there.

When entering information in a particular field, you can copy the entry made in that field from the previous record by pressing Ctrl+' (apostrophe). Press Ctrl+', for example, to carry forward the same entry in the State field of each new record when entering a series of records for people who all live in the same state.

When entering dates in a date field, use a consistent date format that Excel knows. (For example, enter something like **7/21/98.**) When entering zip codes that sometimes use leading zeros that you don't want to disappear from the entry (such as zip code **00102**), format the first field entry with the Special Zip Code number format (refer to Chapter 3 for details on sorting number formats). In the case of other numbers that use leading zeros, you can put an ' (apostrophe) before the first 0. The apostrophe tells Excel to treat the number like a text label but doesn't show up in the database itself. (The only place you can see the apostrophe is on the Formula bar when the cell pointer's in the cell with the numeric entry.)

Press the ↓ key when you've entered all the information for the new record. Or, instead of the ↓ key, you can press Enter or click the New button (see Figure 9-2). Excel inserts the new record as the last record in the database in the worksheet and displays a new blank data form in which you can enter the next record (see Figure 9-3).

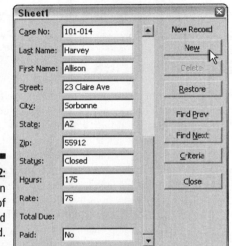

Figure 9-2:
Enter data in
the fields of
the second
record.

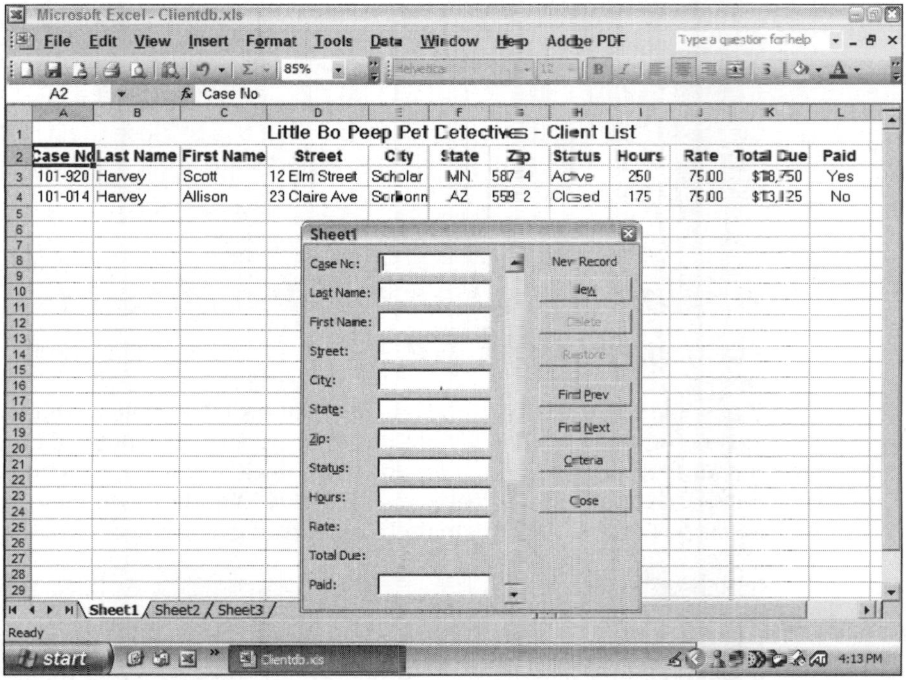

Figure 9-3:
Advance to
a new
record in
the Data
Form, and
Excel
inserts the
previous
record
into the
database.

Calculated field entries

When you want Excel to calculate the entries for a particular field by formula, you need to enter that formula in the correct field in the first record of the database. Then position the cell pointer in either the row of field names or the first record when creating the data form, and Excel copies the formula for this calculated field to each new record you add with the data form.

In the Bo Peep Detectives clients database, for example, the Total Due field in cell K3 of the first record shown in Figure 9-1 is calculated by the formula =Hours*Rate. Cell I3 contains the number of case hours (Hours), and cell J3 contains the hourly rate (Rate). This formula then computes what the client owes by multiplying the number of case hours by the hourly rate. As you can see, Excel adds the calculated field, Total Due, to the data form but doesn't provide a text box for this field (calculated fields can't be edited). When you enter additional records to the database, Excel calculates the formula for the Total Due field. If you then redisplay the data for these records, you see the calculated value following Total Due (although you won't be able to change it).

When you finish adding records to the database, press the Esc key or click the Close button at the bottom of the dialog box to close the data form. Then save the worksheet with the File⇨Save command from the menu bar or click the Save tool on the Standard toolbar.

Adding e-mail and Web addresses to a hyperlink field

When you enter an e-mail or Web site address into a field of the Data Form, Excel converts the address into an active hyperlink (indicated by underlining the address text in blue) in the database itself as soon as you complete the record. Of course, for Excel to create active hyperlinks, you must enter the e-mail address in the anticipated format that goes something like:

```
John9697@aol.com
```

Likewise, you must enter the Web page address in the expected format that goes something like:

```
www.dummies.com
```

Note, however, that no matter how much the e-mail or Web address that you enter *looks* like a real address, Excel has no way of knowing whether or not the address is *valid*. In other words, just because Excel converts your text into a clickable hyperlink, that doesn't mean that following the link will send the intended recipient an e-mail message or take you anywhere on the World Wide Web. Obviously, you must be very careful to enter the correct address (and as you are probably well aware, this is far from easy).

After entering e-mail and/or Web page addresses in a hyperlink database field, you can then use the links to send a particular person a new e-mail message or to visit a particular Web site. Look at Figure 9-4 to see a hyperlink field that adds the e-mail addresses of the clients in the Little Bo Peep Detectives clients' database. Because the hyperlinks are active, all you have to do to send an e-mail message to a particular recipient (especially those who are not currently paid up) is click his or her E-mail entry in the database. Excel will then launch your e-mail program (Outlook Express or the full-blown Outlook in most cases) with a new message already properly addressed.

Figure 9-4:
Little Bo
Peep Client
list with an
E-mail field
full of
working
hyperlinks.

Case N	Last Name	First Name	Street	City	Sta	Zip	E-mail	Stat
101-001	Bryant	Michael	326 Chef's Lane	Paris	TX	78705	mbryant@ohlala.com	Activ
101-004	Cupid	Eros	97 Mount Olympus	Greece	CT	03331	mailto:mbryan@ohlala.com - Click once to follow. Click and hold to select this cell.	
101-014	Andersen	Hans	341 The Shadow	Scholar	MN	53764		
101-014	Harvey	Allison	1st French Manor	Sorbonne	AZ	53912	aharvey@azalia.com	Activ
101-015	Humperdinck	Engelbert	6 Hansel+Gretel Tr	Gingerbread	MD	20815	ehumperdinck@ginger.org	Activ
101-028	Cassidy	Butch	Sundance Kidde	Hole In Wall	CO	80477	bcassidy@sundance.net	Clos
101-029	Oow	Lu	888 Sandy Beach	Honolulu	HI	99909	low@honolulu.net	Activ
101-030	Liberty	Statuesque	31 Gotham Centre	Big Apple	NY	10011	lliberty@elisisland.com	Activ
101-920	Harvey	Scott	12 E m Street	Scholar	MN	53764	shervey@mediacentral.com	Activ
102-002	Gearing	Shane	1 Gunfighter's Enc	LeLa Land	CA	90069	sgearing@nirvana.net	Activ
102-003	Wolfe	Big Bad	3 West End Blvd	London	AZ	85251	bwolf@grandmas.com	Clos
102-006	Cinderella	Poore	8 Lucky Maiden Way	Oxford	TN	07557	pcinderella@fairytale.org	Clos
102-012	Gondor	Aragorn	2956 Gandalf	Midearth	WY	80342	agandalf@wizards.net	Clos
102-013	Baggins	Bingo	99 Hobbithole	Shire	ME	04047	baggins@hobbit.org	Activ
102-020	Franklin	Ben	1789 Constitution	Jefferson	WV	20178	bfranklin@kitesunlimited.com	Activ
102-025	Washington	George	8 Founders Diamond	Hamilton	DC	01776	gwashington@presidents.com	Clos
103-005	Cole	Old King	4 Merry Soul Way	Fiddlers Court	MA	01824	okcole@fiddlersthree.net	Activ
103-007	Baum	L. Frank	447 Toto Too Rd	Oz	KS	65432	fbaum@ozzieland.com	Clos
103-016	Oakenshield	Rex	Mines of Goblins	Everest	NJ	07639	roakenshield@hobbit.org	Clos
103-017	Jacken	Jill	Up the Hill	Pail of Water	OK	45678		Clos
103-022	Dragon	Kai	2 Pleistocene Era	Ann's World	ID	00001	dinc@jurasic.org	Activ

Adding a hyperlink field to a vendor database with the Web site home addresses of the companies from which you routinely purchase makes it extremely easy to go online and check out new products — and, if you're really brave, even order them. Adding a hyperlink field to a client database with e-mail addresses of the key contacts makes keeping in touch extremely easy.

Locating, changing, and deleting records

After the database is under way and you're caught up with entering new records, you can start using the data form to perform routine maintenance on the database. For example, you can use the data form to locate a record you want to change and then make the edits to the particular fields. You can also use the data form to find a specific record you want to remove and then delete it from the database.

- ✔ Locate the record you want to edit in the database by bringing up its data form. See the following two sections "Scrolling the night away!" and "Finders keepers" and Table 9-1 for hints on locating records.
- ✔ To edit the fields of the current record, move to that field by pressing Tab or Shift+Tab and replace the entry by typing a new one.

    Alternatively, press ← or → or click the I-beam cursor to reposition the insertion point, and then make your edits.
- ✔ To clear a field entirely, select it and then press the Delete key.

To delete the entire record from the database, click the Delete button in the data form. Excel displays an alert box with the following dire warning:

    Displayed record will be permanently deleted

To go ahead and get rid of the record displayed in the data form, click OK. To play it safe and keep the record intact, click the Cancel button.

Please keep in mind that you *cannot* use the Undo feature to bring back a record you removed with the Delete button! Excel is definitely *not* kidding when it warns *permanently deleted*. As a precaution, always save a back-up version of the worksheet with the database before you start removing old records.

Scrolling the night away!

After you display the data form in the worksheet by positioning the cell pointer somewhere in the database and then choosing Data⇨Form from the Excel menu bar, you can use the scroll bar to the right of the list of field names or various keystrokes (both summarized in Table 9-1) to move through the records in the database until you find the one you want to edit or delete.

✔ **To move to the data form for the next record in the database:** Press ↓, press Enter, or click the down scroll arrow at the bottom of the scroll bar.

✔ **To move to the data form for the previous record in the database:** Press ↑, press Shift+Enter, or click the up scroll arrow at the top of the scroll bar.

✔ **To move to the data form for the first record in the database:** Press Ctrl+↑, press Ctrl+PgUp, or drag the scroll box to the very top of the scroll bar.

✔ **To move to a new data form immediately following the last record in the database:** Press Ctrl+↓, press Ctrl+PgDn, or drag the scroll box to the very bottom of the scroll bar.

Table 9-1	Ways to Get to a Particular Record
Keystrokes or Scroll Bar Technique	*Result*
Press ↓ or Enter or click the down scroll arrow or the Find Next button	Moves to the next record in the database and leaves the same field selected
Press ↑ or Shift+Enter or click the up datascroll arrow or the Find Prev button	Moves to the previous record in the base and leaves the same field selected
Press PgDn	Moves forward ten records in the database
Press PgUp	Moves backward ten records in the database
Press Ctrl+↑ or Ctrl+PgUp or drag the scroll box to the top of the scroll bar	Moves to the first record in the database
Drag the scroll box to the bottom of the scroll bar	Moves to the last record in the database

Finders keepers

In a really large database, trying to find a particular record by moving from record to record — or even moving ten records at a time with the scroll bar — can take all day. Rather than waste time trying to manually search for a record, you can use the Criteria button in the data form to look it up.

When you click the Criteria button, Excel clears all the field entries in the data form (and replaces the record number with the word *Criteria*) so that you can enter the criteria to search for in the blank text boxes.

For example, suppose that you need to edit Old King Cole's file status. Unfortunately, his paperwork doesn't include his case number. All you know is that currently his case is open (meaning the Status field for his record contains Active rather than Closed), and you're pretty sure that he spells his last name with a *C* instead of a *K*.

To find his record, you can at least use the information you have to narrow the search down to all the records where the last name begins with the letter *C* and the Status field contains Active. To limit your search in this way, open the data form for the client database, click the Criteria button, and then type the following in the text box for the Last Name field:

C*

Also enter the following in the text box for the Status field (see Figure 9-5):

Active

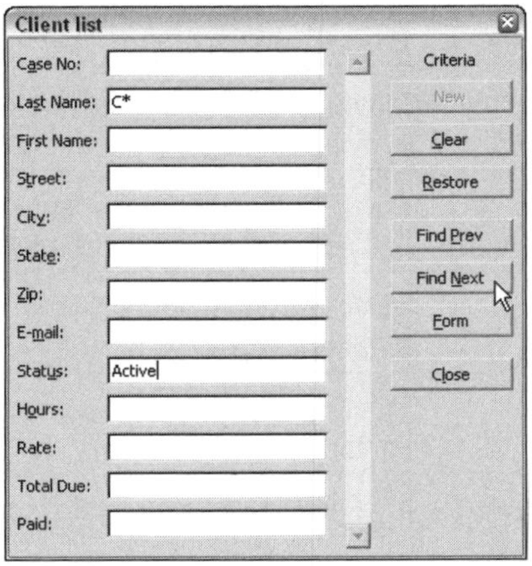

Figure 9-5:
Use the
Criteria
button in the
data form to
enter
search
criteria for
finding a
particular
record.

When you enter search criteria for records in the blank text boxes of the data form, you can use the ? (for single) and * (for multiple) wildcard characters. In Chapter 6, I show you how to use these wildcard characters with the Edit⇨Find command on the menu bar to locate cells with particular entries.

Now click the Find Next button. Excel displays in the data form the first record in the database where the last name begins with the letter *C* and the Status field contains Active. As shown in Figure 9-6, the first record in this database that meets these criteria is for Eros Cupid. To press on and find our Old King Cole's record, click the Find Next button again. Old King Cole's record shows up in Figure 9-7. Having located Cole's record, you can then edit his case status in the text box for the Status field. When you click the Close button, Excel records his new Closed case status in the database.

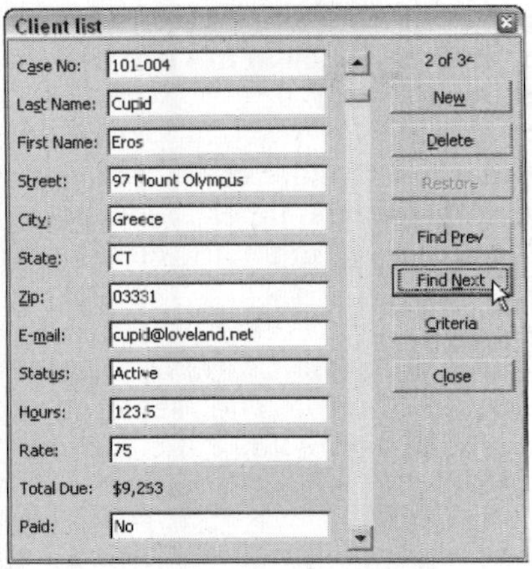

Figure 9-6:
The first record in the database that meets the search criteria.

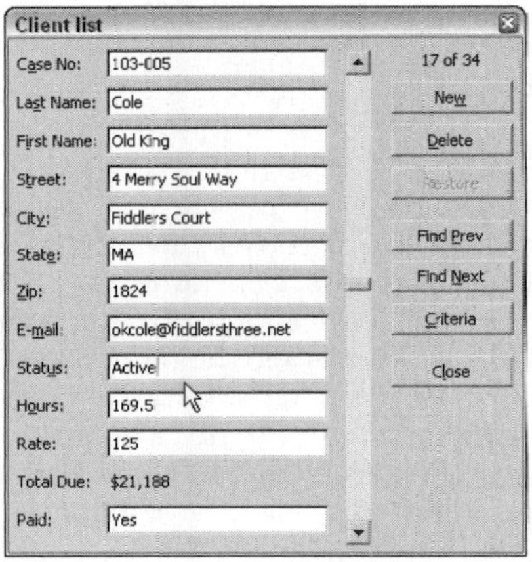

Figure 9-7:
Eureka! The King's long lost record is found in the database.

When you use the Criteria button in the data form to find records, you can include the following operators in the search criteria you enter to locate a specific record in the database:

Operator	Meaning
=	Equal to
>	Greater than
>=	Greater than or equal to
<	Less than
<=	Less than or equal to
<>	Not equal to

For example, to display only those records where a client's total due is greater than or equal to $50,000, enter >=**50000** in the text box for the Total Due field before clicking the Find Next button.

When specifying search criteria that fit a number of records, you may have to click the Find Next or Find Prev button several times to locate the record you want. If no record fits the search criteria you enter, the computer beeps at you when you click these buttons.

To change the search criteria, first clear the data form by clicking the Criteria button again and then clicking the Clear button. Then select the appropriate text boxes and clear out the old criteria before you enter the new. (You can just replace the criteria if you're using the same fields.)

To switch back to the current record without using the search criteria you enter, click the Form button. (This button replaces the Criteria button as soon as you click the Criteria button.)

Sorting It All Out

Every database you put together in Excel will have some kind of preferred order for maintaining and viewing the records. Depending on the database, you may want to see the records in alphabetical order by last name. In the case of a database of clients, you may want to see the records arranged alphabetically by company name. In the case of the Little Bo Peep Client database, the preferred order is in numerical order by the case number assigned to each client when he or she hires the agency to find his or her pets.

When you initially enter records for a new database, you no doubt enter them either in the preferred order or the order in which you get a hold of their records. However you start out, as you will soon discover, you don't have the option of adding subsequent records in that preferred order. Whenever you add a new record with the New button in the data form, Excel tacks that record onto the bottom of the database by adding a new row.

Suppose you originally enter all the records in alphabetical order by company (from *Acme Pet Supplies* to *Zastrow and Sons*), and then you add the record for a new client: *Pammy's Pasta Palace.* Excel puts the new record at the bottom of the barrel — in the last row right after *Zastrow and Sons* — instead of inserting it in its proper position, which is somewhere after *Acme Pet Supplies* but definitely well ahead of Zastrow and his wonderful boys!

And this is not the only problem you can have with the order used in originally entering records. Even if the records in the database remain fairly stable, the preferred order merely represents the order you use *most* of the time. But what about those times when you need to see the records in another, special order?

For example, although you usually like to work with the clients database in numerical order by case number, you may need to see the records in alphabetical order by the client's last name to quickly locate a client and look up his or her total due in a printout. When using the records to generate mailing labels for a mass mailing, you want the records in zip code order. When generating a report for your account representatives that shows which clients are in whose territory, you need the records in alphabetical order by state and maybe even by city.

Flexibility in the record order is exactly what's required to keep up with the different needs you have for the data. This is precisely what the Data⇨Sort command offers you after you understand how to use it.

To have Excel correctly sort the records in a database, you must specify which field's values determine the new order of the records. (Such fields are technically known as the *sorting keys* in the parlance of the database enthusiast.) Further, you must specify what type of order should be created using the information in these fields. Choose from two possible orders:

- **Ascending order:** Text entries are placed in alphabetical order (A to Z), and values are placed in numerical order (from smallest to largest).

- **Descending order:** This is the exact reverse of alphabetical order (Z to A) and numerical order (largest to smallest).

When you sort records in a database, you can specify up to three fields on which to sort. (You can also choose between ascending and descending order for each field you specify.) You need to use more than one field only when the first field you use in sorting contains duplicate values and you want a say in how the records with duplicates are arranged. (If you don't specify another field to sort on, Excel just puts the records in the order in which you entered them.)

The best and most common example of when you need more than one field is when sorting a large database alphabetically in last-name order. Say that you have a database that contains several people with the last name Smith, Jones, or Zastrow (as is the case when you work at Zastrow and Sons). If you specify the Last Name field as the only field to sort on (using the default ascending order), all the duplicate Smiths, Joneses, and Zastrows are placed in the order in which their records were originally entered. To better sort these duplicates, you can specify the First Name field as the second field to sort on (again using the default ascending order), making the second field the tie-breaker, so that Ian Smith's record precedes that of Sandra Smith, and Vladimir Zastrow's record comes after that of Mikhail Zastrow.

To sort records in an Excel database, follow these steps:

1. **Position the cell pointer in the first field name of the database.**

2. **Choose Data⇨Sort from the menu bar.**

   Excel selects all the records of the database (without including the first row of field names) and opens the Sort dialog box, as shown in Figure 9-8. By default, the first field name appears in the Sort By drop-down list box, and the Ascending radio button is selected at the top of the Sort dialog box.

Figure 9-8:
Set up to sort records alphabetically by surname or first name.

3. **Select the name of the field you first want the database records sorted by in the Sort By drop-down list box.**

   If you want the records arranged in descending order, remember also to select the Descending radio button to the right.

4. **If the first field contains duplicates and you want to specify how these records are sorted, select a second field to sort on in the Then By drop-down list box and select either the Ascending and Descending radio buttons to its right.**

5. **If necessary, specify a third field to sort the records by (use the second Then By drop-down list box and decide on the sort order to use).**

6. **Click OK or press Enter.**

   Excel sorts the selected records. If you see that you sorted the database on the wrong fields or in the wrong order, choose the Edit⇨Undo Sort command from the menu bar or press Ctrl+Z to immediately restore the database records to their previous order.

When completing the steps to sort a database, don't inadvertently select the No Header Row radio button in the Sort dialog box (refer to Figure 9-8), or Excel will make hash of your field names by sorting them in with the data in the actual records. Read to the upcoming sidebar "Sorting something besides a database" for clarification on when you would select this radio button.

Up and down the ascending and descending sort orders

When you use the ascending sort order with a key field that contains many different kinds of entries, Excel places numbers (from smallest to largest) before text entries (in alphabetical order), followed by any logical values (TRUE and FALSE), error values, and finally, blank cells.

When you use the descending sort order, Excel arranges the different entries in reverse: numbers are still first, arranged from largest to smallest; text entries go from Z to A; and the FALSE logical value precedes the TRUE logical value.

Check out how I set up my search in the Sort dialog box in Figure 9-8. In the Bo Peep Client database, I chose the Last Name field as the first field to sort on (Sort By) and the First Name field as the second field (Then By) — the second field sorts records with duplicate entries in the first field. I also chose to sort the records in the Bo Peep Client database in alphabetical (Ascending) order by last name and then first name. See the clients database right after sorting (in Figure 9-9). Note how the Harveys — Allison, Chauncey, and Scott — are now arranged in the proper first name/last name alphabetical order).

Figure 9-9: The Client database sorted in alphabetical order by last name and then by first name.

Microsoft Excel - Bo Peep Clientdb.xls

	A	B	C	D	E	F	G	H	I
1					Little Bo Peep Pet Detectives - Client List				
2	Case I	Last Nam	First Nar	Street	City	Sta	Zip	E-mail	Stat
3	101-014	Andersen	Hans	341 The Shadow	Scholar	MN	58764	handerser@mediacentral.co	Clos
4	103-023	Appleseed	Johnny	6789 Fruitree Tr	Along The Way	SD	66017	jseed@ppplemedia.com	Activ
5	102-013	Baggins	Bingo	99 Hobbithole	Shire	ME	04047	baggins@hobbit.crg	Activ
6	103-007	Baum	L. Frank	447 Toto Too Rd	Oz	KS	65432	fbaum@ozzie-and.com	Clos
7	104-026	Brown	Charles	59 Flat Plains	Saltewater	UT	84001	cbrown@snoopy.net	Activ
8	101-001	Bryant	Michael	326 Chef's Lane	Peris	TX	78705	mbryant@ohlala.com	Activ
9	101-028	Cassidy	Butch	Sundance Kidde	Hole In Well	CO	80477	bcassidy@sundance.net	Clos
10	102-006	Cinderella	Poore	8 Lucky Maider Way	Oxford	TN	07557	pcinderella@fairytale.org	Activ
11	103-005	Cole	Old King	4 Merry Soul Way	Fiddlers Cour	MA	01824	okcole@fiddlersthree.net	Activ
12	101-004	Cupid	Eros	97 Mount Olympus	Greece	CT	03331	cupid@loveland.net	Activ
13	103-022	Dragon	Kai	2 Pleistocene Era	Am's World	ID	00001	dinc@jurasic.org	Activ
14	104-031	Eaters	Big	444 Big Pigs Court	Dogtown	AZ	85257	pigcy@oinkers.com	Clos
15	106-022	Foliage	Red	49 Maple Syrup	Waffle	VT	05452	riddinghood@grandmas.com	Activ
16	102-020	Franklin	Ben	1789 Constitution	Jefferson	WV	20178	bfranklin@kitesunlimited.com	Activ
17	104-019	Fudde	Elmer	8 Warner Way	Hollywood	CA	33461	efudd@wabbit.org	Activ
18	102-002	Gearing	Shane	1 Gunfighter's End	LaLa Land	CA	90069	sgearing@nirvana.net	Activ
19	102-012	Gondor	Aragorn	2956 Gandelf	Micearth	WY	80342	agandalf@wizards.net	Clos
20	104-005	Gookin	Polly	4 Feathertop Hill	Hawthorne	MA	01824	pollyanna@roseglasses.net	Activ
21	101-014	Harvey	Allison	1st French Manor	Soibonne	AZ	53912	aharvey@azalla.com	Activ
22	105-008	Harvey	Chauncey	60 Lucky Starr Pl	Shetland	IL	50080		Activ
23	101-920	Harvey	Scott	12 Elm Street	Scholar	MN	58764	sharvey@mediacentral.com	Activ

Client list

Sorting something besides a database

The Sort command is not just for sorting records in the database. You can use it to sort financial data or text headings in the spreadsheets you build as well. When sorting regular worksheet tables, just be sure to select all the cells with data to be sorted (and only those with the data to be sorted) before you choose Sort from the Data pull-down menu.

Also note that Excel automatically excludes the first row of the cell selection from the sort (on the assumption that this row is a header row containing field names that shouldn't be included). To include the first row of the cell selection in the sort, be sure to select the No Header Row radio button in the My List Has section before you click OK to begin sorting.

If you want to sort worksheet data by columns, click the Options button in the Sort dialog box. Select the Sort Left to Right radio button in the Sort Options dialog box, and click OK. Now you can designate the number of the row (or rows) to sort the data on in the Sort dialog box.

You can use the Sort Ascending tool (the button with the A above the Z) or the Sort Descending tool (the button with the Z above the A) on the Standard toolbar to sort records in the database on a single field.

✔ To sort the database in ascending order by a particular field, position the cell pointer in that field's name at the very top of the database and then click the Sort Ascending button on the Standard toolbar.

✔ To sort the database in descending order by a particular field, position the cell pointer in that field's name at the very top of the database and then click the Sort Descending button on the Standard toolbar.

You AutoFilter the Database to See the Records You Want

Excel's AutoFilter feature makes it a breeze to hide everything in a database except the records you want to see. All you have to do to filter a database with this incredibly nifty feature is position the cell pointer somewhere in the database before you choose Data⇨Filter⇨AutoFilter from the menu bar. When you choose the AutoFilter command, Excel adds drop-down list buttons to every cell with a field name in that row (like those shown in Figure 9-10).

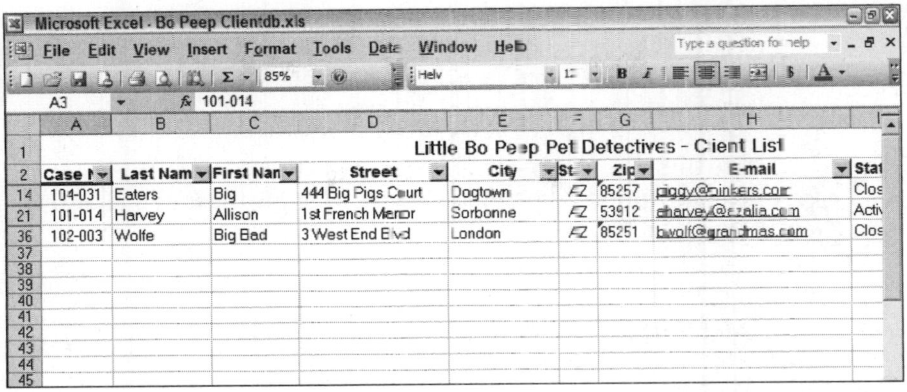

Figure 9-10:
The Client
database
after
filtering out
all records
except
those with
an AZ
State field.

	A	B	C	D	E	F	G	H	I
1					Little Bo Peep Pet Detectives - Client List				
2	Case N	Last Nam	First Nan	Street	City	St	Zip	E-mail	Stat
14	104-031	Eaters	Big	444 Big Pigs Court	Dogtown	AZ	85257	piggy@oinkers.com	Clos
21	101-014	Harvey	Allison	1st French Manor	Sorbonne	AZ	53912	aharvey@azalia.com	Activ
36	102-003	Wolfe	Big Bad	3 West End Blvd	London	AZ	85251	bwolf@grandmas.com	Clos

To filter the database to just those records that contain a particular value, you then click the appropriate field's drop-down list button to open a list box containing all the entries made in that field and select the one you want to use as a filter. Excel then displays only those records that contain the value you selected in that field. (All other records are temporarily hidden.)

For example, in Figure 9-10, I filtered the Little Bo Peep Client database to display only those records in which the State field contains AZ (for Arizona) by clicking the State's drop-down list button and then clicking AZ in the drop-down list box. (It was as simple as that.)

After you filter a database so that only the records you want to work with are displayed, you can copy those records to another part of the worksheet to the right of the database (or better yet, another worksheet in the workbook). Simply select the cells and then choose Edit⇒Copy from the menu bar (Ctrl+C), move the cell pointer to the first cell where the copied records are to appear, and press Enter. After copying the filtered records, you can then redisplay all the records in the database or apply a slightly different filter.

If you find that filtering the database by selecting a single value in a field drop-down list box gives you more records than you really want to contend with, you can further filter the database by selecting another value in a second field's drop-down list box. For example, say that you select CA as the filter value in the State field's drop-down list box and end up with hundreds of California records still displayed in the worksheet. To reduce the number of California records to a more manageable number, you could then select a value (such as San Francisco) in the City field's drop-down list box to further filter the database and reduce the records you have to work with on-screen. When you finish working with the San Francisco, California, records, you can display another set by choosing the City field's drop-down list box again and changing the filter value from San Francisco to some other city (such as Los Angeles).

When you're ready to once again display all the records in the database, choose Data⇨Filter⇨Show All from the menu bar. You can also remove a filter from a particular field by clicking its drop-down list button and then selecting the (All) option at the top of the drop-down list.

TIP

Note that if you've only applied a single field filter to the database, choosing the (All) option is no different from selecting the Data⇨Filter⇨Show All command from the menu bar.

Viewing the Top Ten records

Excel contains an AutoFilter option called Top 10. You can use this option on a numerical field to show only a certain number of records (like the ones with the ten highest or lowest values in that field or those in the ten highest or lowest percent in that field). To use the Top 10 option to filter a database, follow these steps:

1. **Choose Data⇨Filter⇨AutoFilter from the menu bar.**

2. **Click the drop-down list button in the field that you want to use in filtering the database records.**

3. **Select the Top 10 option in the drop-down list box.**

   Excel opens the Top 10 AutoFilter dialog box, similar to the one shown in Figure 9-11.

   By default, the Top 10 AutoFilter chooses to show the top ten items in the selected field. You can, however, change these default settings before filtering the database.

4. **To show only the bottom ten records, change Top to Bottom in the leftmost pop-up list box.**

5. **To show more than the top or bottom ten records, enter the new value in the middle text box (that currently holds 10) or select a new value by using the spinner buttons.**

6. **To show those records that fall into the Top 10 or Bottom 10 (or whatever) percent, change Items to Percent in the rightmost pop-up list box.**

7. **Click OK or press Enter to filter the database by using your Top 10 settings.**

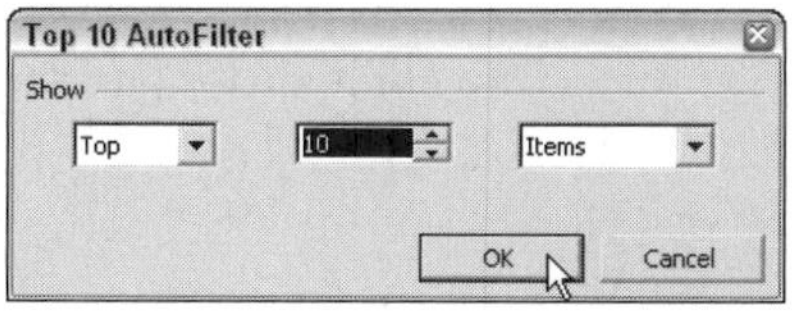

Figure 9-11:
The Top 10
AutoFilter
dialog box.

Top 10 AutoFilter			⊠
Show			
Top ▼	10 ⏶⏷	Items ▼	
	OK	Cancel	

In Figure 9-12, you can see the Little Bo Peep Client database after using the Top 10 option (with all its default settings) to show only those records with Total Due values that are in the top ten. David Letterman would be proud!

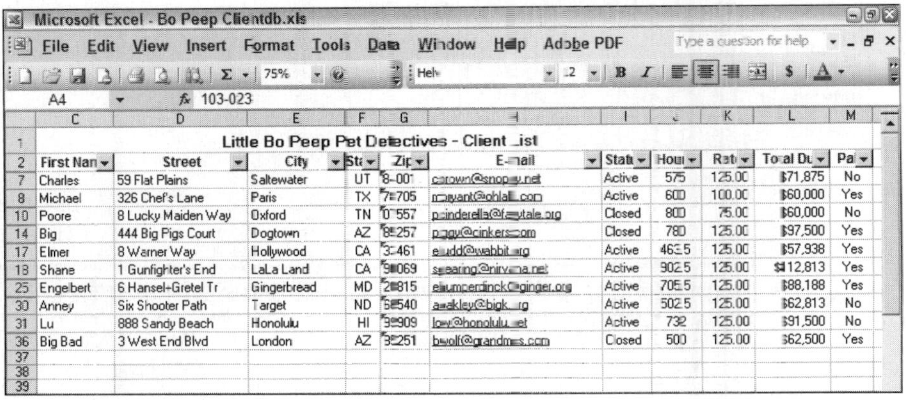

	First Nan	Street	City	Sta	Zip	E-mail	Stat	Hou	Rat	Total Du	Pa
7	Charles	59 Flat Plains	Saltewater	UT	8-001	cbrown@snoopy.net	Active	575	125.00	$71,875	No
8	Michael	326 Chef's Lane	Paris	TX	7-705	mbryant@ohlala.com	Active	600	100.00	$60,000	Yes
10	Poore	8 Lucky Maiden Way	Oxford	TN	0-557	pcinderella@fairytale.org	Closed	800	75.00	$60,000	No
14	Big	444 Big Pigs Court	Dogtown	AZ	8-257	piggy@cinkers.com	Closed	780	125.00	$97,500	Yes
17	Elmer	8 Warner Way	Hollywood	CA	3-461	efudd@wabbit.org	Active	463.5	125.00	$57,938	Yes
18	Shane	1 Gunfighter's End	LaLa Land	CA	9-069	sshearing@nirvana.net	Active	902.5	125.00	$112,813	Yes
25	Engelbert	6 Hansel+Gretel Tr	Gingerbread	MD	2-815	ehumperdinck@ginger.org	Active	705.5	125.00	$88,188	Yes
30	Anney	Six Shooter Path	Target	ND	5-540	aoakley@bigk.org	Active	502.5	125.00	$62,813	No
31	Lu	888 Sandy Beach	Honolulu	HI	9-909	low@honolulu.net	Active	732	125.00	$91,500	No
36	Big Bad	3 West End Blvd	London	AZ	3-251	bwolf@grandmas.com	Closed	500	125.00	$62,500	Yes

Figure 9-12: The database after using the Top 10 AutoFilter to filter out all records except for those with the 10 highest Total Due amounts.

Getting creative with custom AutoFilters

In addition to filtering a database to records that contain a particular field entry (such as *Newark* as the City or *CA* as the State), you can create custom AutoFilters that enable you to filter the database to records that meet less-exacting criteria (such as last names starting with the letter *M*) or ranges of values (such as salaries between $25,000 and $50,000 a year).

To create a custom filter for a field, you click the field's drop-down list button and then select the Custom option at the top of the pop-up list box — between Top 10 and the first field entry in the list box. When you select the Custom option, Excel displays the Custom AutoFilter dialog box, similar to the one shown in Figure 9-13.

In this dialog box, you first select the operator that you want to use in the first drop-down list box. (See Table 9-2 for operator names and what they locate.) Then enter the value (text or numbers) that should be met, exceeded, fallen below, or not found in the records of the database in the text box to the right. Note that you can select any of the entries made in that field of the database by choosing the drop-down list button and selecting the entry in the drop-down list box (much like you do when selecting an AutoFilter value in the database itself).

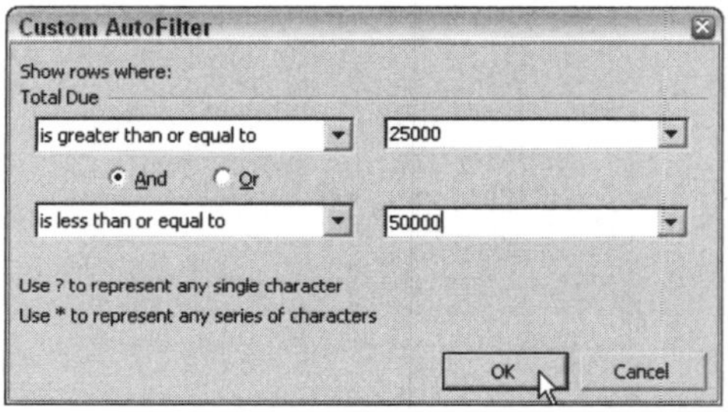

Figure 9-13:
Use the
Custom
AutoFilter to
display
records with
Total Due
amounts
between
$25,000 and
$50,000.

Table 9-2	**Ways to Get to a Particular Record**	
Operator	*Example*	*What It Locates in the Database*
Equals	Salary equals 35000	Records where the value in the Salary field is equal to $35,000
Does not equal	State does not equal NY	Records where the entry in the State field is not NY (New York)
Is greater than	Zip is greater than 42500	Records where the number in the Zip field comes after 42500
Is greater than or equal to	Zip is greater than or equal to 42500	Records where the number in the Zip field is equal to 42500 or comes after it
Is less than	Salary is less than 25000	Records where the value in the Salary field is less than $25,000 a year
Is less than or equal to	Salary is less than or equal to 25000	Records where the value in the Salary field is equal to $25,000 or less than $25,000
Begins with	Begins with d	Records with specified fields have entries that start with the letter *d*
Does not begin with	Does not begin with d	Records with specified fields have entries that do not start with the letter *d*

Operator	Example	What It Locates in the Database
Ends with	Ends with ey	Records whose specified field have entries that end with the letters *ey*
Does not end with	Does not end with ey	Records with specified fields have entries that do not end with the letters *ey*
Contains	Contains Harvey	Records with specified fields have entries that contain the name *Harvey*
Does not contain	Does not contain Harvey	Records with specified fields have entries that don't contain the name *Harvey*

If you only want to filter records in which a particular field entry matches, exceeds, falls below, or simply is not the same as the one you enter in the text box, you then click OK or press Enter to apply this filter to the database. However, you can use the Custom AutoFilter dialog box to filter the database to records with field entries that fall within a range of values or meet either one of two criteria.

To set up a range of values, you select the "is greater than" or "is greater than or equal to" operator for the top operator and then enter or select the lowest (or first) value in the range. Then make sure that the And radio button is selected and select "is less than" or "is less than or equal to" as the bottom operator and enter the highest (or last) value in the range.

Check out Figures 9-13 and 9-14 to see how I filter the records in the Client database so that only those records where Total Due amounts are between $25,000 and $50,000 are displayed. As shown in Figure 9-13, you set up this range of values as the filter by first selecting "is greater than or equal to" as the operator and $25,000 as the lower value of the range. Then, with the And radio button selected, you select "is less than or equal to" as the operator and $50,000 as the upper value of the range. The results of applying this filter to the clients database are shown in Figure 9-14.

To set up an either/or condition in the Custom AutoFilter dialog box, you normally choose between the "equals" and "does not equal" operators (whichever is appropriate) and then enter or select the first value that must be met or must not be equaled. Then you select the Or radio button and select whichever operator is appropriate and enter or select the second value that must be met or must not be equaled.

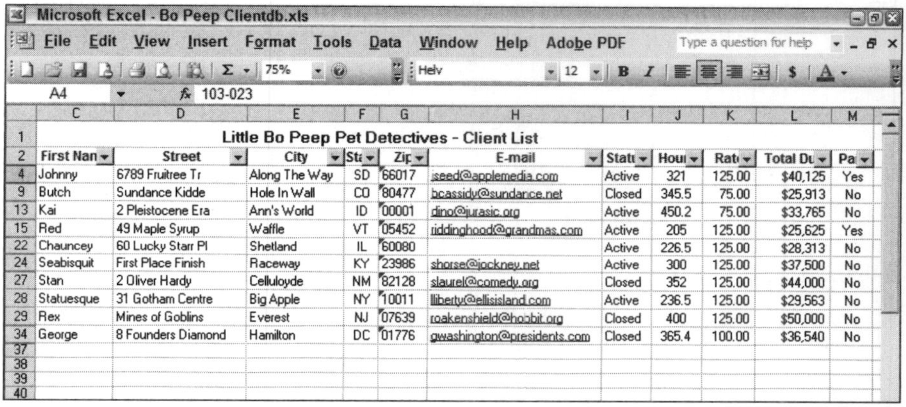

Little Bo Peep Pet Detectives - Client List

	First Nam	Street	City	Sta	Zip	E-mail	Statu	Hour	Rate	Total Du	Pa
4	Johnny	6789 Fruitree Tr	Along The Way	SD	66017	jseed@applemedia.com	Active	321	125.00	$40,125	Yes
9	Butch	Sundance Kidde	Hole In Wall	CO	80477	bcassidy@sundance.net	Closed	345.5	75.00	$25,913	No
13	Kai	2 Pleistocene Era	Ann's World	ID	00001	dino@jurasic.org	Active	450.2	75.00	$33,765	No
15	Red	49 Maple Syrup	Waffle	VT	05452	riddinghood@grandmas.com	Active	205	125.00	$25,625	Yes
22	Chauncey	60 Lucky Starr Pl	Shetland	IL	60080		Active	226.5	125.00	$28,313	No
24	Seabisquit	First Place Finish	Raceway	KY	23986	shorse@jockney.net	Active	300	125.00	$37,500	No
27	Stan	2 Oliver Hardy	Celluloyde	NM	82128	slaurel@comedy.org	Closed	352	125.00	$44,000	No
28	Statuesque	31 Gotham Centre	Big Apple	NY	10011	lliberty@ellisisland.com	Active	236.5	125.00	$29,563	No
29	Rex	Mines of Goblins	Everest	NJ	07639	roakenshield@hobbit.org	Closed	400	125.00	$50,000	No
34	George	8 Founders Diamond	Hamilton	DC	01776	gwashington@presidents.com	Closed	365.4	100.00	$36,540	No

Figure 9-14: The database after applying the custom AutoFilter.

For example, if you want to filter the database so that only records for states WA (Washington) or IL (Illinois) are displayed, you select "equals" as the first operator and then select or enter WA as the first entry. Next, you select the Or radio button, select "equals" as the second operator, and then select or enter IL as the second entry. When you then filter the database by clicking OK or pressing Enter, Excel displays only those records with either WA or IL as the code in the State field.

Chapter 10

Of Hyperlinks and Web Pages

In This Chapter

▶ Creating a hyperlink to another Office document, Excel workbook, worksheet, or cell range

▶ Creating a hyperlink to a Web page

▶ Changing the Hyperlink and Followed Hyperlink styles

▶ Saving an Excel worksheet data and charts in static Web pages

▶ Creating Web pages with interactive worksheet data and charts

▶ Editing Web pages with your favorite Web Page editor or Word

▶ Sending worksheets via e-mail

*N*ow that everyone and his brother seems to have a heavy dose of Internet fever and the World Wide Web has become the greatest thing since sliced bread, it should come as no surprise to discover that Excel offers a whole bunch of exciting Web-related features. Chief among these features are the ability to add hyperlinks to the cells of your worksheet and the ability to convert your worksheets into Web pages that you can publish on your Web servers.

Web pages that you create from Excel worksheets make your Excel calculated data, lists, and charts available to anyone who has a Web browser and Internet access (which is pretty much everyone in business these days), regardless of what type of computer is used and whether Excel is used. When you save worksheets as Web pages in Excel, you now have a choice between making your worksheet data static or interactive.

When you save a worksheet as a static Web page, your users are limited to simply viewing the data without being able to make any changes to it. When you save a worksheet as an interactive Web page, however, your users (provided that they are using Microsoft Internet Explorer 4.0 or later) not only can view the data but also can make certain changes to it. For example, if you save an order form that calculates subtotals and totals as an interactive Web page, your users can edit the quantities ordered, and the Web page will automatically recalculate the totals. Or if you save a database list (like the ones I describe in Chapter 9) as an interactive Web page, your users can sort and filter the data in their Web browsers just as you do in the Excel program!

Adding Hyperlinks to a Worksheet

Hyperlinks in a worksheet make the opening of other Office documents and Excel workbooks and worksheets just a mouse click away. It doesn't matter whether these documents are located on your hard drive, a server on your LAN (Local Area Network), or Web pages on the Internet or a company's intranet. You can also set up e-mail hyperlinks that automatically address messages to co-workers with whom you routinely correspond, and you can attach Excel workbooks or other types of Office files to these messages.

The hyperlinks that you add to your Excel worksheets can be of the following types:

- Hypertext that normally appears in the cell as underlined blue text
- Clip art and graphics from files that you've inserted into the worksheet
- Graphics that you've drawn with the tools on the Drawing toolbar — in effect, turning the graphic images into buttons

When creating a text or graphic hyperlink, you can make a link to another Excel workbook or other type of Office file, a Web site address (using the URL address — you know, that monstrosity that begins with http://), a named location in the same workbook, or even a person's e-mail address. The named location can be a cell reference or named cell range (see Chapter 6 for details on naming cell ranges) in a particular worksheet.

To create the text in a cell to which you attach a hyperlink, follow these steps:

1. **Select the cell in the worksheet of the workbook that is to contain the hyperlink.**

2. **Enter the text for the hyperlink in the cell; then click the Enter button on the Formula bar or press the Enter key.**

To insert a piece of clip art or a graphic image (stored in its own graphics file) into the worksheet to which you attach a hyperlink, follow these steps:

1. **From the menu bar, choose Insert⇨Picture⇨Clip Art or Insert⇨ Picture⇨From File; then find the piece of clip art or select the graphics file with the image you want to use for the hyperlink.**

   After Excel inserts the clip art or file graphic image into your worksheet, the image is selected (as evidenced by the sizing handles around the boundary box that surrounds it).

2. **Use the sizing handles to size the graphic image; then drag it to the place in the worksheet where you want the hyperlinked image to appear.**

To add the hyperlink to the text or graphic image in your worksheet, follow these steps:

1. **Select the cell with the text or click the graphic to be linked.**

2. **Choose Insert⇨Hyperlink from the menu bar, press Ctrl+K or click the Insert Hyperlink button (the one with the picture of a piece of chain link in front of the globe) on the Standard toolbar.**

   Excel opens the Insert Hyperlink dialog box (similar to the one shown in Figure 10-1) in which you indicate the file, the Web address (URL), or the named location in the workbook.

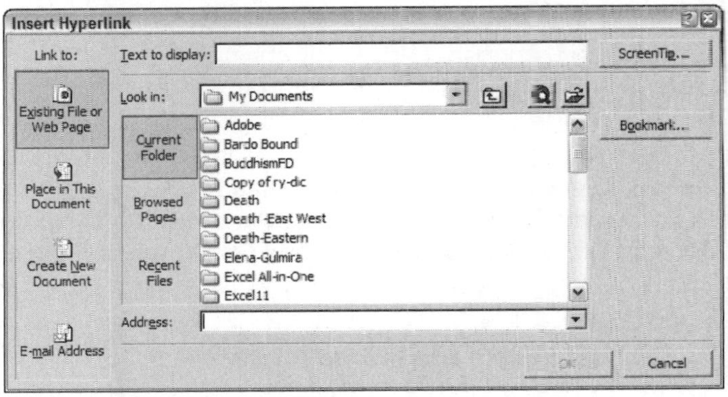

Figure 10-1:
Linking to a
Web page in
the Insert
Hyperlink
dialog box.

3a. **To have the hyperlink open another document, a Web page on a company's intranet, or a Web site on the Internet, click the Existing File or Web Page button if it isn't already selected; then enter the file's directory path or Web page's URL in the Address text box.**

   If the document you want to link to is located on your hard drive or a hard drive that is mapped on your computer, click the Look In drop-down button and select its folder and then select the file in the list box below. If you've recently opened the document you want to link to, you can click the Recent Files button and then select it from the list box.

   If the document you want to link to is located on a Web site and you know its Web address (the www.dummies.com/excel2k.htm-like thing), you can type it into the Address text box. If you recently browsed the Web page you want to link to you can click the Browsed Pages button and then select the address of the page from the list box.

3b. **To have the hyperlink move the cell pointer to another cell or cell range in the same workbook, click the Place in This Document button. Next, type in the address of the cell or cell range in the Type the Cell Reference text box or select the desired sheet name or range name from the Or Select a Place in This Document list box (shown in Figure 10-2).**

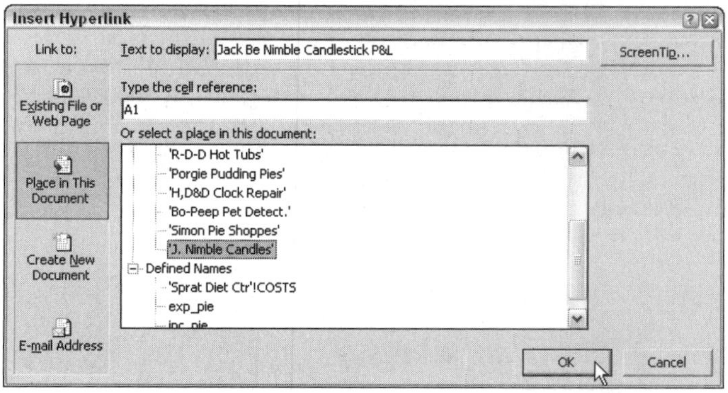

Figure 10-2:
Linking to a worksheet range name or cell reference in the Insert Hyperlink dialog box.

> **Insert Hyperlink**
>
> Link to: Text to display: Jack Be Nimble Candlestick P&L   ScreenTip...
>
> Existing File or Web Page
>
> Type the cell reference:
> A1
>
> Or select a place in this document:
> 'R-D-D Hot Tubs'
> 'Porgie Pudding Pies'
> 'H,D&D Clock Repair'
> 'Bo-Peep Pet Detect.'
> 'Simon Pie Shoppes'
> 'J. Nimble Candles'
> ⊟ Defined Names
>   'Sprat Diet Ctr'!COSTS
>   exp_pie
>   inc_pie
>
> Place in This Document
>
> Create New Document
>
> E-mail Address
>
> OK   Cancel

3c. **To open a new e-mail message addressed to a particular recipient, click the E-mail Address button and then enter the recipient's e-mail address in the E-mail Address text box (as shown in Figure 10-3).**

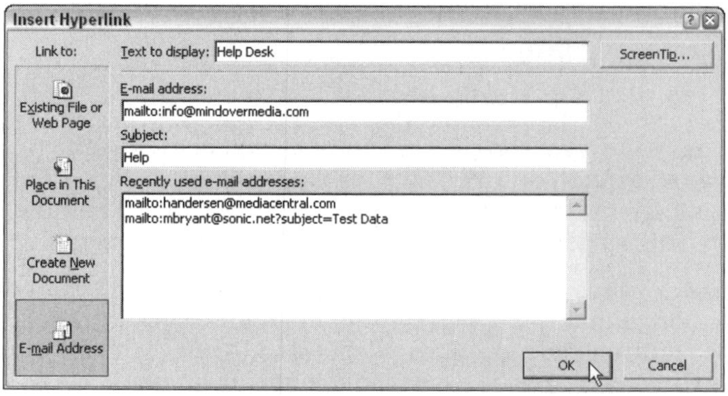

Figure 10-3:
Linking to an e-mail address page in the Insert Hyperlink dialog box.

> **Insert Hyperlink**
>
> Link to: Text to display: Help Desk   ScreenTip...
>
> Existing File or Web Page
>
> E-mail address:
> mailto:info@mindovermedia.com
> Subject:
> Help
> Recently used e-mail addresses:
> mailto:handersen@mediacentral.com
> mailto:mbryant@sonic.net?subject=Test Data
>
> Place in This Document
>
> Create New Document
>
> E-mail Address
>
> OK   Cancel

In most cases, your e-mail program is Outlook Express — it comes with the Internet Explorer 6.0, which ships with Office 2003.

As soon as you begin typing the e-mail address in the E-mail Address text box, Excel inserts the text `mailto:` in front of whatever you've typed. (`mailto:` is the HTML tag that tells Excel to open your e-mail program when you click the hyperlink.)

If you want the hyperlink to add the subject of the e-mail message when it opens a new message in your e-mail program, enter this text in the Subject text box.

If the recipient's address is already displayed in the Recently Used E-mail Addresses list box, you can enter it into the E-mail Address text box simply by clicking that address in this list box.

4. **(Optional) To change the hyperlink text that appears in the cell of the worksheet (underlined and in blue) or add text if the cell is blank, type the desired label in the Text to Display text box.**

5. **(Optional) To add a ScreenTip to the hyperlink that appears when you position the mouse pointer over the hyperlink, click the ScreenTip button, type in the text that you want to appear next to the mouse pointer in the ScreenTip Text box, and click OK.**

6. **Click OK to close the Insert Hyperlink dialog box.**

Follow those hyperlinks!

After you create a hyperlink in a worksheet, you can follow it to whatever destination you associated with the hyperlink. To follow a hyperlink, position the mouse pointer over the underlined blue text (if you assigned the hyperlink to text in a cell) or over the graphic image (if you assigned the hyperlink to a graphic inserted in the worksheet). When the mouse pointer changes to a hand with the index finger pointing upward, click the hypertext or graphic image, and Excel makes the jump to the designated external document, Web page, cell within the workbook, or e-mail message. What happens when you make the jump depends on the destination of the hyperlink, as follows:

- **External document hyperlinks:** Excel opens the document in its own window. If the program that created the document (such as Word or PowerPoint) is not already running, Windows launches the program at the same time that it opens the target document.

- **Web page hyperlinks:** Excel opens the Web page in its own Web browser window. If you are not online at the time you click this hyperlink, Windows opens the Connect To dialog box, and you need to click the Connect button. If Internet Explorer is not open when you click this hyperlink, Windows opens this Web browser prior to opening the Web page with the URL address listed in the hyperlink.

- **Cell address hyperlinks:** Excel activates the worksheet in the current workbook and selects the cell or cells of the sheet and cell range address listed in the hyperlink.

- **E-mail hyperlinks:** Excel launches your e-mail program, which opens a new e-mail message addressed to the e-mail address you specified when creating the hyperlink.

After you follow a hypertext link to its destination, the color of its text changes from the traditional blue to a dark shade of purple (without affecting its underlining). This color change indicates that the hyperlink has been used. (Note, however, that graphic hyperlinks do not show any change in color after you follow them.) Also, Excel automatically restores this underlined text to its original (unfollowed) blue color the next time that you open the workbook file.

When following hyperlinks within a worksheet, you can use the buttons on the Web toolbar. To display the Web toolbar, choose View⇨Toolbars⇨Web from the Excel pull-down menus.

You can use the Back and Forward buttons on the Web toolbar (shown in Figure 10-4) to jump back and forth between the cell with the internal hyperlink and its sheet and/or cell address destination. After clicking the hyperlink in a cell and jumping to its destination, you can click the Back button on the Web toolbar to jump right back to its cell. When you're back at the cell with the hyperlink, you can jump right to the destination again by clicking the Web toolbar's Forward button.

Figure 10-4:
You can use the buttons on the Web toolbar to jump back and forth between links.

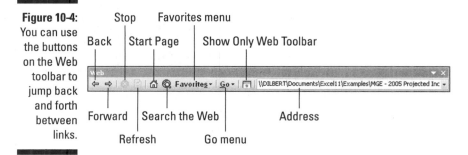

In Figures 10-5 through 10-7, I show you how you might use hyperlinks to jump to different parts of the same workbook. Look at Figure 10-5 to see a worksheet that contains an interactive table of contents to all the Profit and Loss data tables and charts in this workbook. This interactive Table of Contents consists of a list of the data tables and charts contained in the workbook. A hypertext link to the appropriate worksheet and cell range has been added to each entry of this list in the cell range B4:B15. (I removed the gridlines from this worksheet to make it easier to see and use the hyperlinks).

When I click the <u>Mother Goose Enterprises P&L</u> hyperlink, shown in Figure 10-5, Excel immediately takes me to cell A1 of the Total Income worksheet. In this worksheet, the graphic image for the Home button (made from the outline of a house on a page of paper) appears to the right of the worksheet title in cell A1, as shown in Figure 10-6. This graphic contains a hyperlink that, when clicked, takes me to cell A1 of the Workbook TOC worksheet (the one shown in Figure 10-5).

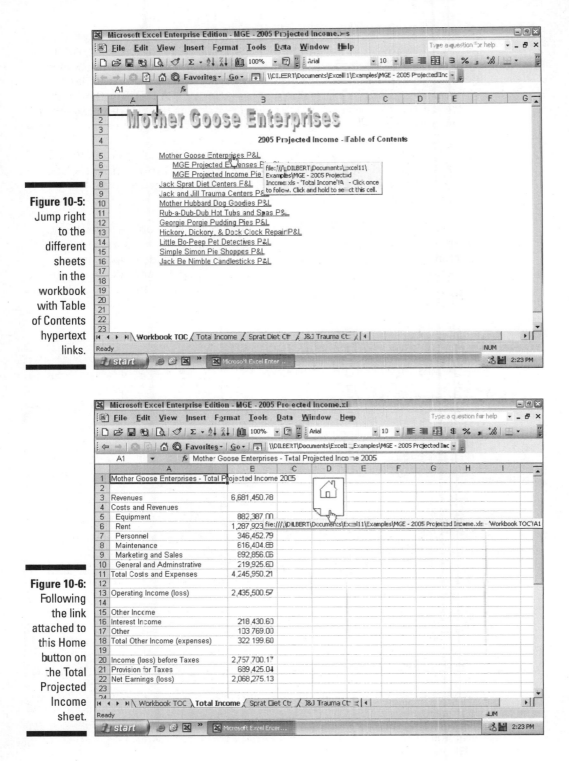

Figure 10-5:
Jump right
to the
different
sheets
in the
workbook
with Table
of Contents
hypertext
links.

Figure 10-6:
Following
the link
attached to
this Home
button on
the Total
Projected
Income
sheet.

When I click the <u>MGE Projected Expenses Pie Chart</u> hypertext link partially shown directly under the Mother Goose Enterprises P&L link in Figure 10-5, the result is shown in Figure 10-7. This hyperlink is attached to the named cell range, Exp_Pie (this range name appears on the Name box on the Formula bar). This cell range encompasses the cells A28:D45 in the Total Projected Income worksheet. Note that clicking this hypertext link selects all cells in this named cell range, which just happen to be the ones that lie under the 3-D pie chart that shows the breakdown of the projected expenses anticipated in 2005. Because you have no way to attach a hyperlink directly to a chart that you add to a worksheet, you have to resort to selecting the underlying cells when you want a hyperlink to display a particular chart that's been added to a worksheet.

To the right of the MGE Projected Expenses pie chart, you see a starburst graphic (that I created with the Drawing toolbar, using the Stars and Banners option on the AutoShapes pop-up menu). This handmade graphic image contains the same hyperlink as the home page Clip Art graphic (shown in Figure 10-6) so that, when clicked, it, too, takes me back to cell A1 of the Workbook TOC worksheet.

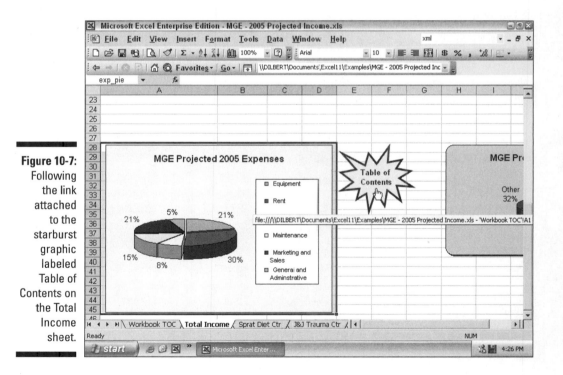

Figure 10-7:
Following the link attached to the starburst graphic labeled Table of Contents on the Total Income sheet.

Editing and formatting hypertext links

The contents of cells that contain hypertext links are formatted according to the settings contained in two built-in workbook styles: Hyperlink and Followed Hyperlink. The *Hyperlink* style is applied to all new hypertext links you set up in a worksheet that you haven't yet used. The *Followed Hyperlink* is applied to all hypertext links that you have used. If you want to change the way used and unused hypertext appears in the workbook, you need to change the formatting used in Followed Hyperlink and Hyperlink styles respectively. (Refer to Chapter 3 for information on modifying styles.)

If you need to edit the contents of a cell containing a hypertext link, you must be careful that, when getting Excel into Edit mode so that you can change the text, you don't inadvertently follow the link. This means that under no circumstances can you click the cell with the hypertext link with the (primary) mouse button because that's the way you follow the hypertext link to your destination! The best way to get around this problem, if you're used to selecting cells by clicking them, is by doing the following:

1. **Click a cell right next door to the one with the hypertext link (above, below, right, or left), provided that this neighboring cell doesn't contain its own hyperlink.**

2. **Press the appropriate arrow key to then select the cell with the hypertext link to be edited ($\downarrow$, $\uparrow$, $\rightarrow$, or $\leftarrow$).**

3. **Press F2 to put Excel into Edit mode.**

4. **Make your changes to the contents of the hypertext in the cell; then click the Enter button on the Formula bar or press the Enter key to complete your edits.**

If you need to edit the destination of a hypertext link (as opposed to contents of the cell to which the link is attached), you need to right-click the cell with the link to open the cell's shortcut menu (and avoid following the hyperlink) and then select the Edit Hyperlink command from this shortcut menu. Doing this opens the Edit Hyperlink dialog box (which looks suspiciously like the Insert Hyperlink dialog box shown in Figure 10-1 after you've filled it in) in which you can change either the type and/or the location of the hyperlink.

To get rid of a hyperlink while still retaining the cell's text entry, right-click the hyperlink and choose Remove Hyperlink from the cell's shortcut menu. To get rid of the hyperlink along with the cell's text entry, select the cell and then press the Delete key (the equivalent of choosing Edit➪Clear➪All from the menu bar).

Editing and formatting graphics with hyperlinks

When it comes to editing the graphics images to which you assign hyperlinks, you can edit the graphic image by right-clicking the image and selecting Show Picture Toolbar from its shortcut menu. Doing so selects the graphic and opens the Picture toolbar from which you can modify various and sundry attributes of the image. You can change the color, fill, brightness, and contrast, how it's cropped, and whether the image moves and is resized when you edit the underlying cells. You can also open the Format Picture dialog box by right-clicking the image and choosing Format Picture from its shortcut menu and use its options to edit certain properties of the graphic (such as the color, fill, transparency, line style, size, and protection).

If you want to manually resize the graphic image or move it to a new place in the worksheet, you need to Ctrl+click the graphic (by holding down the Ctrl key while you click) and then manipulate it with the mouse. To resize the graphic image, you drag the appropriate sizing handles. To relocate the graphic image, you drag the graphic (when the mouse pointer changes to an arrowhead pointing to two double-headed arrows in the form of a cross) to its new position in the worksheet.

To copy a graphic image along with its hyperlink, you can click the image while you hold down the Ctrl key and then (without releasing the Ctrl key) drag a copy of the image to its new location. Alternatively, you can right-click the graphic image and then put it into the Clipboard by choosing the Copy command from the graphic's shortcut menu. After you copy the graphic with its hyperlink to the Clipboard, you can paste it into a worksheet by choosing Edit⇨Paste from the regular Excel menu bar (or press Ctrl+V) or by clicking the Paste button on the Standard toolbar.

To delete a graphic image and at the same time remove its hyperlink, you Ctrl+click the graphic to select it and then press the Delete key. To remove a hyperlink without deleting the graphic image, right-click the graphic and then choose Remove Hyperlink from the shortcut menu.

To edit the hyperlink's destination, right-click the graphic and then select the Edit Hyperlink command from the image's shortcut menu. This opens the Edit Hyperlink dialog box, from which you can modify the location to be followed.

Spreadsheets on the Web?

Actually, the concept of publishing Excel spreadsheet data on the World Wide Web makes a heck of a lot of sense, both from the standpoint of the worksheet's tabular layout and the worksheet's calculated contents. Excel enables you to create Web pages that either display your worksheet data in a static, look-but-don't-touch mode, or in an interactive, let's-have-some-fun mode. When you create a Web page with static worksheet data, your users can view the Excel data only with their Web browsers. When you create a Web page with interactive worksheet data, however, your users can continue to play around with the data by editing and formatting its values. Depending upon the nature of the spreadsheet, your users can even continue to perform calculations and, in cases of data lists, manipulate the data by sorting and filtering it.

Saving an Excel worksheet as a Web page is as easy as choosing the File⇨ Save as Web Page command from the Excel menu bar. When you select this command, Excel opens the Save As dialog box, as shown in Figure 10-8. As you may notice, the Web-page version of the Save As dialog box contains the same basic controls as the regular workbook version. The Web-page version differs from the worksheet version in the following controls:

✔ **Entire Workbook** or **Selection: Sheet:** When you select the File⇨Save as Web Page command, Excel gives you a choice between saving all the data on all the worksheets (with the Entire Workbook radio button, which is selected by default) and saving just the data selected on the current worksheet (with the Selection: Sheet radio button). When no particular chart or cell range is selected in the current worksheet, this button appears as Selection: Sheet, and when you choose the Selection: Sheet radio button, Excel puts all the data on the current worksheet into the new Web page. When you've selected a chart in the workbook, this button appears as Selection: Chart. When you've selected a cell range, this button appears as Selection:, with the cell addresses of the range following the colon.

✔ **Publish:** Click the Publish button to open the Publish as Web Page dialog box (as shown in Figure 10-9) in which you specify a number of different publishing options. This dialog box enables you to

  • Select which items in the workbook to include in the new Web page

  • Edit the type of interactivity if any to use

  • Edit the filename of the new Web page

  • Decide whether to open the Web page in your computer's Web browser

✔ **Add Interactivity:** Select the Add Interactivity With check box when you want your users to be able to edit and recalculate the worksheet data or filter or, in the case of database lists, sort and/or filter the records. Note that Excel 2003 automatically adds interactivity to your data when you elect to publish the entire workbook as a Web page.

✔ **Title:** Click the Change button to the right of the Title heading to open the Set Page Title dialog box in which you add a title to your new Web page. The title that you add here appears centered at the top of the Web page right above whatever worksheet data or charts the page contains. (Don't confuse the Title with the Web page header that appears on the title bar of the user's Web browser.) Whatever title you enter in the Set Page Title dialog box then appears in the Save As dialog box following the Page Title label when you click OK.

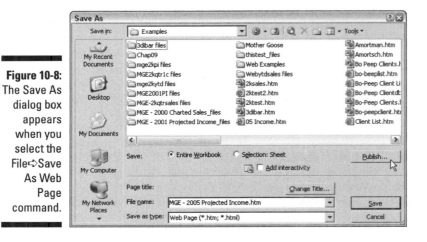

Figure 10-8: The Save As dialog box appears when you select the File⇨Save As Web Page command.

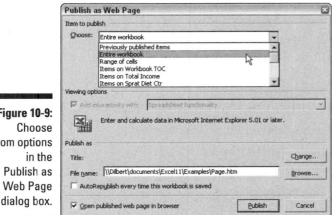

Figure 10-9: Choose from options in the Publish as Web Page dialog box.

Saving a static Web page

Static Web pages enable your users to view the data but not change it in any way. To create a static Web page, you follow these general steps:

1. **Open the workbook with the data to be saved as a Web page.**

2. **(Optional) When saving something less than the entire current worksheet, select the chart or range of cells. For example, if you're inserting a chart, click the chart, and if you're inserting only a range of cells, just select the range.**

   If you know that you want to save a particular chart or particular range of cells of a worksheet in the new Web page, you should select the chart to be saved before you open the Save As dialog box (as I outline in Step 3). Selecting the chart ahead of time changes the Selection: Sheet radio button to the Selection: Chart radio button. In the case of a cell range selection, the Selection: Sheet radio button changes to a Selection: radio button followed by the address of the cells selected.

3. **Choose File⇨Save as Web Page from the menu bar to open the Save As dialog box (refer to Figure 10-8).**

4. **Indicate which part of the workbook is to be saved in the new Web page.**

   To save only the data in the current worksheet, choose the Selection: Sheet radio button instead. *Note:* If you clicked the chart in the worksheet that you intend to convert into a Web page graphic before opening the Save As dialog box, you need to choose the Selection: Chart radio button (which replaces the Selection: Sheet button). If you selected a cell range, you need to choose the Selection: radio button followed by the address of the selected cell range. Remember that if you choose the Entire Workbook option, Excel automatically makes the resulting Web page interactive.

   To save the contents of a worksheet other than the one currently selected, click the Publish button, and then choose the sheet by its description from the Choose drop-down list box.

   To save a chart that you didn't select prior to opening the Save As dialog box, click the Publish button, and then select the chart (identified by its description) from the Choose drop-down list.

   To save a specific range of cells that you didn't select prior to opening the Save As dialog box, click the Publish button. Then select Range of Cells from the Choose drop-down list before you type the range address in the text box immediately below or enter its address by selecting the range of cells by highlighting them in the worksheet.

5. Specify a filename for the new Web page.

Enter the name for the new Web page in the File Name text box. Note that Excel appends the filename extension .htm (which stands for HyperText Markup, indicating that this is an HTML text file) or xml (Extensible Markup Language) to whatever filename you enter in this text box, depending upon which type is selected in the Save as Type drop-down list box — see Step 8). If you plan to publish the Web page on a Unix Web server, keep in mind that this operating system is sensitive to uppercase and lowercase letters in the filename. (The Macintosh and Windows operating system are both case-blind when it comes to filenames.)

6. Designate the location where the Web page is to be saved.

When saving the new Web page on your computer's hard drive or even on a network drive, you need to indicate the drive and directory in the Save In text box just as you do when saving a regular Excel workbook file. (Consult Chapter 2 for more on saving workbook files.) To save the page to a folder:

- To save the new Web page directly on your company's Internet or intranet Web site, click the My Network Places button in the panel on the left, and then open the folder in which you want the page saved.

- To save the new page on an FTP (File Transfer Protocol) site that your Web administrator or favorite IT person has set up, click FTP Locations at the bottom of the Save In drop-down list box (opened by clicking its drop-down button), and then open the FTP folder in which you want the page saved.

In both cases, you (or a qualified Web-head) must have already set up the Web folders or FTP locations before you can save your worksheet Web pages there.

7. (Optional) Specify a title for the Web page.

If you want Excel to add a title (which appears centered at the top of the page before any of the data or charts), click the Change Title button in the Save As dialog box. Then type the text for the title in the Set Page Title dialog box and click OK. Note that you can also add or edit a title with the Change Title button in the Publish as Web Page dialog box (which you open by clicking the Publish button in the Save As dialog box).

8. Specify the type of Web page.

By default, Excel saves the worksheet data you select in a single file Web page (with the .mht file extension). If you want to save the file as a regular Web page, select Web Page (*.htm; *.html) from the Save as Type drop-down menu. To save the data as an XML file, select XML Spreadsheet (*.xml) from this drop-down menu.

9. Save the Web page.

To save your new Web page using the settings you designate in the previous steps, select the Save button in the Save As dialog box (refer to Figure 10-8). If you want to preview your Web page immediately upon saving it, click the Publish button to open the Publish as Web Page dialog box. Next, select the Open Published Web Page in Browser check box before you click the Publish button or press Enter.

Note: Upon saving your worksheet data in the new Web page, Excel automatically creates a new folder with the same name as the .mht, .htm, or .xml file that contains all the supporting files, including such things as the graphics files and charts among the numerical data. Thus, if you move the Web page from a local drive to a Web server of some sort, you need to copy the supporting files' folder as well as its Web page file to ensure that the user's browser can successfully render the entire contents of the page.

If you would prefer that Excel not create a separate folder with the supporting files, you can change this setting in the Web Options dialog box (opened by choosing Tools⇨Options and then clicking the Web Options button on the General tab). In the Web Options dialog box, simply remove the check mark from the Organize Supporting Files in a Folder check box on the Files tab.

Saving an interactive Web page

The interactive Web pages feature is one of the coolest features in Excel. This is because interactive Web pages enable the users who view your Web pages with Microsoft Internet Explorer (Version 4.0 or later) to make changes to the worksheet data — all without any kind of scripting or programming on your part. (Put that in your Java cup and drink it!) These changes can include any of the following elements covered elsewhere in this book:

- **Worksheet data tables:** In interactive worksheet tables, you can edit the values and have the formulas automatically (or manually) updated in the tables. You can also change the formatting of the data and what parts of the worksheet are displayed in the Web page. (Refer to Chapters 3 and 4 for information on formatting and editing worksheet data including formulas.)

- **Database lists:** In interactive database lists, you can sort and filter the records more or less as you do in normal Excel database (see Chapter 9 for details on setting up and maintaining an Excel database) as well as edit the data and change the list's formatting.

- **Charts:** In interactive charts, you can edit the supporting data and have the chart automatically redrawn on the Web page. You can also make changes to the chart itself, including chart type, titles, and certain chart formatting.

To create an interactive Web page, you follow the same steps as outlined in this chapter's section "Saving a static Web page," with the following exception: When saving anything less than the entire workbook, you must select the Add Interactivity check box prior to saving or publishing the new Web page.

Keep in mind that when creating a Web page with an interactive chart, you need to click just the chart before opening the Save As dialog box with the File⇨Save as Web Page command. Excel automatically will add the supporting worksheet data to the new Web page (provided that you don't forget to select the Add Interactivity check box prior to saving or publishing the page) beneath the interactive chart.

Note that when you publish an entire workbook, Excel enables you to select individual worksheets and chart sheets in the Web page equivalent of the workbook by clicking the sheet tab at the bottom of the interactive Web table (known as the Sheet Selector) and then clicking the name of the sheet in the pop-up menu that appears.

Acting out with interactive worksheet data

Look at Figure 10-10 to see a new Web page containing a fully interactive first-quarter sales table (created from the Mother Goose – 2004 Sales workbook) as it appears when opened with Microsoft Internet Explorer 6.0 that ships with Office 11. I created this interactive Web page by clicking the Selection: Sheet option button and the Add Interactivity check box in the Save As dialog box, which I had opened by choosing File⇨Save As Web Page on the Excel menu bar.

The biggest tip-off in the Internet Explorer that you're dealing with an interactive worksheet table rather than a static one is the display of the toolbar at the top of the data table. You can use these buttons to edit the table's data as well as to alter how the information is displayed.

You can use any scroll bars that appear along the right and lower edge of the table to bring new worksheet data into view. You can also manually modify the widths of the columns or height of the rows by dragging their borders left and right or up and down, or you can use the AutoFit feature to size columns by double-clicking the right border of the cell with the column letter. (See Chapter 3 for more on resizing columns and rows.)

Changing the contents

To change a particular cell of the worksheet data, double-click the data to select its contents. If the cell contains a label or value, this text is selected, and you can replace it by typing the new label or value. If the cell contains a formula, the calculated result is replaced by the formula, which you can edit.

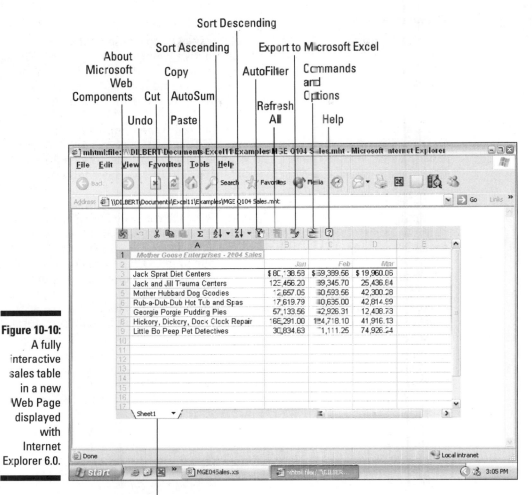

Figure 10-10: A fully interactive sales table in a new Web Page displayed with Internet Explorer 6.0.

Sheet Selector

If you want to prevent your users from being able to change particular cells in the worksheet data, you need to protect the table or sheet prior to saving its data as a Web page. You can enable your Web users to change particular cells (such as the quantities they want to order) without letting them edit others (such as the cells that contain the prices and those with the formulas that calculate the totals). To accomplish this, you need to unlock the cells that you want them to be able to edit before protecting the worksheet (which prevents them from changing any other cells). See Chapter 6 for details on how to do this.

Changing the data display

The Commands and Options dialog box is the key to changing the way that worksheet data is displayed in your interactive Web page. To open this dialog box, you click the Commands and Options button on the toolbar above the worksheet data. (If this toolbar is not displayed, right-click the worksheet table and choose the Commands and Options from the shortcut menu.)

You can see the first-quarter 2004 sales table with the Commands and Options dialog box displayed in Figure 10-11. This dialog box contains four tabs (Format, Formula, Sheet, and Workbook) with various options for modifying the appearance and functionality of the interactive sales table.

Although the Commands and Options dialog box affords you quite a number of editing and formatting opportunities, be aware that any changes you make to the worksheet data table with these options are temporary: You cannot save your changes to the Web page. The best you can do is print the Web page by using the browser's File⊅Print command to get a hard copy of the edited and reformatted table data. Or if you have Excel on your computer, export the Web page to a read-only Excel workbook by clicking the Export to Microsoft Excel button on the toolbar above the table of data. (See the section "Exporting an interactive Web page to Excel," later in this chapter, for details.)

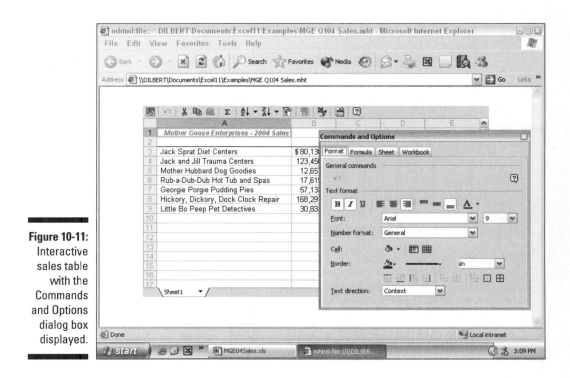

Figure 10-11:
Interactive sales table with the Commands and Options dialog box displayed.

In Figure 10-12, check out the Web page with the first-quarter 2004 sales table after I removed the display of the sheet tab, the column and row headings, and the gridlines. I removed them by deselecting their check box options in the Show/Hide area on the Sheet tab, and I removed the Sheet Selector by deselecting its check box option in the Show/Hide area on the Workbook tab.

More often than not, instead of making changes to the look of the worksheet data table, you'll be making changes to its contents. Figures 10-13 and 10-14 illustrate just this kind of change. In Figure 10-13, you see a new Web page created from an Excel worksheet containing a blank Georgie Porgie Pie Palace order form. This order form contains all the formulas necessary to compute the extended prices for each type of pie ordered as well as the subtotal for all pies ordered, any applicable tax, and, finally, the order's grand total. Figure 10-14 shows the same Web page after entering all the order information in the various blank cells.

To prevent unwanted (not to mention unwarranted) changes in the pie ordering form, I made sure that the user can edit only the shaded cells in the worksheet data table of the Web page shown in Figures 10-13 and 10-14. I did this in Excel prior to creating the Web page by unlocking shaded cells and then turning on the protection for the worksheet. (See Chapter 6 for details on how to do this.)

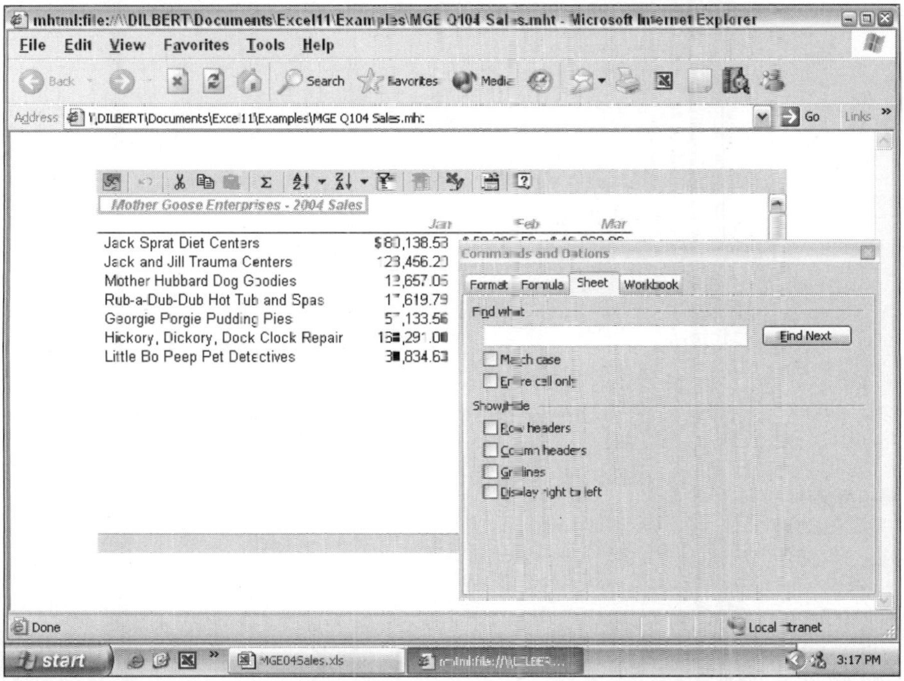

Figure 10-12:
The Web page with interactive sales table after making several formatting changes.

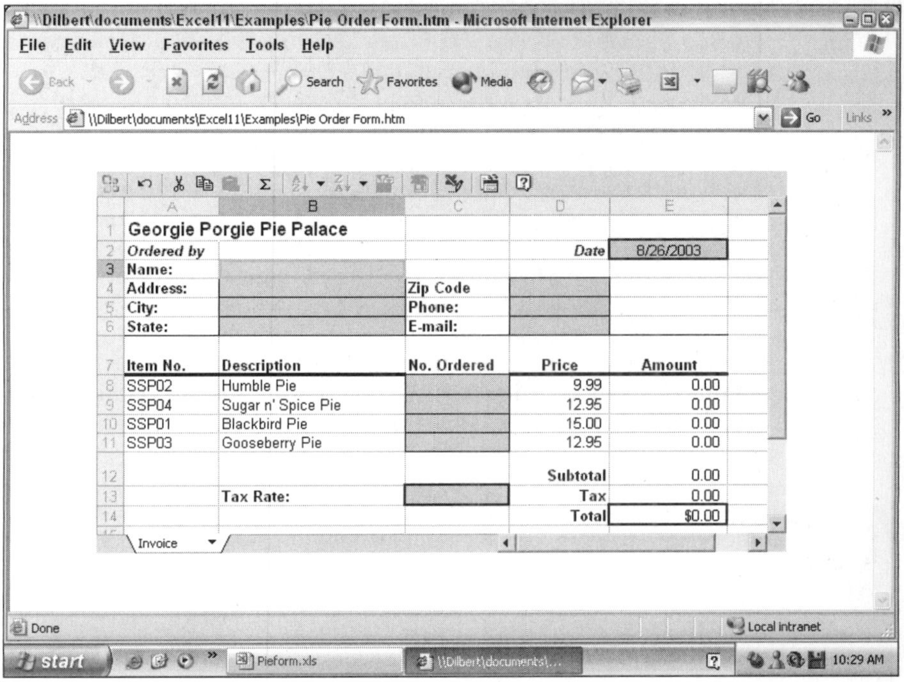

Figure 10-13:
A Web page containing an inter-active order form.

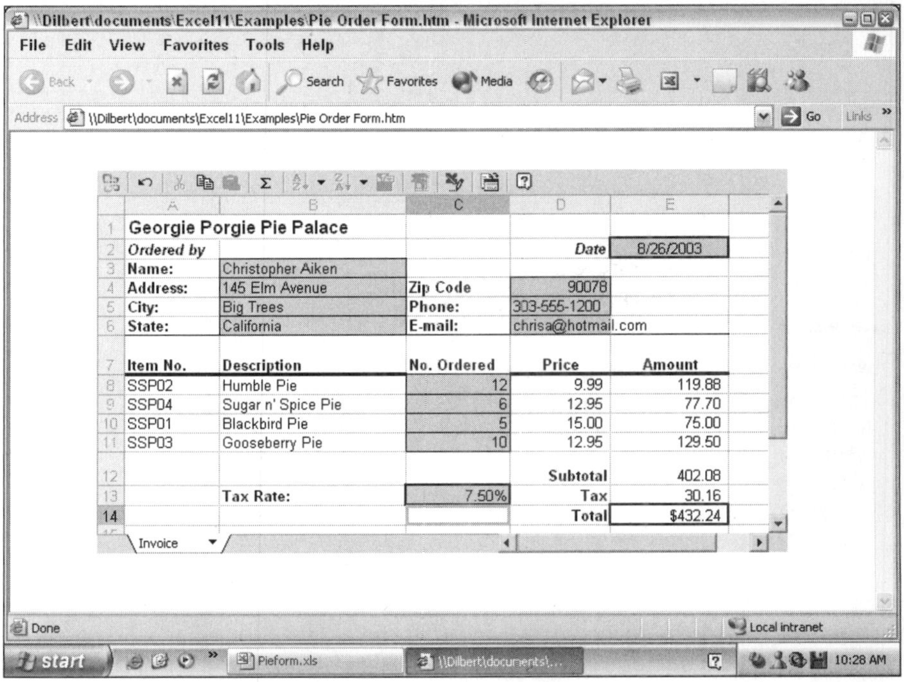

Figure 10-14:
A Web page with filled-in and calculated order form.

Acting up with an interactive database

Web pages containing an interactive list of data arranged as a database (as I detail in Chapter 9) enable you to make all the same type of content and formatting changes as standard worksheet data tables. In addition, you can also sort the records in the data list and use a slightly modified form of the AutoFilter capability to filter out all but the desired records.

Peruse Figures 10-15 and 10-16 to see how to use the AutoFilter feature on a Web page containing an interactive database. Figure 10-15 shows the Bo Beep Client List database after saving it in an interactive Web page.

To sort this database, do one of the following:

- ✔ Click the column (field) on which you want the records sorted and then click either the Sort Ascending or Sort Descending button on the toolbar.

- ✔ Right-click the database, and choose Sort Ascending or Sort Descending from the shortcut menu. Then, from the pop-up list that appears, choose the name of the field on which to sort the database.

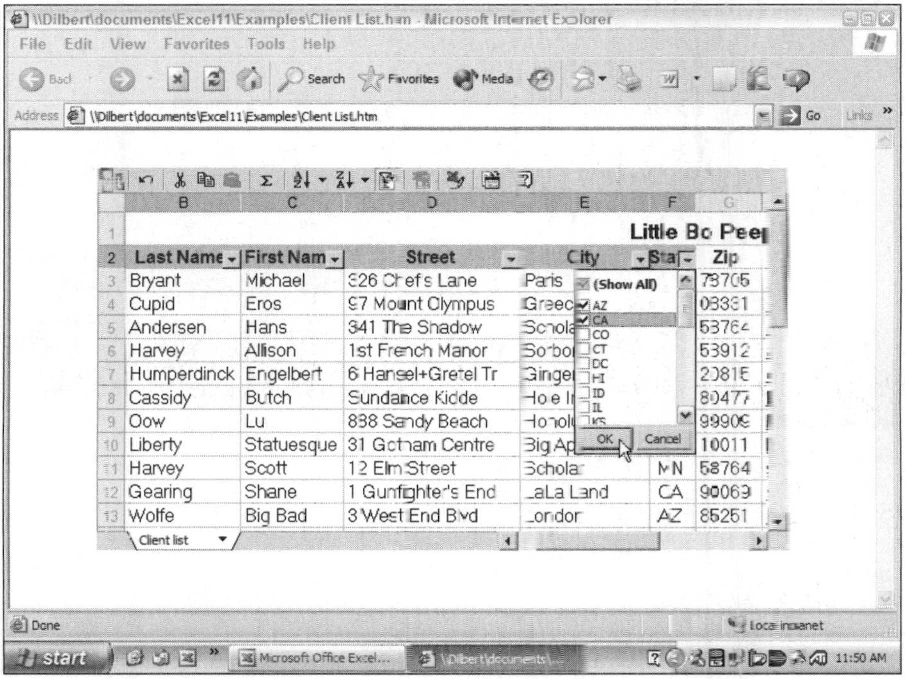

Figure 10-15: Web page with interactive database showing the AutoFilter buttons to the right of each field.

To filter the records in a database, you display the AutoFilter pop-up buttons by clicking the AutoFilter button on the toolbar or the AutoFilter command from the database's shortcut menu. After the AutoFilter pop-up buttons are displayed in the cells with the database field names, you can filter the records by selecting the desired entries from the appropriate field's drop-down list.

See the results in Figure 10-16 of the Bo Peep Client List after I filtered its records so that only those containing either AZ (Arizona) or CA (California) appear. To do this, I clicked the AutoFilter button in the State field to open the State drop-down list where the Show All check box was selected (thus selecting the check boxes for all the individual state entries as well). I then selected the (Show All) check box to deselect (or clear) it, thus automatically deselecting the check boxes for all the individual state entries. Next, I selected the AZ and CA check boxes before clicking OK at the very bottom of the drop-down list.

TIP

To restore a database list after filtering its records, click the AutoFilter button in the field or fields involved in the filtering and select the Show All check box to restore its check mark (and the check marks in all the boxes for all the individual entries as well) before you click OK at the bottom of the drop-down list.

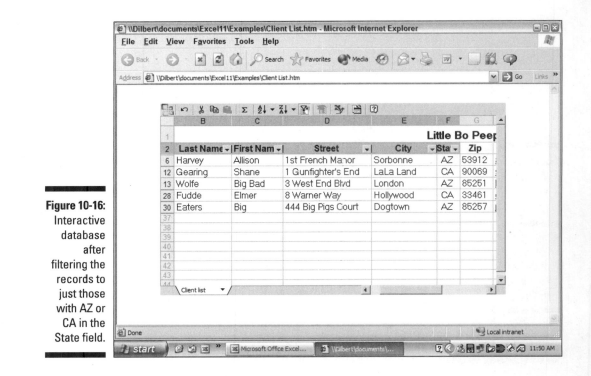

Figure 10-16:
Interactive database after filtering the records to just those with AZ or CA in the State field.

Acting on an interactive chart

Web pages with interactive Excel charts display both the chart and supporting worksheet data. When you make changes to supporting data, the chart is automatically updated in the Web page. In addition to being able to update the chart by editing supporting data, your users can also make certain editing changes to the chart (such as changing the type of chart or editing the chart title).

Figure 10-17 shows a new Web page with an interactive chart created from a Clustered Column chart added to the Mother Goose first-quarter 2004 worksheet that graphs the January, February, and March sales for the various Mother Goose companies. As you can see in this figure, the supporting worksheet data appears beneath the cluster chart with the now familiar interactive toolbar.

If you change the values in the supporting worksheet data, the chart is automatically updated, as Figure 10-18 clearly shows. In this figure, I increased the February sales for Jack Sprat Diet Centers from $59,389.56 to $259,389.56 in supporting data. To verify that the Clustered Column chart has been updated to match this increase, compare the size of the middle column in the first cluster in Figure 10-18 with that of the middle column in the first cluster in Figure 10-17.

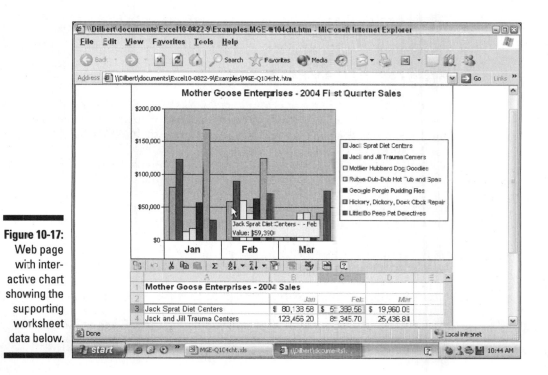

Figure 10-17:
Web page with interactive chart showing the supporting worksheet data below.

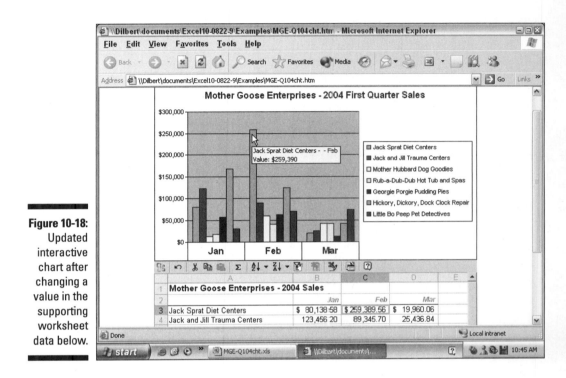

Figure 10-18:
Updated
interactive
chart after
changing a
value in the
supporting
worksheet
data below.

Adding worksheet data to an existing Web page

You don't always have to save your Excel worksheet data in a brand-new Web page. You can, in fact, add the data to any existing Web page. Just keep in mind that anytime you add worksheet data to an existing Web page, Excel always appends the data to the very bottom of the page. If you want the data to appear earlier in the Web page, you need to edit the Web page as I describe in the upcoming section "Editing your worksheet Web pages."

To append Excel worksheet data to an existing Web page, you follow all the same steps as saving it in a new Web page, with the following exception: Instead of specifying a new filename in which to save the data, you need to specify (usually by browsing) the name of the existing file to which the data is to be added.

After selecting the name of the existing file to which to append the selected worksheet data or chart and then clicking the Save button in the Save As dialog box, Excel displays an alert box containing three buttons: Add to File, Replace File, and Cancel.

Be sure to select the Add to File button instead of the Replace File button. If you choose the Replace File button instead of Add to File, Excel replaces the existing page with a new one, containing only the selected data or chart, rather than adding it to the end of the existing file. Be aware, however that when you click the Publish button in the Publish as Web Page dialog box, Excel automatically appends the selected worksheet or chart data to the existing Web page file you selected without displaying this alert dialog box.

Editing your worksheet Web pages

So what do you do, you may ask, if you add some worksheet data or an Excel chart to an existing Web page but don't want the information stuck down at the very tail end of the page? In that case, you need to edit the Web page and move the worksheet data or chart to the desired position in the Web page.

You can edit the new Web pages that you create in Excel or the existing pages to which you've appended worksheet data with any Windows-based Web page editing tool. If you don't have a favorite Web page editing program, go ahead and use Word (that comes as part of the Office suite of applications) as your Web page editor. It's actually quite adequate and really good about shielding you from the behind-the-scenes HTML tags and weird XML scripts.

Keep in mind that double-clicking a Web page file icon in Windows Explorer or My Computer will only result in opening the Web page in your favorite Web browser (where you can look but you can't touch). To open a Web page for editing, you must remember to launch a Web editor (such as Word or, in some cases, Excel) first and then use the editing program's File⇨Open command to open the Web page that needs changing.

To open a Web page for editing in Word, you follow these steps:

1. **Launch Word.**

   You can launch Word by clicking the Microsoft Word button on the Office toolbar or by clicking the Start button and choosing Programs⇨ Microsoft Word from the pop-up menus.

2. **Choose File⇨Open from the Word menu bar or click the Open button on the Word Standard toolbar to display the Open dialog box.**

3. **In the Open dialog box, select the folder that contains the Web page you want to open from the Look In drop-down list box at the top; then click the name of the file with the Web page in the central list box.**

   After you select the Web page file you want to edit, you open the file in Word by clicking the Open button. Because Office keeps track of which program creates the Web page (indicated by the addition of the particular program icon on top of the normal Web page icon), you may have to use the Open in Microsoft Word command instead of simply clicking the Open button if the Web page file you created is associated with Excel rather than Word.

4. **If you are opening a Web page that was created in Excel and has never been edited in Word, choose the Open in Microsoft Word option from the Open button's pop-up menu. If you are opening a Web page that was lasted edited in Word, just click the Open button or press Enter.**

When you have the Web page open in Word, you can then edit its contents and alter its formatting as needed. For example, to move a worksheet data table or chart that's been appended to the bottom of a Web page, you select the table or chart and then employ either the good old cut-and-paste or drag-and-drop method to position your selection at the desired place in the Web page. When moving an Excel worksheet table, keep these things in mind:

- To select a worksheet data table and all its contents, position the Word mouse pointer somewhere along the top of the table. When the pointer assumes the shape of a downward-pointing arrow, click the mouse, and Word will select all the cells in the table.

- To use the drag-and-drop technique to move a worksheet table that you've selected in Word, position the mouse pointer on the box with the double-cross that appears in the very upper-left corner of the selected table. When the pointer itself assumes the shape of a double-cross, use this pointer to drag the outline of the table to the desired place in the Web page document. When you've dragged the pointer to the beginning of the line in the document where the top row of the table is to appear, release the mouse pointer.

- To use the cut-and-paste technique to move a worksheet that you've selected in Word, choose Edit⇨Cut (or press Ctrl+X) to place the table in the Windows Clipboard. Then position the insertion-point cursor at the beginning of the line where the first row is to appear and choose Edit⇨ Paste (or press Ctrl+V).

When moving an Excel chart, keep these things in mind:

- To select a chart in Word, click somewhere on the chart just as you would in Excel. As soon as you click, the selection handles appear around the chart's perimeter and the Picture toolbar appears on the screen.

- To move a chart that you've selected in Word using the drag-and-drop technique, position the mouse pointer somewhere in the selected chart. When the pointer assumes the shape of an arrowhead with the outline of a tiny box below it, drag this pointer to the desired place in the Web

> page document. When you've dragged the pointer to the line in the document where the top of the chart is to appear, release the mouse pointer.
>
> ✔ To move a chart that you've selected in Word using the cut-and-paste technique, choose Edit⇨Cut (or press Ctrl+X) to place the chart on the Windows Clipboard. Then position the insertion-point cursor at the beginning of the line where the top of the chart is to appear and choose Edit⇨Paste (or press Ctrl+V).

Editing a worksheet Web page in Excel

There's no rule saying that you can't open and edit a Web page in Excel. In fact, if you only want to change some data in a worksheet data table or correct some entries in an Excel database list, opening the Web in Excel and making the changes there is definitely the best way to go. To open a Web page in Excel, you simply follow the procedure for opening a standard workbook file, (For details on opening files in Excel, refer to Chapter 4.)

If the file icon for the Web page file you want to open does not display an *XL* on top of the page with a globe (as would be the case if you edited the Web page in another program, such as Word, and saved the changes), clicking the Open button won't open the page for editing Excel. In such cases, you need to click the pop-up button attached to the Open button and select the Open in Microsoft Excel option from the pop-up menu.

After opening the Web page and making your editing changes to its data, you can save your changes to the Web file (in the original HTML or XML file format) by choosing the File⇨Save command (or by clicking the Save button on the Standard menu, or by pressing Ctrl+S). If the page you edited is located on a Web server, Excel will open a LAN or dial-up connection to the Internet so that changes are saved directly on the server.

If you have to make editing changes, such as moving a worksheet data table or Excel chart or changing the Web page background or inserting graphic images, then you really should use a full-fledged Web page editor (such as Word) because Excel's cell-based orientation makes these kinds of edits almost impossibly difficult.

If you work with a spreadsheet that you must be continually edit and then publish as a Web page in its updated form, you can have Excel automate this process. Simply select the AutoRepublish Every Time this Workbook is Saved check box in the Publish as Web Page dialog box (refer to Figure 10-9) the first time you publish the worksheet as a Web page. Thereafter, Excel will always automatically republish the Web page with your edits at the same time that it saves your changes to your workbook file.

Exporting an interactive Web page to Excel

You cannot save the changes that you make to the interactive data on the Web page in the Web browser. If you decide that you want to save your changes (as you might when experimenting with various what-if scenarios), you need to export the Web page to Excel and then save the updated data either as a Web page or an Excel workbook file.

To save the editing changes that you make to an interactive data table, database list, or supporting chart data (you can't save any of the editing changes made to the chart itself, unfortunately), you simply click the Export to Excel button on the toolbar that appears above the data. This is the button with a picture of a pencil underneath a green X.

Clicking the Export to Excel button launches Excel and simultaneously opens the Web page with the edited data. (In the case of interactive charts, the table with the edited supporting data appears without the associated chart.) On the Excel title bar, you'll see that exported Web page has been given a temporary filename like OWCsheet1.xml (Read Only). OWCsheet stands for Office Web Components sheet, by the way.

Because Excel opens the Web page with the updated worksheet data in read-only mode, the only way you can save the updated data is by choosing the File⇨Save As command and giving the Web page a new filename. If you choose Save rather than Save As, Excel displays an alert dialog box reminding you that the file is read-only.

By default, Excel saves the Web page in the XML file format. If you want to save the file with the updated worksheet data as a regular Excel workbook file, you need to remember to change the Save as Type setting from XML Spreadsheet (*.xml) to Microsoft Excel Workbook (.xls) at the same time you modify the filename in the File Name text box in the Save As dialog box.

If you don't have Excel on the computer that you're using at the time that you edit the interactive worksheet Web page in the Internet Explorer, try sending the OWCsheet.xml Web page file that the Internet Explorer generates to a co-worker whose computer is running Excel. The OWCsheet files are located inside the Temp folder within the Windows folder on your computer's hard drive. To send the Web page file to a co-worker, just insert the file in an e-mail message that you send to him or her.

Sending Worksheets via E-Mail

The last Internet-related feature of note in Excel is its ability to send the current worksheet to e-mail recipients either as the body of a new e-mail message or as an attachment. This feature makes it easy to send financial figures, lists, and charts to co-workers and clients.

If you want to share only the data with your e-mail recipient, you send the worksheet as the body of the e-mail message. Just be aware that when you do this, the only place where you can add your own text is in the Subject area of the e-mail message and the Introduction area in the message header.

If you want your e-mail recipient to be able to interact with the data (such as updating certain financial information or adding missing data), then you need to send the worksheet as an e-mail attachment. When you do this, your recipient receives the entire workbook file, and you type your own e-mail message (complete with any caveats or special instructions). Just be aware that in order for your e-mail recipient to be able to open the workbook file, he or she must have access to Excel 97, 2000, 2002, or 2003 (or Excel 98 or 2001 on the Macintosh) or some other spreadsheet program that can open Microsoft Excel 97/2000/2002/2003 files.

To send a worksheet as the body of a new e-mail message, follow these steps:

1. **Open the workbook and select the worksheet you want to send via e-mail.**

2. **Click the E-mail button on the Standard toolbar or choose the File⇨Send To⇨Mail Recipient command from the menu bar.**

   Excel displays the E-mail dialog box with option for sending the workbook as an e-mail attachment or sending the current sheet as the body of an e-mail message.

3. **Click the Send the Current Sheet as the Message Body radio button in E-mail dialog box and then click OK or press Enter.**

   Excel adds an e-mail header with its own toolbar, To, Cc, Bcc, and Subject fields at the top of the current worksheet (similar to the ones shown in Figure 10-19).

4. **Type the recipient's e-mail address in the To field or click the To button and select the address from your Outlook or Outlook Express address book (if you keep one).**

5. **(Optional) If you want to send copies of the worksheet to other recipients, enter their addresses in the Cc field separated by semicolons (;) or use the Cc button to select their addresses from your Outlook or Outlook Express Address book.**

   You can also enter this information in the Bcc (blind carbon copy) field instead. Click the drop-down button attached to the Options button at the end of the e-mail toolbar and then click Bcc on its menu, if this field isn't already displayed in the header. Do this when you want to send copies to each of the recipients without any of them knowing who else got a copy of the worksheet.

6. **By default, Excel enters the name of the current workbook in the e-mail message's Subject field. If you want, edit the Subject field to something more descriptive of the worksheet's contents.**

7. **To send the new message with the worksheet as the contents, click the Send This Sheet button on the e-mail toolbar (as shown in Figure 10-19).**

When you click the Send This Sheet button, Excel sends the e-mail message (connecting you to your Internet Service Provider, if need be), closes the e-mail toolbar, and removes the To, Cc, Bcc, and Subject fields from the top of your Excel worksheet.

To send a worksheet as an e-mail attachment, choose the File⇨Send To⇨Mail Recipient (as Attachment) command from the menu bar or click the E-mail button on the Standard toolbar and then click OK or press Enter when the Send the Entire Workbook as an Attachment radio button is selected in the E-mail dialog box that appears.

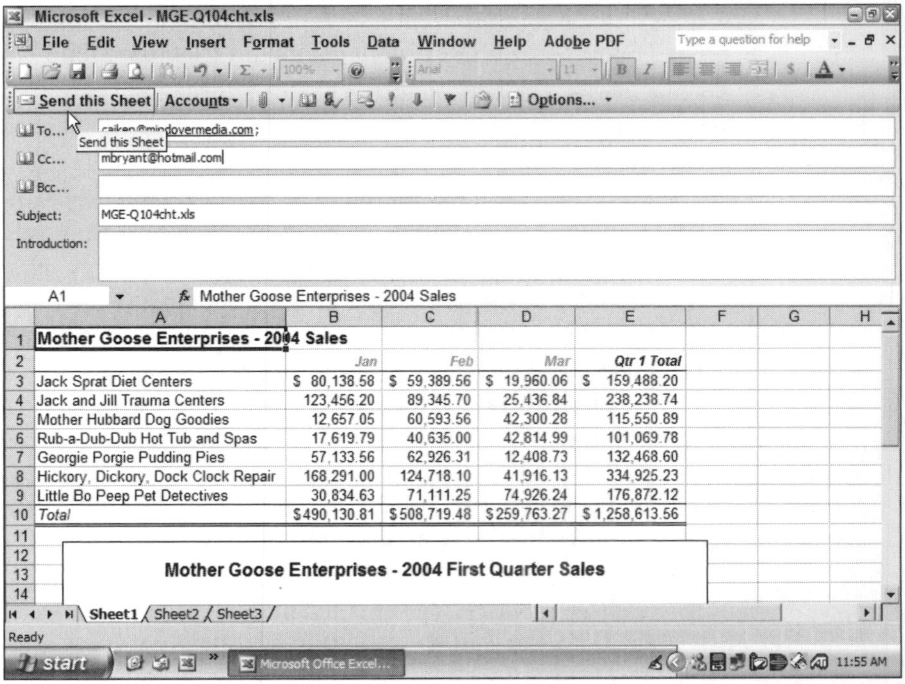

Figure 10-19:
Sending a worksheet as the body of an e-mail message.

The first time you choose this command, Excel opens the Internet Connection Wizard in which you enter the settings for your e-mail account, including your user name, password, and the addresses of the incoming (POP3) and outgoing (SMTP) mail servers. After that, choosing this command opens your e-mail program by using your account settings with a new e-mail message (like the one shown in Figure 10-20) complete with To, Cc, Bcc, and Subject fields and a place in which to type the text of your message. Excel also automatically attaches a copy of the current workbook (including all its worksheets) to the new message. You'll know the workbook is attached when you see the workbook's filename and file size in the Attach field, which appears right above the place for the message text.

After filling in the To, Cc, Bcc, and Subject fields and entering your message, send this message-cum-workbook to the e-mail recipient by clicking the Send button on the window's toolbar. You can also press Alt+S or choose File⇨Send Message from the window's menu bar. Sending your message closes the e-mail windows, as well.

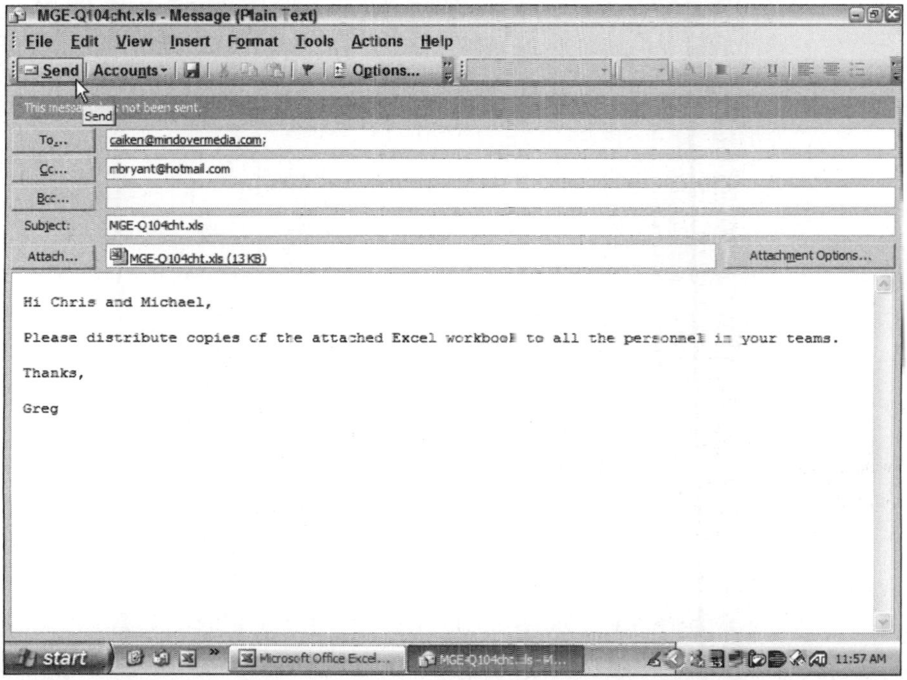

Figure 10-20: Sending a workbook file as an e-mail attachment.

Part V
The Part of Tens

The 5th Wave   By Rich Tennant

"MY GIRLFRIEND RAN A SPREADSHEET OF MY LIFE, AND GENERATED THIS CHART. MY BEST HOPE IS THAT SHE'LL CHANGE HER MAJOR FROM 'COMPUTER SCIENCES' TO 'REHABILITATIVE SERVICES.'"

In this part . . .

Finally, you come to the fun part of this book where the chapters all consist of lists with the top ten Excel tips on this, that, and everything in between. In homage to David Letterman (Indiana's favorite son), you'll find chapters on the top ten features in Excel 2003 and the top ten beginner basics. And, in homage to Cecil B. deMille, Moses, and a much higher power, I've even included a chapter with the Ten Commandments of Excel 2003 that, although not written in stone, when followed faithfully are guaranteed to give you heavenly results.

Chapter 11

Top Ten Features in Excel 2003

If you're looking for a quick runcown on what's cool in Excel 2003, look no further! Here it is, my official Top Ten Features list. Just a cursory glance down the list tells you that the thrust of the features is auto this 'n' that, such 'n' such tips, and so 'n' so Wizards.

And just in case you're interested in more than just a brief feature description, I've included a cross-reference to any place in this book where I cover the feature in more detail.

10. **Quickly and easily do a side-by-side comparison of any two worksheet windows that you have open:** Excel 2003's new Compare Side by Side With command on the Window pull-down menu enables you to tile the active workbook window with any other that you have open (or select, if you have more than two windows open). When you use this command, Excel places the active window over the one to which it's being compared and automatically synchronizes all scrolling in the active window with the one below. See Chapter 7 for details.

9. **Get help on using Excel by typing your question in the Ask a Question text box on the Menu bar or in the Search text box in the Microsoft Excel Help Task pane:** Excel 2003 makes it really convenient to ask for help on using the program. Just click the Ask a Question text box on the right side of the Menu bar or in the Search text box in the Microsoft Excel Help task pane (opened by pressing F1), type in your question, and press the Enter key. Excel responds by displaying a series of links to potentially relevant help topics that you can pursue in the new Microsoft Excel Help task pane. See Chapter 1 for more on using this feature.

8. **Modify the paste options after copying or filling a selection using the Fill handle:** This nifty Excel 2003 feature enables you to copy or fill a range of cells with the Fill handle and then apply new options to the copied or filled cell selection. For example, when Excel automatically copies a value to the cell range, you can change the copies into a filled series of values by selecting the Fill Series item on the Paste Options pop-up menu. Likewise, when Excel automatically fills out a series of values, you can change them to a copy of the initial value by selecting the Copy Cells item on the Paste Options pop-up menu. A similar Paste Options pop-up icon appears when you paste objects that you have cut or copied into the Windows Clipboard. See Chapter 4 for details.

7. **Search for the workbook files you need to edit in the Basic Search task pane:** This dandy task pane that opens when you choose File➪ File Search on the Menu bar or click the File Search button on the Standard toolbar enables you to search for the workbook files you need to edit from right within the worksheet work area. You can switch between the Basic Search and Advanced Search task pane to perform all types of file searches from the simple to the complex. For more on using the Basic and Advanced Search task pane to locate and open workbook files, see Chapter 4.

6. **View and insert stuff copied to the Windows Clipboard from the Clipboard task pane:** The Clipboard task pane automatically appears whenever you copy or cut two or more objects to the Clipboard, or you can open it manually by pressing Ctrl+CC (two Cs in a row). This task pane visually represents each object (up to the last 24) that you've cut (Edit➪Cut) or copied (Edit➪Copy) to the Clipboard. To paste an object that appears in the Clipboard task pane into the current cell in a worksheet, you simply click the object in the task pane. See Chapter 4.

5. **Search for and insert clip art from the Clip Art task pane:** The Clip Art task pane that automatically appears when you choose Insert➪Picture➪ Clip Art on the menu bar or click the Insert Clip Art button on the Drawing toolbar enables you to use key words to search for different types of images stored in your computer's Media Gallery. Results of the search then appear as thumbnails in the task pane, which you click to insert into the current worksheet. For more on searching for clip art in the Clip Art task pane, see Chapter 8.

4. **Open new and existing Workbooks from the New Workbook task pane:** Whenever you first open Excel with a blank worksheet, the program automatically opens the Getting Started task pane at the right side of the worksheet work area. You can use the links on this task pane to open any of the last four workbooks you edited or to open a new workbook, either based on an existing workbook file or on one of the templates at your disposal. For more on using this cool feature, see Chapter 1 and Chapter 4.

3. **Have Excel read back your cell entries so that you can validate their correctness with the Text-to-Speech feature:** The Text-To-Speech feature of Excel 2003 enables you to have the entries made in any group of cells read aloud to you. You can also set this feature so that it will tell what you've just entered in a new cell as soon as you press the Enter key. For more on how you can use this feature to catch and eliminate data entry errors, see Chapter 4.

2. **Get Excel to take dictation and follow your commands with your voice:** If your computer is properly equipped (that is, has speakers, a fast enough processor, and a very sensitive microphone), you can use the speech recognition features to do voice data input and give voice commands. For details on how to train the speech recognition software and use it to enter data and/or give voice commands in Excel 2003, see Chapter 2.

1. **Retrieve unsaved edits after a crash with the AutoRecover feature:**
   The most practical feature in Excel 2003 has to be its ability to recover
   unsaved data after you experience some sort of computer malfunction
   or crash. AutoRecover automatically saves changes to your to any open
   workbook file in ten-minute intervals (provided that you've manually
   saved it at least once with File⇨Save). If your computer crashes, the
   next time that you start Excel, the program automatically opens a
   Document Recovery task pane (this one on the left side of the work
   area) where you can open the most complete version of the recovered
   file. For details on setting the interval for the AutoRecover feature and
   making sure that it's turned on, see Chapter 2.

Chapter 12

Top Ten Beginner Basics

* *

*1*f these ten items are all you ever really master in Excel 2003, you'll still be way ahead of the competition. When all is said and done, this top ten list lays out all the fundamental skills required to successfully use Excel 2003:

10. **To start Excel 2003 from the Windows XP or 2000 taskbar,** click the Start button, highlight All Programs on the Start menu, and then choose Microsoft Excel on the All Programs continuation menu.

9. **To automatically launch Excel 2003 at the same time that you open an Excel workbook that needs editing** (in the My Documents or My Computer window), simply locate the folder containing the Excel workbook you want to edit and double-click its file icon.

8. **To locate a part of a worksheet that you cannot see on-screen,** use the scroll bars at the right and bottom of the workbook window to bring new parts of the worksheet into view.

7. **To start a new workbook (containing three blank worksheets),** choose the New tool on the Standard toolbar (or choose File⇔New on the pull-down menus or press Ctrl+N). To insert a new worksheet in a workbook (should you need more than three), choose Insert⇔Worksheet from the menu bar or press Shift+F11.

6. **To activate an open workbook and display it on-screen** (in front of any others you have open), open the Window menu and select the name or number of the workbook that you want. To locate a particular worksheet in the active workbook, click that worksheet's sheet tab at the bottom of the workbook document window. To display more sheet tabs, click the sheet scrolling arrows on the left side of the bottom of the workbook window.

5. **To enter stuff in a worksheet,** select the cell where the information should appear; then begin typing. When you finish, click the Enter button on the Formula bar (the one with the check mark) or press Tab, Enter, or one of the arrow keys.

4. **To edit the stuff you've already entered into a cell,** double-click the cell or position the cell pointer in the cell and press F2. Excel then locates the insertion point at the end of the cell entry and goes into Edit mode (see Chapter 2 for details). When you finish correcting the entry, click the Enter button on the formula bar or press Tab or Enter or one of the arrow keys.

3. **To choose one of the many commands on the Excel menu bar,** choose the menu name (on the menu bar) to open the menu and then choose the command name on the pull-down menu. To choose a command on a shortcut menu, right-click the object (cell, sheet tab, toolbar, chart, and so on).

2. **To save a copy of your workbook on disk the first time around,** choose File⇨Save or File⇨Save As from the menu bar (or click the Save button on the Standard toolbar or press Ctrl+S); then designate the drive and folder directory where the file should be located in the Save In drop-down list box, replace the temporary BOOK1.XLS filename in the File Name text box with your own filename (up to 255 characters long, including spaces), and then click the Save button. To save changes to the workbook thereafter, click the Save tool on the Standard toolbar (or choose File⇨Save or press Ctrl+S or Shift+F12).

1. **To exit Excel when you're done working with the program,** choose the File⇨Exit command on the menu bar or click the program's close box or press Alt+F4. If the workbook you have open contains unsaved changes, Excel 2003 asks whether you want to save the workbook before closing Excel and returning to Windows. Before you shut off your computer, be sure to use the Shut Down command on the Start menu to shut down the Windows operating system.

Chapter 13

The Ten Commandments of Excel 2003

● ●

*W*hen working with Excel 2003, you discover certain do's and don'ts that, if followed religiously, can make using this program just heavenly. Lo and behold, the following Excel Ten Commandments contain just such precepts for eternal Excel bliss.

10. **Thou shalt commit thy work to disk** by saving thy changes often (choose File⇨Save or press Ctrl+S). If thou findest that thou tendeth to be lax in the saving of thy work, thou shalt maketh sure that thy Auto Recover feature is engaged. Choose Tools⇨Options, click the Save tab, and then select the Save AutoRecover Info check box to have thy program automatically save thy work at no more than every ten minutes.

9. **Thou shalt nameth thy workbooks** when saving them the first time with filenames of no more than twelve score and fifteen characters (255), including spaces and all manner of weird signs and symbols. So, too, shalt thou mark well into which folder thou savest thy file lest thou thinkest in error that thy workbook be lost when next thou hast need of it.

8. **Thou shalt not spread wide the data in thy worksheet,** but rather shalt thou gather together thy tables and avoideth skipping columns and rows unless this is necessary to make thy data intelligible. All this shalt thou do in order that thou may conserve the memory of thy computer.

7. **Thou shalt begin all thy Excel 2003 formulas with = (equal)** as the sign of computation. If, however, ye be formerly of the Lotus 1-2-3 tribe, thou shalt haveth special dispensation and can commence thy formulas with the + sign and thy functions with the @ sign.

6. **Thou shalt select thy cells before thou bringeth any Excel command to bear upon them,** just as surely as thou doth sow before thou reapeth.

5. **Thou shalt useth the Undo feature (choose Edit⇨Undo or press Ctrl+Z)** immediately upon committing any transgression in thy worksheet so that thou mayest clean up thy mess. Should thou forgeteth to useth thy

Undo feature straightaway, thou must select the action that thou wouldst undo from the pop-up menu attached to the Undo button that thou findest on the Standard toolbar. Note well that any action that thou selectest from this menu will undo not only that action but also the actions that precedeth it on this menu.

4. **Thou shalt not delete, neither shalt thou insert, columns and rows in a worksheet** lest thou hath first verified that no part as yet undisplayed of thy worksheet will thereby be wiped out or otherwise displaced.

3. **Thou shalt not print thy worksheet lest thou hath first previewed the printing (choose File⇨Print Preview)** and art satisfied that all thy pages are upright in the sight of the printer. If thou art still unsure of how thy pages break, be sure that thou useth the View⇨Page Break Preview command to seeth how Excel doth divide thy pages.

2. **Thou shalt changeth the manner of recalculation of thy workbooks from automatic to manual** (choose Tools⇨Options⇨Calculation tab⇨ Manual) when thy workbook groweth so great in size that Excel sloweth down to a camel crawl whenever thou doeth anything in any one of its worksheets. Woe to thee, however, should thou also removeth the check mark from the Recalculate Before Save check box when thou setteth up manual calculation or should thou ignoreth the Calculate message on the status bar and not presseth the Calculate Now key (F9) before such time as thou mayest print any of thy workbook data.

1. **Thou shalt protecteth thy completed workbook and all its worksheets from corruption and iniquities** at the hands of others (choose Tools⇨ Protection⇨Protect Sheet or Protect Workbook). And if thou be brazen enough to addeth a password to thy workbook protection, beware lest thou forgeteth thy password in any part. For verily I say unto thee, on the day that thou knowest not thy password, that day shalt be the last upon which thou lookest upon thy workbook in any guise.

Index

Custom Lists box, 94, 95
cut and paste, 178–183
Cut tool, 25

• *D* •

data entry. *See also* cell entries; number
    formats; text entries
  accented letters, 88, 96
  dates, 65–68
  decimal places, 62
  decimal points, 64
  dollar amounts, 62
  formatting, 113
  fractions, 63
  guidelines, 56–59
  Handwriting recognition feature, 87–88
  mathematical symbols, 96
  money amounts, 62
  negative numbers, 62
  numbers, 61–64
  numeric keypad, 64–65
  percentages, 63
  replacing cell entries, 75
  Speech Recognition feature, 77–87
  speeding up, 98
  text, 59–61
  times, 65–66
data forms
  creating from field names alone, 303
  designing, 301–303
Data Labels tab (Chart Options dialog
  box), 286
data lists. *See* databases
data series, 279
Data Table button (Chart toolbar), 282
Data Table tab (Chart Options dialog
  box), 286
data types, 59–62
databases (data lists). *See also* records,
  database
  adding e-mail and Web addresses to a
    hyperlink field, 306–308
  adding records, 304–306
  AutoFilter feature, 316–322

calculated field entries, 306
creating from field names alone, 303
designing the data form, 301–303
interactive, 337, 343–344
sorting records, 312–316
date formats, 66
Date number format, 127
dates
  entering, 65–68
  formatting, 133–134
  in headers or footers, 208
  searching for workbook files, 160
  stored as serial numbers, 67
  in the twenty-first century, 67
decimal places
  Comma Style format, 130
  Currency number format, 127, 128
  entering numeric values with, 62
  fixing the number of, 63–64
  General number format, 128
  increasing or decreasing, 27
  increasing or decreasing number of,
    131–132
decimal points
  automatically added, 64, 65
  entering numbers without, 64
  normal data entry, 64
  zero before, 62
Decrease Decimal tool, 27, 131
Decrease Indent tool, 27, 142
Delete dialog box, 184
Delete key, 76
deleting
  cells, 183, 184
  comments, 231
  graphic images along with their
    hyperlinks, 332
  records, 308
  worksheets, 255
descending order, 313, 315–316
Desktop button (Open dialog box), 159
Desktop button (Save As dialog box), 107
desktop shortcut, starting Excel 2003
    with a, 17–18

• Z •

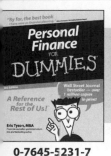

FOR DUMMIES®

A world of resources to help you grow

HOME, GARDEN & HOBBIES

Feng Shui FOR DUMMIES
A Reference for the Rest of Us!
0-7645-5295-3

Gardening FOR DUMMIES 2nd Edition
A Reference for the Rest of Us!
0-7645-5130-2

Guitar FOR DUMMIES
Play-along audio CD included!
A Reference for the Rest of Us!
0-7645-5106-X

Also available:

Auto Repair For Dummies
(0-7645-5089-6)

Chess For Dummies
(0-7645-5003-9)

Home Maintenance For Dummies
(0-7645-5215-5)

Organizing For Dummies
(0-7645-5300-3)

Piano For Dummies
(0-7645-5105-1)

Poker For Dummies
(0-7645-5232-5)

Quilting For Dummies
(0-7645-5118-3)

Rock Guitar For Dummies
(0-7645-5356-9)

Roses For Dummies
(0-7645-5202-3)

Sewing For Dummies
(0-7645-5137-X)

FOOD & WINE

Cooking FOR DUMMIES 2nd Edition
A Reference for the Rest of Us!
0-7645-5250-3

Cookies FOR DUMMIES
A Reference for the Rest of Us!
0-7645-5390-9

Wine FOR DUMMIES 2nd Edition
Winner of the Georges Duboeuf Book of the Year Award.
A Reference for the Rest of Us!
0-7645-5114-0

Also available:

Bartending For Dummies
(0-7645-5051-9)

Chinese Cooking For Dummies
(0-7645-5247-3)

Christmas Cooking For Dummies
(0-7645-5407-7)

Diabetes Cookbook For Dummies
(0-7645-5230-9)

Grilling For Dummies
(0-7645-5076-4)

Low-Fat Cooking For Dummies
(0-7645-5035-7)

Slow Cookers For Dummies
(0-7645-5240-6)

TRAVEL

Italy FOR DUMMIES 2nd Edition
A Travel Guide for the Rest of Us!
0-7645-5453-0

Hawaii FOR DUMMIES 2nd Edition
A Travel Guide for the Rest of Us!
0-7645-5438-7

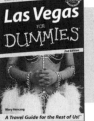

Las Vegas FOR DUMMIES 2nd Edition
A Travel Guide for the Rest of Us!
0-7645-5448-4

Also available:

America's National Parks For Dummies
(0-7645-6204-5)

Caribbean For Dummies
(0-7645-5445-X)

Cruise Vacations For Dummies 2003
(0-7645-5459-X)

Europe For Dummies
(0-7645-5456-5)

Ireland For Dummies
(0-7645-6199-5)

France For Dummies
(0-7645-6292-4)

London For Dummies
(0-7645-5416-6)

Mexico's Beach Resorts For Dummies
(0-7645-6262-2)

Paris For Dummies
(0-7645-5494-8)

RV Vacations For Dummies
(0-7645-5443-3)

Walt Disney World & Orlando For Dummies
(0-7645-5444-1)

Available wherever books are sold. Go to www.dummies.com or call 1-877-762-2974 to order direct.

FOR DUMMIES®

Plain-English solutions for everyday challenges

COMPUTER BASICS

0-7645-0838-5

0-7645-1663-9

0-7645-1548-9

Also available:

PCs All-in-One Desk Reference For Dummies
(0-7645-0791-5)

Pocket PC For Dummies
(0-7645-1640-X)

Treo and Visor For Dummies
(0-7645-1673-6)

Troubleshooting Your PC For Dummies
(0-7645-1669-8)

Upgrading & Fixing PCs For Dummies
(0-7645-1665-5)

Windows XP For Dummies
(0-7645-0893-8)

Windows XP For Dummies Quick Reference
(0-7645-0897-0)

BUSINESS SOFTWARE

0-7645-0822-9

0-7645-0839-3

0-7645-0819-9

Also available:

Excel Data Analysis For Dummies
(0-7645-1661-2)

Excel 2002 All-in-One Desk Reference For Dummies
(0-7645-1794-5)

Excel 2002 For Dummies Quick Reference
(0-7645-0829-6)

GoldMine "X" For Dummies
(0-7645-0845-8)

Microsoft CRM For Dummies
(0-7645-1698-1)

Microsoft Project 2002 For Dummies
(0-7645-1628-0)

Office XP For Dummies
(0-7645-0830-X)

Outlook 2002 For Dummies
(0-7645-0828-8)

Get smart! Visit www.dummies.com

- **Find listings of even more *For Dummies* titles**
- **Browse online articles**
- **Sign up for Dummies eTips™**
- **Check out *For Dummies* fitness videos and other products**
- **Order from our online bookstore**

Available wherever books are sold. Go to www.dummies.com or call 1-877-762-2974 to order direct.

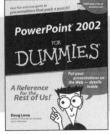
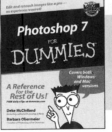

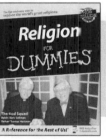
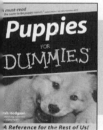